OPINIONS, CONFERENCES, SAYINGS AND INSTRUCTIONS OF MARCELLIN CHAMPAGNAT

OPINIONS, CONFERENCES, SAYINGS AND INSTRUCTIONS OF MARCELLIN CHAMPAGNAT

Translated by Leonard Voegtle, FMS
Edited by José Diez Villacorta, FMS

IVE Press

New York–2010

Cover Design
    © IVE Press

Cover Art
    © IVE Press

Text
    © Marist Brothers.

Institute of the Incarnate Word, Inc.

All rights reserved.

Manufactured in the United States of America

113 East 117th Street
New York, NY 10035
Ph. (212) 534 5257
Fax (212) 534 5258
E-mail ivepress@ive.org
http:// www.ivepress.org

ISBN: 1-933871-22-9

© Catalogued in the Library of Congress of the US.

Printed in the United States of America ∞

Library of Congress Control Number: 2009925169

TABLE OF CONTENTS

TRANSLATOR'S PREFACE

Not having been able to think of a 'catchy' English translation of Avis, Leçons, Sentences, I decided to create my own title instead! In what I am sure was a moment of inspiration, I decided on a quotation from Marcellin's own Spiritual Testament, 'Listen to the words of your father,' which to my mind, signifies for us the full value and import of these chapters.

These pages open for us several windows on our Marist past, and reveal many elements that shaped the attitudes and actions of Marcellin and our first brothers.

They give us insights to their attitudes about God, vocation, community, the spiritual life, the vows, and education. Some of those attitudes are still current. Others may jolt us, especially the often negative and Jansenistic vision of 'the world', of human nature in general, and most particularly of human sexuality.

The conferences reproduced here are also a good example of the didactic style of the day, which favored many quotations from spiritual writers, illustrations from the lives of the saints, and 'horror stories' about the terrible fate awaiting even occasional sinners.

Unfortunately, it is impossible to distinguish today exactly how much of the text is directly quoted from Father Champagnat, and how much represents Br. Jean-Baptiste's edited recollection and reproduction of conferences he had heard, and perhaps summarized in his notebook, twenty or thirty years previously. Contemporary research seems to indicate that Br. Jean-Baptiste was sometimes fairly free in adapting Marcellin's words to his own purposes and in coloring them with his own decidedly more conservative and even Jansenistic personality.

In any case, these texts do reveal the areas of concern which were most important to Marcellin, and which Br. Jean-Baptiste felt should be equally so to succeeding generations of Marists. They may also indicate the areas in which our chronicler felt that abuses were already arising, in the form of departures from the way his generation had been taught to live, think and act during our Founder's lifetime.

Hence, it is important for us today to read these pages with an open mind. Although the mentality, the spirituality, and the view of society and of the Church reflected in them did indeed shape the lives of Marcellin Champagnat and our first brothers, and through succeeding generations, the lives of the men who formed us, they still represent a historic and cultural reality vastly different from our own.

Like the householder in the parable, we must pray for the grace to be able to bring forth from our Marist treasures—and this book is certainly one of them—things new and old for our spiritual and cultural enrichment.

A final note: since many of the persons whom Br. Jean-Baptiste quotes or uses as examples are not all that well known today I have added an appendix of biographical notes on those who can be clearly enough identified.[1]

Br. Leonard Voegtle

---

1 This edition of Opinions, Conferences, Sayings and Instructions of Marcellin Champagnat does not contain the appendix of biographical notes.

CHAPTER ONE

WHAT A BROTHER IS,
ACCORDING TO FATHER CHAMPAGNAT

Our holy Founder had a high opinion of the brothers' religious vocation and their ministry. In his conferences, he often praised the value and merit of the exalted function of catechist. He went on and on whenever he was praising this task, which he called an apostolic ministry, and whenever he was speaking of all the good which can be done by a brother who really has the spirit of his state.

To engrave his teachings on this point more deeply on the minds of the brothers, in a sort of outline form, he usually limited himself to answering this question: What is a brother? Here is the substance of his answers. We think they contain what is best suited to make the brothers understand the holiness of their vocation, and give them a high esteem for their task of catechizing children.

I. A brother is someone predestined for great piety, a very pure life and solid virtue; a soul for whom God's mercy has special plans.

He is a soul called to study Jesus Christ in a special way, to follow in his footsteps, to imitate him to the extent human weakness allows; to love, praise, and bless him; to remain in his presence and thus make up for the indifference and ingratitude of other people.

He is a soul, as St. Bernard says, called to love God without measure. The ordinary Christian should serve God; the religious should remain glued to his heart and do whatever his good pleasure indicates. The ordinary Christian should believe in God, know him and love him; the religious should understand him, savor him, devour him.

He is a man totally and forever dedicated to God and involved in serving him. He is bound to God's service by the same commandments as everyone else, and by the three vows of religion.

He is a soul predestined for more abundant redemption and greater glory in heaven; all the means of salvation and perfection have been given to him. If he uses them well, if he is faithful to the special graces bestowed on him, a magnificent reward is waiting for him in eternity, a reward which Jesus Christ calls a treasure, because it is so superior to that of the other elect, where it referred to as a penny.

He is a soul who cannot be satisfied with anything here on earth; a soul for whom the world is not vast enough, and who will be happy only when he possesses heaven.

II. A brother is God's co-worker and Jesus Christ's partner in the holy mission of saving souls.

What a noble task it is to carry on the work of Jesus Christ, doing what he did on earth, that is, instructing the ignorant, teaching them the science of salvation, the science of religion, the science of the saints! «No matter how hard I look,» said Gerson, «I cannot find anything greater than teaching catechism to children and snatching them away from the contagion of vice and sin.»

What a holy undertaking it is to ruin the devil's work, to pull these young souls back from the gates of hell, to plant in the garden of the Church these tiny shoots in which Jesus Christ is so delighted, to cultivate and water them, to prepare them for the marriage-feast of the Lamb, for their first communion! «It is the most beautiful of all tasks, for the most exalted, the most divine of all ministries,» says St. Denis, «it is cooperating with God to save souls.»

«Brothers who are teaching and forming children to virtue gather the fruit of the cross and of the blood of Jesus Christ; with St. Paul, they can say, 'We are God's coadjutors' (1 Cor 3:9) in the ministry of saving souls. What an honor and glory for a brother!»

If, as St. John Chrysostom put it, heaven were starting to fall apart, and God deigned to say to you, «Help me to hold it together,» wouldn't he be doing you a great favor, and wouldn't it be to your glory? Well, that child whom you sometimes find so disgusting, so contemptible, is in God's eyes nobler and greater than heaven. It was for him that God made heaven and earth; God dwells in him with greater dignity than in his heavenly home. He honors you by choosing you to uphold this living heaven which is falling apart, to repair the holes which ignorance and sin have left in his soul—what an honor and glory!

To be associated with God, to cooperate with him in preserving and rehabilitating his most perfect creatures—what a task, what a vocation! There is really something so great and sublime about it that I would need the tongue of an angel to speak to you about it worthily and properly (Bishop Devie).

III. A brother is the wise man Isaiah speaks of, who spends his life laying foundations and rebuilding ruins.

1. «He lays the foundations of fear of sin, by forming children's consciences and preserving them from evil.» The heart of a child is a blank page, a canvas on which nothing has yet been painted, ready to receive whatever colors one might wish to use on it. If one imprints on it very early the fear of God and horror of sin, those sentiments will remain there for life; they will serve as a brake to halt all the disorderly movements of his soul, control his passions, moderate his language and regulate all his

actions. This fear of God and horror of evil were at the root of the virtues of all the saints, and led them to flee from sin even more than from death.

2. «He lays the foundations of every virtue, by forming the child's heart.» If a child has had a good education, virtues appear by themselves in his soul; religious habits and practices are a necessity for him and become second nature to him. «You can harvest from a field only what you have sowed in it; if it was wheat, wheat you shall have; if you sowed weeds, all you can harvest is weeds. A child who receives the beginnings of virtue produces the fruits of virtue. One who is left to himself or who receives a bad education, will produce fruits of death. A life of virtue and a life of vice are both rooted in one's education.»

3. He lays the foundation of prosperous families. Cardinal De la Luzerne once said, «Look at those honorable families which from one generation to the next have preserved the integrity of their principles, their probity, their good morals, religion, and all the Christian and social virtues. Ask the heads of those families where they got those virtues and how they have been handed down. All of them will tell you that they are the result of a good education, which they gave or had others give to their children.»

4. He lays the religious foundations of parishes. «Children are the Church's greenhouse; through them it renews itself and preserves faith and piety.» Just as a flowing fountain in the middle of a garden assures its beauty and fertility, a good Christian school in a parish produces the fruits of every virtue. From a class of children who are trained in piety and solidly instructed in Christian virtue will come forth a parish of fervent Christians. Just as the People of God came from just one man, Abraham, so a nation of saints can come from just one truly religious school, as Cardinal De la Luzerne also remarks.

5. He lays the foundation of the Church's ministry. The fruit which will be produced by the ministry of the pastors of the Church is contained, as in its seed, in the first education given to

the child; the success of the priest's work is totally dependent upon it. What good is it for the priest to proclaim the word of God if no one understands him? And how will anyone understand him, if the children are left in ignorance? To neglect the instruction and education of children is therefore to nullify the Church's ministry; it cuts children off from all the resources they might have one day found in the homilies of their pastors. «Children left without instruction,» says Massillon, «are like plants which are allowed to dry up from the time they sprout; it will be a waste of time to water them later on—the harm will have been done and they will no longer be able to grow.»

6. Finally, he lays the foundation of the child's eternity. It is not only the child's life which is rooted in his early education, but also his salvation and his eternity. A child's salvation or damnation depends largely on the education given him and the path he was made to follow in his youth. The child is then at a crossroads and quite willing to follow the one pointed out to him. Ordinarily, if you set him on the path of virtue, he will reach heaven; if you leave him on the path of vice, he will go straight to hell. The brother who dedicates himself to the instruction of children is therefore laying the foundations of virtue, piety and salvation in time and in eternity. What a beautiful mission it is to bring up children!

IV. A brother is a substitute father and mother.

The great evil of our century is the almost universal destruction of education in the home. Most parents no longer give their children any religious instruction, either because they do not know their religion well enough, because they themselves were not instructed as children; or—and especially—because they are irreligious and consequently unconcerned about their children's salvation. Oh, yes, they are lovingly solicitous about giving them food and clothing, setting them up in the world, setting aside money for them; but they don't give a thought to their soul, their instruction, their eternity, as though it were a matter of indifference whether or not these young children had any religion, piety or virtue.

How many children today could say with St. Cyprian, «Our own parents have proved to be murderers. We owe them our bodily life, but within our families we quickly lost the life of grace, because those who brought us into existence neglected to instruct us in the truths of salvation and to teach us to fear God!»

Like Gerson, I would tell you, «Poor children, I am deeply touched by your situation. How many shoals surround you on all sides, at an age in which one is so susceptible to impressions, especially the kind made upon us by our fallen nature. What do you see and hear at home? Dissolute and impious parents, who make your ears ring with blasphemies, who make fun of piety, who teach you by their bad example to transgress the laws of God and of the Church, who teach you the maxims of this age and infect you with all their vices and defects.»

When Gerson spoke that way, was he not describing today's parents? Was he not describing the pitiful state of today's children? It is only too true; hence «a great number of children would remain in ignorance, grow up in vice, and lose their souls, if God in his infinite mercy had not had pity on them and raised up pious teachers to take care of them and bring them up in a Christian manner. That is why the brothers' schools exist, and that is what God had in mind in founding them.»

V. A brother is the assistant of the pastors of the Church.

In the first centuries of the Church, the bishops themselves were the catechists. If later on, when the number of the faithful increased, they were obliged by force of circumstances to hand over this responsibility to others, they were careful to choose only the most capable and virtuous men in their church. So we find in Church history that the greatest doctors felt it an honor to serve as catechists. St. Cyril of Jerusalem, St. Ambrose of Milan, St. Gregory of Nyssa, and St. Augustine even wrote books to train catechists and teach them how to teach children the truths and mysteries of the faith.

Down through the centuries, the greatest scholars and the greatest men also felt honored to teach catechism. St. Gregory the Great, St. Francis de Sales, St. Ignatius of Loyola, St. Francis Xavier, St. Vincent de Paul, Gerson, St. Robert Bellarmine and a host of others often taught catechism. So it is a privilege for the brothers to share with the priest the glorious function of catechizing children; by doing so, «they are the aides, the co-workers of the pastors of the Church, who being too taken up with other aspects of their holy ministry, cannot give to the instruction and education of children all the time which such an important task requires.»

And in fact, the instruction a child receives in church, in preparation for first communion, is far from enough to make him a well-formed and educated Christian. If he did not receive instruction and education at home or in school, we could say of him what Tertullian said of those who had been poorly instructed in his day: they are Christians, yes, if you wish, but Christians who are up in the air.

VI. A brother replaces soldiers and police officers.

Why are there so many soldiers? Why so many police officers? Because the number of criminals keeps multiplying almost to infinity. But the only reason there are so many criminals is because children are not instructed or are not brought up properly. «If parents,» says St. John Chrysostom, «worked at giving their children a good education, we would no longer need laws, police, courts, sentences or executioners, because the only reason there are prisons and executioners is because there is absolutely no religion or morality.»

There was a great king who often said that if his subjects would become more religious, he would be able to reduce his army and his courts. «By giving children a good education, a truly Christian education, a brother prevents crime and therefore replaces the police, judges and law courts.»

VII. A brother is the children's guardian angel.

Innocence is the greatest of all possessions and the most excellent of all gifts. In God's eyes, a child who has preserved his baptismal innocence is a treasure more precious than all the kingdoms of the world. But since the child does not know the value of that innocence, nor the dangers which threaten it, God has entrusted the protection of that infinitely valuable treasure to the Christian teacher. «I have appointed you,» he says in Ezekiel, «as a watchman over the house of Israel»; in other words, over that gathering of children you are responsible for bringing up. When he entrusts a child to a brother, God as much as says to him what Jacob said to his children when he entrusted Benjamin to them, «Swear to me that you will take care of this child; know that I will demand an accounting from you, and if you do not give him back to me as innocent as I gave him to you, I will never forgive you.»

«In order to be the children's guardian angel, a brother should exercise continual vigilance over them, and that vigilance should include all the children, all their senses, all their actions.» «Do your best,» Our Lord said to St. Mary Magdalen de' Pazzi, «within the limits of your power and the grace I will give you, to have as many eyes as there will be souls entrusted to your care.»

«Regardless of your children's good qualities,» said Cardinal De la Luzerne, «watch them day and night, never let them be masters of their own actions. If possible, even watch over their thoughts. Don't expect to keep them pure otherwise. What does it take for the devil, that roaring lion, to devour a child and snatch away his purity? A single moment of negligence on your part. It takes only a spark to start a fire, and the human heart is made of sulfur. No matter how wise and virtuous your children may be, I say the same thing: watch them. The most exquisite wine, if it is not properly cared for, quickly turns to vinegar; the most delicious fruit goes wild when the tree that bears it is not pruned; the fattest sheep waste away if they are not cared for by a careful and vigilant shepherd.»

But what should one be most vigilant about?

1. About friendships: a bad friendship is the most common and most natural source of corruption.

2. About posture: a child caught in a suspicious posture, especially if he blushes and hurriedly begins to do some work, should be reprimanded and watched very closely.

3. About bad students and bad companions: contagious diseases are spread by contact. A single rotten apple can spoil the whole barrel; one sheep with mange can spread it to the whole flock; one plague victim can infect an entire city; a single corrupt and licentious child, like an evil sort of yeast, can spoil a whole class, a whole house full of young people.

4. About conversations, tastes, inclinations, and anything else which might endanger children's virtue.

A vigilant brother will be able to rejoice that he preserved the innocence of little children, and he will often bring them to the age of their first communion without their having committed any grave faults.[1] He will help them all to avoid many sins; he will keep the contagion of evil from spreading; he will force perverse children to repress their evil inclinations and struggle in spite of themselves against their passions. What a beautiful mission it is for a brother to be the guardian angel of his students!

---

[1] In Father Champagnat's time, the normal age for First Communion was eleven or older.

VIII. A brother is a model and a living gospel for the children and for everyone else.

Forgetfulness of God, love of money, love of pleasure, the spirit of independence or false freedom, and selfishness, are the five main disorders or defects which reign in society and which the child has constantly before his eyes. To keep him from letting himself be seduced by so many causes of depravation, God has given him, in the person of the brother, a model who constantly gives him an example diametrically opposed to these five worldly vices.

For example:

1. The brother spends his life studying, meditating and teaching the law of God; he spends several hours in prayer every day. His example is therefore well suited for overcoming forgetfulness of God and forming children to piety and the duties of a Christian.

2. He has left his possessions, his parents, everything he had in the world, everything he could claim later on; in a word, he has made the vow of poverty, the only inheritance he wants is Jesus. This heroic behavior loudly condemns uncontrolled love of wealth, honors, worldly vanity, and constantly gives the children an example of detachment from material goods and of humility.

3. He has renounced all sensual pleasures and made a vow of perpetual chastity. So he is well equipped to inspire children with love for the most beautiful of virtues and horror of the most shameful and most dangerous of all vices.

4. He has made the vow of obedience and spends his life in absolute obedience; all his actions, from morning till night, are regulated by obedience. So no one is in a better position than he to train souls to this virtue, to correct that independence which is the scourge of our times and to inspire children with submission and obedience to God, to the pastors of the Church, to the civil authorities and to parents.

5. His life is one of devotedness; he did not want possessions, family or material interests of any sort on earth, so that he could give himself totally to the service of children, living among them, devoting all his solicitude, care, activities, work, strength and even his very life, to their education. Such an admirable example condemns the selfishness of the world and ceaselessly preaches charity, humility and every other Christian virtue.

6. By his gentle charity towards his students, his patience in putting up with their defects, his zeal for training them in virtue and useful knowledge, his vigilance in eliminating anything that might harm them, his daily devotedness to their spiritual and temporal welfare, the brother is a perfect model for fathers and mothers. He gives them a continual lesson in what they should do and be to bring up their children in a Christian manner. Such is the model which God has given to the child and to all the faithful in the person of the brother. After all that, should we be surprised if everyone loves, respects and sides with the brothers?

IX. A brother is a sower of the gospel.

Please note that I said sower and not harvester. Why? In order to teach some of us who complain about their lack of success and who think that the children do not get anything out of their teaching, because the latter aren't very pious, stay away from Church services and the sacraments. and drift with the current of bad example as soon as they have left school. Listen, those of you who talk that way. The season for harvesting crops is not the one when you cultivate the ground to make it fit to produce them. The seed doesn't spring up the minute you drop it into the furrow. For a while, it almost seems lost; but bad weather and even all the rigors of winter do not destroy it. Even while you are complaining, the seed is sprouting in the hearts of your children, and it will appear on the surface in its own time.

When the prophet Elisha thought that all was lost and that his preaching had been useless, God told him that the evil was not so great as he imagined, and that more than seven thousand men had remained faithful.

To remove children from the dangers of the world and keep them away from bad example, to preserve them from sin or at least from serious faults, until the age of ten, twelve and sometimes fifteen, to give them the habit of religious practices, to teach them about the truths and mysteries of the faith, to obtain for them the grace of a good first communion—these are the certain and tangible fruits produced by the brothers' zeal, and that is certainly no mean accomplishment.

More than that, your instructions prepare those children who stray to return to virtue. How many persons who seem to have forgot the lessons of their pious mother or the instruction of their virtuous teacher, after straying far and long, returned to the path of wisdom, and through a life of genuine virtue brought honor to the religion which formed them in childhood? Even while he strayed, St. Augustine could never forget the teachings of his pious mother, nor erase from his memory the name of Jesus which she had so often repeated to him. If this great saint had not been instructed in his religion and formed to virtue in his youth, he would probably have remained a Manichean heretic, and the Church would not have had him as its «Doctor of Grace.» What means of salvation is there, what plank after shipwreck, for those who have been deprived of the benefits of religious education? None.

X. A brother is a man who, following the example of Jesus Christ, passes through this world doing good.

He does good to everyone: to the children he brings up and improves by Christian instruction and education; to the families he assists; to the parishes he builds up, preserves and improves;

to the entire country for which he prepares virtuous citizens; to the Church by assisting its pastors in instructing the most appealing part of its beloved flock, by constantly forming new generations of Christians who are instructed, convinced and faithful.

He devotes himself totally to the service of religion, the service of his country, and gives his strength and his life to procure the glory of God and the sanctification of his neighbor.

XI. Finally, a brother is a very effective bulwark against the evil and contagion of the world.

His mission is to combat vice and sin, to ruin the empire of the devil, to spread the seeds of virtue in the hearts of children, to weaken and destroy the man of sin, to form the man of grace, the heavenly man, the man of glory. Such is the vocation and mission of a brother.

CHAPTER TWO

WHAT A YOUNG BROTHER IS AND HOW NECESSARY IT IS TO TRAIN HIM WELL

An old brother director who was a bitter, difficult and narrow-minded character, being annoyed one day by the presence of the youngest brothers[1] and the noise they were making, burst out impatiently with, «What good are so many 'quarter-brothers'? All they do around here is create disorder, disturb recollection and use up the Institute's money. And in the schools, they are good for nothing except to make people laugh and talk, embarrass the brothers, and impede the success of the schools.»

Father Champagnat happened to be passing by and heard what the brother said. He just laughed and replied, «A 'quarter-brother'! Now, that's really not enough! That shows too much contempt for these youngsters; at least admit that they are good 'half-brothers'!» But he took advantage of the occasion to give the older brothers several solid conferences on the esteem they should have for the young brothers, and the care they should take to help them become attached to their vocation, and to train them in virtue. What follows is a summary of the conferences he gave them on this important topic.

«A religious vocation is a great grace for all those to whom it is given, at whatever age it is received. After baptism, it is the

---

[1] In Father Champagnat's day, some of «the youngest brothers» would have been in their early teens; a few were even younger.

greatest grace God can give a soul. It is a mark of predestination, a second choice, a second selection for the glory of heaven.

«But in my opinion, it is a very special favor, I would even say a first-class gift, to be called to the religious life in one's youth, to be taken out of the world before having known evil, before having lost one's innocence and contracted bad habits. This choice is proof that God has special plans for a person when he calls him to a high degree of virtue and wants to use him for his own glory and for the sanctification of others.

«To be called while young is the surest guarantee of a fidelity to one's vocation, because he who gives himself to God from his childhood has greater strength and facility for practicing virtue; religious observance and regularity become second nature to him.

«Lastly, he has his whole youth during which to acquire the knowledge he needs and to become capable of fulfilling the end of his vocation. That is why the young brothers, if they are well brought up and well trained, are a blessing for our institute. They are its hope, its wealth, its treasure, and one day they will become its adornment, its glory, its pillars and its supports.»

In order to better understand the care required in the formation and education of young brothers, let us state clearly what they are, and let us not minimize any of their defects or weaknesses. In that way, we will have a realistic idea of their needs.

I.

A novice is a young plant which needs to be grafted if it is wild, that is to say, if he has been neglected or received a bad formation in the world, if he has unfortunately suffered from the atmosphere where he first grew up, or if he has already been contaminated by the world he has just barely left. If this brother is given good principles and solid instruction, and helped to make a good general confession, then sanctifying grace, the Christian virtues, and the good dispositions he needs to start out on the road to perfection will all be grafted onto his soul.

II.

A young brother is a plant that needs pruning. Now, pruning is done differently according to the type of tree. Trees standing in open spaces need only to be pruned yearly and to have their dead branches lopped off. That sort of pruning is easy and requires little care, and anyone can do it. This is an image of the care and education needed in the case of ordinary Christians.

The pruning of dwarf trees, or espaliered trees, is totally different. There are two procedures; the first involves shaping: sometimes trees are pruned into pyramids, cones, etc., and sometimes they are extended along walls, or arranged so as to form parallel rows in a sort of palisade. This is a good image of a religious formed according to the rule he has embraced, according to the end of his vocation. He is worked on and shaped until the spirit of his institute is personified in him.

The second procedure furthers and improves upon the first. It involves cutting out, once or twice a year, all suckers, woody branches, and misshapen branches, so as to channel all the sap into the fruit-bearing branches. This pruning is also a good image of the way a religious is continually tested, by cutting away and correcting everything defective in his spirit, his heart and his character.

Note that the more a tree is pruned, cultivated, and trained, the more fruit it produces, and that the biggest, best and most beautiful fruit is always found on trees which have been pruned and fastened, as if crucified, to a frame or a wall. In the same way, the religious who are the best formed, the most tested, the most subjected to obedience, give the best and most abundant fruit— that is to say, the most solid and sustained virtue, the greatest and highest perfection. It is the most tested religious who are best suited to procure God's glory, to serve their institute well, and to always and everywhere do the most solid, lasting and far-reaching good. In a word, such religious are usually fit and ready for any function and capable of doing all sorts of good.

Pruning is also absolutely necessary for a good tree. Look at the grapevine. Left to itself, it is a shapeless shrub which creeps over the ground, exhausts its strength producing sterile branches, produces only sour grapes or none at all, and simply grows wild. If it is pruned once a year, the vine produces good grapes, but not many of them. If it is pruned in the spring and in July, and staked, or trained against a wall, it becomes a large plant and produces a large quantity of excellent grapes. This is a touching image of the religious who, the more he is trained, tested and subjected to a rule, to obedience, becomes more obedient and virtuous, and more suited for various tasks in the Institute. On the other hand, the more he is neglected and left to himself, the less virtue and the more vices he has, and the more worthless he becomes.

And note, finally, that a good and prudent gardener does not allow a tree to bear too much fruit, for fear of wearing it out. So he removes some, and leaves only enough for the strength and size of that particular tree. The effects of a religious' virtue should also be in proportion to his age and the graces he has; too much meditation would disturb his mind or dry up his heart; too many privations or penances would ruin his health; too much practice of virtue would give birth to the worm of pride, self love and singularity. Everyone realizes that the piety, modesty, mortification, in one word the virtue, of a young brother is not that of an older religious, and that one should ask and allow the former less than the latter.

III.

A young brother is a flower. The flower is the beginning, the embryo of the fruit. But how tender and delicate a flower is! How many accidents can kill it! A gust of wind can make it fall, just as a violent temptation is sometimes enough to make a young brother fall. A sudden freeze can kill a flower; in the same way, too much severity or too little fatherliness on the part of a superior or principal are often enough to discourage this young brother and lead him to give up entirely. Too much rain can rot the flower and make the fruit-bud fall. Likewise, too much gentleness and indulgence on the part of a superior, too many emotional devotions, can soften a young brother, and breed in his mind the worm of pride, presumption and self-will, which will soon endanger and finally destroy all his budding virtues.

IV.

A young brother is like an unripe fruit which is threatened by a thousand things which can cause it to die before it matures. He can dry up for lack of sap, that is, for lack of piety; he can be eaten by a worm, that is, by some passion or a bad habit. He can be spoiled by bad air and miasmas, this is, by bad example, bad companions, bad reading, and the contagion of the world, which create a sort of deadly fog around his virtues. It can be bitten or eaten by some poisonous creature, damaged, knocked down by accident. Yes, he can be bitten by some vice, eaten by the devil who is always lurking around him; he can die from a thousand dangers if no one watches over him, if he is not guarded and surrounded by all sorts of care on the part of vigilant superiors.

Moreover, the fruit, and even the whole tree, can be destroyed by caterpillars, which eat first the leaves, then the flowers and the fruit, and finally kill the whole tree. A nest of caterpillars can kill a tree. But what does a nest of caterpillars symbolize? A defect which one cultivates, into which one falls often and easily, and which produces a habit of venial sins.

This young brother, full of self-love and vanity, who entertains a thousand proud thoughts; who is only interested in pleasing people, who is always boasting; who in a word, nourishes the detestable worm of pride, commits a great number of venial sins every day, and they eventually undermine his virtue. That other one, whose main vice is sensuality, does not control his greed, eats and drinks between meals, is always looking for ways to satisfy human nature, is afraid of work and looks for comfort; he thus builds up a dangerous habit of venial sins which will lead him to the evil vice which St. Paul forbids us to name, and sadly, perhaps even to eternal death.

Yes, experience teaches us that anyone who feeds a habit of venial sins sooner or later falls into mortal sin. It is very necessary to instill in young brothers a great horror of minor faults, and to make them really understand that one of the devil's most dangerous snares is to let oneself slide into them without remorse. So wage war on the caterpillars' nests! Wage war on habitual faults!

A serpent in a tree is less to be feared than a tiny worm who burrows into it and kills the trunk. The serpent here is a figure of some violent passion which one recognizes and combats, of a grave fault into which one has fallen by surprise and from which one rises at once. The tiny worm who hides in the pith and eats it, is the figure of a slight defect which one loves and maintains, and which becomes a source of habitual venial sins. This defect becomes a habit, gnaws at the heart, weakens the soul, destroys all its good dispositions, and causes its total loss. So wage war on those gnawing little worms!

V.

A young brother is a child who cannot walk by himself. He needs to be taught how; he needs to be supported by a halter like the ones used for little children. In other words, he needs to be guided along the path to virtue.

A young brother does not know how to walk alone with God, in his prayers. He does not know how to go about them, nor what he should ask for. So help him with your advice and your encouragement, and make him give you a frequent account of the way he uses his time during prayer, meditation, examen and spiritual reading.

He does not know how to walk alone by himself. His defects and his needs irritate and discourage him; his imagination leads him astray; if he has a lively character, it overwhelms him; if he is easy-going, it plunges him into apathy and laziness; his heart seduces him and turns its affections towards things it ought to detest; his vacillating will does not know what it wants and leaves him floating at the mercy of every impression he receives from outside.

He does not know how to act with his brothers. When his passions begin to simmer, if he does not have a good religious formation, he lets himself be swept away by the outbursts of his character, and can easily appear to be lacking in consideration, respect or charity towards the others. Since he considers only his own needs and interests, he thinks everyone else is there to keep him happy and satisfy his whims.

He does not know how to act in his work. Besides the fact that he is a novice in every area, the little difficulties he encounters discourage him and make him want to give up entirely.

Finally, he does not know how to act along the way to virtue and perfection; he needs an enlightened guide. He therefore needs to be supported, directed, helped, encouraged, instructed; for if you leave him alone, he will lose his way, and once he is on the wrong road, he will ruin everything, both spiritually and materially speaking. He will soon become discouraged, abandon his best resolutions and then his vocation, and be in danger of losing his soul.

VI.

A young brother is weak, inconstant and inexperienced. He is weak: in terms of his intellect, which is not yet sufficiently formed, developed and enlightened. Think of a two-year-old child, who is unable to understand the nature of things, their good or bad qualities, and how to use them. He does not know how dangerous it is to play with a sharp instrument, and cuts and slashes his hands without realizing it, while playing. He puts poison into his mouth as though it were a delicious piece of fruit. He sings and jumps for joy at the edge of a cliff.

That is an image of an inexperienced young brother who does not comprehend the value of his vocation, his salvation, his eternity. He does not know how dangerous it is to become intimately linked with this or that person who gives him bad advice and leads him into evil; or to read this book which awakens his passions; or not to reveal the serious dangers which surround him in his work and which are a proximate occasion of sin for him. He will be hurt, he will fall and will infallibly perish, if no friendly hand is stretched out in time to pull him back from the edge of the cliff or to remove whatever could cause his downfall.

The young brother is lacking in light and instruction. Therefore, he is not sufficiently aware of what he is, what he can do, what he should be. He has only an imperfect idea of his faults and his good qualities, and he lacks the prudence he needs to choose the safe road, between the impulses of grace which draw him toward God and the inclinations of fallen human nature which push him away from Him.

He is also weak in his religious and moral formation. He cannot distinguish clearly enough what is merely an attraction to evil from consent to evil, inconstancy of heart from inconstancy of will, the withdrawal of tangible graces from the withdrawal of necessary actual grace which is never lacking to anyone who asks for it in prayer.

Moreover, he needs—and this is the way God wants it—a wise and enlightened mentor who will stimulate him to do his duty and help him to use the faculties of his soul, and to reform what may be defective in them. Since he is not accustomed to reflection, he has only a vague idea of God's plans for him; so why be surprised that he does not throw himself zealously into carrying them out?

He is not sufficiently aware of his predominant passion and how to overcome it. He does not see clearly the snares set for him by the devil, the world and the other enemies of salvation. Being constantly on the edge of the precipice which threatens every soul, he so much needs a wise and friendly hand to guide and uphold him! Without it, inexperienced as he is, there is good reason to fear that he will not realize the danger he is in until he has fallen into the abyss.

The young brother is weak in virtue. Was he well brought up? He will tend toward what is good. Was he badly brought up? He will tend toward what is bad. Is he with good people? He will be good. If he eventually lives with lax confrères, he will easily become lax himself.

The principles and beauty of virtue, and solemn religious ceremonies, all please and touch him, arouse his enthusiasm and lead him toward God, to whom he gives himself heart and soul. But if the world smiles on him, shows him its deceitful pleasures and its vanities? His weakness and the innate tendencies of human nature will leave him open to throwing himself blindly at them, without even thinking about what he has promised his Creator. His virtue lacks manly firmness. He changes with the moods and instability of his heart: today he is pious and enthused about doing good; tomorrow he is dissipated, frivolous, disgusted with prayer, never thinks of God. Today he is active, in high spirits, obedient, because he likes his work; tomorrow he is lazy, rebellious, has no follow-through, because he doesn't like the orders he is given. His inclinations, tastes, and imagination play a large role in his life; not only that, but sometimes it is not virtue or a sense of duty which motivates him, but his whims and fantasies.

The young brother has a weak character and a weak will. He easily makes good resolutions, but does he always keep them? In the morning, at meditation and Mass, he is full of ardor and fire, but the difficulties and contradictions which arise later in the day are enough to extinguish that ardor and make him abandon everything.

He thinks he can do anything, whereas a mere trifle makes him waver and give ground before his enemy. If he succeeds, if someone praises him, he's elated, full of joy. If he suffers some setback, he is dejected, sad, sometimes even reduced to tears.

Discouragement and inconstancy are his major sicknesses; how can he react and struggle with any success against these two formidable foes if he is left to himself and to the whims of his imagination? Since he is still not used to the spiritual combat, temptations weary and worry him. In that condition, which is dangerous for his vocation and his soul, he is very much at risk of losing both if he does not receive wise and fatherly direction.

This is the critical moment when his vocation will be decided. If he opens up and asks advice, you must welcome him with great charity, be full of compassion for him, rekindle his courage, stir up his good will, nourish his piety by prayer, and show him that the source of consolations, light and strength lies in assiduous prayer and fervent reception of the sacraments.

***

Now let me say a few words about the means we should take and how we should act in order to form and direct these young brothers, correct their faults and assist them in their many needs.

1. The older brothers, and especially the directors, should give the young brothers good example. Good example is, in fact, the quickest way to form young religious to virtue, because they more readily believe what they see others doing than the instructions they are given; because example shows that virtue is easy; because young people are natural imitators. Besides, they are so weak that it is very hard for them to bring themselves to do good unless they see the same being done by those who are ahead of them.

A brother director has as many copies of his actions, as many imitators of his conduct, as he has brothers to direct. So he should always act in such a way as to be able to say to them what St. Paul said to the first Christians, «Be followers of me, as I also am of Christ» (*1 Cor* 4:16; 11:1). Caesar never told his soldiers, «Do this,» but rather, «Let's do this»; he was always at their head and shared all their hardships. That is how a director should act and speak. A master forms his disciples in his own image. A director who is pious, regular, humble, silent, modest and zealous will enjoy the consolation of seeing all his virtues reproduced in the members of his community.

2. A brother director should stir up the spirit of piety in the young brothers. He who knows how to pray well knows how to live well, as St. Augustine said. Yes, he who knows how to pray well knows how to live as a good religious, knows how to bring up children well, knows how to do his work well, knows how to practice every virtue. To form brothers to piety is, so to speak, to make them capable of doing everything; it is to make holy religious of them, because, as our Founder said, «To be genuinely pious and to be a holy religious is the same thing.»

To inspire them to genuine piety, make them read books about asceticism, books likely to make them love their holy state; make them give you an account of their meditations, help them to make them, and to say all their other prayers well. Suggest that they make some novenas to the Blessed Virgin and to the Sacred

Heart to obtain the gift of piety. But above all, insist that they perform all the spiritual exercises prescribed by the rule, with exactitude and piety.

3. Young brothers need to be encouraged. The most common temptation the devil uses to destroy young people is to discourage them, to make virtue appear exaggeratedly difficult to practice, and also to exaggerate their faults, in order to make them give it all up. Therefore, if you want your young brothers to avoid this snare of the devil, strengthen and stir up their courage constantly.

People need encouragement at all ages, but this help is especially necessary for young people, because since they lack experience, the least difficulty brings them to a halt and makes them abandon their good resolutions. Since they are simple, naive and honest, they easily believe what they are told, and offer no resistance to the impetus they are given. If they are well directed, if they receive good advice, if they are encouraged, they take the path of virtue and walk it at a steady pace. On the other hand, if they are left to themselves, maltreated, led to believe that virtue is difficult, that they are not up to it, or that they do not have sufficient aptitude for their work or for their state of life, that is enough to discourage them and lead them to abandon everything.

It is a great shame for a young brother to fall into the hands of a severe, hard, uncharitable, imprudent director. Nurturing a newborn child demands goodness, indulgence, care, attention and a mother's heart. And how much more necessary is that mother's heart when it comes to training a young brother! A brother director should be filled with the same motherly feelings for his young brothers as those of St. Paul, who in writing to the early faithful, told them, «My dearest children…by the gospel I have begotten you» (1 Cor 4:14-15).

Why «my dearest children»? What do those words mean? They mean that one must be a father, that one must, if possible, have the feelings of a mother, to win young people over to God and train them in virtue; because the hand and heart of a master are not enough—in fact, they are totally inappropriate.

4. As far as possible, one should avoid scolding young brothers. It may be necessary to make frequent remarks to them; one must warn them when they are not doing things well, teach them how to act, show them how to do things by doing in front of them what they do not know how to do themselves. But one must not scold them or speak rudely to them, because nothing is more likely to turn them away from doing good and make them disgusted with the service of God.

Besides, if a brother director has a habit of scolding, it costs him the esteem of his brothers, destroys the effectiveness of everything he says, causes murmuring and sows bad spirit in a community. Another thing, which is no less important, is not to blame young brothers for too many faults at a time. It is infinitely preferable to show them to them one by one, so as not to discourage them.

5. It is also a duty of justice and prudence for a director always to proportion young brothers' tasks to their strength, intelligence and capacity. To demand of a young religious more than he can do is an injustice. It offers him an occasion for becoming irritated and moody, and abandoning everything. One brother, because he lacks experience, character or aptitude, or because he has not been trained, has no discipline, and his class makes very little progress. Another, in charge of the kitchen, leaves some[thing] to be desired, for the same reasons. Be satisfied with these brothers' good will; don't persecute them, don't nag them, don't discourage them by showing that you are dissatisfied with them, by scolding them, or by demanding of them more than they are capable of producing.

What a beautiful gift, what a delightful quality it is for a superior to realize what task best suits each one, and to be satisfied with what each one can do!

6. Young brothers must be carefully followed up in every detail of their conduct. This is the best way to learn their defects, their good qualities, their progress, and their needs, both spiritual and physical, and to be in a position to correct what is bad and to maintain and perfect what is good. It is also the best way to accustom a young brother to obedience and to preserve him from willfulness which is such a dangerous defect in a religious.

7. Finally, it is a duty for the brothers directors and all the older brothers to respect the young brothers. But what must they respect in them?

a. Their innocence. To do so, one must be very reserved in one's speech, never talk about the world nor of anything whatsoever which might make them aware of evil or start them thinking about it. How many young brothers have told me, «Such and such a conversation which was held in my presence was fatal for me; it brought on dangerous temptations and falls.» What a terrible responsibility a brother director incurs if he is not circumspect in his words and actions.

b. Their virtue, especially their esteem for the Rule, and the veneration, confidence and openness of heart they show toward the Superior General.

c. One must also respect and uphold their authority. To do so, one must be very careful not to reprimand them in front of the children or speak to them without deference and politeness.

d. It is only just to respect their rights, listen to their remarks and their excuses, and accept them when they are well founded, leaving them entire liberty to have recourse to the Superior General when they so wish.

e. It is also an unquestionable duty for the brother director to respect their person, deal courteously with all of them, command them with gentleness, and treat them as his brothers, as members of the same body, as other selves.

f. Finally, one must never lose sight of this particular form of respect which is due to their youth and their weakness. Whatever is weak deserves our concern and our respect. Now, as we have just said, everything about a young brother is weak: his character, his will, his virtue, his intellect, his vocation. Hence, everything needs to be cared for, fortified, treated with care and delicacy, with that sort of respect, in a word, which is simply a mixture of tenderness, condescension and gentleness.

CHAPTER THREE

THE MISFORTUNE OF LOSING ONE'S VOCATION

As Father Champagnat was visiting a classroom one day, he saw one of the most pious brothers on his knees. «What's this?» he said, «You in penance? I'm scandalized!» The brother lowered his head and said nothing. During recreation after dinner, Father ran into him; he could hardly wait to ask him what fault he had committed.

«Father, I talked a little bit too much.»

«I doubt you would have been punished like that just for saying a few idle words.»

«What I said wasn't just idle; it offended one of the brothers.»

«What did you say?»

«While Brother Louis was explaining to us what it meant to miss one's vocation, I said to so-and-so, 'You're nothing but a missed brother.' He got angry and told Brother Louis, who punished me, as you saw for yourself.»

«Did you say that just for laughs, or was there some malice behind it?»

«Well, I must admit that what I said was more or less what I think of him and pretty well expressed my feelings.»

«That's too bad. You would have been better off listening carefully to Brother Louis; at least then you would have learned what it means to miss one's vocation.»

Our Founder, who seized every opportunity of teaching his brothers, seeing that several of them had come over and were listing to this conversation, repeated, «What does it mean to miss one's vocation?»

«Throwing your cassock into the bushes,» said one.

«So you don't see any difference between losing your vocation and missing it? There's a big difference between them. To miss your vocation, to lose your vocation, to profane your vocation, to be unfaithful to your vocation, are definitely very different things.»

«Father,» several brothers said at the same time, «would you explain all those things to us? Brother Louis didn't go into all those details, and we'd like to know about them.»

«All right, so be it,» he answered; «listen to me now, and remember what I'm going to tell you.»

I.

To miss your vocation means to be unaware of God's plans for you. It means not knowing your vocation or having only a confused and incomplete notion of it. For example, there are individuals who are good and pious by nature, which gives them a disposition for religious life, but they stay in the world because they have never had the advantage of seeing religious and they don't know any religious communities, so they never have the opportunity or the means to embrace this way of life. If people like that are faithful to grace, then a well-ordered and pious life in the world will replace the vocation they were unable to follow for lack of sufficient enlightenment and knowledge.

II.

To lose your vocation means that after having known it sufficiently, and having entered a community, you leave before making profession. It means not having known at all how or what to cultivate, maintain, strengthen and preserve a vocation which was really given by God, or not having wanted to do so. It means not having made any profit at all on the talent entrusted to you by the divine Master. It means that after having answered the divine call and embraced a definite vocation, you stop answering and finally end up having that special favor withdraw, for one of the following reasons:

- abuse of grace and contempt for little things;
- uncontrolled passion for study or some material thing;
- infidelity to the Rule;
- neglecting the exercises of piety;
- violent temptations followed by repeated grave faults;
- finally, discouragement, which is the most common cause of the loss of vocation.

«Even just one of these causes, if it is not removed, and if it becomes a habit of venial sin as it usually does, is enough to make one lose his vocation.

«Loss of vocation has the most serious consequences. Here are the three most common ones:

1. An unhappy life. The man who is not where God wants him to be is like a dislocated limb, which suffers and makes the whole body suffer.

2. A long string of related faults. Massillon says that 'Everything becomes a temptation or a stumbling-block for anyone who leaves a holy state to which God is calling him, in order to jump back into the world. The most innocent pleasures soil his heart; the most indifferent objects will be fatal for his innocence; the easiest obligations will arouse in him invincible repugnance; he will corrupt everything by using it improperly; no matter which way he turns, he will find himself caught in snares.'

«There are three disastrous things which follow the loss of one's vocation,» adds Tronson; «deprivation of a great number of graces, a terrifying succession of sins, and the risk of being damned.»

3. Lack of success in everything one undertakes. How can you succeed in a job and in a state of life in which you have

placed yourself and to which God is not calling you? He who resists God cannot count on his protection; so what will happen to him is exactly what the prophet said: 'Unless the Lord build the house, they labor in vain that build it' (Ps 126:1). Such a person will throw himself into all sorts of ventures, will try everything, and more often than not, will fail at everything.

«Now, my friends, let me tell you a little story which you'll enjoy because it confirms what I just told you and because it's about the Blessed Virgin whom you love so much:

«St. Catherine of Sweden, the daughter of St. Bridget, was violently tempted to abandon her vocation. Her mother prayed for her, and the next night, Catherine saw the whole world on fire, and herself totally surrounded by the flames. At that moment, the Blessed Virgin appeared to her, and Catherine cried out to her, 'Help me, holy Mother of God!'

'Oh?' said Mary, 'You show contempt for your vocation, you want to return to the world and all its dangers, you want to deliberately throw yourself into these flames of hell, and now you call on me for help? I don't help those who willingly put themselves in danger!'

«Catherine promised not to pay any attention to the temptation, and to be faithful to her vocation, and the Blessed Virgin immediately extinguished the fire which was threatening to consume everything.

«So, my friends,» added Fr. Champagnat, «if any of you is tempted to abandon his vocation, let him remember this little story, and invoke the Blessed Virgin right away and with fervor.

«The Little Brother of Mary who entrusts his vocation to his heavenly Mother every day, will never lose it.

«Now let's see what it means to profane one's vocation or apostatize from it.»

III.

To apostatize from one's vocation means to abandon it when it is no longer a matter of counsel but one of precept; in other words, after having made profession. Profaning one's vocation and the holy covenant one has made with God often brings on the total ruin of one's salvation. It is like a shipwreck on the high seas; after such a disaster, it will be very difficult, perhaps impossible, to reach port. It is total bankruptcy; the entire economy of one's salvation, one's whole spiritual fortune is endangered and perhaps ruined forever. Apart from mental illness, the only way one reaches such a state is through crimes, the profanation of one's vows and the sacraments, total neglect of duty, or some other enormous failing.

There is nothing worse than apostate religious. St. Augustine's opinion of them was, «I have never seen more perverse and more deeply corrupted individuals than those who went bad in religious life.» According to St. Robert Bellarmine, they were prefigured by the figs which Isaiah saw, so bad, so rotten, that the mere sight of them disgusted people and made them want to vomit. It was of them that Jesus Christ was speaking when he said, «No man putting his hand to the plow, and looking back, is fit for the kingdom of God» (Lk 9:62).

St. Thomas also spoke about them when he stated that one of the strongest signs of reprobation is inconstancy in one's vocation. And finally, St. Paul was talking about them when he stated that it is impossible, meaning really that it is very difficult, for those who have been enlightened, who have tasted the gift of God and have then fallen, to be renewed later on by penance, because they have done all they can to crucify the Son of God all over again and heap scorn upon him. For, he adds, the earth «that brings forth thorns and briers is reprobate, and very near to a curse, whose end is to be burnt» (Heb 6:8). I have finally come to understand the words of St. Ignatius, «For a professed religious,

MARCELLIN CHAMPAGNAT

the most dangerous temptation of all is temptation against one's vocation.»

«Well, my friends, let's leave such a sad and frightening subject, and conclude by saying what it means to be unfaithful to one's vocation.»

IV.

To be unfaithful to one's vocation means:

1. not reaching the degree of virtue and perfection to which one is called; it means not being sufficiently faithful to grace; it means shrinking from being hard on oneself, living in laxity and tepidity;

2. not doing all the good one had the grace to do, that one could and should have done.

Every religious teacher who neglects his own perfection and education is more or less unfaithful to his vocation. These are the sad effects of infidelity to one's vocation:

1. a host of little faults, and sometimes big ones;

2. a restless, unhappy life, in which one is not happy with his confrères, with himself, nor even with God; one is deprived of the hundredfold of consolations and happiness promised by Jesus Christ;

3. the danger of losing one's vocation and being abandoned by God;

4. great fear of death, many regrets and terrible anxiety at that formidable moment;

5. a long and rigorous purgatory.

«There, my dear brothers,» Father concluded, «is the explanation you asked me for. May God help you to be profoundly aware of it. May he help you understand the value of your vocation. May he preserve you in it and keep all of you faithful to it!»

CHAPTER FOUR

HOW THE YOUNG BROTHERS FASTED

During Father Champagnat's lifetime, there was great fervor in the novitiate. All the brothers, even the youngest, strove to become virtuous out of a sense of duty, out of love, and out of a holy desire to imitate Jesus Christ and to become like him. Now, it happened one Lent that all the young brothers decided that they wanted to follow the example of our Savior and fast for the entire forty days. This project of youthful mortification came out of a recreation period.

«Here it is Lent,» they said to one another, «the time to fast and do penance.»

«I intend to fast every day,» said one of them.

«Me, too,» chimed in several others.

«But,» someone interjected, «I heard that they won't let the young brothers fast.»

«Oh, that's too bad,» said all those good young brothers very sadly.

«Well,» put in one of the youngest enthusiastically, «it's true that you have to be twenty-one to fast without any difficulty, but if we ask permission to fast, they'll give it to us, because we're not sick and we're all feeling fine.»

So it was agreed and decided that six of them would go to Father Champagnat to ask permission for all of them to fast. They were so fervent, so simple and so naive that it never even occurred to them that they might be refused. Our six delegates went to the Founder's room; they entered rather timidly, bowed deeply, and then the oldest, who was not yet sixteen, spoke for all of them:

«Very Reverend Father, we have come here humbly and confidently to ask your permission to fast for the whole of Lent.»

«For the whole of Lent?»

«Yes, Father, the whole of Lent.»

«That's a very long time. Do you know how many fast days there are in Lent?»

«Forty days.»

«So you want to fast for forty days?»

«Yes, Father.»

«All six of you?»

«Not just the six of us, but all the other young brothers too. We came to ask your permission in their name.»

«My children, I am impressed by your fervor and your love of penance and mortification, and to encourage you to persevere in the practice of those virtues, I give you permission to fast during Lent. You may go tell the other brothers who sent you. But since you are young and inexperienced, and since you need to be guided in everything, I will tell you tomorrow just how you should carry out this long forty-day fast. Meanwhile, eat a very good supper, so that your stomach will be ready to fast well all through Lent. Now go tell all your confrères that I give them permission to fast, but that I reserve the right to explain to you how to do it well and really sanctify it.»

Our young brothers thanked Father affectionately, left his room full of joy, and could hardly wait to tell their confrères that their request had been granted, and that they could get ready to fast for the whole of Lent.

Soon the whole community knew that the young brothers were preparing to compete with the older ones in penance and mortification. Everyone was delighted, especially the cook, since that would lighten his task considerably, and dispense him from having to make lunch.

The next day, as he had promised, and as was his custom, Father Champagnat gave the community a conference for the beginning of Lent, and he spoke about how to sanctify the fast. Even though it was a day dedicated to penance, he was more cheerful than usual. Everyone could see the contentment and holy joy on his face.

«My dear brothers,» he said, «I am pleased to inform you that all the members of the community are well disposed to sanctify the Lenten season. The proof is that the older brothers' spirit of mortification and penance has fortunately become contagious and spread to all the young brothers, which has led them to come to ask my permission to fast all during Lent.

«Are you surprised that I granted their request? Now, don't be jealous of them, you old brothers; rather, rejoice to see that your example has borne such good fruit!

«Yes, you young brothers will all be fasting, because you all need to do penance in order to preserve your innocence, to imitate Jesus Christ, and to earn the heavenly reward which is waiting for you. But since the Church is a good mother, and takes care of the bodies of all her children as well as their souls, she permits you because of your age to follow a less painful fast than the one she demands of your confrères and all the other faithful who are over twenty-one. She dispenses you from making your stomach fast, and asks of you only four simple practices which will give you the merit and rewards of fasting.

I.

The first observance which Holy Mother Church wants to see you practice, is to make your eyes fast by means of modesty. This type of fasting is very pleasing to God, and will be very meritorious for you, for the three following reasons:

1. Modesty represses the passions, and is a barricade against sin. Do you know what these words of the Holy Spirit mean: «Death is come up through our windows»? (Jer 9:21[20]). They mean that sin, which is death to the soul, enters through our eyes when we are not careful to control them modestly. The holy man Job, who had meditated deeply on those words, said, «I made a pact,» in other words a covenant, «with my eyes, never to think of anything evil» (cf. Job 31:1). Why do you think he said, «not to think,» instead of «not to see» anything evil? Because our thoughts are so closely linked to what we see, that the two always go together. So, modesty keeps us from sinning.

2. Modesty leads to recollection, prevents distractions, and encourages piety and devotion. He who wants to pray well must therefore first of all be very modest, and carefully control all his senses, especially his eyes, because letting one's glance roam freely is an unquenchable source of distractions.

3. Modesty edifies one's neighbor, makes him love virtue and leads him to God. The modesty of holy religious inspires deep remorse in sinners, and puts the brakes on their disorderly lives. That was how St. Bernardine's modesty put a stop to the licentiousness of his fellow-students, who used to say, «Here comes Bernardine; we'd better behave!» It is said that no one could see the great St. Ephrem without experiencing feelings of devotion and without wanting to become better, because his modesty was so great and so obviously inspired by virtue. Likewise, the modesty of the martyr St. Lucian was so powerfully admirable that it compelled even pagans to embrace Christianity. When the tyrannical emperor Maximian heard about this, he sent for Lucian, but he was so afraid of being converted by his modesty that he had a curtain hung between him and the saint.

«Dear Brothers, be recollected, be modest in the way you look at things, in your behavior, in all your actions. Make all your senses fast by means of great self-control, and you will really sanctify the Lenten season. Every single day will be filled with virtues and merits for you.

II.

The second thing the Church expects of you is to make your tongue fast by keeping silence. This kind of fasting has two advantages:

1. It helps you to avoid sin. It is truly written, «In the multitude of words there shall not want sin» (Prov 10:19); and elsewhere, «He that uses many words shall hurt his own soul» (Sir 20:8); and also, «An unbridled tongue,» that is, one which does not keep silence, «is a world of iniquity» (cf. Jas 1:26, 3:6). So, I assure you that if you make your tongue fast, you will cut your daily faults in half. The fast of the tongue is extremely profitable for one's soul and one's conscience!

2. But that's not all; this kind of fasting preserves and nourishes all the virtues and makes them grow, which is why the Holy Spirit has said, «If any man offend not in word, the same is a perfect man» (Jas 3:2). In other words, he would possess all the virtues.

If you want to know if someone is healthy, often all you have to do is look at his tongue; if it's red and inflamed, or dull, or whitish, he's sick, his health isn't good. Likewise, to know the state of soul of a religious, pay attention to his tongue, how he controls and uses it. If he talks a lot, you may be almost sure that his soul is full of faults and sins. If he speaks little, if he is reserved and circumspect in his speech, you may be certain that his soul is adorned with beautiful virtues.

The itch to talk, the habit of mocking, teasing or dissipation, is a sure sign of a vain and dissolute conscience, a superficial mind, a soul which is weak and devoid of virtue. St. Thomas Aquinas was so convinced of this that he stated flatly, «If you see a religious who enjoys idle conversations, mockery, worldly trifles, beware of thinking him spiritual and virtuous, even if he performs miracles.»

To make your tongue fast is therefore a good way to protect yourself from sinning, to increase and develop your virtues, to be pleasing to God and even to learn how to speak well.

III.

The third penitential practice expected of you will be to make your defects and little passions fast. Now, do you know, my dear young brothers, what it means to make your defects fast? It means to fight them, to resist them. Are you inclined, for example, to lie now and then, to speak ill of your neighbor, to make fun of your brothers, to be disrespectful towards them, to come late to certain community exercises, and so on? If you correct these things, if you abstain from them until Easter, you will have made your defects fast.

To make your passions fast means to struggle against temptations and the evil inclinations of our fallen human nature; it means to avoid sin, and to uproot from our heart, by mortification, all the weeds the devil has sown there. Let's imagine you're prone to laziness, pride, envy, gluttony, certain forbidden pleasures, moodiness, and so on. Combat them all; tell these evil passions, «Get away from me; don't come back to bother me until Easter. I've made up my mind to fight you to the death, and I'm going to wage war against you all during Lent and forever after.»

«And that's not all,» you should add; «I'm going to apply myself in a special way to the practice of the virtues contrary to all those passions. I will combat laziness by great fidelity to regulations and by studying and working hard. I will combat pride by offering all my actions to God, by doing them all for him and not to please others, by doing all the little favors I can for my confrères, and by making myself the servant of all. I will combat gluttony by mortifying myself at meals, and sensuality by being careful to refuse myself anything that I don't really need.» What an excellent fast that will be! What a holy Lent you will spend, dear brothers, if you act this way! This is the real way to imitate Jesus, to share in his sufferings, and to guarantee yourselves a treasury of merits for all eternity.

IV.

The fourth observance will be never to make your soul fast, never to give it moldy bread. You make your soul fast when you miss your exercises of piety, such as meditation, examen, spiritual reading, Mass and Communion. You make your soul fast when you neglect the practice of virtues and good works; when you are unfaithful to grace; when you act without any intention or through routine, and therefore without merit. To give your soul moldy bread means to say your prayers badly, to say them without fervor, preparation or devotion; it means to give in to distractions, laxity and a thousand ways of being culpably negligent.

Prayers said negligently, with deliberate distractions; spiritual reading done inattentively, with no desire to profit from it, with no personal application, do to the soul what moldy bread does to the body. It is spoiled, unhealthy food which disturbs your health, weakens it little by little, or even ruins it instead of maintaining and strengthening it. So don't make your soul fast in any way; don't give it moldy bread. In other words, don't drop any of your exercises of piety, don't be satisfied with simply performing them, but perform them well, and be brave in fighting distractions, negligence and routine.

And now, brothers, I must ask you a question. Why does the Church prescribe fasting? You will no doubt tell me that we must do penance, combat and overcome our passions, mortify our bodies, and ultimately, imitate Jesus Christ. Very good; those are definitely the major motives for fasting. But is that all? No, we also fast and deprive ourselves of some food in order to help the poor more, and to distribute more alms by giving to them what we have given up ourselves. That is what good Christians do; they give the poor the benefit of their fasting, that is to say, everything of which they deprive themselves.

Brothers, I want you to do something of the sort. I want you to offer to God, for the conversion of sinners and infidels, for the sanctification of the children in our schools and the relief of the souls in purgatory, all the acts of virtue you will perform through your modesty, your fidelity to silence, and the violence you will do yourselves in order to combat your defects and passions, to pray well and to practice the virtues of our holy state.

This offering and gift will be very pleasing to God, very useful to your neighbor, and much more meritorious for you than depriving yourself of a piece of bread in order to give it to the poor.

«Well, brothers,» concluded the Founder, «are you happy with the fast I'm proposing to you? Does it satisfy your devotion and your love of penance?» He stopped there as if awaiting an answer. All the young brothers who had been listening to him very attentively, even if their pious hopes had been a bit disappointed, lowered their eyes and nodded their heads with a smile, as if to say, «Yes, Father, we're satisfied, and we'll do exactly what you have just advised.»

Then he added, «To show you how much I want to encourage those who love penance and mortification, and to show you how edified and pleased I am with your docility, I give you permission for the fast of the stomach—the regular fast—every Friday in honor of Our Lord's Passion.»

So the young brothers were completely happy, and the older ones felt both satisfied and challenged. As for Father Champagnat, he was delighted. And Our Lord must have spread abundantly over all of them the choicest blessings of his loving heart.

CHAPTER FIVE

THE KINDS OF BROTHERS FATHER CHAMPAGNAT DID NOT LIKE

Father Champagnat was very cheerful and talkative during recreations, and even though his conversations usually centered around serious and edifying topics, he always made them pleasant and lively, which amused his listeners even as he was teaching them. One day, after speaking about the qualities a teacher needed in order to make his students like him, he laughed and said, «Guess what kind of brothers I don't like!» Since no one knew what to say, he answered his own question:

I.

«I don't like brothers who are 'preachers', because they give sermons.» "It's not a brother's job to give long explanations, and ask difficult questions, much less to give sermons. All those things should be left to the clergy. Brothers should stick to having the catechism learned by heart and asking a few pertinent questions to make sure that the children understand what they are reciting. They should strive to engrave deeply in the children's minds the great truths of religion, and come back often to those truths and the principal mysteries of our faith. They should aim at training the children in the practices of Christian piety, and at giving them a great horror of sin, great confidence in Our Lord and great love for him. But they should do all that in a few words, with simple questions, suggestions, and comments, and not with long speeches which wear the children out but don't teach them anything."

II.

«I don't like pretentious brothers, because they parade around the classroom.» "While brothers like this stride gravely around the room and turn their backs on the children, the latter fool around, and sometimes even scandalize each other and teach each other bad things."

So there is good reason why the Rule says a brother should stay in his seat and not leave it without necessity. That way, he can always see the children, he is always aware of everything they are doing, and by that very fact, he makes it impossible for them to disturb, to neglect their work or to elude their teacher's vigilance. Discipline, good spirit, and even the students' progress are fundamentally dependent on the exact observance of this rule.

III.

«I don't like brothers who are 'nannies', because they lack dignity, they caress the children suggestively and spoil their character.» "Experience definitely teaches us that children who are admired, caressed, flattered and praised without good reason and beyond limits, lose all respect and esteem for their teachers. They become proud, hypocritical, self-willed, violent, disobedient, ungrateful, selfish, and very often even licentious and totally depraved."

There are several ways to spoil a child: you spoil his mind with exaggerated praise; you spoil his heart by paying too much attention to him and showing him too much affection; you spoil his will by letting him follow his own whims; you spoil his character by tolerating his defects.

It is mainly through familiarity, and lack of gravity and dignity, that one manages to spoil all of a child's faculties at once in this way. A brother who has good judgment, who values his reputation, who understands his own dignity and that of the child; a brother who, above all, wants to do good and to forestall all danger to himself, shows profound respect for his students. He always speaks to them with reserve, and never touches them, whether to caress or to punish them.

IV.

«I don't like brothers who are executioners. What a terrible defect it is to slap children, to strike them with one's hand, the signal or the pointer, to pull their ears or their hair! Isn't that a bit like what Jesus' executioners did, when they mocked the divine Savior?»

So there is a good reason why our rule tells us that all these ways of correcting children are unbecoming, are opposed to charity, demonstrate anger, and are forbidden to the brothers. Do you raise children properly and train them in virtue with blows of the cane? No, it is courtesy, reason and religion, not corporal punishment, which produce submission and turn the heart towards good.

«But, Father,» objected one brother, «the Holy Spirit recommends chastising children and carefully correcting them.»

«Yes, that's true,» Father answered; «the Holy Spirit wants children to be corrected. He even makes it a duty for fathers and mothers, and therefore for those who take their place. But chastising children does not mean beating them; in Scripture, the word 'chastise' does not mean to inflict corporal punishment, but simply to punish in general.»

«Father,» said another, «may I point out to you that we need to punish in order to obtain the discipline you so much recommend and which you assure us is half of education.»

«My dear friend,» he answered, «discipline is so essential to education that without it no education is possible. But do you believe that corporal punishment establishes order and discipline in a school? In my opinion, discipline is the result of moral authority rather than punishment, which ordinarily produces no other effect than to make children angry and drive them away from the school. And moral authority comes from ability, virtue, consistently edifying behavior, unlimited dedication to the children's education, and a constantly uniform character.

«Besides, what is the point of discipline? Is it simply to create external order in a class, to force the children into submission and subject them willy-nilly to the school regulations? No, the aim of discipline is to win the children's hearts, to train them in virtue, to lead them to do their duty out of love and not to make them tremble. To accomplish all that, discipline must be fatherly; if it is not, it really does not educate a child, and instead of making him better, it only makes him worse. Show yourself to be your children's father rather than their master; then they will respect and obey you without difficulty.»

The spirit in a brothers' school should be that of a good family, not that of a barracks or a prison. What stands out in a good family are mutual respect, love and confidence, not fear of punishment. Anger, brutality and hardness are inspired by the devil to destroy the fruit of the good principles given to the child. Just as weeds choke the wheat, excessive punishment stifles the good attitudes which your teaching and good example can produce in the children's hearts.

At that point, the bell interrupted this interesting exchange, but at the next recreation, the brothers immediately gathered around Father Champagnat and asked, «Father, are there any other kinds of brothers you don't like?»

«Yes, there are—several of them,» he answered.

V.

«I don't like brothers who 'have sore elbows',» for four reasons:

«1. Because lazy people are not fit for religious life, which is by nature a life of work, devotedness and mortification;

«2. Because idleness is the mother of all vices.» St. John Chrysostom says, «Land which is not cultivated or sown produces nothing but weeds, and the man who gives in to sloth is full of defects, vices and sins. The man who works is tempted by only one devil, but the lazy man is pursued by a legion of them.» According to St. Thomas Aquinas, laziness is the bait with which the devil most easily catches souls. Look at Samson: as long as he was fighting the Philistines, he stayed strong and virtuous. As long as David was busy with the work of establishing his kingdom, he stayed out of sin. As long as Solomon was busy with the building of the Temple, he remained wise and in control of his passions. But as soon as these three great men gave in to the dangers of idleness and easy living, they fell and let themselves be overcome by the most shameful passions.

«3. Because idleness is very displeasing to God and enough to cause the loss of a soul.» Jesus teaches us this truth when he condemns the lazy servant and the man who buried his talent, when he curses the fig tree that had nothing but leaves, and when he ordered the sterile tree cut down and burned. St. Paul teaches us the same truth by means of a comparison: «The earth that drinks in the rain which comes often upon it, and brings forth herbs for them by whom it is tilled, receives blessing from God. But that which brings forth thorns and briers, is reprobate, and very near to a curse, whose end is to be burnt» (Heb 6:7-8). The good soil is the symbol of the hardworking man; the bad soil, which produces nothing but brambles and which is condemned and burned over, represents the lazy man.

«4. Because the idle man is useless, an embarrassment to everyone.» That's why the Holy Spirit says, «As vinegar to the teeth and smoke to the eyes, so is the lazy man to those [with whom he lives]» (Prov 10:26). That means that he makes everyone around him, everyone who works with him, everyone who lives with him, suffer and do double work. The lazy man creates trouble and disorder everywhere, because anyone who does not love work does his own job poorly and prevents others from doing theirs well. He who does not do his work increases that of the others; whatever he does not do he passes on to his brothers, who have to do what his laziness led him to neglect.

«The lazy brother will never do any job well. He is not fit for teaching, because instructing others requires ability and devotedness. He is not fit to direct a house, since that responsibility requires knowledge, experience, reflection—all qualities which are acquired only through application and solid studies. He is not even fit for manual labor, because that demands work and tying oneself down to something, both qualities which disgust and frighten a lazy man. So what can a brother who does not like work do? Nothing good, and plenty of evil. He does not fit in anyplace because he isn't capable of doing anything; he spoils everything that passes through his hands, he is the scourge of the houses and a burden for everyone.»

VI.

«I don't like brothers who act like servants. My affection is reserved for the children of the family.» Would you like to know the difference between a brother who is a servant and one who is a child of the family?

1. A servant thinks of his superior as a severe master, as a policeman; he is afraid of him, stays out of his sight and conceals his conduct from him as much as possible. A brother who is a child of the family thinks of his superior as his father; he has total confidence in him, tells him all his defects and needs, and has no secrets from him. His filial spirit makes him consider everything he receives from his superior as a gift, which in turn leads him to accept remarks and reprimands as signs of affection and proofs of a deeply loving friendship.

2. A servant treats his brothers like strangers; he shows them neither charity nor cordiality, and does nothing to help them along, to be of service to them or to make them happy. A brother who is a child of the family considers all the members of the institute as his brothers; he shares their sorrows as well as their joys, he is always ready to help them and console them, and is never afraid to render them even the most humble and most difficult services.

3. A servant considers himself an outsider in the community, and is unconcerned about its best interests. He could care less whether the institute prospers or declines; he shows neither zeal nor devotedness for the common good; he simply goes through the motions of doing his job; he wastes the goods of the institute, lets things be spoiled and go to ruin rather than put himself out to take care of them, he uses them, in other words, as if they were government property.

A religious who is a child of the family considers his institute as his family, and takes nothing more to heart than to see it prosper and be blessed by God. So he strives to acquire its spirit, the virtues and the knowledge he needs to fulfill its aims and to make himself capable of doing the various tasks which may be entrusted to him. Being totally devoted to the good of the institute, he always prefers the interests of the congregation or the common good of a community, to his own. Everywhere he goes he creates good spirit and gives good example; he is always ready to sacrifice even what is dearest to him: his own tastes, satisfaction, work, health, even his life, for the good of the institute.

A servant lives in religious life as if he were in a foreign country, in exile or in prison. He is an unhappy man who has no friends at all and for whom no one feels sorry. A brother who is a child of the family enjoys all the delightful aspects of family life. He has as many servants, or rather as many friends, as there are brothers in the institute. He finds in religious life the hundredfold of good things and contentment which Jesus promised; to him, everything is a source of happiness and consolation.

VII.

«I don't like nonchalant brothers, because they belong to the race the Holy Spirit is talking about when he says, 'Fools change like the moon' (Sir 27:12). That sort of person is not attached to his vocation and limps along all his life.»

Nonchalant brothers are not very suited for virtue, which demands a firm character and a strong will; they are worthless for teaching, which is a ministry made up of patience and constancy. «A holy man,» says the Holy Spirit, «continues in wisdom, like the sun» (Sir 27:12), that is to say, he is firm and constant in his vocation and does not regret leaving behind the fleshpots of Egypt. He is firm and constant in his daily good resolutions, in his studies, in his work and in everything he takes in hand; he is firm and constant in fighting temptations; he never makes peace with his defects and is not afraid to do holy violence to himself in order to avoid sin, preserve the grace of God and practice virtue.

VIII.

«I don't like brothers who go looking for advice in Egypt.»

When a brother needs advice about how he himself should act or how he should direct his school, he should ask his superior. If he asks elsewhere, he risks getting advice which will not meet his needs or be in keeping with the spirit of his state.

The great remedy for temptations is openness of heart and submission to one's confessor or superior. This total openness of heart is necessary above all in temptations against one's vocation.

«He who, in such cases, wants to guide himself will only get lost; he who, instead of consulting his superior and following the latter's advice, seeks advice elsewhere, will also get lost, for he who seeks advice in Egypt will perish with the advice of Egypt.»

No one is better suited than the superior to make judgments about the vocations of his religious, because he has the grace of state to do so, and he is the guide appointed by God to lead those entrusted to him. A brother who, on such occasions, hides things from his superior or rejects his advice and follows that of someone else, is often deluded and runs headlong toward ruin.

IX.

«I don't like proud, vain brothers.» All my affection goes to the little brothers, «that is to say, the humble ones who hide like violets and always take the last place.» God loves the humble and blesses everything they do. On the other hand, he detests the proud and refuses to give them his help and his grace, because they steal his glory and attribute to themselves all the good they do, or think they do.

«In my opinion, there is no defect more harmful to the work of God and more likely to make it fail than vanity, faith in our tiny talents and confidence in ourselves. I am also convinced that unless they are humble, brothers who are very talented are the least likely to do good, because they count only on themselves and not on God. One does not need to be a genius to do God's work, but one does need a lot of piety, devotedness, confidence in God and good spirit.»

A brother who is humble and little in his own eyes pleases everyone by his modesty, his politeness and the way he treats everyone. His humility ennobles everything which flows from him; it sets his virtues in relief, makes his every least action valuable, adds weight to his words. It gives him authority, and wins him everyone's respect and esteem.

The proud brother is hateful to God and man. «The heart of the vain man,» says the Holy Spirit, «is like the breath of someone with a bad stomach; no one can come near him nor remain in his company.» The proud man stirs up trouble wherever he goes. A proud spirit created division among the angels in heaven. It takes only one proud, arrogant, haughty person to sow trouble and disorder in a family or community. What a terrible vice pride is! I'm not surprised that St. John Chrysostom calls it the height of folly, because while the madman creates problems for himself, the proud man creates problems for everyone else.

X.

Lastly, I don't like brothers who are slowpokes. To accustom the brothers to being very punctual, the Founder established a penance for the last one to arrive at community exercises. That is the kind of brother he called a slowpoke. Negligent brothers who readily break the Rule are ranked among the greatest enemies of the Institute; they are the ones who make others lose respect and love for the rules, who lead others to consider them a burden and a heavy yoke which one must throw off as much as possible. It is they who destroy regularity, who become the fomenters of bad spirit, abuses, and all the disorders which creep into communities.

«You all understand, my friends,» Father Champagnat said by way of conclusion, «that it is not really the brothers about whom I have just spoken that I dislike, but rather their defects. I love all the brothers, and if I feel any special attraction for any of them, it is for those who have the greatest needs and to whom I can be the most helpful.»

CHAPTER SIX

THE FIRST PLACES

One Sunday in July, during a conference on the gospel for the feast of St. James, which fell the next day, one of the brothers, in a reply to a question from Father Champagnat, said he was amazed at the request of the mother of the two sons of Zebedee. Father replied, «Brother, mother love makes women say many things we must overlook, even though they don't appear to us to be very well founded.

You think this woman was too ambitious; well, I must admit I am much more ambitious than she was! She asked for only one first place for her sons, whereas I want and ask every day for three of them for each of you. Do you know what are the three first places I request for you? They are the first place in the stable of Bethlehem, the first place on Calvary, and the first place at the altar.»

The virtues which give us the first places in the stable of Bethlehem are modesty, simplicity and the hidden life. The Little Brothers of Mary should therefore love those virtues very much. They should also love the cross, sufferings and mortification, because it is the practice of those virtues which win us the first places on Calvary. And they should love holy Mass, communion, and frequent visits to the Blessed Sacrament, because these are the money which buy us the first places at the altar where Jesus offers himself and remains day and night. The Little Brothers of Mary should have a heart of gold, burning with love, because the first places everywhere are reserved for those who love Jesus.

I want the Little Brothers of Mary to be faithful followers of the newborn Jesus, of the dying Jesus, and of Jesus immolated on the altar. May they be faithful followers of Jesus in all his mysteries: his life, his activities, his sufferings; these should be the main subject of their meditations. They should follow Jesus at every moment of his life, but it is most proper that they keep him company and contemplate him especially in the crib, on the cross and on the altar. May they make their own and carry out the prophecy of Isaiah, as expressed in the Chaldean text: «The just will be the belt around the Savior's waist, and they will always remain close to him» (Is 11:5). How do just persons become Jesus' belt? By accompanying him in everything he does, by following him in all the mysteries of his life, and by daily meditation on his holy life, his sufferings, and his favors to them.

Do you know, brothers, why I want you to be faithful followers of Jesus in his crib, on Calvary and on the altar? Because those three places are the three great fountains of grace; it is there above all that Jesus distributes it abundantly to his chosen ones. Listen once again to the prophet Isaiah exclaiming, «You shall draw water with joy out of the Savior's fountains» (Is 12:3); there you will find every grace. Yes, at these divine and saving fountains you will find the grace of mercy, in which you can wash away all the stains of your sins; you will find the grace of peace of soul, of divine consolation, of holy joy, of good will, of strength and holy courage to overcome yourself, to avoid sin and to combat your defects. You will find the grace of divine enlightenment which will help you to know the greatness of God, his sovereign right to be served by you, the excellence of your vocation, the price of your soul, the esteem you should have for holy things and for your rule.

You will also find the grace of devotion and of genuine piety. How pious one will become, how much he will grow in virtue, if he meditates regularly on the Incarnation, the Redemption and the Eucharist, and on everything that Jesus Christ has done for us! The crib, the cross and the altar are three inexhaustible fountains of piety, graces and fervor. The brother who goes regularly to those three sacred fountains will become like the tree planted near running water, which as the prophet says, bears fruit every month of the year.

There you will find above all the love of Jesus, which is the greatest of all graces. «God is love» (1 Jn 4:8), says St. John.

Yes, God is charity everywhere, but particularly at the crib, the cross and the altar; in other words, it is in those three places above all that his infinite love appears and reveals itself. It is in those three places above all that he inflames the hearts of the saints with his divine love. It is in those three places that our poor hearts can better understand and feel how much he loves us. «I have come to cast fire on the earth,» Jesus says, «and what do I want but that it be kindled» (Lk 12:49) and set the hearts of all men on fire.

Jesus came to bring sacred fire to earth; he spreads it everywhere in a thousand ways, but he has built three great hearths where all the saints and all fervent souls come to be set on fire. These hearths are: the stable of Bethlehem, Calvary and the altar. Oh, brothers! Go to the Savior's fountains and draw from them abundantly! Did you hear that word, draw? Don't say that grace is measured out to you, or given to you stingily, or that you have to wait for it. Stop complaining that you ask for it but don't get any. It's not the priest who gives it to you, it's not even the generous hand of Jesus who bestows it; it's you, yes, it's you yourself, who draw it freely. You can take as much as you want, so if you have only a little, it's your own fault; it's because you're using a container that's too small, your heart is too closed, not open enough to love. So go to the Savior's fountains, go there often and always draw from them freely and abundantly.

Rich people, the great ones of society, own several houses, villas or châteaux where they live in turn according to the season of the year and to gratify human nature. The saints, the friends of Jesus, also have several homes, but they particularly like three rooms.

First, they like the stable of Bethlehem, in which they shut themselves up to meditate on the wonderful mystery of the Incarnation, and to contemplate the Baby Jesus. Second, they like the room of Mount Calvary, where they spend Lent and every Friday of the year, talking with Jesus crucified, meditating on his sufferings and humiliations, and still more on the immense love of his divine Heart. «How good it is to be here,» St. Bonaventure cried out, when his mind and heart withdrew to Calvary, near the cross of Jesus; «I am going to build three dwelling places in my crucified Jesus: one in his hands, another in his feet and the third in his adorable heart; there I will obtain everything I want.» St. Augustine said, «I live in the rooms of my Jesus' wounds, and there I take everything I lack, because his wounds are full of mercy.» Finally, the room the saints spend most time in is the altar, where they go every day to love and adore Jesus, keep him company and tell him what they need. St. Elzéard wrote to his wife St. Delphine, «If you are looking for me, if you want to see me, you will find me only in the Heart of Jesus, before the Blessed Sacrament; that is where I spend all my time.» And how many other examples I could mention!

For the saints, these three rooms become three hearths where their soul is consumed in the flames of divine charity. In these furnaces of love they become seraphim on earth, receiving strength and help to advance continually from virtue to virtue, to the very peak of perfection.

Like the saints, the Little Brothers of Mary should live by turns in these three dwellings; they should go from the stable of Bethlehem to Calvary, and from Calvary to the altar. They should ardently desire the first places at the crib, the cross and the altar, but in order to obtain them, let them always remember to be humble, mortified, and burning with love.

CHAPTER SEVEN

THE ANEURYSM:
AN IMAGE OF INFIDELITY TO THE RULE

Any and all occasions suited Marcellin Champagnat for working on the religious formation of his brothers, helping them become more attached to their holy vocation, inspiring them with love for it, and describing to them its responsibilities. Therefore, every important event inside or outside the community gave him material for his conferences which were always very interesting as well as profitable for his brothers. So it was with the death of Brother Pacôme in 1839, which was so sudden that it shocked the whole community at the Hermitage.

Brother Pacôme, whose secular name was Jean-Marie Revoux, died suddenly of a hemorrhage. Like many other men, he had unfortunately lived for a long time far from God. He was converted by one of Fr. Champagnat's sermons on the uncertainty of the moment of our death, and his conversion was so perfect that he left the world and became a religious. During the 1838 retreat, he had a presentiment of his approaching death, and so he made that retreat as if it were to be the last one of his life.

He had acquired the good habit of choosing a quotation from scripture or from the Fathers of the Church at the beginning of each month, and then trying to put it into practice for the whole month. The quotation he had picked for December that year was, «Be ready, because the Son of Man will come when you least expect him» (*Lk* 12:40). He considered those words a warning that his end was near, so he prepared for it by redoubling his vigilance, piety and fervor.

Even though he was as healthy as ever, as the end of the month drew nearer, the stronger became his presentiment that death was approaching with it. On 9th January he was suddenly stricken by a massive hemorrhage, which carried him to the tomb in less than two days. But since he had been preparing for death for a long time, he calmly watched it come and accepted it with resignation and even with holy joy.

So Fr. Champagnat profited by his death to give the brothers an excellent conference. He spoke of the danger in which the religious who is unfaithful to his rule puts his soul.

«The rule,» he said, «is the soul of a religious house; it is the heart of the perfection of each religious. That is why the habit of breaking the rule is a defect just as dangerous for a brother's perfection and salvation as an aneurysm is for a man's health and life. To know if a man is sick, and just how sick he is, you take his pulse. On the moral level, to know the level of a religious' spiritual health or perfection, take the pulse of his regularity; you will never make a mistake if you use his fidelity to the rule as the thermometer of his virtue.

«A brother who keeps his rule well is a holy religious; a brother who readily breaks his rule is a tepid religious; one who attaches no importance to it and habitually neglects it is a bad religious.»

An aneurysm creates disorder and disturbances throughout the body; it brings on headaches and causes pain in all the limbs.

Habitual irregularity kills community life, sows disorder in a house, and endangers the success of the schools. Every religious who is habitually unfaithful to his rule damages his Institute, dishonors and vilifies it, and deprives it of God's blessings.

He scandalizes his brothers and becomes a stumbling-block for them. If someone living alone leads a disorderly life, he loses his soul, but his loss is not contagious; on the contrary, in community, and without committing any major crimes, a religious who is unfaithful to his rule, who is lax and dispenses himself from observing certain points, may be the cause of serious disorder for the whole house, and a fatal example for a certain number of his confrères. To be habitually unfaithful to the rule draws down a frightful curse on oneself, for Tronson says that if the founder of a community shares in all its good works, and has as many jewels in his crown as they are souls who sanctify themselves in it, he who sows disorder in a community by his irregular conduct will be guilty of all the faults of those he has scandalized, and also of the faults of those whom they will scandalize in their turn. Salvien says that a religious house where the rules are no longer observed is no longer a shelter and a safe harbor, but a place full of reefs where all those who enter will be shipwrecked.

So woe to those who violate the rules, because they cause souls to be lost.

An aneurysm, properly speaking, is a swelling caused by the dilation of an artery; but the name is also applied to the unhealthy dilations of the heart and various lesions of the veins and arteries. When it takes place in the heart or in certain other organs, it disturbs their proper functioning and its rupture is very dangerous. In many cases, it can produce instantaneous death.

Infidelity to the rule produces the same effects. It makes the exercises of piety defective, for the sole reason that they are not performed at the indicated time and according to the spirit of the rule. It interferes considerably with the exercise of the virtues and seriously reduces their merit, because they are then practiced out of self-will and not out of obedience. It obstructs the good effects of the sacraments, and paralyzes all the means of salvation or renders them useless. It creates disorder in all the faculties of the soul: in the mind, which wanders, becomes upset and deceives itself, because it is not keeping itself busy according to the rule; in the heart, which loses its taste for piety and becomes tepid and corrupt, because it gives its affection to trifles or often even to bad things, instead of giving it to its duties, its perfection, its rule and Jesus Christ; in the will, which since it is not disciplined, trained, strengthened and governed by regularity and punctuality, becomes capricious, inconstant, weak, and thereby incapable of a generous act of virtue.

An aneurysm leads to loss of strength, energy and health; it reduces the body to a state of continual suffering. Infidelity to the rule also saps the soul's strength and energy to combat evil and practice good, because it makes it lose grace. Blood runs through the veins to every part of the body, and grace runs through our obedience to the rules, to every power of the soul. So to the extent you violate the rules, you lose that many graces. But what graces do we lose through infidelity to the rule? The graces attached to time and place, to obedience to each article of the rule; graces of state, of choice, of supererogation, of privilege, without which there is absolutely no solid virtue, true piety, perfection, nor often even salvation, since, according to St. Francis de Sales, the predestination of a religious depends on how faithfully he observes his rules.

An aneurysm is a mortal illness. Habitual infidelity to the rule is also a defect or illness which leads to death, to mortal sin. When it represents a habit, the breaking of a rule is no small offense, especially because of the effects which these oft repeated infractions can have. To burst a single vein puts a man's life in danger.

It takes only a spark to cause a fire. It takes only a small breach in the wall to admit the enemy and allow him to take a city.

Only one stone need fall from a vault to make the whole vault come down. The tiniest hole in a bowl is enough to let all the water out.

All these comparisons teach us that little faults weaken the soul, deprive it of grace and lead it to serious faults, to mortal sin, to death. This is confirmed by the words of Jesus Christ, «He that is unfaithful in that which is little is unfaithful also in that which is greater» (*Lk* 16:10). Finally, it is a constant that no one ever sanctified himself in a community without observing its rules. «He that breaks a hedge, a serpent shall bite him,» says the Wise Man (*Eccles* 10:8). The hedge is the rule; the serpent is mortal sin. Yes, habitual infidelity to the rule is a mortal illness; that is to say, it leads to mortal sin.

An aneurysm puts us in danger of instantaneous death. A drop of blood falling on the heart, a spasm in the brain, or a hemorrhage, can lead a man with an aneurysm to the tomb in the space of a few hours.

Infidelity to the rule produces the same effects and exposes the soul to the same dangers. The religious who violates his rule is constantly walking on the brink of the abyss; he cannot promise himself a single day of security. Absence from an exercise of piety, a visit contrary to the rule, an act of laziness, a lack of mortification, the violation of any article whatever of the rule, can lead to a serious fall and become the cause of his damnation.

Why does this religious fall so easily?

1. Because his repeated infidelities have weakened his soul, sapped the strength of his will, made his conscience lose its horror of sin, and thus prepared the way for serious falls, for mortal sins.

2. Because a religious who is not where he should be does not have grace of state, graces of protection, or superabundant help to avoid evil. Helps and graces are to be found in the place where he ought to be; so he is left to his own weakness, he is surrounded by enemies and he has no defenders. Is it any surprise that he falls into sin and stays there? How such a religious is to be pitied!

CHAPTER EIGHT

WHAT SIN IS

Like all the servants of God, like all the saints, Fr. Champagnat had an extreme horror of sin. The most irritating developments, afflictions, human contradictions, the loss of material possessions—none of those could affect the peace of his soul and his normally cheerful character. Only sin visibly affected him, and made his face assume a sad and pained appearance. «To see God offended and souls lost,» he said, «are two things I cannot stand; they make my heart bleed.»

In his conferences to the brothers, he repeatedly came back to the topic of sin: how much it offends God, how much it hurts us, the terrible punishments God has attached to it, how horrified of it we should be, and what we must do to avoid it. It would be too long to repeat here everything we heard him say on this important point; suffice it to analyze a few of his instructions.

What Is Sin?

There you have a question that wise men, teachers, and the greatest saints have been asking for six thousand years, a question they studied and pondered their whole lives, and to which none of them, nor all of them together, ever found the perfect answer. No, neither wise men, nor the most famous teachers, nor the saints, nor even the angels, understand and can say what sin is. Only God knows its entire enormity and malice, and he alone is capable of repairing the damage it does wherever it penetrates.

I.

Sin wrongs God.

1. It is opposed to all his perfections, it attacks them, dishonors and outrages them. God is truth; sin is error and lies. God is infinite goodness; sin is wickedness and malice itself. God is the essence of purity and holiness; sin is filth, abomination and disgrace. God is infinite justice; sin is disorder and injustice. God is the necessary being; sin is nothing and nothingness. Sin is therefore the exact opposite of God, the antithesis of all his divine attributes. God is the supreme good; sin is the sovereign evil.

2. Sin wrongs God because it upsets the harmonious course of his works and sows disorder everywhere; because it creates obstacles for all his plans, detracts from his glory and turns creatures away from the purpose of their existence, which is to glorify God.

3. Sin wrongs God because it negates the merits of Jesus Christ, because it makes the death he suffered for us useless, and because it causes the loss of souls which the divine Savior came to redeem by his entire life-work.

4. Sin wrongs God because it grieves him, because it made Jesus Christ suffer and die, and because, in a certain sense, it renews his sufferings and death every day. St. Paul describes anyone who gives in to his passions and commits a mortal sin as «crucifying again to themselves the Son of God» (*Heb* 6:6).

II.

Sin wrongs man, because it strips him of all good and brings him all evil. Mortal sin does to the guilty soul what death does to the body.

1. Death takes away the body's life, the first and greatest of all natural goods. In the same way, sin takes the soul's life, that is to say, sanctifying grace, charity, God's friendship, and God himself, who is the true life of the soul. «The soul that sins, the same shall die» says the prophet Ezekiel (18:4), and St. James adds, «Sin, when it is completed, begets death» (*Jas* 1:14). «The body,» comments St. Augustine, «dies when the soul leaves it; the soul dies when God withdraws from it, and God withdraws from the soul as soon as it commits mortal sin.»

2. Death takes away the body's beauty. No matter how beautiful a person was, as soon as he is dead, all that remains is a hideous cadaver, horrible to look at. The soul in the state of grace is admirably beautiful; it is more brilliant than the sun, and nothing on earth can be compared to the glory surrounding it. St. Catherine of Siena once saw a soul in the state of grace, and was so delighted and drawn by the sight that she said that if her faith had not assured her that there is only one God, she would have taken that soul for a divinity. «My Jesus,» she exclaimed, «I am no longer astonished that you underwent the death of the cross for such a beautiful creature.»

Now, as soon as the soul falls into mortal sin, it totally loses its beauty, and is now only an object of horror. «Oh, how the old gold has tarnished,» says the prophet (*Lam* 4:1). This soul which was whiter than snow has become black as coal. This soul which was like the angels and which shone brighter than the sun has become like a demon. All its beauty disappeared with the loss of grace; it has become more ugly, more repulsive, more horrible, more degraded than if it were changed into a filthy animal. If it showed itself in this frightful state, those who saw it would die of fright. How horrible and terrifying is a soul which has lost the life of grace! But that is not all.

3. Death strips a person of all his possessions. No matter how much gold, silver, or property a man has, no matter how many beautiful houses, no matter how skilled or brilliant he may

be, when he dies, he takes nothing with him, he leaves everything behind. He came into the world naked and he will leave it naked. No king or emperor, St. Ignatius tells us, took a single gold thread with him into the next world as a token of the grandeur and wealth he was leaving behind.

Likewise, when a man dies in mortal sin, farewell to all his spiritual wealth. Along with charity, or the life of grace, he loses his virtues, his merits, his good works, etc. «If the just man,» says the prophet, «shall commit iniquity... the justice which he has done shall not be remembered» (*Ezek* 3:20). Imagine a man who has given everything he owns to the poor, who has fasted on bread and water for fifty years, who has practiced all the virtues all his life, and who performed every possible good work. If he commits one mortal sin, he loses everything; yes, all his merits, virtues, works, prayers, communions—everything is forgotten, everything is dead. None of it will be counted in his favor if he dies in this accursed sin! So what a great evil mortal sin is!

4. Death takes away all a person's senses—sight, smell, hearing, feeling; a dead man no longer sees, speaks or moves. That is an image of what happens to someone who falls into mortal sin. Sin takes away the soul's sight, its light, its understanding, its feeling. It is useless to tell him that he is in a bad way, that he is going to be lost, that he is going to be damned. He neither sees nor understands anything; he goes along like a blind man, like a crazy person falling into one pit after another.

Mortal sin ruins all the faculties of the soul: it destroys the memory, darkens the intellect, disturbs the reason, corrupts and hardens the heart, ruins the conscience, weakens the will and makes it dissolute, makes the soul brutish and animalistic. That is why our Savior called the Jews, «serpents, a generation of vipers» (*Mt* 23:33). Worse yet, sin turns man into a demon: «The devil is your father» (*Jn* 8:44), Jesus told the same Jews; and elsewhere, speaking of Judas, «One of you is a devil» (*Jn* 6:71). God, what a terrifying thing sin is!

III.

Sin is the cause of all the material ills that afflict humanity.

1. Sin leads to loss of possessions, honors and everything that makes life pleasant. «You have polluted the land with your prostitution and your vices,» says Jeremiah, «this is why the showers have been withheld, the late rains have not come» (*Jer* 3: 3). What snatched the crown of Israel from Saul's head? His disobedience. What brought Nebuchadnezzar down from his throne? His pride.

2. Sin ruins and destroys families. «You have committed a crime,» the prophet told David, «so now the sword will never be far from your house» (*2 Sam* 12:10). Sin destroyed the families of Eli, Ahab, and a thousand others.

While Emperor Phocas of Constantinople was having his palace fortified, he heard a voice one night, which told him, «Your Majesty, you are wasting your time defending yourself and building walls for protection. The evil is within; your sin will destroy you.» And the very next day, he and his whole family died.

3. Sin shortens one's life. «The days are coming,» God told Eli, «when I will break your strength and the strength of your father's house, till there is not one old man left in your father's house» (*1 Sam* 2:31). The years of the sinner will be shortened; «bloody and deceitful men shall not live out half their days» (*Ps* 54[55]:24). «The life of sinners is cut off like the weaver's cloth; when he cannot untangle his thread, he breaks it and throws it away.» Such are the pronouncements of the Holy Spirit. On Judgment Day, we will see that a great number of people died prematurely because of their sins.

IV.

Sin is the great evil of our origin and of every generation.

If you want to know what an evil sin is, judge it by the terrible punishments inflicted on Adam, for a simple act of disobedience.

Adam had hardly tasted the forbidden fruit when God's anger fell on him with every imaginable evil:

1. He was stripped of innocence, of original justice and of all the natural gifts which came with them.

2. He lost God's friendship and grace.

3. He became subject to ignorance, weakness, concupiscence and pain.

4. He was chased out of the earthly paradise and condemned to eat his bread in the sweat of his brow for more than 900 years.

5. Everything revolted against him: his body against his soul, his passions against his spirit and intellect; all the elements, the seasons, the animals, and men themselves, declared war on him.

6. He was condemned to death, to the corruption of the grave. Is that all the punishment inflicted on Adam? No, that is the least of it. Consider these other consequences of original sin as well:

7. Because of sin, all men come into the world subject to every form of misery: suffering, pain, hunger, thirst, fatigue, illness, death, and the corruption of the grave.

8. All are born children of anger, enemies of God, slaves of the devil, unworthy and incapable of possessing heaven.

9. All come into the world in a state of ignorance and concupiscence or inclination toward evil, and with a multitude of other miseries.

10. What is most deplorable is the loss of an infinite number of children, who die every day without having been baptized, among infidels, heretics, schismatics and even Catholics. All these

children will never see God, because they die without having been purified from Adam's sin.

11. Heap together all the evils in the world: famine, wars, the destruction of so many cities, infirmities, sufferings, illnesses, the calamities of all sorts which overwhelm mankind. Then say, without fear of error: the sin of Adam is the baneful source of all these evils. Conclude from all that what sin is, how terrible it is, how great is its malice. The one sin of Adam drew down, draws down and will draw down, all these evils on his posterity, until the end of the world. But if God thus punishes in his children Adam's sin which they did not commit, how will he punish the sins which each of us commits voluntarily?

If he thus punishes in this life both innocent children, and still more the just and the saints, for the simple disobedience of Adam, how will he punish all the impurities, blasphemies, scandals and murders which great sinners accumulate every day without remorse! Oh, God, how terrible is your justice! How great is the malice of sin!!

V.

Sin is an infamous act, which dishonors humankind, which is why St. Paul told the Corinthians, «We renounce the hidden things of dishonesty» (*2 Cor* 4:2) and also, «The evildoer loves the darkness.»

Seneca, pagan though he was, understood that sin is infamous and dishonorable, and so he said, «Even though I knew that no one would be aware of it and that God would forgive me for it, I would not commit evil, because such an act would be unworthy.»

Only sin dishonors a man and makes him blush. Tell someone he is poor, ignorant, sick, crippled, covered with mud, poorly dressed—does that dishonor him? No. But if that same man is surprised in the act of stealing, lying, etc., and you tell him he is a thief, a liar, immodest, he will immediately blush—proof positive that sin is infamous and that it dishonors a person.

VI.

Sin is an act of madness.

What do you think of Esau, who sold his birthright for a plateful of lentils? What would you say of someone who, for a taste of honey, would risk perpetual imprisonment or burning for a year in a fire? What would you think of someone who, for a toy or an hour's pleasure, would sell his freedom, give up his entire fortune, and consent to live as a slave, in total deprivation, until his death? You would say that they are all crazy.

The man who, for a pleasure, a momentary sin, a shameful, transitory satisfaction, sacrifices his soul, his God, and heaven, and condemns himself to hell, to frightful, incomprehensible, eternal torments—isn't his folly ten times more unbelievable? How true it is that sinners are madmen, as the Holy Spirit assures us.

Every sinner is crazy, because sin is the height of folly. He is crazy, because he cannot distinguish what is in his own best interest, he prefers the creature to the Creator, mud to gold, deadly poison to grace, hell to heaven, a shameful satisfaction to eternal glory. He is crazy because he is happy to be sick, he loves his sickness, he runs away from remedies, scorns warnings; he thinks he is wiser than everyone else. What stupidity! The sinner has lost his mind; he is crazy, because he deliberately kills himself. Yes, you sinful men, even though in the eyes of your peers you may pass for intelligent men who give good advice, when you commit sin you give clear indications of insanity.

If someone told you, «So-and-so jumped off the roof of his house; he broke all his limbs and has cuts and bruises all over his body,» you would answer, «What a shame; he must have been crazy; some fit of insanity must have snapped his mind and destroyed his reason.»

He was crazy? Well, aren't you just as crazy as he, and even more so? You were in the state of grace, you were the child of God, and you lightheartedly threw it all away, lost it all; you killed your soul, you made yourself the slave of Satan! Can there be any greater insanity than yours? How right the Holy Spirit is to call sinners madmen, because they prefer evil to good, death to life. Plato said that Jupiter had removed half of the brains of slaves; we have even more reason to say that sin removed all of it from sinners.

VII.

Mortal sin is a fever which makes the soul delirious and quickly kills it.

1. Fever begins with chills, an all-over feeling of discomfort, and ends with burning heat. Mortal sin begins with tepidity, negligence and laziness, and culminates in the fire of the passions of pride, lust and gluttony. Minor vices and defects open the door to the great passions; minor faults lead to major falls, mortal sins; neglect of minor obligations and the duties of one's state disposes the soul to ignore one's major obligations as a religious and a Christian.

2. Fever distorts the sense of taste, takes away appetite and the desire to eat. Mortal sin kills piety; the soul in sin no longer has the strength to raise itself to God, it finds prayer distasteful, and nothing is more painful than performing this holy exercise. It does not dare appear in God's presence; like Adam, like Cain, it flees from the Lord's face, that is to say, from prayer, the sacraments, mortification, the practice of virtue, spiritual reading. All of those things become unbearable.

3. Fever saps a person's strength and beauty. Mortal sin damages all the faculties of the soul, ruins one conscience,

weakens one's will. In abandoning itself to sin, the soul puts itself on the slope of the abyss and it is almost impossible for it to hold itself back. Its passions have taken over, its temptations have become more violent, it is crushed under the weight of its sin as if under a mountain; the slightest temptation makes it fall, and it slides from one abyss to the next; it has lost grace, the real strength of the soul; it has lost security, the virtues, the supernatural gifts which adorned it, everything that made it beautiful in God's eyes.

Its sin makes it appear deformed, horrible; that deformity, that ugliness sometimes appears even in the body—the eyes become dull, the expression hesitant, the brow wrinkled, the face clouded; the complexion, which was so lovely, so rosy, becomes blotchy and gray; the cheeks become livid and sunken; the step heavy and uncertain. Mortal sin has changed everything; it has destroyed everything beautiful in this body and left on it all the marks of the passions.

4. Fever destroys one's reason and leads to delirium. My God, we have already seen that; is there a crazier man than the sinner? How many young people have we not seen, who after giving in to an evil passion, become so frantic that they run wildly through the fields. Ask that discouraged young brother why he wants to abandon his vocation; if he is sincere, he will answer, «I can no longer put up with myself; I have been suffering horribly ever since I gave in to that unfortunate sin. I no longer have control over my imagination, over my head; my mind, my intellect are disturbed; I must wander the world to calm down, and besides, I no longer know what I'm doing—I've lost my head!!!»

5. Fever makes one suffer cruelly. Dear God! Who can describe the sufferings of the man in mortal sin? Who can tell us what remorse, anguish, and all sorts of pains he suffers in this world? But even more, who can tell us what the damned suffer in hell? Oh, how cruelly sin makes one suffer!!!

6. Fever causes a fiery, burning thirst, which nothing can slake. Mortal sin kindles in the soul the fire of all the passions. The man in mortal sin is burning up with the fire of pride. Look at him turn purple with anger as soon as someone offends his self-love. Look at his heart, dried up like tinder by the fever of the impurity which is consuming it. Watch all his feelings become aggravated and perverted by ambition and love of worldly things. The man in mortal sin is burning with the fire of every passion. What a sad state he is in!

7. Fever is often intermittent, periodic and progressive. One attack follows another. The man in the state of mortal sin goes from fall to fall, from grave sin to still graver sin. He commits almost as many faults as he takes steps. He reaches the point where he drinks iniquity like water, to use the expression of Holy Scripture.

8. Fever can be diagnosed from an irregular pulse. The state of sin reveals itself through remorse, worries, preoccupations, fears, and the irresistible need sinners feel to distract themselves with new pleasures. Look at that man who has just performed an evil act. His imagination is excited, his intelligence and reason are disturbed. His heart is agitated, his conscience is upset, all the faculties of his soul are in disorder. How feverish is the condition of a soul in mortal sin! But what a horrible thing sin is! What a frightful thing a man in mortal sin is! His soul is abominable in God's sight; even his body sometimes bears its frightful marks; his sin is reflected in his person; the ugliness of vice is imprinted on him and he becomes totally deformed, emaciated, shaky and hideous.

VIII.

Mortal sin is irreparable once we die.

It completely extinguishes the life of grace in the soul which commits it, and makes its death and condemnation eternal. He who has once renounced God renounces him forever. What a terrifying duration for an action which seemed so brief! A hundred years from now, or a thousand, or ten million, if you ask a lost soul, «What's keeping you in hell?,» he will tell you, «My sin.»

«But you've been in that fire such a long time! Isn't your sin burned away yet? Iron, steel, marble, even the purest diamond would long ago have been melted, burned up, destroyed, reduced to nothing!

«No, my sin has not been destroyed, not one bit diminished; it is still as whole, as horrible, as diabolical, as at the moment when I committed it!»

Hell cannot destroy sin. Nor can the penances, tears and merits of the saints, by themselves, erase one single mortal sin. A man in this sad condition cannot expect anything from angels or men; they may pray for him, but not remove his sin. Only God, only the merits of Jesus Christ, can draw the sinner up from the abyss into which he has fallen, blot out his sins and reconcile him with heaven, but always on condition that he repent sincerely. Oh my God, what a great evil sin is! Why do we understand it so little?

God has a sovereign hatred of sin. God's hatred for sin is implacable, inextinguishable, infinite and necessary. He hates it as much as he loves himself, for he is the sovereign good and sin is the sovereign evil. God's hatred for sin is so great that he arms all the elements and arouses all creation to combat sin and punish it. He used fire from heaven against Sodom, the deluge in the time of Noah, lightning against Julian the Apostate, the wind against Jonah, the sea against Pharaoh, the earth against Korah and his accomplices, bears against the children who made fun of Elisha, lions against the Babylonians, worms against Herod, grasshoppers against the Egyptians, the plague against David, flames against those offering false sacrifices. All the scourges which afflict the earth are sent to punish and combat sin.

To combat sin, he sent his son from heaven, and delivered him up to death. To combat sin, Jesus Christ instituted the sacraments, established the priesthood, and gives us his grace. Finally, to combat and punish sin, God created hell, and condemns to it all those who commit iniquity and who die in sin.

Fear and hatred of sin are attitudes common to all the saints. All of them have said, like the Wise Man, «I would give up all I possess, and suffer every evil, rather than commit sin.» Look at the martyrs. What did they not suffer? They were stripped of all their possessions, clapped into irons, cruelly whipped, broken on the wheel, subjected to horrible tortures. Ask them why they exposed themselves to such sufferings, and they will tell you, «It was to avoid sin, which we detest above all else.» They will all tell you, like the first Christians, «Death rather than a lie; we accept every torment rather than offend our conscience.» Oh, if we only had a bit of that light which enlightened the saints and showed them that sin is the greatest of all evils, the only real evil in the world, then instead of complaining about our sufferings or becoming discouraged by our temptations, we would say, like them, «For a Christian, only one thing is necessary: never to sin!»

With such instructions, which he repeated frequently, Fr. Champagnat instilled the fear of the Lord and the horror of sin in the hearts of his brothers, and gave them a timorous conscience, which fears even the shadow of [s]in, and which, in the opinion of St. Gregory, is a sure proof of a beautiful soul. This fortunate attitude was the foundation of that solid virtue we find in all our first brothers. They not only feared grave faults, but the least venial sins frightened them, and their maxim was, «Let us wage relentless war against venial sin, so that we will never be in danger of falling into mortal sin.»

May all present and future Brothers of Mary, take that beautiful motto as their standard of conduct: fear and flee sin, even venial sin, more than every other evil in the world!

CHAPTER NINE

THE HUNDREDFOLD TO ALL,
OR TO EACH ACCORDING TO HIS WORKS

Jesus Christ has said, «Everyone who has left... father, or mother... or lands for my name's sake, shall receive a hundredfold, and shall possess life everlasting» (*Mt* 19:29). Now, just as there is a hundredfold of blessings, peace, joy, and all sorts of spiritual goods for good and fervent religious, there is also a hundredfold of bitterness, anguish, grief, and all sorts of tribulations, for tepid religious, and still more so for bad religious. This can be seen very clearly from the following story or parable, and the reflections which accompany it. In the Middle Ages, the religious in a certain monastery lived so fervently that the Queen of Virgins often appeared to them to encourage them. The religious of that holy house gathered in the chapel every day around three o'clock, to chant the Magnificat before the altar of the Mother of God.

That was the moment the divine Mother chose to appear to them and bless them. After that, the religious retired to their cells to eat the bread that an angel brought to each one, by order of the Mother of God. This bread tasted delicious; more than that, it had a special ability to give strength, peace of soul, and holy fervor in the service of God.

That was the great effect it produced in the heart of all the good religious. But just as the laxest communities always have a few holy religious, who keep themselves free of contamination, and who seem to have been placed there to condemn their irregular brothers, there is no community, no matter how regular and perfect it may appear, which does not have a few sick or gangrenous members, who abuse grace and become perverted even among saints. God permits this as if to prove over and over again the terrible truth that one can lose one's soul anywhere, and that it is not where we are that makes us holy, but what we do.

Now, this is what happened in the community we are talking about. One day, a young religious, after the visit to the Blessed Virgin, went to his cell to eat his bread as usual; but to his great surprise, the piece he found there was moldy, dry, black and disgusting! Two mouthfuls were enough to turn his stomach, bring on vomiting, give him chills and make him deathly ill.

Highly indignant, he took the bread to his superior, and said bitterly, «Look at what the Blessed Virgin sent me. Some food this is! How can anyone put up with the demands of religious life after something like this? Good God, how difficult this life is!» The virtuous superior began to cry, and said to the young brother, «My son, your heart has dried up and turned away from God; you let yourself become bored, you turned your eyes toward the world and its vanities, you became tepid and negligent. So why are you surprised that God treats you according to your works?»

The venerable old man had hardly finished speaking when another monk, looking very grim and with fire in his eyes, came in and held out the bread he had found in his cell, and said, «This bread is revolting; it is covered with dust and dirt, full of worms, and smells rotten! The little bit I tasted poisoned me, and those worms became real snakes which are eating away at my stomach and intestines. God, how I am suffering! What torture I am going through! It is like the torments of the damned.»

«My son,» said the superior, «your heart is evil, criminal and depraved. It has abused the gifts of God, and profaned holy things. God is treating you as you deserve; he is paying you back according to your works.»

At that very moment, the other religious of the monastery arrived, their faces bright and beaming with joy. Forming a circle around their venerable superior, they told him, «Father, we have come to share with you the favor which the Queen of Heaven has just done for us. As you know, she cares for us with tender solicitude, and every day she sends us the bread we need to live on. But today, this bread, which is always excellent, was so delicious that it filled our souls with sweetness and overwhelmed them with so much happiness that only the happiness of heaven could be greater. How true the words of Jesus Christ are: A hundredfold in this life and life everlasting in the next.»

«Yes, dear brothers,» the good superior replied calmly and authoritatively, «the words of Jesus Christ are infallible; the hundredfold of happiness and all sorts of good things is for good religious. The hundredfold of anguish, bitterness and tribulations is for all bad religious. God, you are just and equitable; you give to each one according to his works. Today I have tangible proof of that right before my eyes!»

So what is religious life then? According to the story we have just heard, it is evident that there are various answers to that question.

I. For brothers who are pious and solidly virtuous, religious life is a real paradise.

1. It is a paradise through charity and union of hearts. This union brings peace of soul, calmness of mind, it destroys all worries, all regrets, and gives perpetual joy. Solidly virtuous religious truly have the right to say, with the Prophet-King, «How good and how pleasant it is for brothers to live together in unity» (Ps 132:1). Where there is union and charity, there is Jesus Christ, there is God, there is the Blessed Trinity, and there, consequently, is paradise and perfect happiness!

2. Religious life is a paradise through peace of soul and the joy of a good conscience. A good conscience, says the Holy Spirit, is an endless feast. And St. Ambrose adds, «What food could be more pleasant than the witness of a good conscience and the delights reserved for the pure soul?» «Such a soul,» continues St. John Chrysostom, «enjoys so much happiness that words are powerless to express it.» Compared to the happiness produced by a good conscience, everything pleasant and consoling on earth is mere bitterness!

3. Religious life is a paradise through our being spared the problems, worries and miseries of this life; by being distanced from perils and from the danger of offending God; through the consolations, the holy joy, the unction of grace, and all sorts of good things which Jesus Christ showers on religious who have left everything to serve him and who belong completely to him.

The sweetness God reserves for those who love him is ineffable and human words cannot express it. That is why the Holy Spirit says, «Oh, taste and see that the Lord is sweet; blessed is the man that hopes in him» (Ps 33[34]:9). The sweetness, consolation and joy of the servants of God are, in fact, incomprehensible to all those who are not fortunate enough to experience them.

St. Francis of Assisi, who had left all for the sake of Jesus, was so filled with consolation and joy in the midst of the greatest deprivation, that he thought he was already in heaven and exclaimed, «The happiness I feel is so great that all my pains make me happy.»

The joy that overflowed in the heart of St. Francis Borgia prevented him from sleeping at night, to the point where he had to ask God to reduce it, for the sake of his health.

St. Philip Neri loved Jesus beyond measure; he would have preferred to die rather than commit the slightest venial sin, or fail in the least point of his rule. But that fidelity and love were well rewarded: the divine Savior flooded him with so much consolation that while he was in bed, he sometimes cried out, «That's enough, Jesus! Hold back your sweetness and let me get to sleep!»

St. Ephrem felt exhausted because of the weight of the consolations he experienced, and humbly asked Our Lord to lessen them, saying, «Withdraw from me, Jesus! The weakness of my body can no longer bear the full extent of your pleasures and the happiness with which you intoxicate me.»

St. Teresa stated that a single drop of heavenly consolation gives more contentment than all the pleasures and amusements of the world.

St. Augustine did not know how to explain the happiness he experienced in God's service. «Jesus,» he exclaimed, «you sometimes give me absolutely extraordinary feelings, and you make me taste a sweetness I cannot describe, but which so penetrates me that if it grew anymore and completely overwhelmed me, I don't know what would become of me.» Worldly people who judge only by their senses would find that hard to believe, which doesn't surprise me, because you have to have experienced it to understand it. Give me a religious who loves Jesus, and he will easily understand me; but if I am speaking to a religious who is cold, lacking in piety, tepid, unfaithful to grace, he will not understand anything, because he has no taste for it.

God's promises are unfailing. Jesus has promised a hundredfold of good things, happiness and joy to those who give up the pleasures of the world to attach themselves to him. All his servants are present to testify that he gives even more than he promised.

II. For pious and solidly virtuous brothers, religious life is a real martyrdom.

Yes, the religious is a martyr because of the chastity and poverty he practices his whole life. «To subject the flesh to the spirit is a sort of martyrdom,» St. Bernard says; it is less frightening to the eyes than martyrdom by steel and fire, but it is more painful because of its duration. St. Jerome adds, «To keep one's purity intact is to be a martyr»; and St. Bernard also says that «Voluntary poverty is a real martyrdom.»

The religious is a martyr because he sacrifices his will and his freedom, because of the constant violence he has to practice on himself in order to observe his rule, because of his zeal for the glory of God, and his dedication to the instruction of children. «Shedding one's blood for the faith is not the only martyrdom,» St. Jerome tells us; «obedience to God and to one's superiors also deserves to bear that name.» «It is a great and sublime martyrdom,» St. Lawrence Justinian states, «to spend one's life for Jesus Christ and to wear oneself out for him.»

The religious who leaves his parents in order to serve children, to teach them and win them over to God, the religious who consecrates all of his work, who uses up all his strength, his health and his life in training children to virtue, and preserving them from eternal death, is truly a martyr. «I die every day for your glory,» St. Paul told the first faithful; in other words, he used up all his strength and sacrificed himself to win them over to Jesus Christ. That is what the holy religious does. Yes, if the three vows of religion are observed exactly, they are a continuous martyrdom, and they receive all the merit of one.

But perhaps you will ask me, if religious life means suffering, pain, continual sacrifice, in a word, martyrdom, how can it be a paradise of delight? It is a martyrdom because the body and soul of the religious are actually immolated, and because such a religious, as St. Bernard says, gives his blood, so to speak, drop by drop.

It is a paradise of delight because this immolation is voluntary, and as one author has nicely put it, when pain becomes pleasure, pain is no longer pain. This is so because love is stronger than pain, and even stronger than death, and it changes sacrifices and torments into enjoyments. As witnesses to this we have St. Paul: «I exceedingly abound with joy in all our tribulations» (2 Cor 7:4); St. Francis Xavier, who in the midst of total deprivation, was giddy with happiness; St. Lawrence on his gridiron and St. Vincent in his cell, who sang and could not hold back their joy. There are also the holy religious we spoke of in our story, who tasted indescribable happiness amid privations, fasts, austerities and penances which were most fearsome to human nature. The loaf of bread which the Blessed Virgin sent them brought them more delight, consolation and happiness than worldly people experience in a lifetime of pleasures.

We can say of the religious, in a way, as we do of Jesus Christ, that he has arrived and is still on the way, that he enjoys and suffers; the joy of his soul is so great that he does not feel, so to speak, his pains and sufferings. Rather, far from drying up or diminishing the joys and consolations of a holy religious, crosses, privations and sufferings only increase them.

III. Religious life is a life of pain and disappointments.

That is the way tepid men speak, religious who have only one foot in religious life, and who have never worked wholeheartedly at fulfilling their obligation, the exact observance of the Rule; sensual, worldly, carnal religious, who perhaps were unhappy at home with their parents, and lacked the necessities of life, and who still feel unhappy because they do not have the luxuries, superfluities and enjoyments of the celebrities of this world; religious who do not know the value of their soul, and what Jesus Christ did to save it; who have never grasped what God is, the excellence of the religious life, the happiness and the consolations which flow from virtue, because they have never been fervent; religious who came into religious life, not to suffer, not to immolate themselves to God, but for enjoyment, to have a soft life, and to be better off than they were in the world; lax religious who are unfaithful to grace, trapped in habits of venial sin, and who experience only anguish, regret, and bitterness in religious life, like the young monk whose only food was moldy bread.

IV. Religious life is a prison for every religious who violates the sacred commitment he made to God and who profanes his vows.

It is a prison and a hell for the sacrilegious religious, who is in the state of mortal sin; his conscience is prey to constant remorse and puts him through cruel tortures; it torments him like an executioner.

The religious state is a prison for him who has lost the spirit of his holy state and his love for it, who stays in his vocation only because he does not know what else to do. Such a person has only his body in religious life. Like someone condemned to the galleys, he is a captive, a slave; he drags his ball and chain all through life. This ball and chain are the religious observances and exercises of piety which displease him mightily and which he performs only under duress and constraint, and because he cannot do otherwise.

Finally, religious life is a prison, or rather a hell, for every religious who is dissolute and addicted to vice, because such a man, through his bad conduct, his self will and his evil character, is necessarily in opposition to his superiors and at war with all his brothers; because he is continually doing the opposite of what he would like to do, and experiences no consolation at all. For him, everything is painful, everything is a torture, because he has been handed over to the tyranny and fury of all his passions, without being able to get away from them; because everything he sees, everything he does, everything he hears, torments him and brings him remorse; because his conscience, like that of the monk with the grim expression in our story, is a den of serpents, that is, of passions, sins and demons who bite and devour and oppress him constantly. Like that evil monk, he cries out, «Good God, how I am suffering! What torture I am going through! My torments are like those of the damned!»

So it is true that religious life is either the happiest or the unhappiest life there is. It is what you make it: a life of happiness for solidly virtuous religious, a life of anguish and many afflictions for the tepid religious, a life of torments and misfortune for the vice-ridden, criminal, sacrilegious religious. Like manna, it has many tastes; it is delicious for pure and mortified souls; it is unpleasant and disgusting for lax and ill-advised religious, who do not know the gift of God; it is full of gall, a torture, for carnal souls. In a word, religious life is whatever religious make of it for themselves—no more, no less!!!

CHAPTER TEN

SIN IS AN EVIL FOR THE ONE WHO COMMITS IT, FOR HIS FAMILY AND FOR HIS COMMUNITY

I.

One of our old brothers recalls that the first realization that Fr. Champagnat tried to make sink into a soul was fear and horror of sin. He never let slip an opportunity go back over this point, because he understood that flight from sin is the foundation of all sanctity. I received a lesson from him on this subject which I think would be very useful to share. I once accused myself in confession of having lied. When I added that this fault had not hurt anyone, he reacted energetically:

«What did you say, brother? Sin, any sin at all, always hurts the one who commits it, and it is not possible for someone to offend God without wounding his own soul, and without doing himself harm. The fault of which you just accused yourself is therefore a real evil for you, and it is not correct to say that it didn't hurt anyone!»

«I understand, Father, but I only wanted to say that my lie wasn't the kind they call pernicious, and that it didn't do any harm to my neighbor.»

«Yes, I understood what you meant, brother, but I am speaking to you this way so that you will understand very clearly that a fault is always pernicious for the one who commits it, and if you should avoid lying because it wrongs your neighbor, you should avoid it even more because it wrongs you yourself, since you should love yourself more than you love your neighbor. Besides, you must know that just as our virtues and good works profit everyone through the communion of saints, we can say that our faults always hurt everyone in one way or another. We may at least be sure that they hurt our brothers, our parents, those with whom we live, and those with whom we have anything in common.»

Since this instruction of Father's made such a strong impression on me, I brought up the same topic a few days later in a spiritual conversation I had with him. Here is the gist of what he told me on this important point:

II.

«It is very certain, brother, that the good works and virtue of a good religious are a blessing and a treasure, not only for himself but also for his brothers and for all those with whom he lives.

1. «A holy religious is a treasure for his family, his community and for the entire country. He brings God's blessing wherever he goes, God makes everything he does and everything obedience entrusts to him succeed; because of him, God often blesses all those who are associated with him or who live in the same house. Have you not read in holy scripture that the patriarch Jacob, who was a saint, brought God's blessing and prosperity with him to Laban's house, and that Joseph, who was a saint, likewise brought God's blessing and prosperity on the house of Putiphar and on all of Egypt?

2. «A holy religious is a means of salvation and sanctification for his family; his prayers and his good works bring down a shower of graces and blessings on his father and mother, his brothers and all his relatives. The father of St. Aloysius Gonzaga understood this truth and on his deathbed, he exclaimed tearfully, 'It is to Aloysius that I owe my conversion; it was his prayers which obtained for me sorrow for my sins and a full and total

confidence in God's mercy.' While working zealously at his own perfection, therefore, a religious is working for the salvation of his parents, and nothing he can do is more likely to obtain it than for him to become very faithful to grace and to respond to God's plans for him. By so doing, even without thinking about it, he is working on behalf of those near to him; his letters, a single word from him, even the thought of him, stirs them up, gives them good thoughts, leads them toward good and makes them better.

3. «A holy religious is a source of graces for all those with whom he lives, and one holy religious is often all it takes to sanctify a whole community and a whole country. Through her heroic virtue and fervent prayers, St. Teresa reformed the Carmelite Order, and obtained the conversion of several thousand sinners. One day, Our Lord told St. Margaret of Cortona, 'Because you make every effort to belong entirely to me, I will grant the grace of conversion to all those for whom you pray, and even those who will hear about you.' We can say about all the saints what St. John Chrysostom said about Elias, 'Elias is the mediator between God and the people; he snatches sinners from the hands of divine justice; he calls the forgetful people and brings them back to their heavenly homeland; he establishes peace between God and humankind, between the Creator and the creature.'

4. «A holy religious is a protector and defender, who diverts the plagues of heaven from his community, his family and his entire country. 'Everyone knows,' says St. Ambrose, 'that the saints are a solid and valuable rampart for their homeland? Their faith protects us, their justice preserves us from punishment and extermination.' If the city of Sodom had had ten saints, it would not have perished. God spared the world because of Noah, who was a saint. Because of St. Paul, God spared all two hundred and twenty people who were shipwrecked with him.

5. «A holy religious draws down God's blessing on his brothers; he is a guarantee of prosperity for the house where he

lives and for the institute to which he belongs. Just as a fire warms all the bodies gathered around it, so the piety and fervor of a holy religious spreads imperceptibly and enters all the brothers who live with him.

III.

«But what is really upsetting is that it is no less certain that the sins and bad conduct of one single religious are a misfortune for all his brothers and for all those who have anything to do with him. His irregularity and bad example weaken the others' virtue; his sins draw down God's curses upon them, upon the establishment and upon the entire institute . Holy Scripture offers numerous proofs of that truth. The prophet Nathan told David, 'You have committed adultery. Know then that God's scourge will not leave your house and that divine vengeance will fall upon your children and upon everything you own.' Seventy thousand of that ruler's subjects were swept away by the plague in three days, because he allowed himself to dwell on thoughts of vanity. Achan's sin was imputed to all of Israel, and God told Joshua, 'The anathema is in the midst of you and you cannot stand before your enemies till he be destroyed who is defiled with this wickedness' (*Josh* 7:13).

«The disobedience of Jonah drew down God's wrath on the whole vessel in which he was sailing, and the storm would have swallowed up and killed the crew and all the passengers if Jonah had stayed with them instead of being thrown into the sea.

«Sometimes we are amazed to see the prosperity of an establishment suddenly cut short by some unfortunate event, and we wonder why the children have changed almost overnight and no longer respond to the care they are given? Why have the parents, who were so good to the brothers, now become hostile? How did it happen that so-and-so has become the enemy and persecutor of the brothers?

We come up with all sorts of reasons; the real one is the one nobody thinks of—anathema is in the house. The cause of all these adversities is a brother who has violated his vows, a brother who let himself fall into mortal sin, perhaps a sacrilegious brother, perhaps a brother who is sweepingly unfaithful to grace, who lives in tepidity and in the habit of venial sin. There you have the one and only cause of all the misfortunes of the establishment. As long as it persists, as long as the anathema remains among you, don't look for God's blessing and the prosperity of the school.

A brother who would let himself fall into mortal sin would therefore be a·real scourge for his brothers and for the house where he lives; he could believe with good reason that he is the cause of all the adversities and all the annoyances that afflict the community and jeopardize the schools.

«God looks kindly on convents inhabited by holy religious, and he overwhelms them with blessings; but he turns his eyes away from those where there are men who, forgetful of the holiness of their state, allow the demon to enter their heart and commit iniquity. A religious in mortal sin! Good God! What a misfortune for him and for all his brothers! St. Ignatius Loyola sensed how dangerous it was to be in the company of such a man when he said, 'I would not dare spend the night and go to bed in a house where I knew there was a man guilty of mortal sin; I would be afraid that the roof would fall in and crush us all.'

«My God, deliver us from mortal sin, which is our great enemy and the scourge of our houses, and if some brother, through human weakness, ever falls into it, give him the grace to rise again immediately.»

CHAPTER ELEVEN

THE ORIGIN OF AND REASON FOR VARIOUS PRACTICES CUSTOMARY IN THE INSTITUTE

A good religious holds to the rules and pious practices of his order from the very bottom of his heart. The older these practices are, the dearer they are to him, and the more faithful he is to them. In order to give our brothers greater esteem for our holy customs, we recall here their origin and why they were established.

Our Founder used to say that there are five great devotions which nourish the piety of the good Christian and the fervent religious. These are: devotion to Our Lord, devotion to the Blessed Virgin, devotion to St. Joseph, devotion to the guardian angels and patron saints, and devotion to the souls in purgatory.

A brother, he added, will never be solidly pious if he does not excel in these five devotions; the piety of him who lacks them is dry, arid, and he will never taste the ineffable consolations of religious life. Our Father ceaselessly presented and recommended these devotions to his brothers; he never lost an opportunity to make them sink into their hearts. That is the major reason for the pious practices we are going to list here.

I. Devotion to Our Lord

Solid virtue consists in knowing, loving and imitating Jesus Christ. Therefore, Father Champagnat called devotion to Our Lord the first of all devotions. To study Jesus Christ, to meditate on his holy life, to follow him in all its mysteries, was his daily occupation.

1. Every year he carefully prepared for the feast of his birth, and celebrated it with the utmost solemnity. On Christmas Eve he made a crib to represent the divine birth and the main circumstances surrounding it. He went with the community to adore the divine infant lying in the crib on a little straw, and addressed to him the most fervent prayers.

«Brothers,» he said, «let us love the divine infant of Bethlehem; it was for our sake that he came down from heaven and became a poor, suffering human being. Let us go to Jesus, whose heart contains every divine and human perfection; but let us go to him by the road of humility and mortification; let us ask him for those virtues, for his love, and for everything we need. He cannot refuse us anything.»

The custom of setting up the crib and adoring the holy infant Jesus at Christmas has always been observed in the novitiates of the Institute.

2. Father Champagnat meditated on the sufferings of Jesus all during Lent; he considered, and rightly so, that this was the subject which could best nourish the brothers' piety and give them a tender affection for our divine Savior. Consequently, it was the only topic he gave them for their meditation, spiritual reading and even the reading in the dining room, where every year The Sufferings of Jesus Christ by Fr. Allaume was read.

On Good Friday, for many years, Father and the whole community fasted on bread and water. On that day, there was no recreation after dinner, and profound silence reigned throughout the house. Every moment of the day was devoted to participation in liturgical services, and to reading or meditation on the sufferings of Jesus Christ. The solemn singing of the office during Holy Week, as well as on Christmas Eve, was begun in 1824, as soon as there was a chapel. Even though the community then were few in number, and few of the brothers could help with the singing, Father still sang the entire office, including the nine lessons of Matins. The singing of the office during Holy Week was maintained in the novitiates, but the Christmas Eve office was dropped. Instead, the «*Venite Adoremus*» and «*Te Deum*» were sung before Midnight Mass. The community remains standing during the singing, and the brothers come two by two to adore the infant Jesus in the crib.

3. The processions of the Blessed Sacrament at the mother house of the Hermitage began that same year, 1824. These processions did not glitter with sumptuous vestments, because the house was poor, but they were noteworthy for the piety of the brothers and the graceful simplicity of the repositories decorated with flowers and foliage and spaced out along the route of the procession.

4. The visit to the Blessed Sacrament is one of the practices which Father recommended most. Even in the days when they were in La Valla, the brothers went regularly to the church three times a day: in the morning for Mass, after dinner, and after supper when the days were long, to visit the Blessed Sacrament. The same was done in the establishments; the brothers brought the children to Mass before morning classes, and to make a first visit at eleven-thirty, and a second at the end of the afternoon classes.

Fr. Coeur, the parish priest of Mornant, once reproached Fr. Champagnat: «Your brothers are too pious; it seems to me that they go to church too often with their children.»

«Let them,» he answered, «and pray to God that no one may ever say of them, 'Those brothers aren't pious enough; they don't go often enough to adore the Blessed Sacrament; they don't train their children sufficiently in that holy practice.»

Once they had a chapel in La Valla, over and above Mass and the private visits which each one could make during the day, the whole community went to the chapel three times a day to adore the Blessed Sacrament: when they got up in the morning, when they left the table after dinner, and at night before retiring.

5. True devotion to Our Lord, Fr. Champagnat used to say, takes in all his mysteries, his entire life, and consequently includes devotion to his holy childhood, to the holy name of Jesus, to the passion, to the Sacred Heart and to the Blessed Sacrament. Anyone who loves Our Lord and who wants to make new progress in divine love [every] day, follows Jesus in all his mysteries and in all his actions, and works unceasingly to acquire his spirit and imitate his virtues.

II. Devotion to the Blessed Virgin

The five principal feasts of the Blessed Virgin: her Immaculate Conception, Purification, Annunciation, Assumption and Nativity, have always been holidays and solemnly celebrated in the institute since 1824. There has always been general communion, Mass with deacon and sub-deacon, and benediction in the evening.[1] Father always had several favors to request on the occasion of these feasts. His loving devotion to Mary, and his inventive zeal, suggested to him a thousand ways to spread this priceless devotion, and to stir up the brothers' piety.

Among the feasts of the Blessed Virgin, there are two that the brothers of the institute celebrate with special devotion and solemnity: the Immaculate Conception and the Assumption. They are always prepared for by a solemn novena made in community; each evening, in the chapel, the *Ave Maris Stella* and a hymn are sung, and the litany of the Immaculate Conception is recited in preparation for that feast, or the litany of the Holy

---

[1] In the 19th century, frequent communion was a rarity, even in religious communities, and the Rule specified the days when everyone was permitted to receive.

Heart of Mary in preparation for the Assumption.[2] There is benediction of the Blessed Sacrament on each day of the octave; this was begun for the feast of the Assumption in 1843, and for the Immaculate Conception in 1854, as an expression of thanksgiving for the proclamation of that dogma. The major novenas preparatory to these feasts, and the solemn benedictions during the octave make August and December two months totally consecrated to Mary.

It is customary and traditional in the Institute to ask the Blessed Virgin, during August, for the grace of a happy death, and during December, for the gift of prayer, the holy virtue of purity, and the grace to be preserved from mortal sin.

May devotions date back to our origins. Father Champagnat began them in La Valla as soon as he arrived in that parish. He performed them every morning after Mass. Following his example and suggestion, May devotions were held in all the hamlets of the parish, and soon even each family had its shrine, where they gathered every evening before the image of Mary to request her protection, sing her praises and meditate on her grandeur. As soon as the institute had been founded, May devotions became a community exercise, and the same practice was established in the schools by an article of the rule, which stated that, «All the brothers will take to heart the exact performance of the May devotions, and see to it that their children do likewise with good taste and piety.»

During the revolution of 1830, the brothers in many places were disturbed, and the government even threatened to close the novitiate of the Hermitage and to suppress the congregation. During those critical moments, instead of being frightened and discouraged, Fr. Champagnat turned to the Blessed Virgin as he

---

[2] Since these litanies have not been approved, they are replaced, in community exercises, by the litany of the Blessed Virgin.

habitually did, and entrusted his community to her. Then, after calling together his brothers, who had been alarmed by a search of the house conducted by the royal prosecutor and a contingent of police, he told them, «Don't be upset by the threats made against us and have no fear for your future. Mary, who brought us together in this house, will not let us be driven out of it by human malice. Let us be more faithful than ever in honoring her, in showing that we are her true children, and in imitating her virtues; let us redouble our confidence in her, and let us remember that she is our Ordinary Resource. To earn her protection and avert all danger, we will sing the *Salve Regina* every morning before meditation.»

That was the only precaution he wanted to take, and Mary, in whom he had placed his entire trust, did not fail him, because the Prefect of the Loire, who was plotting to destroy the congregation, was suddenly replaced, and the brothers were not bothered again. Since then, the singing of the Salve Regina has continued in the novitiates and has become an article of rule. The custom of reciting the Salve Regina after Mass in the novitiates is older, and dates from 1824; it was born in the tiny chapel in the woods where Father said Mass during the construction of the Hermitage.

While the Founder was in Paris in 1838, to request government authorization for his Institute, he often went to recommend this important matter to Our Lady of Victory, and enrolled in the Archconfraternity of the Sacred Heart of Mary, which Fr. Desgenettes, the parish priest, had just established. In 1841, the latter granted a diploma of membership to all the members of the institute; that was when the custom of having benediction every Thursday was instituted. The Our Father, Hail Mary and Memorare recited after benediction remind us of the purpose of this benediction, which is to pray for the conversion of sinners in union with all the members of the archconfraternity.

The practice of the Saturday fast dates from the first days of the Institute. But as Father noted, fasting should always be accompanied by prayer, which is why he urged that fervent prayers be said to the Immaculate and Blessed Virgin, in order to obtain purity and the grace of being preserved from mortal sin. Saturday, he added, should be totally consecrated to the Blessed Virgin; one should attend Mass in her honor, one should not fail to speak about her during catechism or to have hymns sung in her praise.

III. Devotion to Saint Joseph

The Little Brothers of Mary have always professed to have great devotion to St. Joseph, the glorious spouse of Mary.

«The Blessed Virgin,» said Fr. Champagnat, «is our mother, and St. Joseph is our first patron.» So, from the beginning, he always wanted the brothers to place themselves under his protection every day and consecrate themselves to him with the prayer, «Glorious St. Joseph...I choose you this day, and all my life, to be my special patron,» which is part of our evening prayer. Later, he added the litany of this great saint to the recitation of the rosary in the novitiates. The feast of St. Joseph has always been celebrated in the institute with great piety, and the Chapter of 1860 prescribed that it would be a holiday in all novitiate houses, and celebrated there with the same solemnity as the feasts of the Blessed Virgin.

IV. Devotion to the Patron Saints and Guardian Angels

At the beginning of each month, Father had a patron saint chosen for that month. After having drawn the name of the patron by lot, his life is read, and he is invoked each day with the prayer, «Saint N., pray for us who have recourse to you, so that we may imitate your virtues and follow in your footsteps,» followed by an Our Father and Hail Mary. On the saint's feastday, his life is re-read, and Mass is celebrated in his or her honor. This practice spread through the schools and has always been maintained in the novitiate houses and in all the establishments where there are pious brothers director.

In a note in the Founder's handwriting, dating from 1818, summarizing the main things the brothers ought to teach the children, we read the following: «The brothers will have great confidence in their guardian angel; they will invoke him often, as well as the guardian angels of the children entrusted to them. A picture of the guardian angel will be placed in every classroom, and the brothers will not fail to profit by all occasions which may arise to remind the children of the outstanding service which our guardian angels perform for us, what we owe them, how advantageous it is to invoke them often and to have great devotion to them.» Father often told stories about the protection afforded by the holy angels, and he urged the brothers to do likewise, but he recommended that these stories be taken, as far as possible, from holy scripture and the lives of the saints.

V. Devotion to the Souls in Purgatory

Devotion to the souls in purgatory was no less dear to Father Champagnat; he recommended it on every occasion, and to stimulate the piety of those whom charity had not sufficiently disposed to pray for the dead, he occasionally recalled the following story.

It is recorded in the chronicles of the order of St. Francis of Assisi, that a brother of that institute appeared after his death to one of his confrères and assured him that he was suffering horribly in purgatory, because he had been lacking in charity towards his brothers, both living and dead. He added that up to that point, he had drawn no benefit from either the good works which had been performed for him, nor from the masses said and the prayers offered on his behalf, because God, to punish his negligence in praying for the souls in purgatory, had applied their merit to other brothers who, during their life, had charitably put up with the defects of their neighbor, and prayed a great deal for the souls in purgatory.

«So you see, brothers,» he would add, «what we have done will be done to us. God will treat us as we have treated others. If we forget our deceased brothers and benefactors, we will be forgotten, and we will have to pay, down to the last penny. A brother who prays a great deal for the souls in purgatory and who teaches his children the same good habit, will spend only a short time in that place of expiation; his charity will cover all his little faults, and what he has done for others will be returned to him a hundredfold.»

Every year, at the end of the retreat, the Founder gave a conference on purgatory and held a solemn service, with a procession to the cemetery, for the deceased brothers and all the deceased benefactors of the society.

On Sundays, after vespers, he recited the *De Profundis* for the same intention. The *Pater* and *Ave* which followed were for the living benefactors. This practice of the *De Profundis*, *Pater* and *Ave* dates from 1824. Father always preceded these prayers with these words, to point out their purpose: «Let us pray for our benefactors, living and dead.»

VI. Other special practices

Evening prayer in the institute has always ended with the *Pater*, *Ave*, and *Miserere*. The *Pater* and *Ave* are for the superiors and the children in our schools; the *Miserere* is to ask God's pardon for all the faults committed during the day by the members of the congregation and to implore divine mercy for those who may unfortunately be in the state of mortal sin.

To go to bed with a mortal sin on one's soul is a frightful thing, a thousand times more dangerous than to sleep with a poisonous snake. «My God,» Father used to exclaim, «do not ever let one of our brothers go to bed with a mortal sin on his conscience. When one has been so unfortunate as to commit a grave fault, he must rise again by an act of perfect contrition and go to confession as soon as possible. 'Let not the sun go down upon your anger' (Eph 4:26), St. Paul told the first faithful; and I say to you, do not let the sun go down on your conscience guilty of mortal sin. Go reconcile yourself with God by a sincere confession, because you could die during the night; even if that misfortune did not happen to you, a religious in mortal sin is a horrible thing. It is Satan in the midst of the children of God, the abomination of desolation in the holy place.» So let us say the Miserere with great compunction, so that God may shield all of us from the misfortune of falling into mortal sin, and forgive us all our faults of the day.

In the constitutions of the Sisters of the Visitation, St. Francis de Sales included the rule that during the day, and even during the recreation periods, there was to be a sister responsible for reminding the others from time to time of the holy exercise of the presence of God, in these words: «May all our sisters remember the holy presence of God.» Our Father praised that rule highly, but he said, with good reason, «The bell will be more exact than a brother in fulfilling that function.» So he specified that a short prayer would be said every hour to remind us of the presence of God, to offer him our actions, to ask his help, and to maintain within us the spirit of fervor.

When a fireplace is burning well, he added, all it takes to maintain the fire and keep the room warm is to put another log on it from time to time. In the same way, when one has made his meditation well in the morning, heard Mass piously and received holy communion, all it takes to preserve fervor and good dispositions of soul is to say the prayer of the hour during the day. He who is faithful to this practice draws abundant fruit from it; he is always ready and eager to pray and to perform his exercises of piety with devotion. Those are the reasons for the prayer of the hour whose practice among us is as old as the institute.

«When one is fervent, when one is zealous to make progress in virtue,» Father used to say, «one often makes novenas. These are a very good way to preserve fervor, sustain the struggle against the great temptations, and to renew one's piety. Making novenas is an indication of zeal for one's perfection, so it hurts me to see that brothers who are tepid and negligent in God's service drop novenas and the other practices of truly pious souls.»

When he left the Hermitage to go found the establishment of Saint-Pol, in the Pas-de-Calais, the brother director asked Father's permission to take with him a book entitled, Formulas of novenas and triduums for all the feasts of Our Lord and of the Blessed Virgin. «Yes, take the book,» he answered, «and use it often. You will need to make novenas up there, if you want God to bless you. You must establish the practice of novenas as much as you can, as well as the good customs of the Institute. Be aware that you are laying foundations, and that those who come after you will do what you have done.»

The exchange of peace dates from our origins. It is exchanged in community on the first day of the year as a way of wishing one another a happy New Year, and at the end of the annual retreat, and on the days of reception of the habit, as a mark of friendship and to preserve family spirit. Since then, it has been limited, at least for all the brothers, to New Year's Day; at receptions of the habit and professions, it is limited to the brothers involved and the superior.

On the day of his election, Brother Superior General and his assistants serve at table in the dining room during dinner. It was Fr. Champagnat himself who put that act of humility into practice in 1839, at the time of the election of Brother François, his successor. He no doubt wanted this gesture to remind the

119

Brother Superior and his Assistants that they had been chosen to serve the brothers and not to lord it over them, to be their fathers and not their masters. He also hoped to make all the members of the institute understand clearly that superiorship is less an honor than a heavy burden, that it is a task calling for devotedness, solicitude and charity, and not a sinecure or a life of pleasure, satisfaction or ease.

CHAPTER TWELVE

NEW YEAR'S EVE, OR GIVING THANKS

Fervor is a rare virtue; it is a gift given to faithful souls, and even in religious life there are few souls who are faithful to grace. Many Christians and most religious serve God as a master; few serve and love him as a father. St. Bernard complained about this error when he told his religious, «God's spirit has been given to each of us to help us save our souls, but that doesn't mean we all work at it fervently.

«Few are filled with this spirit, few strive to obtain it. Some are satisfied with avoiding mortal sin, and they say, 'If I save my soul, that's enough'» What is the cause of that wrong attitude which is so widespread in communities? There are several. The main ones are: firstly, lack of interior life; therefore routine spoils most of what we do. Second, lack of a filial attitude: we do not know God, we have a totally wrong conception of him, we consider him to be a hard and severe master, we act as if we were his slaves, with attitudes which shrivel up the heart and smother piety and the spirit of love.

Third, ignorance of Our Lord and of the infinite wealth we possess in him. We neglect to meditate on his mysteries and to share his outlook. Finally, ingratitude and forgetting to be thankful. In order to be forearmed against such defects, Fr. Champagnat made much of the spirit of faith, confidence in God, meditation on the life of Our Lord, and giving thanks.

Listen to the great esteem he had, and inspired in others, for the latter virtue, the horror he had of ingratitude, and the way he gave thanks to God.

1. The spirit of gratitude is characteristic of all the saints. «Bless the Lord, my soul, and never forget all he has done for you; let all that is within me bless his holy name» (*Ps* 103:1). This was the daily prayer of the prophet-king, and the Holy Spirit bears witness that «in all his works he gave thanks to the Holy One, and to the Most High, with words of glory» (*Sir* 47:9). «My soul magnifies the Lord, and my spirit has rejoiced in God my savior, because he has regarded the humility of his handmaid, [and has filled me with graces]» (*Lk* 1:46), the Blessed Virgin exclaimed.

St. Bonaventure assures us that the august Mother of God never ceased thanking the Lord, and for fear that ordinary human politeness might distract her from praising God, she was accustomed to reply, «Thanks be to God,» when anyone greeted her. St. Paul says, «I give thanks to God,» over and over again on every page of his letters, and he never failed to urge the faithful to fulfill this duty faithfully.

2. «Gratitude,» says St. John Chrysostom, «is normal for a solidly virtuous soul,» and St. Jerome assures us that it is normal for Christians to thank God for all his gifts. Holy Scripture gives this beautiful testimony to Tobias: «He never murmured against God who afflicted him, but remained unshakable in his fear of him, and thanked him every day of his life.» Gratitude was so habitual to the first Christians that they greeted each other by saying, «Alleluia,» or «Let us thank God.» Thanksgiving always had a place in their prayers, which is why they added the «Glory be» at the end of each psalm. When St. Jerome arrived in the Mideast, he was so taken with this prayer, and this devotion became so dear to him, that he asked Pope St. Damasus to introduce it in the Western Church, where it has been in use ever since.

In order to imitate the first Christians and be in tune with the spirit of the Church, Fr. Champagnat wanted the «Glory be» to be the brothers' ejaculatory prayer and the prayer of the hour.

«The Church,» he told us, «ceaselessly sends up a concert of praise to God and makes thankful voices heard everywhere, by repeating and singing at every hour, 'Glory be to the Father, to the Son, and to the Holy Spirit'. What prayer could be more pleasing to God than the one holy Church offers him? The «Glory be» will therefore be our ejaculatory prayer every hour, and through it we will imitate not only the Church militant, but also the Church triumphant, the angels and saints who eternally sing the Gloria Patri.

«After all, my dear brothers, when you look at things from the right perspective, what is our life on earth? A preparation for eternal life. Now, I have just insinuated that praising, blessing, thanking and loving God is the task of the heavenly court. The language of the saints comes down to these words: love, blessing, glory, wisdom, thanksgiving and praise be to our God for ever and ever. If the life of the saints in heaven is devoted to glorifying God and thanking him, it should be just the same on earth. Every prayer must end one day, except the prayer of thanksgiving, which will last forever. But in order to earn the right to say in eternity the prayer of thanksgiving which is the glory and happiness of the elect, we must begin it in time, we must learn to do on earth what we want to do in heaven.»

Let me repeat, so as not to forget, that the spirit of gratitude is characteristic of the saints, which is why the Holy Spirit says, «Bless the Lord, you his elect, glorify him for his gifts.» Do you understand those words—«Bless the Lord, you his elect»? Have you meditated attentively on them? What do they mean? They mean that gratitude is the constant cry and sentiment of the elect, just as ingratitude is the ordinary vice and disposition of the damned. Yes, thanksgiving is the prayer of all God's friends; they begin it in time and will continue it in eternity.

3. Gratitude, along with giving thanks, is a great way to obtain new favors. That is why a wise old man said, «The best way to ask for anything is to say thank you.» And St. John

Chrysostom assures us that nothing makes us grow more in virtue, and unites us more closely to God, than continually thanking him. «Rivers of graces come down from heaven,» adds St. Bernard, «and rivers of thanksgiving should ascend there, because if this heavenly water returns to its source through gratitude, it will fall again upon us, even more abundantly.»

The apostle Paul knew this secret, and that is why, as much out of gratitude as from his desire to advance in virtue, he began everything by giving thanks. «First, I give thanks to my God... for you all,» he told the Romans (*Rom* 1:8). «[Give] thanks always for all things,» he says elsewhere (*Eph* 5:20). And again, «Whatsoever you do in word or in work, do all in the name of the Lord Jesus Christ, giving thanks to God and the Father by him» (*Col* 3:17). And to make us really understand that praising, blessing and loving God, and growing in virtue, are one and the same thing, he adds, «Grow in the love of Jesus Christ by continually giving thanks.»

4. Gratitude is an act of love and a powerful means of perfection. When Fr. Champagnat decided, on the advice of the principal brothers, that the «Glory be» would always be part of the prayer of the hour, one of the brothers asked him, «Wouldn't it be better, Father, to say an act of charity?»

«Brother,» he replied, «gratitude is an act of love; we thank God because we love him, because his goodness towards us touches us, surprises us and wins us over to him.» Gratitude is so much an act of charity that in heaven we will thank Jesus more than ever, once he has crowned all his gifts by the greatest of all, eternal blessedness. Thanksgiving is grateful love, just as contrition is sorrowful and contrite love after having displeased the infinitely good God. Now, if thanksgiving is an act of love, it is certainly the way most suited to make us advance in perfection, since charity is the most meritorious virtue, the one which most closely unites us to God. On the other hand, ingratitude in religious and in pious souls is one of the worst defects there is.

This defect greatly displeases God and wounds his heart. «I have brought up children,» he says in Scripture, «but they have despised me» (*Is* 1:2). Jesus cured ten lepers, but nine showed themselves to be ungrateful, and only one turned back to thank his benefactor. The heart of Jesus suffers from such ingratitude, and cannot refrain from complaining about it. «Were not ten made clean?» he asks. «And where are the nine?» (*Lk* 17:17). How many times have we not given the heart of Jesus this sad surprise? How many times have we not forgotten to thank him for his graces? I am not surprised to hear St. Bernard exclaim, «I have an extreme horror of ingratitude; and if you ask me why, I will answer you that I am convinced that there is nothing in the children of benediction, in religious, which so much displeases God as ingratitude for his benefits.»

Ingratitude causes three great evils:

1. It dries up the source of grace. Why does God, who is so good, and who has overwhelmed us with so many gifts, even in the world, and without our asking him for them, not grant us just as many now in religious life, when we are constantly begging him to grant us this or that favor? Why does he seem to be deaf to our prayers? Has his power diminished? Are his riches exhausted? Has his goodness towards us changed? No, nothing like that; the true and only cause is that we have been ungrateful, we have forgotten to thank him for his gifts. Ingratitude, by depriving us of grace, leaves us to our own weakness, hands us over to our enemies, and leads us into sin. «God,» says Rupert, «withdrew his hand and his protection from the first man, and let him fall into sin, because he had failed to give thanks for the gift of his creation and all the other gifts God had given him. On the other hand, Scripture teaches us (*Sir* 47:10) that God made David victorious over his enemies to repay him for his gratitude, and because that holy king had loved, praised and thanked God with all his heart.»

2. It is why many lose their vocation. A religious vocation is one of the greatest graces God can give a soul; but those who do not esteem it highly enough, and who are not grateful for it, make themselves unworthy of it, and God, to punish them, takes back this gift and gives it to others who will show themselves grateful for it.

At the chapter of faults, Father often told the young brothers, for their penance, to recite the «Glory be» or the «Magnificat,» to thank God for having taken them out of the world. When the question arose of deciding what prayers would be said at the ceremony of the reception of the habit and profession of vows, he wanted the «Te Deum» always included, so as to thank God for the gift he was giving the Institute in the person of new members, and to teach all the brothers that it is their duty to thank God often for the inestimable gift of their vocation.

A certain brother, who was giving Father an account of his conscience, told him that he was not attached to his vocation and felt tempted to abandon it. «Do you fight this temptation?,» Father asked him.

«Very little.»

«Have you ever thought very highly of your vocation?»

«During my novitiate, I loved and esteemed it quite a bit.»

«Have you often thanked God for calling you to this vocation?»

«Never, or hardly ever.»

«I can understand why you are disgusted with it; you have been ungrateful, the gift of God has been taken away from you, and it will be given to someone else, more faithful and more grateful. Only a moment ago, a brother of your group was sitting right where you are; he had come to ask me for permission to receive a special communion, to end a novena which he is in the habit of making every three months, to thank God for his vocation and for all the other graces he has received because of it.

This brother is fervent, happy and contented in his holy state, and he is so attached to his vocation that he assured me that he would not exchange it for an empire. So his gratitude is helping him keep a gift which your ingratitude is making you lose.»

3. It is the enemy of piety and leads to tepidity. One sees so many religious who perform all their duties poorly because they are not at all happy in religious life, and draw no consolation from their exercises of piety! Everywhere—during meditation, examen, Holy Mass—their heart is covered by a veil which cannot be pierced by either the example of their brothers, the splendor of the ceremonies, or even the spirit of God. God's blessings are as burdensome for such souls as his chastisements are for others. For them, prayer is a penance, confession a torture, communion a real torment. God's blessings irritate them like a burning wound. The graces he showers on them upset them and make them nervous, instead of bringing them peace and happiness. What is the real cause of all that? Ask such religious what they think of God, ask them if they have thanked him regularly, and you will learn the real secret of their sad condition. For them, God has been nothing but a hard, severe master, not a father.

They almost never thought of thanking him. The vice of ingratitude is at the root of their whole life. They fear God, or rather his punishments, and do not love him. They beg him to deliver them from hell, and do not think of praising him and thanking him for his gifts. They are filled with a servile spirit and have never known the filial spirit. There you have the cause of their dryness, the reason for their tepidity. These religious are ungrateful, they do not know the spirit of gratitude, and ingratitude has fastened them in the pillory of imperfection; they will never make a single step towards progress so long as they have that detestable spirit of servility. What a wicked vice ingratitude is! How God detests it! «It is very true,» as St. Bernard says, «that this vice dries up the wellsprings of grace, dries up all the good sentiments of the soul, goes against its best interests, and directly attacks its salvation.»

The practice of gratitude was particularly dear to Fr. Champagnat, and he never received any favor from heaven without acknowledging it with acts of thanksgiving. Father's normal practice was to make novenas and say Holy Mass often to thank God for his blessings. The anniversaries of his baptism, first communion, ordination, and religious profession, and of other days on which he had received special favors, were always for him feast days totally dedicated to thanksgiving.

In the same spirit, he spent the last hour of the year in prayer, to thank God for the graces he had received during it. He was very attached to this exercise, for several reasons. He used to say that it was «a way to make up for the losses of the entire year. If we do not enjoy the consolation of being able to congratulate ourselves for having made good use of every day of the year and for having spent every day well, we can make up for it by sanctifying its last hour through prayer and the holy practice of thanksgiving. It is likewise in our own best interest to deeply humiliate ourselves before God, to ask him to pardon our faults, in order to obtain their total remission, so that they will not follow us into the year which is about to begin.»

It is also of the utmost importance to give to God the first-fruits of the new year and to take the means to spend it in a holy manner. That is what Fr. Champagnat did. Hence, he spent these two hours:

1. asking God's pardon for all the faults he had committed during the year which, according to his expression, was about to drop into eternity;

2. going over the graces and favors he had received from God, and thanking him effusively for them.

There was nothing more moving than to hear him exclaim, «My God, what am I? A composite of your blessings. The graces you have allotted to me are so numerous that I could more easily count the grains of sand at the seashore than list them all. I have had the happiness of immolating the spotless Lamb more than three hundred and sixty times! What a favor! What a favor! What a favor! Oh, good Jesus, I am collapsing under the weight of your blessings! May you be eternally blessed for all the graces I have received from you! May the angels and saints praise and glorify you forever for them! Mary, my august mother, let me use your feelings and your words, and say like you, 'My soul magnifies the Lord...'!»

3. offering himself to God, consecrating to him the New Year and all he planned to do during it;

4. asking God, through the intercession of the Blessed Virgin and his holy patrons, to bless the new year, to accept and sanctify all its works, and to make it a happy year, free from sin and full of graces, virtues and merits.

How ardent and heartfelt was Father's gratitude to God, the sovereign source of all good gifts! And how many beautiful examples he has left for us to imitate, of this virtue as well as of all the others!

CHAPTER THIRTEEN

OUR NEED FOR MEDITATION AND MENTAL PRAYER

«Meditation, prayer, actual grace, habitual grace, perseverance in charity and in our vocation, and our eternal salvation, are six things which are linked together and depend on one another,» Fr. Champagnat used to say. «In the normal course of events, without prayer or mental prayer there are no actual graces; without abundant actual graces it is not possible to resist temptations and to preserve habitual grace and our vocation along with it, because mortal sin, while killing the soul, at the same time kills our vocation and razes the whole structure of our salvation down to its very foundations.»

To explain this maxim of our Founder, we will show that mental prayer, and by that very fact, meditation, which is like an indispensable means to it, is necessary for six fundamental reasons.

I.

We need mental prayer in order to enlighten our mind. We can save ourselves only by serving God; we can serve God only by loving him; we cannot love him with our whole heart if we do not esteem him greatly; and we will never think highly of him if we are not sufficiently aware of his perfection. Now, how can we acquire that awareness except by daily meditation? If God is so poorly served, or to put it more clearly, if we ourselves serve him so negligently, it is because we do not know him. «Father,» Jesus

Christ said, «the world has not known you, [and therefore it has not loved you]» (*Jn* 17:25). «[The source of all disorders, of all sins,]» says the prophet Hosea, is the fact that «there is no truth, and there is no mercy, and there is no knowledge of God in the land» (*Hos* 4:1).

To win salvation it is not enough to know God well; one must also know oneself. Since St. Augustine was convinced of this truth, he said this prayer every day: «My God, may I know you and know myself. May I know myself in order to despise and hate myself, and may I know you in order to esteem and love you.» And, in fact, to work effectively at our perfection, we must know:

1. the depths of corruption within us, in order to humble and mistrust ourselves;

2. our violent tendency toward evil, in order to repress it;

3. our total helplessness, so that we never to count on ourselves, but place all our confidence in God;

4. our dominant passion, in order to combat it, and all our defects, in order to correct them;

5. our sins, in order to weep over them and erase them by our tears. Now, it is very evident that in order to acquire this self-knowledge, we absolutely need daily reflection and meditation.

Moreover, in order to attain salvation, we must necessarily know the duties of our state, as Christians and as religious. It is only by studying the law of God and meditating diligently on it that we can come to know and observe them. Hence this precept given us by God himself: «These words which I command you this day shall be in your heart. You shall meditate upon them sitting in your house, and walking on our journey, sleeping and rising. [For fear of forgetting them] you shall bind them as a sign on your hand, and they shall be and shall move between your eyes, and you shall write them in the entry and on the doors of your house» (*Deut* 6:6-9).

It is not enough to be instructed in the law of God, we must also love and observe it; but in order to love and observe it, we must know its beauty, its fairness, its advantages; the rewards attached to practicing it; the threats, penalties and punishments inflicted on those who violate it. That is why, after giving his law to the Israelites, God enumerated for them, on the one hand, all the blessings and rewards which would be granted to those who would observe it, and on the other hand, he placed before their eyes all the misfortunes and all the chastisements he would inflict on those who would violate it. If we could ask the Christians who are in hell the cause of their damnation, they would all answer that it was nothing else but forgetfulness of God, of his holy law, and of the rewards attached to its observance and the chastisements drawn down by its transgression.

Without meditation there is no light, that is, there is no true knowledge of God, of ourselves, of our duties, or of our destiny, and consequently, no assurance of salvation. «He who keeps his eyes closed,» says St. Augustine, «cannot see the road which leads to his homeland, and he will never reach it.» The first thing the Philistines did to Samson after they captured him was to gouge his eyes out. That is a parallel to what the devil does to a soul when he becomes its master: he blinds it and prevents it from meditating and practicing mental prayer.

The Holy Spirit, who wants all souls to be saved, ceaselessly cries out to them, «[Approach God, meditate on his holy law and you will be enlightened]» (*Ps* 37:6). What the sun does exteriorly to the world, meditation does interiorly to souls. The sun warms, enlightens, gladdens, gives life; mental prayer pours torrents of light into our understanding, inflames and strengthens our will, spreads joy and happiness in our heart, vivifies and nourishes our soul with the graces it brings us. Take the sun away from the earth, and you will have nothing but darkness, ice, sadness, death; take meditation away from a man, and his mind will be filled with darkness and ignorance, his will with weakness and apathy, his heart with hardness, bitterness and anguish; his soul will die of starvation, as St. Chrysostom says. St. Thomas Aquinas was so convinced of that truth that he did not hesitate to state that no one deserves the name of religious if he is not faithful to the practice of mental prayer; for just as one cannot obtain an effect without its cause, so one cannot have enlightenment without reflection, grace without prayer, and in a word, virtue and salvation without mental prayer.

II

We need meditation to strengthen our heart, make it good, sensitive and docile to the impressions of grace. Of itself, our heart is hard, stubborn, insensitive, cold and evil; so it will certainly be lost, for the Holy Spirit assures us that, «A wicked heart will be laden with sorrows» (*Sir* 3:29).

But what is a hard heart? St. Bernard says it is one which is not contrite, torn by compunction and the pain of its sins; one which is not softened by piety nor warmed by the love of God; one which is ungrateful, which does not think of the blessings it has received and does not thank God for them; one which is not touched by prayers nor shaken by threats, and which even punishments find insensitive; one which does not blush for its crimes, which forgets the past, neglects the present and does not think at all about the future; one, finally, which is not zealous for its salvation and has no fear of the damnation which awaits it if it remains in that sad condition.

What is the remedy for such a sickness? The only infallible remedy is meditation and prayer. Hardness of heart can be cured only by daily mental prayer. Mental prayer does to the heart what fire does to iron; when iron is cold, it is extremely hard, and impossible to work, but fire softens it and makes it docile, so to speak, to the will of the blacksmith. In the same way, mental prayer warms the heart, softens it, and leads it to embrace fervently the practice of virtue. The holy prophet king, who meditated assiduously on the law of God, exclaims, «My heart grew hot within me» (*Ps* 38[39]:4). Then he adds, «I run!» Where are you running, holy king? «In the way of the commandments of my God»; that is to say, in the practice of all the virtues. And how long have you been running like this? «Since God opened my heart through mental prayer» (*Ps* 118).

Later on, in a moment of forgetfulness and weakness, he complains that his heart has become dry. «I found myself dried up like hay, because I forgot to eat my bread.» What bread? The bread of meditation and prayer, all the Holy Fathers reply.

No matter how good a field may be, St. John Chrysostom tells us, to make it really fertile, it must be frequently watered by the rain; in the same way, our heart must often be watered by prayer, if we want it to bear the fruit of virtue and sanctity. In order to observe the divine precepts and the evangelical counsels, adds Bartholomew of the Martyrs, we must have a tender heart, meaning one which easily receives the impressions of grace and puts them into practice. Now, it is mental prayer which gives us this tenderness and docility of heart. Solomon understood this truth, which is why he told God, «Give your servant an understanding heart» (1 Kings 3:9). Finally, St. Paul teaches us the same thing when he says that, in order to make us practice virtue, God gave us the sentiments and the heart of children, and that the Holy Spirit makes us cry out constantly, «Father! Father!»

III.

We also need mental prayer to avoid sin and preserve the life of grace. Prayer is as indispensable for our soul to preserve the life of grace, as food is for our body to preserve our health and natural life. A man who would refuse all nourishment would inevitably die; likewise, anyone who gives up meditation and prayer, which are the nourishment of the soul, will lose the life of grace and end up by falling into mortal sin, which is the death of the soul. The saints and masters of the spiritual life are unanimous in affirming this truth. St. John Chrysostom was not afraid to say and to repeat, «I consider any religious who gives up mental prayer as not only sick, but dead. Just as we judge a body to be dead when it no longer breathes, so we can be certain that a soul is dead when it has stopped praying.»

St. Bonaventure states that a religious who gives up mental prayer is not only miserable and useless, but in addition, in the sight of God he has a dead soul in a living body.

In St. Alphonsus Liguori's opinion, a religious who does not meditate on the eternal truths and who drops mental prayer is nothing more than the corpse of a religious.

According to St. Teresa of Avila, a religious who gives up mental prayer does not need the devil to lead him to hell, because he goes there himself and throws himself in of his own free will.

The holy abbot De Rancé, the reformer of the Trappists, states that a religious who neglects meditation is neglecting his salvation and heading for ruin. Such a person, he adds, is like a soldier who throws down his weapons in the middle of a battle; like a shipwrecked person who, instead of grabbing the rope thrown to him, lets the current carry him away; like a sick person who refuses the only remedy that can cure him; like a starving person who refuses to take nourishment. Those unfortunate people will certainly die, and the same holds true for anyone who does not pray.

It is morally impossible, says St. Robert Bellarmine, for anyone who does not meditate to remain free from mortal sin. Gerson adds that, barring a miracle, anyone who does not meditate cannot live as a Christian.

Abbot Diocles regarded meditation as so necessary to religious that he said, «He who gives up meditation soon becomes either a brute or a demon; rather, he becomes both—a brute because of his ignorance, a demon because of his malice, wickedness and hardness of heart.»

Mental prayer is the weapon which God has given us to fight the devil, resist his temptations and preserve ourselves from sin. According to St. Alphonsus, without meditation and prayer, we will never have the strength to resist temptations and to control our passions. Prayer is the door through which the Lord hands us his graces of light and strength; if that door remains closed through our own fault, what will become of us? We will inevitably fall. Look at the martyrs; where did they get the energy and strength to resist tyrants and endure tortures? From prayer.

St. Theodoret, after having suffered great torments on a bed of red-hot potsherds, feeling his entire body racked with pain (*au fond de ses entrailles*) and no longer able to endure it, loudly called on God for help, and was immediately given so much strength that he endured his sufferings with joy until he died. On the contrary, some Christians, when tortured, denied their faith because they had neglected to pray.

«It made me very sad,» St. Cyprian said, «to see strong and generous men who had suffered for a long time and were close to receiving the crown, suddenly deny their faith because they had taken their eyes off him who gives strength to the weak; that is to say, they had stopped praying.»

The necessity of praying in order to resist the devil becomes even more evident from the following facts of history. During the terrible tortures inflicted on the martyrs, men were sometimes seen to grow pale and renounce the faith, but there is no mention of a single virgin who trembled, or at least who died an apostate. This is a clear and striking proof that it was grace alone which sustained the martyrs; but it is no less certain that they obtained this grace only through persevering prayer. In Japan, an old man who had been condemned to be sawed into little pieces with a reed was strong enough to endure this torment for several hours; but before breathing his last, having stopped recommending himself to God, he renounced the faith and died that instant. A terrifying example, which once again confirms the truth that whether we are resisting torture or temptation, it is prayer which gives us strength and wins us the victory.

«It is a matter of experience,» says St. Alphonsus, «that mental prayer and sin cannot dwell together. Those who practice mental prayer regularly do not fall into sin; and if that misfortune should occur through surprise or weakness, they promptly get up again.» St. Teresa adds that, «We may be certain that a soul who perseveres in mental prayer will never let itself slip into sin, and will never be lost, no matter how violent and how many its temptations may be.» Mental prayer is the pipeline which brings us the water of grace, the help and strength with which we avoid sin. In order to break that pipeline, the devil makes all sorts of efforts to prevent us from praying, because he knows that souls who are unswervingly faithful to their daily meditation and their exercises of piety are lost to him. Being convinced of that fact, St. Teresa also said that the most fatal and most dangerous of all temptations is the one which leads us to neglect meditation and prayer; and St. Lawrence Justinian said that the devil's most successful ruse for causing souls to be lost is to turn them away from prayer or meditation, because their giving up those practices guarantees the success of his temptations.

IV.

We also need to pray in order to correct our defects. Father Rodriguez says that, «The entire conduct of our lives depends on prayer; it is well or poorly regulated depending on whether we perform our mental prayer well or badly.»

«So therefore,» adds St. Alphonsus, «if you see a religious who is tepid, unmortified, vain, disobedient, lax in observing the rule, quick-tempered, quarrelsome, you can say, 'He does not meditate,' and you will not be mistaken.»

«Meditation,» says St. Bernard, «teaches us to know ourselves and shows us our defects; prayer gives us the grace to overcome and correct ourselves; meditation shows us the virtues we lack, prayer obtains them for us; meditation shows us the road which leads to heaven, prayer makes us travel it surely and diligently; meditation shows us the perils which surround us, the enemies we have to combat; prayer helps us to avoid those perils and gives us the strength to attack and overcome our enemies.

«Meditation enlightens and purifies the soul, controls our inclinations, directs our actions, corrects our defects, improves our manners and puts order in the way we live our whole lives. Anyone who stops meditating will never know his defects, and consequently will never be able to correct them. He will never see the snares of the devil and will let himself be caught in them. He will never know the risks his salvation is running, and will not even dream of avoiding them.

«Finally,» he concludes, «without mental prayer, one stops being reasonable; one lets oneself be deluded by the devil, dominated by one's passions, eaten up by one's defects; without mental prayer, there is only ignorance in one's mind, weakness in one's heart, infidelity in one's will; life is one long string of defects and sins.»

According to Theodoret, «Mental prayer is a universal remedy for curing the illnesses of the soul, an infallible way to remove the rust of our defects.» Developing that thought further, he adds, «The medical profession treats each physical ailment with some specific remedy, and often applies several of them to cure just one disease, because all these remedies are weak and have only limited power; but mental prayer is a universal and infallible remedy for correcting every sort of defect and repelling all the attacks of the devil, because it applies to all the sicknesses of the soul an infinite good who is God, from whom it draws all its strength. That is why it is called all-powerful.»

Prayer is to the soul what the hand is to the body. The hand is the instrument of the whole body and of itself in particular. It works to feed and clothe the body and to meet all its other needs, and it also works for itself. If one hand is sick, the other hand bandages it; if one hand is dirty, the other washes it; if one hand is cold, the other warms it. In the final analysis, the hands do everything, and the same holds true for prayer.

«Brother,» a young religious once asked an old Father of the Desert, «what must I do in order not to give in to the bad thoughts which overwhelm me?»

«Pray, brother.»

«And to repress my intemperate tongue?»

«Pray.

«And so as not to give in to the suggestions of my enemy who urges me to leave my cell and waste time with my brothers?»

«Pray.»

«And to uproot and destroy the pride, lack of mortification, and self-will of which I am full?»

«Pray.»

«But Father, why do you give me just one single means to do so many different things?»

«For two reasons: first, because it is a universal and effective way to obtain everything; and second, because it includes and can replace all the others.»

V.

Mental prayer is also an absolute necessity for practicing virtue in an outstanding manner and for living as a good and fervent religious. «The soul,» says St. Augustine, «has received the faculty of improving itself, with the help of God, and of being able, through works of piety, of acquiring all the virtues and gifts which raise it to the height of perfection.» Now, this faculty is the power and grace of prayer.

«Every perfect gift,» says St. James, «is from above, coming down from the Father of lights» (*Jas* 1:17). What do these words of the holy apostle mean? According to St. John Chrysostom, they mean that mental prayer is the cause and mother of all virtues, and that not a single one of the things which are necessary for holiness can enter a soul which fails to communicate with God via mental prayer.

According to Pope Innocent I, they mean that we will try in vain to win the victory over our vices, and to raise the edifice of virtues and perfection, unless grace is drawn into us through constant, fervent prayer.

By the words, «Every perfect gift comes from above,» the Holy Spirit wanted to teach us, says St. Bonaventure, that not a single grace comes down from heaven, and one cannot acquire a single solid and perfect virtue, without prayer and mortification.

Finally, concludes Cardinal Cajetan, just as one cannot obtain an effect without its cause, nor an end without the means, it is not possible to practice virtue without mental prayer. So, no one who fails to make mental prayer can be called a religious, because he does not have the virtues of his state.

On the contrary, a prayerful soul is «like a tree which is planted near the running waters, which shall bring forth its fruit in due season. Whatever he shall do shall prosper» (*Ps* 1:3). Notice the phrase, «in due season,» which means «at the right moment.» A pious religious will be patient, obedient, humble, regular, modest, charitable, zealous, mortified, and so on. According to St. John Chrysostom, mental prayer does for the soul what an abundant fountain does for a garden; without it everything is dry and sterile, everything dies; with it, everything is flourishing, fresh and delicious, and every plant produces good fruit. Likewise, prayer keeps the holy plants of obedience, humility, love of God and all the virtues perennially fresh and beautiful.

The gift of mental prayer is proof of solid virtue. «If,» says St. Gregory, «you see a soul favored with a great gift of piety, you may be sure that that is an indubitable sign that God is calling it to great perfection, and to do great things for his glory.» St. John Chrysostom is of the same opinion: «If I meet a religious who loves meditation and is faithful to performing all his exercises of piety well, I immediately judge that grace abounds in his heart; for if one becomes wise by remaining in the company of wise men, as the Holy Spirit tells us, what wisdom does one not acquire from conversing familiarly with God, and how perfect must one's virtues be!»

«God,» the holy doctor goes on to say, «would not put up with a home that was poor, undecorated, and messy. So as soon as he enters a soul through meditation and mental prayer, he puts order in it and fills it with his divine gifts; he first imprints on it great delicacy of conscience which cannot stand even the slightest faults; he then gives it a generous heart and noble thoughts which make it despise earthly goods, pleasures and honor, so that the most beautiful things in the world look like mere trifles and manure. Moreover, he fortifies its will, gives it generous courage, which makes it rise above work, tribulation, pain, and even death, and leads it to the most heroic virtues. Finally, God helps that soul to find in prayer a thousand ways and means to make its life pure and holy, and to help it practice profitably all sorts of good works.

VI.

Finally, it is absolutely necessary for us to practice mental prayer every day, in order to persevere in our vocation and to fulfill its purpose. No one keeps anything he despises or has no use for. Therefore, in order to preserve our vocation, we must appreciate and esteem it as something very precious. To do so, we must often meditate on its excellence and advantages, the graces of which it is the source, the dangers from which it preserves us, the pleasant and virtuous life it provides for us, the problems and misfortunes from which it preserves us.

A religious does not lose his vocation all at once, but bit by bit. Step by step and by degrees, he reaches the stage of infidelity and apostasy; first he says his prayers poorly, then he shortens them, and then he lets them go altogether. The onset of that fatal eclipse, by which God hides himself totally from us, is like the onset of an eclipse of the sun—hardly noticeable at first, it finally leaves the soul in total darkness. To prevent such a misfortune, we must meditate on the great truths and never lose sight of the great task of our salvation.

«You asked me,» says Bourdaloue, «if meditation is really necessary. Let me ask you a question in return: is it really necessary to love God, to avoid sin, to correct your defects, to preserve charity, and to persevere in your holy state and in doing good? In other words, is it really necessary to guarantee your salvation, to save your soul, to avoid hell and win heaven? If you tell me that all of that is necessary, I will reply that meditation and prayer are even more so, since it is through mental prayer that you will obtain all the rest.»

St. Vincent de Paul says that, «Perseverance in one's vocation, success in the assignment one has been given, victory over temptations, our return to God after our falls, and final perseverance in doing good, should all be considered as the effects of meditation.»

We can feel sure about the virtue of a religious, no matter what danger he is exposed to, if he is faithful to mental prayer, his examination of conscience and reception of the sacraments. On the contrary, if he neglects them, even if he is a saint today, he will never survive; and if he is imperfect, he will soon begin to despise his most essential obligations. All those who become bored with their state, all those who lose their vocation, or who, by their disedifying conduct, deserve to be considered and treated as useless individuals, reach that terrible position only because they neglected their exercises of piety. That was the origin of all the rest.

«All those religious,» says Bellecius, «who fall into serious sin, who abandon their holy state, who scandalize the Church and the faithful, reach that point only because they abandon mental prayer or perform it in a lax fashion or only to keep up appearances.»

«Not only that,» says St. Bonaventure, «but all it takes is relaxation in the habitual practice of meditation to make a house, or even a whole religious order, lose its fervor and its original regularity, and eventually fade away.»

If you ever meet a religious who is bored, dissatisfied, and has little esteem for his holy state, and if you say that he does not meditate, you will not be mistaken.

«On the contrary,» says Fr. Judde, «I dare you to show me a religious who is very exact in making his meditation and examen, in attending Mass, in reciting his rosary and his office, and so on, who is not happy in his state, who does not love his vocation, who does not possess its virtues and fulfill its purpose and obligations.»

«How many religious,» says St. Alphonsus, «sin, grow old in their bad habits and defects, are finally lost and fall into hell, because they do not meditate and pray.»

Religious, pray, pray, never stop praying and meditating on the eternal truths. If you do this, your perseverance and salvation are guaranteed; if you give up meditation and prayer, you will certainly be lost.

«We must be firmly convinced,» concludes Massillon, «that praying is a man's normal condition, his first duty, his greatest need, his only resource, his greatest consolation; it is man himself.»

CHAPTER FOURTEEN

THE FIVE TYPES OF DEVOTION OR PIETY

The spirit of piety is the best of all gifts, a treasure for a religious, the infallible means of acquiring solid virtue and responding perfectly to God's plans for us. «Of all the things one can prize in life,» says St. Gregory of Nyssa, «there is none which should be preferred to the spirit of prayer, because prayer is the universal and most effective means for carrying out everything God has ordained for the eternal predestination of his elect.»

«You may be sure of this,» says St. Francis of Paola; «it is not possible for human words to express the great benefits which the gift of piety brings to a soul. Prayer has infinite excellence, power and merit; it is the origin and the source of all gifts, all graces, all virtues.» And this great saint went on to say, «Recommend unceasingly to all the brothers to devote themselves to it constantly and to ask Our Lord every day for the gift of piety.»

Father Champagnat called piety the main point. In his opinion, to have the gift of solid piety is to possess all the virtues. «If God grants you the gift of piety,» he used to say, «by the same token he gives you all the virtues, because we can say of piety what Solomon said about wisdom: 'Everything good came to me together with it.' As a matter of fact, it is not possible to speak often with God without absorbing his spirit, without becoming like him through imitating his virtues; it has always been my experience that anyone who had the spirit of piety also had the spirit of obedience, mortification and zeal, and was totally involved in his own perfection. Pious brothers are precious men, the pillars of the institute; whatever talents, strength and health they may have, they make themselves useful wherever they go, because they bring their good spirit with them, and God blesses everything entrusted to them.

«On the contrary, a brother who is lacking in piety does nothing good, either for himself or for others. He is powerless to do good, because he does not have the right means for doing so, which are piety and union with God. Long experience has taught me that a brother without piety is a worthless man; he is never at home anywhere and he is an embarrassment for everyone. St. Benedict had good reason to say, 'Never expect anything good from a religious who is not pious, no matter how many other talents he may have.'»

But what does 'solidly pious' mean? To have the gift of piety, to be solidly pious, means to love prayer, to enjoy the exercises of piety, to struggle forcefully and perseveringly against the obstacles to prayer, such as distractions, to feel a constant need for prayer, to spend as much time as possible in prayer, to experience complete happiness and consolation in one's conversations with God. To help us know where we stand in terms of piety and to know to what extent we possess this precious gift, or how weak we are on this major point, here is a brief explanation of the five types of devotions or piety.

I. Piety of the mind

This consists of knowledge of the mysteries of Our Lord, and in great esteem for prayer, for the service of God, for virtue, and for everything which has to do with salvation.

«An object,» says St. Thomas, «can cause us pleasure in two ways: first, in itself, when it actually makes an impression on our senses, when we see or taste it. In this case, it produces devotion in the heart; that is to say, good feelings, fervor, etc. Second, through the image we create of it when our mind dwells on the positive attitude we have toward it, and through the esteem we have for it when we discover its value and its good qualities.

Now, it is this esteem which produces devotion or piety of the mind. We acquire and develop this devotion through spiritual reading and above all through meditating deeply on the mysteries of Our Lord, and the dogmas and truths of religion. This devotion is very necessary, very advantageous, because it produces, nourishes and develops all the others and helps them to grow. It is to devotion and piety of the heart what the seed is to the fruit, what wood is to fire.

II. Piety of the heart

This consists of having a taste for prayer, feelings of confidence in God, gratitude for his gifts, love for Our Lord, praise for his divine perfection, and contrition for our sins; in a word, fervor and palpable devotion.

This devotion is an outstanding grace and a priceless benefit, provided one does not become too attached to it, that one submits with resignation to its withdrawal when that happens, and that we carefully avoid making it a question of emotion.

Devotion of the heart enhances all the others; it ennobles and sanctifies them. It is sweet, full of consolation; it makes virtue easy; it helps us to make constant progress, for nothing is difficult when one is in love. Love is stronger than death, so the greatest sacrifices are nothing to someone who loves.

Devotion of the heart is the devotion of great souls, of good, generous, fervent hearts. It is the devotion of heaven—the saints are filled with love, praise, gratitude and holy joy, which constitute their full-time occupation and their happiness.

III. Piety or devotion of the conscience

This consists in the horror and fear of venial sin and flight from it and everything else which displeases God.

Devotion of the conscience is the surest and the least subject to illusions. In fact, when someone is faithful to God and carefully avoids everything that could displease him, one may be sure that one is on the right road and advancing in perfection, even if one's mind is troubled, or unable for whatever reason to think about God and to understand the value of divine things.

IV. Devotion or piety of the elbow

This consists of acting well, of being a man of work and of good work, of being totally dedicated to one's work, of making sacrifices in order to do it well and to make oneself useful to one's neighbor.

This devotion was familiar to all the saints; they were all people of action; they were all faithful to the duties of their state; they all devoted themselves to the common good; they were all full of charity for their neighbors, and performed for them every service which lay in their power; all were full of zeal and sacrificed themselves in order to procure God's glory and the sanctification of others.

V. Piety or devotion of the tongue

This consists of saying many vocal prayers. This devotion, which is the least of all, is still useful, and it brings the soul great benefits, if one is careful to say these prayers in a modest posture, to pronounce them well and to bring them to life with good intentions.

When this devotion is the result and fruit of the other devotions, as is the case with fervent souls and holy religious, it is of great value and excellence. These prayers or multiple actions are the burning sentiments of the soul which, escaping in the form of jets of fire—ejaculatory prayers turn the actions of the day into a continuous prayer.

This devotion is very easy; when it is performed well, it becomes a source of actual graces, it maintains and feeds the soul's good sentiments, it sanctifies all our actions, and is the best preparation for mental prayer, communion, and the exercises of piety.

It will be easy now for each one to know if he is pious; to do so, he needs only to examine to what degree he possesses the devotions of which we have just spoken. Can he who has no esteem for prayer, virtue, salvation, and the service of God be pious? No, he has no foundation for solid piety.

Can he who has a hard, icy, dry heart, who does not nourish himself on feelings of confidence, gratitude, love, and so forth, be pious? No, he does not possess the elements of solid piety. True piety is in the heart, and when the heart is a stranger to prayer, there is absolutely no true piety.

Can he who does not take care of his conscience, who has little fear of venial sin and falls into it easily and without remorse, be truly pious? No, he has only a hollow piety, even though he may say many prayers.

Can he who performs his duty negligently, and who does not include care and devotion in performing his tasks among the first duties of his state, be truly pious? No, his piety is only an illusion.

On the other hand, he who is very careful to keep his conscience pure, and who fears and flees sin, has a good deal of piety. He who is faithful to the duties of his state, who is entirely devoted to his assignment and sacrifices himself to perform it well, has a good deal of piety. And he who has a serious mind, who does not take lightly the matter of his salvation, his vocation, his eternity, has a good deal of piety, even if he finds it very difficult to pray and feels little attraction for prayer.

Finally, in order to grasp the excellence of the gift of piety and how much we need to acquire it, let us often recall the three following points of our Rule:

The first says that, «The religious exercises of the community are, for the brothers, the most proper and efficacious means of avoiding sin, correcting their defects, and doing all things well, according to these words of the Apostle: 'Godliness is profitable to all things' (*Tim* 4:8).»[1]

And the second tells us, «There is nothing they should so much desire as the spirit and gift of prayer; for 'He who prays well, lives well,' says St. Augustine. On this important point depends the tenor of their life, which will be regular or irregular according as they acquit themselves well or ill of their religious exercises.»[2]

And finally, the third states that, «They will often ask God for the spirit of prayer, and will take every means to acquire and preserve it. If they find themselves becoming lax about this essential element, they should ask permission to spend several days on retreat, in order to renew their piety and spirit of prayer, because without them, a brother will never be a good religious.»[3]

In an instruction he gave on prayer, our revered Father told us, «In order to become solidly pious, we must fulfill two conditions: the first is to remove the obstacles to solid piety. These obstacles are: dissipation and vain or bad thoughts in our minds, uncontrolled affections in our hearts, and faults and stains on our conscience.»

So watch over your mind: keep it recollected, and never abandon it to vain or dangerous thoughts and chimerical projects. Watch over your heart: never allow an improper affection for any creature to enter it; never let the love of vice enter it, nor anything which might captivate it, tie it down and enslave it. Watch over your conscience; never put up with sin or anything

---

[1] Common Rules, 1947 edition, art. 8.
[2] Idem., art. 9.
[3] Règles Communes, 1852 edition, chapter II, article 11.

which might diminish its purity. Remember these words of St. Augustine, «The eye of the soul is purity; one cannot see anything of divine things without that eye, and the first requirement for praying well is a conscience free from sin, or filled with sorrow for having offended God.» The three focal points of piety, therefore, are the mind, the heart and the conscience; when all three are in good condition, that is to say when the mind is free from thoughts about the world or trifling things, when the heart is free of all improper affections, when the conscience is free from all sin, then prayer is easy. The soul tastes God and has no trouble uniting itself to him.

«The second requirement for becoming solidly pious is to pray a great deal, because we learn to do something well by doing it often.» That means reading books likely to inspire piety, for good reading is the inexhaustible source of holy thoughts, good and noble ideas, and lofty sentiments, which create a supernatural mindset. Good reading is substantial food, easy and always within reach, for true piety and solid devotion. Finally, it means studying your Lord in a special way, and meditating seriously on his life, his sufferings and his virtues, for nothing is better suited to act effectively on our imagination, our mind, and our heart, and consequently make us determined to become more attached to Our Lord, and to acquire more solid devotion and more solid piety.

CHAPTER FIFTEEN

THE OFFICE

The Office of the Blessed Virgin was one of the first pious practices that Fr. Champagnat prescribed for his brothers. He had even thought of giving them the full office of the Church and had spoken publicly to them about it several times. The brothers would have accepted it with pleasure, but the Founder returned to his original idea, and told them, «If the brothers must have an office, it should be that of the Blessed Virgin, for it is appropriate that they recite the office of her whose name they bear, and whom they choose for their mother, their patroness, their model and their first meditation. They felt that this exercise would have been less difficult and more advantageous for the brothers, who generally did not understand Latin and would certainly find it very difficult to remain recollected and fervent during such a long vocal prayer.

Father did not agree with them, and told them that the brothers, whose heads were splitting from teaching and their problems with the students, were much more capable of reciting a vocal prayer than making a meditation. In another context, he added, «The office must be very pleasing to God and to the Blessed Virgin, since it has many enemies; but that is exactly why we should love it and strive to make it always one of our major exercises.» So he often urged the brothers never to omit it, and he wanted those who could not say it to be sure to replace it by three rosaries.

In his informal instructions on how to say it well, our Founder often suggested to the brothers all sorts of pious strategies for maintaining their fervor and fighting distractions. «Why is it, brothers,» he once asked, «that we say the office so poorly? I am going to point out to you first of all five very common reasons. Then we will look at the consequences of our poor recitation, and the means to take to say it well.»

I. Reasons Why We Recite the Office Poorly

1. We do not sufficiently appreciate the holy Office. Remember that this prayer is one of the holiest and most agreeable to God; that it is one of the oldest and most common prayers in the Church for honoring the Blessed Virgin; that it contains in substance all the other prayers to Mary; that it was created to honor daily and simultaneously all the privileges of the Blessed Virgin which the Church celebrates at different times of the year. Then you will recite it with piety.

2. We often start to recite the Office without any preparation. The Holy Spirit, through the mouth of the Wise Man, forbids praying without preparation. That is tempting God, he says, by wanting him to give up his usual way of acting and to perform a miracle. But far from tolerating the negligence of those who tempt him, God punishes them and abandons them to their tepidity. «You may be sure,» says Cassian, «that during your prayer you will be exactly the way you were before it. If you are dissipated, full of thoughts about the world or business matters, that dissipation and those thoughts will follow you to the office, and you will pray poorly. If, on the other hand, you are recollected and totally taken up with holy thoughts, you will be filled with good feelings and your prayer will be fervent.»

3. We too often say the Office through routine. Routine spoils prayer, engenders negligence and leads to tepidity. «There are many people,» says St. Augustine, «who at first pray with fervor, but then let themselves go into a deplorable routine, and slip into apathy, negligence and indifference.

«The demon is watching,» the holy Doctor goes on, «he is right beside you to snatch away the fruit of your prayers, to make you fall into his snares, and look how careless you are!» So remember that you are speaking to God, that you are discussing with him the important question of your salvation, and that routine and negligence should have no place in such a serious matter.

4. We are careless about combating distractions, or else we let ourselves be easily caught in this trick of the devil which consists in dividing us—in other words, in keeping us preoccupied during the office with some holy project or some other business we have to attend to later. To avoid this trap, remember Our Lord's words, «Martha, Martha, you are careful and are troubled about many things» (*Lk* 10:41). Imagine that Jesus Christ is asking you, «Why are you involved in that business now? Right now, only one thing is necessary for you, to say your office well.» Or do what St. Bernard did, and say with him to the things that preoccupy and worry you, «Wait right there, and let me say my office in peace; I'll come back to you afterwards.»

«He who combats distractions prays well,» says St. Thomas, «and often, the violence one is obliged to do oneself in order to preserve modesty, remain united to God and fight against troublesome thoughts, makes one's prayer more meritorious and more pleasing to God.»

5. We say the office too hurriedly and as if we begrudged God the time. «Haste,» says St. Francis de Sales, «is the scourge of devotion.» He who mumbles his prayers and rushes through them to get them over with more quickly, will never be pious. St. Augustine assures us that God is more pleased with barking dogs than with the office of someone who recites it hurriedly and without devotion. «Each word of your office,» adds St. Francis de Sales, «should be for you the source of new merit, if you recite it attentively and piously. If, on the contrary, you recite it poorly, it will mean another loss for your soul.»

II. The Consequences of Reciting One's Office Poorly

1. It is a definite failing to say one's office poorly. «Those persons,» says St. Thomas, «who while reciting a prayer, even if they are not obliged to, willingly allow their mind to wander, cannot be excused from sin, for it appears that these sorts of persons want to despise God, like someone who, while carrying on a conversation, pays no attention at all to what the other person is saying.» Yes, you who say your office negligently or hurriedly, you are committing a fault, because you are insulting God, to whom you are speaking without respect; you are insulting and saddening the Holy Spirit, who wants to make you pray with piety; you are dishonoring Jesus Christ, in whose name you are saying this prayer; you are making the devil happy, and saddening the angels and the saints, you are abusing your senses, you are wasting your time, you are turning against God something that should give him glory. «Are you not afraid,» asks St. Cesarius, that what should sanctify you may make you more of a criminal, and that what should serve as a remedy for your soul may instead poison it?»

2. It is a misfortune to say one's office poorly. In fact, each voluntary distraction wounds your soul, and makes you worthy of additional punishment. Each fault you commit during the office, besides the stain it imprints on your soul, deprives you of a degree of grace, a degree of merit and charity and a degree of glory. In addition, you deprive God of the glory you owe him and can give him by saying your office devoutly. Isn't that a great misfortune from every point of view? Can a brother who has a conscience and who fears sin be satisfied with saying his office poorly? Can he be indifferent to the harm he is doing himself and the losses he is sustaining?

III. Ways and Means to Say the Office Well

And now, brothers, here are several ways and means which I consider very suitable for helping you to recite your holy office worthily and profitably.

1. To say your office well, remind yourself that prayer is the food of your soul. If our body is to stay healthy, we must give it food several times a day. Now, prayer is the food of the soul, and that food is as necessary to it, in order to live the spiritual life, as bread is necessary to the body, in order to live the natural life.

«What happens,» asks St. Nilus, «to a man who neglects to eat? He becomes weak, listless and sick. If he falls, he cannot get up; if he is attacked, he cannot defend himself; if he is injured, he does not heal; if someone calls him, he has no voice to answer; if he must act, he has no energy, no strength, no courage; if he has a relapse, he may well die.» That is the portrait and image of the religious who says his office poorly, and who is not pious; he often falls and rarely rises again; he is often led along by his passions and rarely resists them; he is often wounded by sin and his wounds rarely heal; he is often called by God and rarely responds to his voice. The religious who neglects prayer or who prays badly, loses his spiritual health and brings death to his own soul, which is why St. Bonaventure said, «He who abandons prayer is carrying a dead soul in a live body.»

2. In order to say your office well, imitate David; remember your many needs, your defects, your misfortunes, your sins, your lack of virtue. Like this holy king, say, «My God, I am poor in your sight, I have no graces at all, no virtue, no light, no strength for doing good; I am filled with vices and defects, but in your presence I do what a beggar does before a generous rich person: I cry out unceasingly before your divine majesty for mercy, and I

157

beg you to correct my defects, uproot my vices, heal my soul, and give it the virtues of a good religious.

3. In order to say your office well, remember that prayer, said in the state of grace and with piety, is a meritorious work. In other words, it gains you numerous degrees of merit and glory for heaven. It is an expiatory work for your sins, and consequently it can earn for you the remission of the temporal punishment for which you are answerable in the sight of God's justice, and thus serve as your purgatory. It is a work of petition for grace, whence it follows that if you say your office well, you will obtain an increase of sanctifying grace, and many actual graces, which will fill you with consolation and make it very easy for you to carry out your assignment and practice the virtues of your holy state.

4. To say your office well, remember that you are praying in the name of the entire Church. You recite your office in the name of the congregation of which you are a member, or rather in the name of the entire Church, which has appointed you before God to celebrate his praise and speak on behalf of sinners. Yes, you are the spokesman of the Church Militant, and you ask for grace and assistance for all those who are struggling; you pray for the Church Suffering, and the souls in purgatory are depending on you for their deliverance; you mingle your homage with that of the Church Triumphant, and you do what the angels and saints do in heaven. These are all powerful motives for praying well and they should give you unlimited confidence.

5. To say your office well, remember that you are praying for the entire universe, and for the needs of all men and women. Remember the huge number of infidels who populate Asia, Africa, America, Oceania, for whom you should solicit the gift of faith; the huge number of heretics and schismatics for whom you are deputed to request their return and submission to the Church. If you have charity, you must love all men and women and pray for them all, so that all may be saved. «That is the spirit of the Church,» says St. Chrysostom; «it is the spirit of Jesus Christ. The

heart of St. Paul, which asked for grace for all his brothers, was the heart of Jesus Christ.» And so it should be with you. Unite yourself therefore to all the holy souls who pray and who unceasingly send up their wishes and sighs to heaven, to obtain mercy for all men and women.

6. To say your office well, remember that prayer is the Church's strength and safeguard, and its strongest bulwark. But to whom has the defense of this bulwark been entrusted? To you who are responsible for defending its children. It is up to you to obtain victory for those who are attacked by temptation and the devil, consolation for the afflicted, help for all those who are in need. It is you who, by your prayers, must obtain gospel workers for countries which lack them, and holy priests for every parish. Listen to Jesus Christ telling you, as he did St. Mary Magdalen de Pazzi, «My child, help me to save souls, to destroy sin, and to spread the reign of God on earth; pray, pray fervently, so that my death and my blood will not be useless for so many souls who are likely to be lost.» Good heavens! Who would dare refuse to pray, or who would be lax and tepid in prayer, if he reflected on these truths?

7. You will say your office well if you do not forget in whose presence you are praying. You are in the presence of the devil, your greatest enemy. So be on your guard, watch over your senses, your imagination and your heart, because the devil is counting and marking down all your faults. You are in the presence of the angels and the saints who are all burning with fervor; could your prayer mingle with theirs if it were cold and poorly said? You are in the presence of your guardian angel, who is responsible for presenting your prayer to God, and marking it down in the book of life. See if that prayer is worthy of the one who is offering it and of him to whom it is offered, and if it deserves an eternal reward. You are in the presence of the Holy Trinity. «Remember,» says St. Cyprian, «that God sees and hears you; strive to please him, by your modest bearing and your respectful tone of voice.»

8. You will say your office well if you remember that this prayer makes you like the angels and saints, whose functions you fulfill on earth. What do the angels and saints do in heaven? They praise, bless, love and honor God; and you do the same thing when you pray. In a few more years, you will be with them. So when you say your office, imagine that you are already among them. «Put Jesus on your right hand,» says Thomas à Kempis, «Mary on your left, and all the saints around you. Imagine that your confrères are the angels. Stir up your fervor by thinking that you will soon be singing God's praises in heaven, together with those who are reciting the psalms with you now on earth. Unite yourself to the whole court of heaven, to praise God as he deserves.»

9. You will say your office well if you stop to think that this prayer sanctifies your entire person. Does it not sanctify your memory to recall the principal truths of the faith, to picture the mysteries of the Savior's life and death? Does it not sanctify your intelligence to use it to meditate on God's law and word? Does it not sanctify your will to make it produce acts of love? And that's not all; you also sanctify your conscience by fulfilling your duty to pray; you sanctify your heart by filling it with good sentiments; you sanctify your mouth by using it to bless the Lord; you sanctify your body by using your strength to celebrate God's praises; you sanctify your time by consecrating it to such a holy occupation; you sanctify your whole life by assuring yourself of the graces you need. So you cannot do anything better, more useful and more advantageous than to say your office well.

10. You will say your office well if you are careful to make one of the following reflections from time to time. While you are reciting God's praises in the psalms, many sick people are experiencing extreme suffering; many people are at the point of death and will breathe their last while you are praying; many are undergoing terrible temptations and may perhaps fall into the abyss of sin for lack of help if you pray badly. A vast crowd of people are blaspheming God, outraging him, insulting his divine

majesty, and raising their insolent voices to heaven. How many sinners, in the depths of the most frightful despair, are on the point of becoming the prey of the devil and of being damned to eternal torments without recourse. Can you be insensitive to so much misery? Will you not hold out a helping hand to these unfortunate people? Good Lord, how many reasons we have for saying our office well!

11. You will say your office well if you recall that you are not praying alone, but that a host of holy religious, priests and lay persons are praying at the same time as you, and saying their office with great fervor. Others, during this time, are offering to God great sacrifices or hard penances, or risking their lives to glorify Our Lord, to make him known and win souls to him. Can you be negligent or feel disgusted, when you think of so much heroic virtue? How hard, insensitive, blind and unhappy you would be if such examples left you unmoved in your laxity and tepidity!

12. Finally, you will say your office fervently if you remain united to Jesus Christ by remembering that he himself is praying with your mouth and heart. «Our divine Savior,» says St. Augustine, «prays for us as our pontiff; he prays in us as our leader, and we pray to him as our God.»

Another Father of the Church says, «Your mouth should be the mouth of Jesus Christ, so that it is he who pronounces with your tongue the words of your office, he who adores his Father when you adore him, he who sings his praises when you sing a psalm or a canticle; he who works or suffers when you work or suffer.» «A very good way to pray,» says St. Teresa of Avila, «is to picture Our Lord praying in us and with us.» Let us pray with him, and consequently like him; that is to say, with the same interior and exterior respect, the same love, the same constancy, the same perfection. That is the real way to make our prayer divine.

Those are the thoughts and sentiments with which we should busy ourselves to arouse our piety and bring ourselves to say our office well.

CHAPTER SIXTEEN

BROTHER HIPPOLYTE AND HIS LAMP

Brother Hippolyte was a young man of twenty-six when he entered religious life. He had been trained as a tailor, and in fact was a good one. He could have done very well for himself in the world, but his desire to guarantee his salvation urged him to give himself to God. Caught in the middle of his internal struggle between the world and grace, Brother Hippolyte hesitated; religious life had its attractions, but so did the world. In his hesitant state, he came to see Fr. Champagnat, to speak with him about his vocation; but so as not to take any risks, he asked to try out the community for just a few days.

Father Champagnat welcomed him warmly, but did not want to receive him on a trial basis, nor without his first having paid for his novitiate, because he feared that he would recoil in the face of the first trials, which are always the most painful to nature, especially when one has not yet broken entirely with the world.

In the end, grace triumphed over the resistance of nature. Our pious young man definitively renounced the world and everything he had hoped to obtain there. He went to the Hermitage with the money for his novitiate expenses, and gave it to Fr. Champagnat, assuring him that all he wanted now was to work at becoming a good religious.

Delighted with his good dispositions, Fr. Champagnat received him gladly, for he badly needed a tailor. That same evening, speaking about him with one of the oldest brothers, he said, «Thank God! Today he sent us someone for our tailor shop. I am counting on his persevering, because he came with a good sign of a vocation.»

«And what might that be, Father?»

«The three hundred francs he gave me. This young man was doing well in the world; he earned the money for his room and board. He would not have broken this way with his entire future, and he would not have sacrificed his savings, if he were not detached from the goods of this world and determined to persevere in his vocation.»

Father was not mistaken; Brother Hippolyte did not miss the world, became truly attached to his holy state of life, and was soon put in charge of the tailor shop, a post he occupied with great skill until his death, and one in which he was noted for his total devotedness and unalterable patience and gentleness.

I.

Brother Hippolyte spent forty-one years in community; during that whole time, those who knew him assure us that he was outstanding for four main qualities.

1. Brother Hippolyte was remarkable for his constancy in his vocation and his love for his holy state. From the day he entered religious life, he never once regretted what he had left behind in the world, and never thought of returning to it. He was never tempted by a false idea of freedom or the vanity of worldly possessions. «I am in God's service,» he used to say; «I am happy here and I will stay here my whole life.» He particularly admired the reply of St. Polycarp to the tyrant who was urging him to renounce Jesus Christ: «I have been in the service of Jesus for eighty-four years; he has always been good to me, so why should I deny him? May God preserve me from such ingratitude!» In his simplicity, Brother Hippolyte used to say, «That seems to me a very just and reasonable answer. Like that great saint, I am satisfied with God, I am pleased to be serving him and that makes me happy, so why should I leave? I belong to God, and I will stay with him all my life and for all eternity.»

Brother Hippolyte was often in contact with those who were leaving the congregation, because he was usually responsible for giving them secular clothing. «That is the only part of my job which I find painful,» he used to say; «I always suffer when I see these poor young men with no experience take the road back to the world.» And he sometimes told them, «You don't know what you're giving up, nor what awaits you. Just be careful that the best days of your life haven't passed you by, and then you begin to miss the happy days you devoted to God's service. I know the world; it looks beautiful from a distance, but it's frightening from close up. It promises a lot but gives very little consolation, satisfaction or real happiness.»

2. Brother Hippolyte was constantly noted and admired for his gentleness. It is a fact known to all the brothers that Brother Hippolyte did not know how to be angry, and that no one had ever seen him lose his temper, nor even show any of those momentary irritations or flare-ups which are so common in busy persons. He was often disturbed, often surrounded by a large number of brothers asking for whatever they needed; but Brother Hippolyte was always calm, always impassive, and had a kind word for everyone. «I'm here to serve you, brother, please wait a moment; be patient and you'll all be waited on,» and so on. No one ever heard him rebuff anyone; never did a sharp word issue from his mouth. If he did not have what someone asked for, or if he was not permitted to satisfy the requests of certain brothers, he would excuse himself very politely, and one could see that he suffered more from not being able to give what he was asked for, than did the person who had been refused.

3. Brother Hippolyte was always noteworthy for his great benevolence and his constant readiness to be of service to everyone. He made himself the servant of all his brothers. He no longer belonged to himself at all. From morning till night, he took care of other people; at whatever hour of the day or night someone went to him for help, he found him always ready to be of service. Like St. Francis de Sales, he found his happiness in

serving his neighbor, in giving of himself for the good of his brothers and the benefit of the community. His pleasant, gentle and straightforward manner, and the goodness of his character all added a special charm to the good he did and the service he gave. Like all of the elect, Brother Hippolyte had a tender, loving, sensitive heart, naturally inclined to be merciful and indulgent. That is no doubt why he did not know how to refuse anyone, and did not spare himself when it came to being useful to his confrères. Like his divine Master, he spent his life doing good to everyone.

4. Finally, Brother Hippolyte was most especially noteworthy for his love of work and his dedication to his task. His task was one of the most important and the most confining, and words cannot express the persevering zeal with which he made, cared for, repaired and organized the brothers' entire wardrobe for more than forty years. Almost as soon as he had entered the Institute, he was put in charge of the tailor shop; he stayed there, asking and desiring nothing more than that, until the day he died. He spent days and entire weeks rearranging and putting in order all the used clothing, so that nothing would be lost or ruined. Brother Hippolyte died at his task; he was devoted and faithful to the end, and death took him by surprise with his tools in his hand.

II.

But these four characteristic qualities of Brother Hippolyte were not the only virtues that shone in him. This excellent brother was also very pious. The multiple demands and vexations of his work never led him to neglect his religious exercises. But his piety was never affected; it was in keeping with his character—simple, peaceful, calm, constant and steady. Devoted as he was to his brothers, very much attached to his Institute, submissive to his superiors, full of a childlike spirit towards God, he spent his life serving others without offending anyone.

Nonetheless, our venerated Father, who dearly loved economy, occasionally reprimanded him because he had the habit of carrying a little lamp to light his way on his nocturnal rounds of the building. He scolded him, even in public sometimes, for not always putting it out soon enough, or for using it without real necessity. Brother Hippolyte received these reprimands humbly and without saying a word; but they didn't change him one bit, because he believed that with his lamp he could go faster and lose less time, and especially that he was in no danger of bumping into walls or furniture. Even though he blamed Brother Hippolyte on the point of economy, Father said that he liked to see this brother with lamp in hand, because it was for him an image of the wise man who is always enlightened by a reflective spirit and guided by prudence. «Like Brother Hippolyte,» he used to say, «the virtuous man, the good religious, the wise director, never goes anywhere without his lamp; his reflective spirit enlightens everything he does, and prudence directs and guides all his undertakings and everything he does.»

III.

On another occasion, our Founder told us, «There is one quality and one virtue whose necessity you do not sufficiently grasp; the quality is the spirit of reflection, and the virtue is prudence. Now, my dear brothers, prudence, which is the fruit of the spirit of reflection is so necessary that St. Thomas calls it the eye and the pilot of the soul. That means that this virtue is just as necessary for man's moral behavior as his eyes are for his physical behavior.

«This virtue is so necessary that the great patriarch St. Anthony did not hesitate to state that it should hold the first place among the moral virtues. Once, while he was having a discussion with several other desert fathers, the question arose: What virtue is most likely to protect religious from the snares of the devil and lead them most surely to perfection? One said it was fasting and mortification; another, vigilance; a third, detachment from material possessions; a fourth, charity towards one's neighbor. After listening to all of them, St. Anthony decided that it was prudence, because, as he told them, «Even though all the virtues you have just mentioned are necessary for those who want to serve God, what we have learned from the falls of many does not admit of our finding in those virtues the principal and most infallible way to reach our goal. We have often seen religious who were very exact in observing the fasts and in keeping vigilance; others practiced great poverty; others devoted themselves to all the ways of practicing fraternal charity; but they still fell into the snares of the devil and had regrettable falls, because they were not prudent and discreet in continuing the good they had begun.»

Prudence is so necessary that St. Bernard did not fear to say that without it, virtue becomes vice. Perhaps you would like to ask me how that can possibly be. A few examples will help you understand it better.

1. Take prudence away from a young religious full of generosity and enthusiasm, who wants to belong entirely to God and advance in virtue day by day, and you will soon see him so overburden himself with exercises of piety that his days will not be long enough for him to perform them all and his mind will be affected by his lengthy meditations. Soon you will see him carry the spirit of penance so far that, refusing his body the rest and food it needs, he will ruin his health, and will no longer be able to perform the penances prescribed for the ordinary faithful. Soon you will see him chasing after an imaginary perfection, or one which is not in keeping with the spirit of his state; he will give his imagination free rein and expect to acquire in a few months a degree of holiness which demands long years of work, and which can come only from a long life of effort and the practice of all the virtues.

2. Take prudence away from a brother director who loves regularity and piety, who wants to make them prevail among his

brothers, and then watch what he does and what he accomplishes. He demands exaggerated exactitude and punctuality, which are impossible to obtain. He gives reprimands for failures which he ought to pretend he has not noticed. He punishes for things about which it would be enough to make a gentle comment. He refuses to give the weak, the young and the sick the exemptions which their genuine needs demand, and which charity makes it a duty to grant. His demands are unmerciful and he wants everyone to practice a level of perfection and virtue which are the lot only of elite souls.

With a director like that, regularity, which is a beautiful virtue, becomes a tyranny which destroys his brothers' love, respect and esteem for him, which makes them lose their filial spirit and love for the rule, which makes them find the sweet and light yoke of Jesus Christ hard and heavy, which deprives them of the consolations of religious life and of the hundredfold promised by Our Lord. With a director like that, regularity, instead of bringing about observance of the rule, sows disorder in the house and turns a religious community into an army camp. Exaggerated regularity, because it lacks prudence, turns a director into hard and severe taskmaster, a policeman whom everyone avoids and fears instead of loving him and going to him as to a loving father.

3. Take prudence away from a brother full of zeal and devotedness, and see what becomes of those virtues, and into what errors they lead him. Under the pretext of teaching his students better, he neglects his exercises of piety, and gives to study or classwork the time he should give to prayer, spiritual reading and his own perfection. He is so busy doing good for others that he endangers his own salvation, forgetting Our Lord's words, «What does it profit a man to gain the whole world, and suffer the loss of his soul?» (*Lk* 9:25).

He throws himself into projects in which he is at risk, and his weak virtue cannot help but give way. He undertakes things which God does not want, things which his rule does not ask of him, and for which he has neither the aptitude nor the grace of state.

His supervision of the children is oppressive and it wears them out, makes them malicious, sly, secretive and hypocritical. Or he goes to the other extreme, deceives himself about the dangers they run, places too much confidence in them, does not supervise them, and so lets them spread their vices and defects to one another.

And what is the outcome of all that? For himself, his piety diminishes, his soul grows weaker, he falls into tepidity and sin. For the children, their education is defective, they find danger where they should find security, they lose their virtues and good qualities instead of developing and learning how to preserve them. For the community, he violates its rules, creates disorder, scandalizes his brothers, and compromises their success, because they cannot continue what he has done or begun.

IV.

In the spiritual life, prudence is so important for a man's behavior and for regulating the other virtues, that:

1. The Holy Spirit calls it the knowledge of the saints (*Prov* 9:10), that is to say, the knowledge of elite people, wise people, people who are models, people of lofty mind and great hearts, people who are good and generous, people with will power and with consciences which are upright, enlightened, well-formed—in a word, perfect people, because the saints are all those things.

2. Prudence is the great means and the secret for avoiding the snares of the devil and sin. He who is prudent mistrusts himself and never exposes himself to danger. Following the advice of the Holy Spirit, he does not turn aside either to the right or to the left (*Deut* 17:11), because vice lies to the right and left, and virtue is in the middle. So he walks amid the snares of the devil in total

security, like one who follows a lamp which goes ahead of him through the darkness.

When St. Thomas Aquinas was asked how one could live his whole life without committing serious faults, he answered, «If anyone behaves prudently in everything he does, and in such a way as to be aware of the motives for which he is acting, he will certainly avoid sin.» The imprudent person, on the contrary, always walks in the darkness, does not see danger or the snares of the devil, and falls into them without realizing it. When concupiscence calls, he runs towards its voice; when passion attracts him, he follows it; that is why he falls headlong into the abyss of all sorts of sins.

3. Prudence is the great means, the great secret for preserving the virtues, making them grow, and making constant new progress in them; that is why several Fathers of the Church call prudence the mother and guardian of virtues.

The prudent and reflective man weighs his words; he speaks little and always to the point, so he does not offend against silence, modesty and discretion. He is not stubborn in his opinions, he gives in easily, avoids quarrels and dissensions, and by so doing, he preserves charity, peace, patience and gentleness.

He does nothing without having thought carefully about it and assuring himself that what he intends to do is permitted, fitting and advantageous; in this way, he maintains justice and moderation. He mistrusts himself, which protects his humility; he does not count on his own lights but often asks advice, follows the direction of his superiors, and thus keeps himself under obedience.

Take away prudence, and the works of virtue are not properly performed; they always lack some quality; they are defective and sinful in a thousand ways; consequently, they are not at all pleasing to God.

Prudence is necessary above all for a brother director. «Who will govern others?» asks the Wise Man. «The prudent man,» replies the Holy Spirit.

If you ask me who will do the cooking, I will answer that a brother who is strong, clean and devoted will do nicely. Who will do the teaching? Anyone who is educated, zealous and devoted can be put in charge of that task. Who will carry out the other duties around the house? They can be entrusted to religious who are docile and pious, provided they have a certain aptitude for the task which will be given them. But if there is question of governing and directing the brothers, piety, virtue and education are not enough for that ministry. To carry it out well, one must join to those other qualities an upright mind and a reflective attitude. So entrust it to a man who is prudent, and who like David, says to God, «Lord, let my lamp shine, so that I may not stray from your path either to the right or to the left, and let my torch enlighten the others.»

4. Prudence is the superior's compass. Without a compass, the pilot could not steer his ship; it would go off course and never reach the goal of its voyage, and he would not be able to prevent it from breaking up on the rocks or sinking into the depths of the ocean. In the same way, a superior cannot lead his community well if he does not have a judicious mind, and reflective spirit and the prudence which flows from them. If he lacks that virtue, he will not only be useless to his inferiors, but will become harmful to them. So, like David, he should often pray, «Lord, make my lamp shine, give me an upright mind, a reflective spirit, and grant me prudence.»

If, on the contrary, the superior is full of prudence,

1. This virtue will teach him how to win the esteem of his brothers, by his fidelity to the rule and his good example; to win their confidence and their hearts by his goodness, his charity, his concern and attentiveness to their needs; to obtain their docility by the aptness, wisdom and justice of his orders; to make his

authority loved and lead minds to submit to it, through the care he takes to make it gentle and fatherly.

2. Prudence will teach him that there is a great diversity of characters, and that in order to direct a community of men or a class of children well, he must study the temperament and character of each one, so as to direct him according to the bent of his own mind. Those who are timid must be encouraged; those who are superficial and dissipated need to be restrained by fear and a bit of severity. Some need the spurs to urge them to move along; others, the bridle to rein them in. Some are best led by words, others by example. Praise is good for some, but gives others a swelled head. Some should be corrected in private, others in public. To some, one must speak gently; to others, more severely. Some need to be followed up even in the smallest detail; with others, one must often close one's eyes and pretend not to have seen anything. Finally, if the brother director keeps his lamp firmly in hand, he will see that among those entrusted to him, no two are alike or can be led in the same way, and he will give each one the lessons and remedies which are best suited to him.

3. Prudence will teach him to be discreet with the authorities and with the parents of the students, and to have contact with the world only through necessity. By so doing, she will help him avoid the risks of all kinds which are run by a director who appears in public too often, or who lets the spirit of the world get into his house.

4. Finally, prudence, which is the eye of the soul, meaning the faculty of seeing things as they really are, or the faculty of foreseeing things still a long way off, will show him all the dangers which threaten him, all the snares which are spread for his weakness. She will give him the means to escape them, will help him foresee the obstacles which will block his plans, and what he should do to overcome or go around them. Finally, she will bring him success in all his undertakings, and win for him the approval of men and the blessings of God.

CHAPTER SEVENTEEN

WHY THE DEVIL TEMPTS US

A young brother, who was very virtuous but had a lively imagination and very irritable temperament, often went to speak to Fr. Champagnat about his interior difficulties, and especially his temptations against the holy virtue, which were very violent. Father, who knew this young brother's timorous conscience and his excessive sensitivity, encouraged him and suggested to him that one very effective remedy would be calmness and confidence. The brother, who feared sin more than death, but did not know how to distinguish between feeling and consent, the mere thought of evil and an affection for evil, for sin, was not very satisfied with the suggested cure offered him, and did not understand that one can resist temptation by contempt alone. So one day, he said bitterly to Fr. Champagnat, «My struggles are so great that I can't hold out any longer; if they go on like this, I don't know what's going to become of me! Please give me a strong and fast-acting remedy, to get rid of the enemy who pursues me day and night with diabolical rage.

Don't be afraid to overwhelm my body; I prefer health of soul to health of body, because first and foremost, I have to guarantee my salvation, and therefore I have to avoid sin.»

Father, believing with good reason that the instructions this excellent brother needed to calm him down would be useful for many others, told him, «Brother, one of these days I am going to give a conference on temptations and how to combat them. I hope you will find in that instruction the strong and fast-acting remedy you're asking for. Meanwhile, trust in God and be at peace.»

I.

A few days later, Father did in fact give the promised conference, which he began with this anecdote: «After his conversion, St. Martin made a resolution to serve God perfectly, and to enter a monastery in order to do so. He was on his way to that holy sanctuary of virtue when the devil, amazed at his strength of soul and fervor, made tremendous efforts to upset his plans. He took the form of a traveler, and coming up to St. Martin, asked him in a haughty tone of voice, 'Where are you going?'

«The saint, having immediately recognized him for what he was, answered, 'I am going where God is calling me.' The devil was annoyed at his reply, and could no longer hold himself in or conceal himself. 'Wherever you go, whatever you try to do in the future, you may be sure that you will always find me on your trail, to persecute you, lay snares for you, and destroy your soul.'

«The devil was good to his word; he pursued him his whole life, and even appeared to him at the moment of his death. Amazed at Satan's persistence and rage, St. Martin said to him, 'What are you doing here, cruel beast? What are you waiting for? You won't find anything in me that belongs to you, and in spite of your rage and malice, I will be received into Abraham's bosom.'»

«My dear brothers,» Fr. Champagnat went on, «the war that the devil waged against St. Martin is the same one he has waged against all the saints, and still wages against all good religious. So, he who gives himself to God must expect to find the devil constantly in his path; he must expect the most terrible temptations, and a life-long struggle against this enemy. This is a truth which every page of scripture teaches us: 'My son,' says the Holy Spirit in Sirach, 'when you come to the service of God, stand in justice and in fear, and prepare your soul for temptation' (*Sir* 2:1).

«Many are the afflictions of the just,» says the prophet, «but out of them all will the Lord deliver them.» (*Ps* 33:20).

«Because you were acceptable to God,» the angel told Tobit, «it was necessary that temptation should prove you» (*Tob* 12:13). And St. Paul adds, «Whom the Lord loves, he chastises, and he scourges every son whom he receives» (*Heb* 12:6).

But perhaps you will ask me, «What is the cause or the reason for these temptations?» There are two main ones: God's goodness towards his chosen ones, and the devil's rage against those same persons. God, in his goodness, permits temptation for our own good, to purify us, to humble us, to make us vigilant, prudent and mortified, to force us to pray, to exercise and strengthen our virtue, to increase our merit on earth and our glory in heaven. Those are God's intentions when he subjects us to temptation. Those of the devil are something else again, and today I want to make you well aware of what he has in mind when he buffets us with temptations, so that you will not let yourself be caught in his snares and ambushes.

Since the devil, who is God's enemy, can do nothing against him, he revenges himself on God's image; he wages a relentless war against us, because of God's merciful plans for us, the graces he grants us, the heavenly goods he is preparing for us, and because he has destined us to one day occupy the thrones which the rebellious angels lost through their pride. Being jealous of our good fortune, «the devil, as a roaring lion, goes about seeking whom he may devour,» as St. Peter puts it (1 *Pet* 5:8). Note well that the prince of the apostles does not say that the devil tries to bite us, but to devour us. In fact, what he wants is our complete destruction; you can see that by the detestable intentions he has when he tempts us and wages his unending war against us.

II.

The devil's objectives in this endless war and in the multiple temptations with which he assails us are:

1. To make us offend God and to deprive us of the life of grace, which is the mainstay and pledge of our future life of glory; to stain our soul, to make us his slaves, and to hurl us into hell. Everyone knows this aim of the devil; no one doubts that he wants to destroy us and make us his companions in misfortune and punishment. But how many pious persons, and how many religious, are unaware of the devil's other perverse intentions when he ceaselessly pursues us with his temptations! So educate yourselves today about his pernicious plans and don't let yourselves be caught in his nets.

2. When the devil cannot make us offend God, he hopes, by means of his temptations, to upset us, to exhaust us, to make virtue unpleasant for us and the yoke of Jesus Christ heavy and insupportable, and to make us lose time we should be spending on our sanctification. «When the devil sees that a soul is getting away from him,» says St. Francis de Sales, «and that he will not be able to make it lose its blessed eternity, he rests satisfied with tiring it, beguiling it with his temptations, and making it waste time.»

3. As a result of these annoyances, this fatigue and loss of time in the work of our sanctification, the devil hopes to stop our progress on the road to perfection, to spoil our virtues and good works, to lessen our merits, and consequently to diminish the glory which awaits us in heaven.

4. This enemy of our salvation also plans in his treachery to prevent us from praying and to make us neglect our exercises of piety. The first condition required for praying well is calmness and peace of soul. When we are upset, or when we wonder if we have offended God, we no longer have any taste for prayer, and there is no time when we suffer more than during our exercises

of piety. On the other hand, all we need to do is start to pray, and we become the butt of all the temptations of hell. And why does the devil make such an effort, so much noise and such an uproar? Because he knows that prayer is the source of all graces, and he wants to dry up that source.

5. Not only does he strive to keep us from praying, but also to turn us away from communion. Frequent communion is the means par excellence to set oneself on fire with love for Jesus, to make great progress in virtue and to guarantee our salvation. The devil knows this, and that is why he tempts pious souls with so much cunning and violence, on the days just before their communions. If he succeeds in upsetting them, and in raising doubts or fears about having consented to temptation, in making them decide not to receive communion, he has triumphed and he rejoices, because he has won a great victory. And in fact, to deprive a soul of its heavenly food, to separate it from Jesus Christ, to deprive it of the treasure of graces which one single communion brings us, is a great victory for hell, as well as an immense loss for that soul.

And yet, there are a crowd of religious who let themselves be caught in that crude snare. Knowing their lack of experience and their weakness, the devil assails them roughly, pursues them, wears them down until he managed to disturb their minds and introduce doubts there. Then, to accomplish his work, he leads these poor souls to discouragement and deep sadness.

In that condition, they do not even dare look into themselves; they cannot stand themselves; their confidence in God evaporates; their piety and devotion grow cold; they spend days and weeks in boredom and tepidity; they perform their exercises of piety only to get them over with; they let their communions go; as a result, they fall into an infinite number of venial sins, and remain perpetually imperfect. Isn't that the story of a good number of you who are listening to me right now?

179

6. By means of his repeated attacks, Satan plans to ruin our character. Would you ever have imagined that the devil's aim, in overwhelming you with temptations, was to ruin your character? Well, you may be sure that is one of the most common expressions of his malice. To destroy a man's character makes virtue very difficult for him. To destroy the character of a religious makes community life almost impossible for him, and makes him the scourge of his confrères. To destroy the character of a brother vowed to the education of youth is to paralyze all the good he might accomplish. And after all, what can a man, a religious, of bad character, really accomplish? Nothing, in terms of works of zeal. The devil knows that, and that is why he pursues you with his temptations, in order to throw you into sadness, boredom, and discouragement. When we are in that condition, we get all worked up, our minds are disturbed, our heart dries up, we become exaggeratedly irritable, we are dissatisfied with everything, we become angry, we scold without reason, we become a burden to ourselves, insupportable to others, and find ourselves clashing with everyone.

7. Another motive for the devil's tempting us is to falsify and spoil our conscience, by throwing it into perplexity and scruples. Scruples falsify our judgment, keep us away from the sacraments, disturb our peace and our mind. How many unfortunate people, having been seduced by the devil, began with scruples and ended with insanity! How many even more unfortunate persons began with scruples and ended with impiety and debauchery!

And how does one become scrupulous? Through the devil's suggestions, and through too great a fear of temptations. To seduce a soul and lead it to that state, the devil makes it see sin everywhere, and makes it consider scrupulosity as a virtue, as delicacy of conscience. That is one of the most pernicious errors; scrupulosity is a great defect, the great enemy of the love of God. The wise and pious Gerson did not hesitate to state that a scrupulous conscience often hurts a soul more than one which is too easy and too lax. And Fénelon, gentle as he was, adds these strong words: «Woe to the soul which is shriveled and dried up, which fears everything; because of its fear of sin and temptation, it does not have time to love and to run generously. So flee that frightful poison of piety and say with St. Joseph of Cupertino, 'Away with sadness and scruples; I won't give either of them house room!'

8. Finally, the devil's temptations are also aimed at sapping one's strength, undermining one's health, and making a person totally useless. In fact, it is certain that nothing is more likely to ruin one's health than the mental problems, melancholy and anxieties of a conscience which has lost its peace, which is always troubled, always apprehensive about committing sin and being lost.

III.

Those, my dear brothers, are the pernicious plans of Satan. And what specifically does he use to do so much harm? Our imagination, which he fills with fear, illusions and fantasies. Do you want to keep from being caught in the snares of the devil and avoid all those evils he is preparing for you? Combat temptations calmly and courageously, by the following means:

1. Use preventive measures: flee idleness, contacts with the world, and all dangerous occasions. Also flee pride, gluttony, familiarity with the students, curiosity, and everything else which might awaken the passions, lead you to sin or give rise to temptation.

2. Remember that every perfect gift comes from above, and that by yourself you cannot remain pure. So ask for purity with constancy and perseverance, and let that be one of your main intentions in all your prayers.

3. Consecrate yourself to the Blessed Virgin every morning, commit yourself to several practices to merit her protection, and ask her in particular for the grace never to commit a mortal sin.

Do not fail to make the same request of Our Lord every day at Mass and after your communions.

4. If you take these precautions faithfully and consistently, you need not be afraid of temptations. Be brave and keep yourself always in a state of holy joy. St. Anthony had the habit of saying that one excellent way to overcome temptations was to show resolve and joy during the combat. This joy upsets the devil and makes him lose hope of catching us in his nets. In the Septuagint, the devil is called Myrmicoleon, which means «lion and ant.» «Why such a name?» asks St. Gregory; «why is the devil called a lion?» Because he is, in fact, a raging lion, a real tyrant, for those who fear him and who to him are only ants. «And why is he called an ant at the same time?» Because he really is nothing but a powerless insect, an ant, for courageous souls, who to him are lions. So it was with St. Teresa, who said aloud that she had no more fear of him than of a fly. So it was with St. Pachomius, who told him, «I laugh at you, and I am no more afraid of your presence than of the whisper of a leaf blowing in the wind.»

5. Expect temptations; think of them as something inevitable and even necessary. Remember the story of St. Martin; expect to always find the devil in your path, and resign yourself to it. Don't be surprised at his attacks; they contribute to your glory and your merit. He pursues you precisely because you are virtuous. «The saints, the just,» says the prophet Habakkuk, «are delicious morsels for Satan.» Pirates don't attack empty ships with no cargo, but only those which are loaded with gold, silver or priceless merchandise. Thieves don't attack beggars, but only rich people. In the same way, the devil leaves sinners alone; they are empty ships and real beggars, that have nothing worth taking. But he attacks good religious because they are loaded down with merits and virtues. It gives him hellish satisfaction to defeat them and hateful pleasure to soil them, despoil them and make them unhappy.

6. Resist temptations with contempt. The greatest masters of the spiritual life are in agreement that simple contempt for temptation is a quicker and more effective way to resist the devil and preserve oneself from sin than words and acts of the contrary virtues. This means has the tremendous advantage: first, of not engaging the devil in combat and not wearing oneself out or dirtying oneself by struggling with him; second, of discouraging the devil and putting a rapid end to his struggles and assaults.

Imagine a man who, while walking along quietly, suddenly finds himself harassed by a dog, which barks and runs after him. If that man keeps going without turning his head or paying attention to the barking, without doing a thing to keep him quiet, the dog will stop and go away. But if the traveler becomes frightened, if he chases the dog or throws stones at it, or threatens it with a stick, he simply makes the dog more excited and prolongs the struggle endlessly, with the risk of being bitten.

That is a good picture of what happens when we are tempted. If you treat the devil with contempt, he will leave you alone, or will tempt you only seldom and lightly. If you are too afraid of him, if you let your imagination run wild, if you become upset and fight him off by shaking your head and other such gestures, you will only fix the evil fantasies in your imagination, perpetuate the temptation and disturb your peace of mind. In the long run you will endanger your health and put yourself at great risk of offending God.

St. Francis de Sales is of the same opinion. Here are his exact words: «Recently, I was near a beehive, and a few bees landed on my face. I was about to raise my hand to chase them, when a farmer told me, 'No! Don't be afraid of them and don't touch them, and they won't hurt you at all. If you try to chase them, they will sting you.' I took his word for it, and not a single one of them stung me. Believe me—don't be afraid of temptations, don't be apprehensive about them, and they won't bother you; just keep going and don't stop to play with them.»

There is a sort of exaggerated fear which is more likely to draw us toward the edge of the cliff than make us avoid it. Why is it that a man who walks nonchalantly—even runs—along a narrow plank lying on the ground, doesn't dare try it if the same plank is way up in the air? It's because fear has seized him, vertigo has affected his balance, and his legs will no longer hold him; his head is spinning and the mere thought of danger is enough to make him fall.

That is an image of what happens when we are tempted: if we are too afraid, if our imagination takes over, we become upset, the temptation becomes more violent, we lose courage, and we give in to sin. When a confidence man wants to get hold of some simple and trusting soul's money or valuables, or involve him in some shady business deal, he takes him to the tavern, buys him several large drinks, and when he's tipsy and his mind is fuzzy, he shows him the snare—he takes his money or gets him to sign some fraudulent document.

That is how the devil acts, and that is the ruse he uses; he gets us drunk, he muddles our mind, and once he is in control of our head, he reaches our heart unhindered and obtains the consent of our will. So the important thing to do when tempted is to keep your head. Keep your mind clear and calm, don't get upset or frightened or discouraged, but remain cheerful and fight the temptation with contempt.

Once when several Fathers of the Desert had gathered to discuss spiritual matters, the oldest said to one of the others, «What do you do to fight temptations?»

«I think about how ugly sin is, and that's enough to drive them away.»

«And you,» the old man said to another; «what method do you use?»

«I beg Our Lady to protect me until the temptation passes.»

«And I,» said a third, «I'm satisfied with despising the devil, with not paying any attention to what he tells me, and with carrying on my work in the presence of God.»

«Your conduct,» said the old man, «is the best, for two reasons; first, because it gives you complete freedom of mind and does not tire any of your faculties; secondly, because you can use it at any time.»

And in fact, one cannot always meditate, pray, or take up the sword to fight back; but one can always despise and disdain an enemy. So that way is the best, the safest and the least difficult.

For the rest, the longer the temptation persists, the clearer it is that you have not given in. «It's a good sign,» says St. Francis de Sales, «that the devil makes so much noise and stirs up such a storm around our will; it proves that he hasn't got into it. One does not lay siege to a fortress that is already in one's power; as long as the attack continues, one can be sure that there is sustained resistance and that one has not consented.»

People who fear sin, who ask every day to be preserved from it, who watch over themselves and avoid dangerous occasions, may be sure that the thoughts, temptations and revolts of the flesh which wear them out are not voluntary. So they should not worry about them, but despise them, and abase themselves before God. They should examine their conscience very little on such matters, and confess in very few words any negligences of which they may feel themselves guilty on this point.

Long examinations of conscience before confession, to decide whether one has consented, are very dangerous. First, they stir up the imagination, recall the temptations, keep the fire of concupiscence burning, etc. A wound which is touched too frequently becomes infected instead of healing. Second, they eventually weaken our horror of mortal sin, and make us lose our modesty of soul; for if one should not so much as mention the impure vice, all the more reason not to even think about it. He whose head is always full of bad things, and who is always going over whether or not he consented, will end up no longer fearing evil. He will lose his conscience and expose himself to the greatest dangers. So flee from this snare as one of the most dangerous, do not be afraid of temptations, and fight them with scorn.

CHAPTER EIGHTEEN

OUR LADY OF THE HOLY CINCTURE

Here is a story which Father Champagnat greatly enjoyed telling, as much because it is very suitable for inspiring total confidence in the Blessed Virgin, as for the moral applications which Father drew from it to instruct the brothers.

I.

«At the beginning of the 11th century, the plague ravaged Valenciennes terribly, and carried off eight thousand people in a matter of days. The whole city was in turmoil; all that could be seen on any side was the sad spectacle of death. The distraught inhabitants, who could not hope for anything from this earth or from human resources, turned to heaven and ran *en masse* to seek refuge near the altars of the Mother of mercy.

«At that time, there lived in that region a holy hermit, who, touched by the misfortune of his brothers and sisters, redoubled his austerities and prayers. 'Mary, help of the afflicted,» he cried, «will you allow these people to perish after they have called on you for help and entrusted themselves to you? Will they have to say that they called on you in vain?»

«On the fifth of September, while this holy hermit was saying this fervent prayer, he was suddenly dazzled by a light brighter than the sun. At that moment, the Mother of mercy appeared to him with a most gracious expression, and told him, 'Go to my people of Valenciennes, and assure them that I have disarmed my Son with my prayers. Tell them also that I want the people to go up onto the walls of the city on the night after the vigil of my

Nativity, so that they can see from there the sign of the protection which I want to give them.'

«The pious hermit told the people about this vision, and as the 7th of September began to fade, the city walls and towers, and all the high spots of the city, were covered with people who were deeply moved and eager to see the effects of the heavenly promises. Their confidence was not in vain, for soon the sky brightened as at daybreak, the darkness disappeared and the night was transformed into a beautiful day.

«Then they saw a queen full of majesty, sparkling with light, the light of paradise, like that of the bodies of the blessed, and more brilliant than the sun. This queen, accompanied by an army of angels, held in her hand a cincture or cord which encircled the city in an instant. Nothing can describe the joy and devotion which filled the inhabitants of Valenciennes at this sight. They all fell to their knees and loudly asked the Blessed Virgin to bless them. The Divine Mother did indeed bless them, and delivered them from the plague forever.

«She appeared to the hermit at the same moment, commanded him to tell the people that from now on the 8th of September must be for them a feast day, and that she desired that every year on that day, there be a solemn procession following the route marked by the holy cord. The city, in the person of its magistrates, committed itself by vow to hold a commemorative procession every 8th of September. That procession was held every year until the Revolution of 1793. The holy cincture was picked up with great respect and enclosed in a richly ornamented reliquary.»

II.

«Isn't it true, brothers,» Fr. Champagnat went on, «that you envy the good fortune of the people of Valenciennes, and that you would like to see the Blessed Virgin as they did, to be visibly protected by her and surrounded by her cincture which is the visible sign of her protection? Well, I tell you that you are a hundred times more fortunate than those good people and that the divine Mother encircles you with a cincture far more precious and more sacred than the one with which she encircled the city of Valenciennes. The people of that lucky city saw Mary's cincture for only a short while and were encircled with it for only a moment, whereas the cincture with which you are girded by the Blessed Virgin lasts forever and protects and defends you forever.

«And what is that cincture, you may ask? That holy cincture is:

1. The religious habit, which makes you brothers and children of Mary; it is your habit which sets you apart and distinguishes you from worldly people and which raises an impenetrable barrier between you and them. It is your habit which makes even wicked people respect you; the mere sight of it makes libertines blush, closes their mouth, forces them to compose themselves, and stirs up biting remorse in their conscience. It is your habit which terrifies the devils and makes them flee; it is your habit which makes even the angels respect you and leads them to protect you, help you and defend you. Oh, holy habit! From how many dangers you protect us! I understand now why St. Stanislaus Kostka kissed his habit piously every morning when he put it on. That habit is a pledge of protection; it is Mary's cincture which separates us from the world and its vanities, and which shelters us from their dangers under the protection of the divine Mother.

«When the Blessed Virgin gave the scapular to St. Simon Stock, she told him, 'Take this habit, which is the pledge of my protection; if you wear it until death, you will obtain your salvation.' That is what the Mother of God also says to each of us in giving us the religious habit: 'Take this habit; if you take care of it, if you respect it, if you wear it until death, you will be saved.' Oh, great St. Thomas Aquinas, you understood the happiness of keeping the religious habit and dying in your vocation, you who a few instants before dying, while affectionately embracing your habit, cried out in a great transport of joy and gratitude, 'My God, I thank you for having given me the grace of keeping this holy habit and wearing it until death.'

2. «For us, Mary's holy cincture is also our residence, a blessed place totally dedicated to God. There, we are in a safe harbor, sheltered from the contagion of the vices and scandals of the world. There, we see only good example, we breathe only the good odor of virtues. There, everything leads us towards good, and everything, even the walls, speaks to us of God and inspires us with holy thoughts. There, concupiscence is weakened and controlled by the religious atmosphere which reigns throughout the house, as well as by the graces and helps of all sort which are lavished upon us. There, religious live in total security, while lay people are dashed about by the tempestuous waves of their passions and by the fury of Satan, who reigns as master of the world. I am no longer astonished to read that St. Magdalen of Pazzi hugged and kissed the walls of her convent and cried out, 'O blessed walls, you are my safe harbor! You protect me from so many dangers!'

«That, you young brothers, is why the devil so often shows you the door of your residence and whispers in your ear, 'Here you aren't free; here you live a sad and difficult life; walk through the door of this house which is nothing but a prison for you, and enter the world, where freedom, happiness and a fortune await you.' It is exactly as if he were telling you, 'Here, my hands are tied and my power is chained; I cannot tempt you, I cannot lead you toward evil as I would like, I cannot destroy you and you will escape me if you stay here. So go through that door, go into the world; there, I will rule over you, make you my slave and the slave of all the passions and vices.

«St. Gregory tells us that the devil, speaking like that to a monk, but in more guarded terms, persuaded him to abandon his vocation; but that poor religious had no sooner set foot outside the monastery courtyard, than the devil appeared to him in the form of a mastiff, to devour him. The religious recoiled in horror, and ran to throw himself at the feet of his superior, St. Benedict, who told him, 'I warned you, brother, that the devil was drawing you away from this house, where he cannot ruin you, only to devour and damn you easily in the world. God has been especially merciful to you in showing you the risks you are running. I hope this experience will make you wiser from now on!'

«Another religious, St. Gregory also tells us, urged on by the same promptings of the devil, also left his monastery; but as soon as he reached the boundary of the property, he saw a hideous demon, who threw a rope around his neck and told him, 'Here I am, waiting for you, and I will easily become your master.' The poor religious, being terrified, fell to his knees and made a vow to return to his monastery and die there. The devil immediately took flight, after uttering terrible threats against him.

«Oh monastery walls! You are for us Mary's cincture; you block the devil's fury and preserve us from his ambushes! O precious cincture! You seem to say to the devil, 'You will go no further, your rage will dash itself out against these walls, and the children of the Queen of heaven, who live within them, will sleep in peace here.' Yes, the Little Brother of Mary who loves his residence, who lives there unknown to the world, who hides there and never goes out without real necessity, preserves his vocation and his virtue. He will be blessed by the divine Mother, preserved from the plague of vice, and will progress from virtue to virtue until he reaches eternal life.»

3. For us religious, the holy cincture is our vows of poverty, chastity and obedience, which make us die to the world and all its concupiscences, and which remove the major obstacles to salvation, namely: love of material goods, destroyed by the vow of poverty; love of carnal pleasures, destroyed by the vow of chastity; and lack of control of our self will, destroyed by the vow of obedience. O holy cincture of the vows, you bind religious to

God by a triple bond! O holy cincture of the vows, who can say how many souls you have preserved in their vocation, and hence even in virtue! ... On Judgment Day, we will see millions of religious testify that they owe it to their vows that they avoided sin, practiced virtue and worked out their salvation. I have heard so many brothers say publicly, «Without my vows, I would not be a religious; I owe my perseverance in my vocation to my vows.» O holy Mother of God, how much gratitude we owe you for having encircled us with the holy cincture of the vows. Deign, o good Mother, to complete your work and with your glorious cincture, keep us always on the path of purity, poverty and obedience, which is the way to heaven.

4. Finally, for us Mary's holy cincture is our rules. They form a sort of rampart or barrier around us, which prevent the devil from getting into our souls. So, while people in the world are in the middle of the battlefield, beaten by the enemy of salvation, captured, tied up and garroted like slaves, we religious are in complete security within the fortress created by our rules, we watch the battle without any risk to ourselves. While people in the world wander across the sea which is whipped up by tempests, amid storms and reefs which destroy so many of them, we religious are safe in port, looking on with complete confidence.

The holy cincture of the rule entirely surrounds the brother, and as long as he remains in the circle formed by this precious cord, he cannot be infected by the plague of vice, he cannot offend God, he cannot lose his soul. Dear brothers, observe the rules on modesty, and death will never enter your heart through the windows of your eyes; observe the rule of silence, and you will be preserved from the plague of backbiting and calumny; be faithful to the rules about contacts with persons in the world, avoid lay people, stay inside your houses, do not appear in public, and you will be preserved from the plague of the spirit of the world and from evil passions; keep the rules on humility and simplicity which have been given you, and the plague of pride, vanity, and self will never penetrate your heart; be exact in keeping the rules about the exercises of piety, pray, and you will be preserved from the plague of all the vices. Yes, the brother who keeps his rule, and who does not step outside the circle which this holy cincture forms around him, will keep himself pure and holy; he will never be bitten by the devil; or if he is bitten occasionally as a result of human weakness, he will never be devoured.

Listen to this little story: «Blessed Jordan, who had a special devotion to the Blessed Virgin, had placed his whole community under this divine Mother's protection, and he asked her every day to preserve his brothers from sin. Now, one day, he had a vision: he thought he saw a great queen, accompanied by a long procession, walking through the monastery and blessing all the brothers as they passed in front of her, except for one whom she would not even look at. The holy superior, struck by this, drew closer, and realizing that it was the Mother of God, humbly asked her, 'Divine Mother, why didn't you bless that brother?' 'Because he does not observe his rule, and his infidelities have led him into mortal sin; tell him to convert himself and I will bless him. And, my son, you should know that as a reward for your piety, I have obtained three graces for your order: the first is that your religious will have a great fear of sin; the second, is that none of them will be able to stay long in mortal sin, but will either be converted or discovered; the third is that all those who want to remain in sin in spite of the graces I give them to get out of it, will be banished and expelled from the monastery, so that they will not corrupt the others and dishonor the order. So whoever makes peace with mortal sin will not remain in this monastery.'

«Dear brothers, that is a very special favor, one worth envying. Need I tell you that I am confident that a similar favor will be granted us? Yes, I hope that the Blessed Virgin will preserve from mortal sin all those who are faithful to the rule. I hope that she will grant powerful graces of conversion to all those who will have the misfortune of letting themselves be seduced by the devil and fall into sin, so that they may rise again quickly. And finally, I hope she will not tolerate in her house a religious hardened in sin, who has abused grace, but rather that in one way or another, she will rid the Institute of him.

«Dear brothers, love and venerate the holy cincture of the rule; remain in the enclosure it forms around you. Never step outside it, and I promise you the constant protection of the Good Mother, the happiness of being preserved from mortal sin, the happiness of perseverance and eternal salvation.»

CHAPTER NINETEEN

THE GREAT QUESTION

I. The Saints' Esteem for Purity

1. «Who shall live in the house of God?» asks the holy prophet-king. «He who is pure,» answers the Holy Spirit (cf. *Ps* 24:3-4). Jesus Christ himself promises the vision of glory only to those whose hearts are pure (*Mt* 5:8). Just as the light of the sun can be seen only by clear eyes, St. Augustine tells us, God can be seen only by chaste souls; that is why St. John says that «nothing defiled can enter heaven,» and he adds, «Cast out the impure and drive them away» (cf. *Rev* 20:15).

So what must we do to guarantee our salvation? We must be pure, and wage an incessant war against the evil vice, which is the seal of Satan. Origen tells us that, «He who wants to save his soul must first of all be pure. To think we can reach salvation without practicing the beautiful virtue and while paying tribute to the shameful vice, is an error, an illusion, a folly.»

«Don't be deceived,» adds St. Clement of Alexandria, «the only true Christians are those who are chaste.» According to Tertullian, this virtue is the foundation of sanctity; when this foundation is undermined, everything crumbles and nothing remains but ruins.

«Purity is the salt of the Christian,» to use the expression of Venerable Bede; «he who has lost this salt is devoured by vices just as unsalted meat is devoured by worms.» And lastly, St. Ephrem adds that, «Purity is the life of the spirit and the root of all virtue.»

«Even if a man is humble, mortified and devout,» says St. Thomas of Villanova, «if he is not pure, he is nothing.» Hence, purity is the virtue which makes saints, the virtue which is absolutely necessary for salvation. St. Jerome was so deeply convinced of that truth that he said, «The wise man, the one who really wants to be sure of his salvation, watches over his purity above all, because he knows that everything collapses into ruins when it is lost.»

Let us describe now how evil the vice contrary to purity truly is, and what a horror God and the saints have of it.

2. The impure vice is extremely displeasing to God and destroys everything in a person. «God has such a horror of impurity,» says St. Augustine, «that he prefers the barking of dogs, the lowing of cattle and the grunting of pigs to the prayers and hymns of the impure.» «It is a more serious sin to profane one's body and soul by a shameful sin than to profane a church or a sacred vessel,» St. Peter Damian assures us. «Impurity,» according to St. Thomas, «places us at an infinite distance from God; and whatever hurls us so far away from God has to be a very grave sin.» «Impurity turns man into a demon,» says St. Gregory. «God has reserved the punishment of the wicked, especially the impure, to himself,» adds St. Peter. «Woe, woe woe,» exclaimed St. Bernard, «to those who let themselves fall into this shameful sin!»

Unfortunately, man is subject to many spiritual weaknesses, but as St. Leo tells us, impurity is the most dangerous of all the soul's illnesses. It is a contagious fever, a fire which spreads in all directions, a leprosy which devours everything, a scabies which disfigures everything it touches and makes it hideous. St. Bonaventure says that after having uprooted all the seedlings of virtue, it brings after it and nourishes all sorts of disorders; it is the seedbed of every vice. St. Cesarius tells us that nothing of any value remains in a man subject to this detestable passion; his merits, his virtues, his good qualities both physical and moral, are all depraved, adulterated and ruined.

Impurity is a cancer, an almost incurable disease, according to St. Clement of Alexandria. It is a venom which reaches every part of the soul and corrupts it. Once one is caught in that net, which is Satan's strongest, St. Jerome tells us, one never gets out of it, or only very rarely and with great difficulty. This detestable vice is a muddy swamp; when you try to free one foot, the other sinks into it. The impure person, says St. John Chrysostom, no longer belongs to himself; he is like the demoniac: the devil possesses him and does what he wants with him. The impure vice, affirms St. Cyprian, bastardizes the human race; it destroys all the faculties of the soul, takes away inspiration and judgment, extinguishes intelligence, makes us lose our memory, weakens and breaks our will, depraves our conscience and gives us the heart of an animal, that is to say, a heart without feelings. It ruins the health, weakens the eyesight, diminishes beauty and alters the appearance of the face; it leaves a man dazed, which led St. Eucherius to say that the impure person is no different from a beast, and St. John Chrysostom that if we could see how vile an impure soul is, we would prefer the grave to that miserable condition. In view of such a disgrace, St. Cesarius exclaimed that there are no longer any feast days or joyful days in this life for such a soul; its lot and heritage are tears, regrets, anguish and bitterness.

The saints all had a sovereign horror of impurity. The mere thought of that vice prompted St. Benedict to roll in thorn bushes, St. Francis of Assisi to jump into a frozen pond, and St. Jerome to strike his breast hard with a stone.

3. Our Founder had such a horror of the evil vice that the mere mention of it frightened him. An obvious offense against purity brought tears to his eyes; he was terribly inexorable about it because he was so afraid it might spread. He had no mercy on those who corrupted others, but drove them away without pity.

When he was told about a candidate of that type at ten o'clock one night, an hour after the community had retired, he could not bring himself to let him stay in the house until morning. He made him get up and sent him away at once. The young man begged him on his knees to let him spend the night in a corner of the house or in the stable, saying that it was too late to find anyplace else to sleep.

«No! No!» Father replied, «So long as you are here I will tremble for fear that God's curse may fall upon us.» Even while saying this, he pushed him out the door and closed it behind him. A moment later, one of the brothers remarked that the postulant had left his clothing behind. «Go get his clothes,» he answered, «and throw them across the river, so that we will be totally separated not only from him but from anything that belongs to him, and so that the water will keep the contagion which his belongings will certainly spread from reaching us.»

II. The Excellence and Advantages of Purity

The doctors of the Church call virgins the heroes and heroines of humanity, and purity, the perfection of human life and an initiation into heavenly life. O purity, human beings cannot say what you are, nor worthily express your merit and your glory! One must see you in heaven, by God's own light, to know how beautiful you are. Nonetheless, we will try, brothers, to recall and understand a few of the precious advantages which this heavenly virtue gives us.

1. Purity makes us like the angels. St. John Climacus says that he who has overcome the flesh has overcome nature; now, he who has overcome nature is above human nature and close to the angelic nature. That is why St. Ambrose saw no problem in stating that a pure man is an angel; St. Bernard states that he has the courage, strength and merit of one; Cassian, that he is the equal of those blessed spirits; St. Gregory, that to be a virgin or an angel is one and the same thing.

2. Purity makes us like God and gives us the first seats in the Kingdom. «Out of everything in the world, it is purity which brings us closest to God.» By uniting us more closely with God, it makes us share more fully in his divine perfection and happiness. So it is written that pure souls form a group apart in heaven, that «they follow the Lamb wherever he goes,» make up his heavenly court, and «sing a new song which no other person can learn or sing» (cf. *Rev* 14:3-4).

3. Purity makes us Jesus' well-beloved. This is a truth which Holy Scripture itself teaches us: «He who loves purity will be his prince's beloved.» Jesus therefore has a special love for pure souls; he shares himself in a special way with them and overwhelms them with joy and consolation; he protects them and defends them against the temptations of the devil. At Jesus' order, said a wise man, the holy angels gather around pure souls to incite them to virtue and defend them from the devil. Jesus takes great care with their advancement in virtue, removing the obstacles which might stop their progress, and giving them a wonderful facility in the practice of prayer and all the virtues. Finally, he takes special care of their conduct and everything else that concerns them, because since perfectly pure souls think only of Jesus, he will not let himself be outdone in loving. Besides, it is only normal to take care of rare and precious things, and nothing is more precious in heaven, and still less on earth, than a pure soul. That is why Jesus loves them and takes so much care of them.

4. Purity raises us to a high degree of sanctity. In speaking about the parable of the sower, St. Jerome said that the state of virginity is the one that bears fruit a hundredfold, and that the one which produces only thirtyfold is the lay state in the world. St. Martial states that in heaven, those who have kept their purity will have a hundred times more glory than those who sanctified themselves in the married state. That is why St. John calls them the first fruits of the redemption, meaning that Our Lord gives

them a greater share of his merits and of his blood, and that he will give them greater glory in heaven.

5. Purity earns as much merit and glory as martyrdom. Even in the midst of peace, St. Jerome tells us, with the sword of purity we obtain the palm of martyrdom. Martyrdom of blood, St. Bernard adds, appears more cruel, but its pains do not last so long as those of the martyrdom of chastity. It costs less to lose one's life at a single blow than to mortify one's flesh by a lifetime of purity.

6. Purity is the scourge of the vices; it controls and overcomes all our disorderly tendencies, says St. Cyprian. Experience definitely proves that a person of great purity hates, detests and flees from all sin. He cannot stand evil and combats it everywhere, because the effect of purity is to make one's conscience timorous and very delicate.

7. It perfects and embellishes all the faculties of the soul.

a. It is a source of light for the intellect. Purity, says St. Adelelmus, is a sun for our mind; it makes one an angel. And St. Thomas assures us that because of their purity, the angels come closer to God and share more abundantly in his light, his intelligence and all his perfections.

St. John was a virgin; that is why he rose like an eagle toward God, and drew from the bosom of eternal wisdom the most sublime knowledge and ineffable secrets.

St. Thomas was a virgin, and we know that in order to be associated with the knowledge of the angels and to be called the Angelic Doctor, he had to have the purity of the angels, and an angel put a cincture around him.

St. Jerome assures us that the sibyls had obtained from God the gift of prophecy as a reward for their celibacy. Everyone knows and history proves that humanity's greatest works and most astonishing wonders have been accomplished by persons who were pure. Yes, the crown of intelligence and reason belongs to pure souls.

One day, a religious of great simplicity said to St. Pachomius, «Father, please tells us about some of your visions; we hear that you have had some marvelous ones.»

«It is not for a sinner like me to desire visions,» the saint replied, «but do you know, brother, what is the most marvelous vision of all? It is the sight of a pure and humble person. Perfect purity lets us know and see God and holy things more perfectly than the greatest knowledge and all visions put together.»

On the contrary, the first effect of impurity is to weaken the intellect. St. Thomas says that the impure vice blinds the mind and makes us lose our reason. The soul which has fallen under the yoke of this infamous passion is no longer intelligent; it is stupefied. When it is devoured by the impure fire, says St. Gregory, it can no longer see the sun of justice. Its passions hurl it into a deep ditch, into dark places and the shadow of the grave.

b. Purity puts fire in the heart; it makes it loving, sensitive, thankful. «I love purity above all the other virtues,» St. Giles exclaimed one day. When someone asked him whether charity was not more valuable, he replied, «Can there be charity without purity?» Purity nourishes love; a carnal heart does not know how to love; the sacred fire cannot be lit in the mud.

This truth is so evident that even the wicked are aware of it. «I maintain, without fear of being contradicted by experience,» said Jean-Jacques Rousseau, «that a young man who has preserved his innocence until the age of twenty is, at that age, the most generous, the best, the most loving and the most lovable of men. On the contrary, young men given to vice have only small souls and hardened, depraved hearts; I have always found them inhuman and cruel; they know neither pity nor mercy; they would have sacrificed their father and mother and the entire universe, for the least of their pleasures.»

What caused the loss of that goodness and meekness for which David gave thanks as for one of the most beautiful gifts he had received from God's goodness? Adultery. After this fault, the gentlest of men became the most cruel. He had previously twice spared Saul, his greatest enemy; afterwards, he had his follower Uriah killed at the very moment when that generous officer was giving him proof of the most inviolable fidelity. «Why be surprised,» exclaims St. Bernard, «that a carnal man is cruel and does not know how to love? He no longer has the heart of a man, but that of an animal.»

c. Purity, St. Cyprian tells us, gives energy and strength to the will. «The Lord will make you strong, because you loved purity,» the Holy Spirit told Judith (cf. *Jud* 15:11).

The virgin St. Agatha, a fifteen-year-old child, told her torturers, «Whip, tear apart, cut and break my body; you will never break my will.» Aphrodius, giving the tyrant an account of the virtue of this holy and heroic girl, told him, «It would be easier to soften granite or to change iron into lead, than to change Agatha's mind and take away her love for Jesus Christ.»

History or legend tells us that Godfrey de Bouillon could cut a man in two with a single blow of his sword. Someone asked him what was the secret of the strength of his arm. «This hand,» he replied, «has never been soiled by a single feminine touch; it is purity which makes my will and my arm strong.»

8. Finally, purity is a great sign of predestination and a pledge of salvation, as St. Cyprian says. That is easy to understand, because if heaven belongs to those who flee sin, purity is the ruin of all vices; if heaven is a reward for our merits, chastity multiplies them infinitely; if heaven is the home of God's friends, pure souls are Jesus' special friends. Pure persons are declared blessed by Jesus himself: «Blessed are the pure of heart for they shall see God» eternally (*Mt* 5:8). To sum it all up in one word, purity is the seal with which Jesus marks his chosen ones, just as the impure vice is the seal which Satan stamps on the reprobates.

III. Vigilance, a Necessary Means to Purity

Who is pure? That is an important question, but a very easy one to answer. «The man who is pure,» replies St. Augustine, «is the one who watches over his five senses and who carefully refrains from everything illicit in the use of his sight, hearing, speech, touch, smell and taste.»

Therefore, to preserve your purity, brothers, you must:

1. Watch over your eyes and observe great modesty. It is through the eyes, according to St. Jerome, that poisoned arrows enter to pierce the heart. That is why Jeremiah says, «Death has come up through our windows (*Jer* 9:20) and, «My soul became the victim of my eyes.» A single look can become a fixation, the beginning of our ruin, and the cause of our fall. That is no doubt why Hugh of St. Victor calls the eyes dangerous reefs on which ships loaded with wealth have been wrecked; cruel and terrible rocks, against which a multitude of souls have been sadly broken.

The eyes, St. Gregory tells us, are our masters and teachers in all things; so do not let them see carnal objects, if you do not want them to persuade you to be carnal. Thought and desire follow so closely upon sight, that we are not permitted to look at what it is not licit to desire. «Accustom yourself then,» says St. Francis de Sales, «to see persons of the other sex in a general sort of way, and not with a steady, direct and discerning gaze.»

St. Aloysius Gonzaga never looked at the empress of Austria when he was her page; after several months at the palace, he still did not know what she looked like. For that matter, he never looked steadily even at his own mother.

St. Hugh, the bishop of Grenoble, did not know his mother by sight, since he had never looked directly at her.

St. Peter of Alcantara kept such great modesty of the eyes that he did not even know the monks in his monastery; the only way he could tell them apart was by their voices.

Another holy religious, who had received the great gift of purity, told those who asked him why he was so reserved in looking at women, «When one avoids the occasions, one is protected by God himself. But when one puts oneself in danger by giving one's eyes too much freedom, one is abandoned by God and falls into grave faults.»

Do not rely on the virtue of anyone who does not control his eyes. «Whoever has an impure eye,» says St. Cesarius, «cannot have a chaste soul, because purity of the eyes creates that of the heart.»

2. Watch over your tongue. «Our tongue strips bare our habits; people picture our heart just as our language depicts it,» says St. Isidore. The modest man always uses modest language. The devil lies in ambush for us on all sides, especially so for our tongue. No other organ, St. John Chrysostom tells us, serves him so well for killing souls; no other member works so well with the devil for the ministry of death and sin. It is that harmony which prepares our falls, perdition, the shipwreck of purity and the death of the soul. According to St. Augustine, the tongue is a furnace of impurity in a man who has been ruined by the evil vice. That is why St. Paul warns us, «Be not seduced: evil communications corrupt good manners» (*1 Cor* 15:33) and elsewhere, «Let no evil, indecent or mocking speech come from your mouth; such things are not fitting for holy people.» Still less should the impure vice be mentioned among you.

A careless word made St. Stanislaus Kostka faint, so afraid was he of anything which might wound the beautiful virtue.

St. Charles Borromeo drove from his house a servant who described to him in vulgar terms a crime committed in the city.

St. Francis de Sales did not even want people to speak about purity. «There are two virtues,» he used to say, «which we must practice constantly without ever naming them; they are humility and chastity.»

«But why not praise purity?» someone once asked him. «For fear,» he replied, «of leaving in the mind a hidden and almost imperceptible fantasy about the contrary vice, and thus exposing it to temptation.»

St. John Chrysostom wanted people to be brief even in confession, and carefully to avoid needless repetition and details. «How often,» he said, «our poor human nature, under some frivolous pretext, having been weaned of everything else, seeks some sort of compensation in sight or speech.»

Do not count among the number of chaste men he who is not very modest and very reserved in his speech; avoid him, for such a man, says St. Gregory, is the devil's associate in destroying souls. His tongue is fiercer than that of wild beasts and more venomous than that of serpents. The mouth speaks from the abundance of the heart; so obscene words indicate one which is corrupt. But how many people delude themselves on this point and allow themselves to use words which kindle fires in souls! «But I was just joking,» they'll tell you. So, you joke with sin while violating the law of God and scandalizing and destroying souls and spreading the contagion of vice! Come on, come on, you perverse men; you are Satan's agents; God's curses will certainly fall on you!

3. Watch over your hands. A speck of dust irritates the eye, a breath tarnishes a flower, a slight shock shatters crystal. What does it take to wound the soul, to tarnish the lily of purity, to shatter the vessel in which, as St. Paul says, we carry our treasure, and on which is written in big letters, fragile? A mere trifle!

So avoid external signs of attachment, not only those which make the angels cry and the devils laugh, but even those which appear most innocent.

«Familiarity and playing hands,» says St. Jerome, «indicate a purity which is in its last agony and a virtue which is dying.»[1]

«Flee the least attachments,» wrote Fr. Lambert, superior general of the Dominicans; «I mean not only with shameless persons but even with the most upright. Earth is good and rain is good, but together they make mud. If you touch tar, your fingers get dirty.»

St. Aloysius Gonzaga would never let anyone else bandage a cut he had on his arm.

So long as there's a spark of life in us, the fire of concupiscence is still lit. The coals under a shallow layer of ashes often appear to be dead; but as soon as you touch them, they flare up again. And often enough, a coal which goes out when it is isolated and put to one side, will light again if brought near another. That is the devil's great artifice, to stir up coals which are nearly extinguished, bring them together, and relight them by blowing on them.

After St. Ursinus became a priest, he lived with his wife as with his sister, in perfect continence. When he was at the point of death, she put her face close to his to see if he was still breathing; the saint realized what she was doing, gathered all his strength and told her, «Get away from me, woman; the fire is not yet out, so keep the straw away from it!»

Fresh water, says St. Francis de Sales, loses it clarity if an animal steps in it and stirs it up; a piece of fruit which is often handled loses its freshness and beauty; it fades and goes bad and then no one wants it. The religious who allows himself any leeway and familiarities, even thoughtlessly and with no evil intention, loses the flower of his purity. Our bodies are like glasses which shatter each other at the slightest touch; they are like pieces of

---

[1] An expression familiar to older generations of religious, «playing hands» referred to just about any physical contact between two persons.

fruit which bruise one another and rot when they bump together, even though each remains whole and entire.

St. Nizier, the bishop of Lyons, never touched children's faces or hands. No touch is without danger. A very pious companion of Blessed Marie d'Oignies one day took her hand without thinking. At that very instant she heard a voice from heaven saying, «Don't touch me.» And in fact, at that moment the saint warned the other person, and told her that she had felt some disorderly emotion.

The abbot St. Gerard had been miraculously cured of a paralyzed arm. His brother's wife, a very pious woman, came one day to congratulate him. Her joy was so great that she took hold of the arm which had been sanctified by a miracle, and kissed it; at that instant, the paralysis struck again. God wanted to show how carefully we should avoid all touches.

4. Watch over your taste. An uncontrolled sense of taste is a dangerous reef for our purity. Listen to the teachings of the saints on the subject.

St. Jerome and St. Augustine assure us that gluttony is the mother of impurity and that those two vices always go together.

St. Gregory states that impurity is drawn by two wild horses: gluttony and sloth, and that a sensual man will never be pure. He adds, «Gluttony, sloth, the devil and impurity are four similar things, four inseparable companions.»

According to St. John Chrysostom, the devil has no closer friend than the glutton, because that vice is the source of all the others and especially of impurity.

He also says that a stomach too full of food is like an overloaded ship, which goes to the bottom if a storm blows up, that is to say, a temptation.

St. Catherine of Sweden often told the novices in her convent, «It is impossible for anyone who is not mortified in eating to preserve his or her innocence, since that is how Adam lost his.»

«Never, never,» exclaimed St. Jerome, «will I believe that anyone who is not sober and mortified in drinking and eating, is a chaste person.» He also said, «If I may be permitted to give a bit of advice, if anyone wants to profit by my experience, let him think of wine drunk without moderation as a poison, as oil thrown on a fire.» And he ended with these words, «Wherever there is excess in drinking and eating, the impure vice is in control and rules as master.»

«That is why,» St. Leo remarks, «all the saints, our teachers and models, began fighting temptations of the flesh by abstinence and mortification in drinking, eating and sleep.» «Linen can be whitened only by being scrubbed and beaten,» says St. Ivo of Chartres, «and the body becomes chaste only by means of privation and penances.»

«My son,» St. Philip Neri told one of his penitents who had the habit of eating and drinking between meals, «if you do not correct this defect, you will never take a single step on the road to perfection, and you will always be in danger of losing your purity.»

St. Lawrence Justinian did not even drink water between meals, and refused that refreshment even on the hottest days of summer. He answered someone who found him too strict on that point, «I do so to preserve my purity and to avoid purgatory.»

Sobriety and mortification are among the first means to take to preserve purity, because, as St. Thomas says, «When the devil is repelled and vanquished in his temptations to gluttony and sensuality, he doesn't give any impure temptations, because he knows that one who doesn't give in little combats is far from ready to give in big ones.»

5. Watch over your mind, so as not to let in any bad thoughts. Our actions flow from our affections, and our affections from our thoughts. So it is of the utmost importance to set aside perverse, frivolous and even useless thoughts, and to allow into our mind only holy or useful ones. «All our works,

good or bad,» says St. Augustine, «begin with a thought.» A man's innocence or guilt depends on his thoughts; that is why the Holy Spirit tells us in Scripture, «A good thought will save you and a bad thought will condemn you,» because the latter will be the cause of a bad act. And, as St. Isidore assures us, «The devil's job is to suggest criminal thoughts to us.» «Impure thoughts,» adds St. John Chrysostom, «are arrows fired by the devil to wound us.»

Passion is fire, bad thoughts are straw. «How easy it is,» exclaims St. Gregory, «for that straw to catch fire and turn into a blaze!» Do not neglect to combat a bad thought under the pretext that it is a trifle. A spark looks like a trifle; you can hardly see it, but if it falls on dry wood, it produces a fire which can destroy a house or even a whole city. So reject the bad thought as soon as it appears, or despise it. «Kill your enemy while he is weak,» says St. Jerome; don't let him grow stronger.» «Crush the serpent's head,» adds St. Augustine. «What is his head? The first suggestion of evil; crush that head and you will be master of his whole body.»

A good way to stifle bad thoughts is to fill our mind with good ones. So think of death, judgment, hell, eternity or the passion of Jesus Christ. He who does not watch over his mind, but lets in all sorts of vain, useless, and dangerous thoughts, will never be pure and is exposing himself to regrettable falls.

6. Watch over your heart. The life of the heart is love. No heart is totally devoid of love. So, what sort of love do you live on? Think about what you love. «If your heart loves God,» says St. Augustine, «it becomes divine; if it loves the earth, it becomes earthly; if it loves the flesh, creatures, it becomes carnal, it becomes mud.»

The heart is the seat and source of purity; that is why the Holy Spirit says, «Watch over your heart most carefully, for from it proceed both life and death.»

«Nothing is more flighty than our heart,» says St. Gregory; «it constantly runs away from us to chase after evil affections.» The heart is more fickle than all fickle things, it is more slippery than all slippery things. And so St. Bernard adds, «The devil finds no other organ in the human body so useful for his pursuits, snares and illusions, than the heart.» Being convinced of that truth, St. Augustine exclaimed, «A soldier of Christ must guard his heart above all, and most carefully, if he does not want lust to burn him up. Beware, beware of natural and sensual affections, for they are the door leading to carnal and criminal affections. Flee, flee particular friendships; they are one of the most dangerous snares of the devil.»

St. Francis says, «The devil begins to tie up souls with a hair; then comes the string, then the rope, and finally the iron chain.» That too human affection you feel for a woman or for one of your students, and which you do not combat, will grow with sweet words, looks, familiarities, little presents; then passion will erupt and you will find yourself bound with a chain of iron and of death. What danger purity is in when the heart is caught up in a too human affection which is not resisted. That is one of the greatest dangers for the angelic virtue.

«You who love chastity and want to preserve it,» says St. John Climacus, «be forewarned against this snare of the devil. Don't say you don't feel anything, neither a rush of lust, nor wild fantasies, nor disordered affections.» «No, no,» St. John Chrysostom will answer you, «you will never convince me that the two of you are like two blocks of marble, or that heaven will dry up concupiscence, and almost even human nature itself, to facilitate a friendship which is at the very least useless.»

7. Watch out for everything that could be for you an occasion of temptation and the cause of your falling. Never forget these two maxims of Holy Scripture: «He who wishes to keep his soul pure flees the occasions of sin» (cf. *Prov* 22:5), and, on the other hand, «He who loves danger shall perish in it» (*Sir* 3:24).

«Looking for the occasions of sin,» says St. Bernard, «is the sign of a sin already committed and the reason why one will commit it again.»

«You may be sure,» adds St. Cyprian, «that he who exposes himself to the near occasions of sin seduces his soul and slips into total blindness.» Only he who is watchful, who runs away, who is fearful, who mistrusts himself, does not perish. «How many there are who lose their purity through presumption,» exclaimed St. Jerome on his deathbed. That was the last lesson he gave his disciples.

«To throw oneself into the midst of the flames, hoping not to be burned, is insane and, apart from a miracle, impossible» says Cornelius. «God does not owe us a miracle, and we have not merited one; on the contrary, we have done all we could to distance ourselves from God and to destroy ourselves. So we shall perish miserably and scandalously.»

«The temptations we must fight against our will,» says St. Basil, «are an indispensable war; then, with the help of God, we will be victorious. But to willfully start a fierce conflict by exposing oneself to danger is the height of folly.»

«To throw oneself needlessly into the midst of danger is diabolical,» affirms St. John Chrysostom.

Woe to the presumptuous blind man who does not see or does not fear danger, and who plays with serpents; sooner or later, he will be their victim.

Talking about things concerning the sixth commandment and the impure vice, without real necessity, is playing with serpents. Reading a bad book, or even just a dangerous one, in terms of the reader's dispositions, is also playing with serpents.

Studying out of curiosity questions about which it is better to remain ignorant all one's life, is playing with serpents.

Holding long conversations with women, alone and without necessity, is playing with serpents.

Becoming familiar with a child because one feels a natural, sensual attraction for him, is playing with serpents.

Becoming an intimate friend of a brother, or of a not very edifying layman, who is not reserved in his speech, is playing with serpents.

Woe to him who plays such games! Sooner or later he will perish; sooner or later he will be bitten by the impure vice.

Flee idleness, for it is the forerunner of impurity. «The devil,» says the great St. Athanasius, «is filled with joy at the sight of an idle religious.» Why? Because he knows from experience that laziness inevitably leads to impurity. «What is the imagination of an idle religious?» asks St. Bernard. He answers, «It is a highway which all the impure demons take.» «What is his heart? It is a cesspool in which the most hideous temptations are generated and bubble. It is an unfortified city, the target of all the arrows of hell, the bed, the soft cushion, on which Satan loves to recline,» adds St. Bonaventure.

According to St. Jerome, «He who works has only one devil to tempt him, while he who remains idle has a legion of them, who lay waste and ravage his soul.» For a religious who wants to maintain himself and preserve perfect purity, piety is not enough. He must have, somehow or other, a passion for work. «Remember,» says St. John Chrysostom, «that Adam, being idle, was driven out of the earthly paradise, and that St. Paul, busy making tents amid all his missionary travels, was taken up to the third heaven.»

«Let prayer follow work, and work follow prayer,» St. Jerome wrote to Nepotianus. If you love reading good books, prayer and work, you will have no love for the sins of the flesh, and all the fires of concupiscence will be extinguished in you as if by a miracle.

Flee useless conversation with women as you would thorns, the plague and fire. Almost always, you either get burnt by the flame or blackened by the smoke. The tinder is on one side and the match on the other, and the devil is in the middle to bring them together and blow on the fire. This is where Solomon's proverb really fits: «Sin will always be found amid long and useless conversations.» Someone hanging by a thread from the top of a tower is in less danger of losing his life than a religious who has long conversations with women is in danger of losing his chastity. «We must take great precautions with women, and be brief with them,» says St. Alphonsus; «when we have six words to say, we must limit ourselves to three.»

«Can a man hide fire in his bosom and his garments not burn? Or can he walk upon hot coals and his feet not be burnt?» (*Prov* 6:27-28). «And who is the person who hides fire in his bosom?» Cardinal Hugh of Saint-Cher goes on. «It is the one who willingly speaks with persons of the other sex. Who is the person who walks on coals? The one who enjoys lingering looks at them.» There are a great many persons who are lost because they play with fire like that.

St. Thomas Aquinas was very reserved in his conversations with his mother. «But she's your mother!» someone said to him; «Why do you run away from her?» «That's exactly why I'm on my guard,» replied the saint. St. Augustine did not want his own sister to live with him.

The wise and holy Cardinal Bellarmine severely reprimanded the brother who was accompanying him because he had left him alone with a noblewoman of great virtue. In the travels and visits of a religious, his triple safeguard is his habit, his traveling companion and his modesty. Woe to him who eliminates a single one of those guardians! One cannot count on the virtue of anyone who permits himself long private conversations with women; sooner or later he will fall because of his temerity. According to St. Ephrem, it is impossible to avoid bad thoughts and the stirrings and heat of concupiscence, so long as one does not flee dangerous occasions. «He who does not foresee and flee the danger he should foresee and flee,» says St. Augustine, «is tempting God, and he will be abandoned.»

When purity is in danger, the timidity which makes us run away becomes intrepidity. We advance toward victory when we fall back; we multiply our strength a hundredfold when we admit our weakness and ask for help. In other combats, we defy our enemy and shout, «Forward!» In the fight for purity, we put him to flight by shouting, «Every man for himself!»

«He who runs away from persecution and refuses to suffer for God, loses the crown of martyrdom,» says St. Augustine, «and he who leaves the theater of voluptuousness, out of fear of involving himself in danger, wins the crown of chastity.» Vigilance over oneself, avoiding dangerous occasions, are the only safe harbor for purity; he who leaves that port will surely be shipwrecked.

IV. Prayer, the Indispensable Means to Purity

In order to be pure, is it enough for us to watch over our senses? No, for our Lord also adds, «Pray.» Purity is a gift of God, and every good gift comes to us from on high, from the Father of lights, by means of prayer. «When I knew,» says Solomon, «that I could not possess chastity unless God gave it to me, I went to the Lord to beg him to bestow that gift on me.»

«The virtue of purity,» Cassian adds, «is such an exalted and precious thing that it is impossible for a man to rise to it himself, unless the grace of God pulls him out of the mud of his poor nature.» So no one who does not pray perseveringly is pure.

1. To be pure, we must have recourse to frequent confession. This is the most powerful brake we can apply to hold us back in temptation and to raise us up and rehabilitate us after we fall. He who makes use of this divine remedy will always triumph over the devil and the most violent passions.

The two most formidable enemies of purity are presumption and discouragement. He who confronts danger, exposes himself to temptation, or does not watch over his senses and apply the brakes to them, will never be pure; he will inevitably perish. We are tempting God and deceiving ourselves if we think we can remain pure while throwing ourselves into the midst of dangers; such an act is proof that we have already lost the flower of purity. Beware of presumption, which will ruin you; have recourse to the wisdom of your confessor; have recourse to frequent confession; the virtue of the sacrament will give you strength and grace to struggle and to overcome.

Discouragement is a snare equally tragic and perhaps even more common than presumption. It is impossible to acquire great purity without combats, without temptations, and sometimes even without experiencing several moments of weakness. Now, the worst thing we can do in such cases is to give in to sadness and discouragement. He who picks himself up right away through confession, and who returns to the battle with confidence, will always end up winning a complete victory, regardless of the violence of his temptations and the dangers in which he finds himself. The impure vice is a weed which grows only in the shade, in darkness and in secret; he who exposes it to sunlight through confession and direction, makes it wither and die. So wage war on presumption and discouragement.

2. To be pure, we must also have recourse to holy communion. The blood of Jesus Christ is a bath which calms concupiscence and extinguishes the fire of the passions. «The love of Jesus,» says St. Anthony, «is our most powerful weapon to use in fighting hell.» Believe me, brothers, Satan is afraid of vigils, fasting, and prayers, but he fears above all holy Mass and communion. One single sign of the cross, the invocation of the holy name of Jesus, disarms him and puts him to flight. «If you are less tempted, if you preserve your purity,» St. Bernard used to tell his religious, «you owe it to communion.»

3. Finally, in order to remain pure, we must confidently have recourse every day to the Blessed Virgin. Everyone knows that

one of the greatest benefits of devotion to the Blessed Virgin is that it gives us purity. The first grace the divine Mother asks for her servants and her children is preservation from all sin. It is a fact of experience that the souls who are most devoted to Mary are those who excel in purity. In temptation, invoking the holy name of Mary is enough to put the devil to flight. So, dear brothers, prescribe for yourselves some special daily practices to ask the Queen of Angels for this virtue, and you will infallibly obtain it.

CHAPTER TWENTY

WHAT A SAINT IS

In 1822, during the novena in preparation for the feast of All Saints, Fr. Champagnat stimulated and nourished his brothers' piety by saying a few words to them every evening about the reason for that feast. One day, before saying the grace after supper, he asked me this question: «Tell me, brother, how many types of Church are there?»

«There are three,» I answered, «the Church Triumphant, the Church Suffering and the Church Militant.»

«Very good! And can you explain to me what each of those Churches is?»

«The Church Triumphant is the company of saints who have won the victory and who are enjoying forever the sight and possession of God in heaven. The Church Suffering is the company of the faithful departed who are detained for a time in purgatory to purify themselves from slight faults or to satisfy divine justice for the punishment due for their forgiven sins. The Church Militant is the company of the faithful still living on earth, professing the same faith, celebrating the same sacraments, obeying the same legitimate pastors, and fighting the same enemies: their passions, the devil, the world, and sin.»

«You really amaze me,» Father replied; «I didn't think you were so well informed! You answered like a theologian!»

My self-love savored the compliment deliciously, and I felt very proud of having been given such praise before all the brothers. But my joy was short-lived; Father realized that my vanity needed to be pricked, so he asked me a third question: «Do you know what a saint is? I don't mean a saint of the Church Triumphant, or in Paradise, but a saint on earth, a member of the Church Militant. Let's see if you can tell me what a saint is who's still living on this earth.»

Since the answer I gave did not satisfy him, he gave me and the other brothers a day to think about it. I don't need to tell you that I couldn't think about anything else but that answer; I thought about it for part of the night and spent the next day preparing it. The other young brothers and the novices did the same thing, because any of us might be called upon.

The question was posed again next morning, and I was the first one called on, so I rose with assurance and said, «Father, a saint on earth is one who works miracles.»

«A man who works miracles!» Father replied; «In that case, St. John the Baptist, your glorious patron, wasn't a saint, because he didn't perform any during his entire life. Even the Blessed Virgin doesn't seem to have performed any; in any case, neither the gospels nor church history mention any. If the only saints in heaven were the ones who worked miracles, there would be very few of them. So your answer is absolutely worthless.»

While I was silently digesting, with lowered eyes, this little humiliation I had just received, Father questioned several other brothers, who didn't answer any better than I had. But Father, who wanted to instruct us and teach us what solid virtue and true sanctity were, adopted a more serious tone and said, «Brothers, there are unfortunately many Christians who, like you, do not know what sanctity is, and who look for it in extraordinary things, or in works which God does not require of us. So I very much want to make you understand clearly what constitutes sanctity, and what we must do to be saints.»

1. A saint is someone who fears sin more than all the evils in the world, and runs away from it as he would run from death. A saint cannot stand to have sin in his soul; if he commits some fault out of weakness, he immediately feels remorse. Sin weighs

on him like a mountain; he is not at ease, he knows no peace until he has confessed it and vomited it out of his soul. His motto is: «Hatred for sin! No more sin!»

2. A saint is someone who is solidly pious, someone deeply convinced that prayer is as necessary for his soul as food is for his body; someone for whom prayer is a necessity and a consolation, and who consequently remains steadfast in his exercises of piety and who neglects nothing in order to perform them as best he can.

3. A saint is someone who loves Jesus, who empathizes with Jesus, who suffers when he sees him offended, who gladly seizes every occasion which presents itself to give him glory. «Love,» says St. Augustine, «is the sign of the elect; it shows us the children of God and sets them apart from the children of the devil. Love distinguishes the chosen from the damned; it indicates the soul's level of sanctity.» If a soul has a high level of charity, it is great and very high in sanctity; if it has no charity, it is nothing, because St. Paul tells us, «If I do not have charity, I am nothing» (*1 Cor* 13:2).

4. A saint is an obedient person, who has entire confidence in his superiors, and who lets himself be led like a child. St. Philip Neri often told his religious that holiness dwelt in a space four fingers wide, behind our forehead, in other words, in renouncing our own will. In religious life, obedience and sanctity are synonymous; to be perfectly obedient is to be a saint. Obedience is the royal road to paradise; Jesus was the first to walk it as the guide of the predestined. All the saints followed it, and not a single one of them reached heaven by any other route.

5. A saint is a humble person, who constantly fights pride, who far from wanting to dominate others, makes himself the least and the servant of all. «Learn of me,» says Jesus Christ, «because I am meek and humble of heart» (*Mt* 11:29). All the saints attended the school of Jesus Christ; all of them learned

humility from him; all of them were models of this virtue; all of them had this mark of predestination.

6. A saint is a mortified person, who fear neither sufferings, temptations nor trials of any kind. Those whom God has predestined, he made conformable to Jesus Christ crucified; that is, he made them pass through sufferings and trials. «Without trials, temptations and contradictions,» says St. John Chrysostom, «there can be no victory, because there is no struggle; there can be no crown, because there is no virtue.» So a sensual man, a man without temptations and trials, is not a saint.

There is no saint without these six characteristics, and no religious can claim to be holy if he does not possess them or is not working to acquire them. These characteristics are so essential and so fundamental to sanctity that if a single one of them is lacking, there is no sanctity. So a man who does not fear sin and commits it easily, is not a saint, no matter what other good qualities he may have. A proud man is not a saint, even if he works miracles. A disobedient man who ignores the orders of his superiors to follow his own will, is not a saint, even if he spends all his time in prayer and good works.

Fear of sin, solid piety, love of Jesus, humility, obedience, and mortification are the foundations of sanctity. Any edifice of perfection which does not rest on those foundations will collapse or be flattened by the winds of temptation. No man is a saint if he does not avoid sin, if he is not humble, obedient and mortified. «Pride,» says St. Augustine, «does not ascend to heaven; disobedience, greed, lust, sensuality, and all other vices or defects, do not ascend to heaven with Jesus Christ.» So if we wish to be saints and to ascend to heaven, we must combat sin and our passions, correct our vices and defects, and replace them with solid virtues.

CHAPTER TWENTY-ONE

WHAT A SAINT IS (CONTINUED)

During his lifetime, Fr. Champagnat often returned to the topic of sanctity, and he answered the question, «What is a saint?» in many ways. We believe it will please our confrères and nourish their piety if we repeat here the various definitions Father gave for sanctity.

1. He used to tell us that a saint is a light and a sun, who enlightens and gives life to all those around him. We can say of all the saints what Jesus said of John the Baptist—he was a light, burning and shining. The saints are burning lamps because they are afire with the love of God and because they spread around them the gentle warmth of charity. They are shining lamps because they enlighten all those among whom they live, by showing them the way to salvation.

So there is a good reason for the Holy Spirit to say in the book of Proverbs, «The path of the just, like a shining light, goes forward and increases even to perfect day. The way of the wicked is dark; they know not where they fall» (*Prov* 4:18-19).

2. A saint is a model for the whole world; he is like a book from which both the wise and the ignorant can learn everything they have to do to attain salvation.

Tertullian confirms this truth when he says, «A saint is a summary of the gospel; his good example makes others love virtue and leads them to practice it. Each of his actions condemns evil and sin.» That is why, in speaking of the first Christians who were all saints, he says that their mere presence silenced all the vices.

· 3. A saint is the instrument of God's goodness and mercy, a canal through which God lets his graces flow to us, a major means of salvation for an entire people. In fact, it often takes only one saint to sanctify a family, a parish, a province, a whole kingdom. Look at St. Vincent Ferrer, who brought Spain and France back to God; and look at St. Francis Xavier, who conquered whole kingdoms for Jesus Christ.

4. A saint is a weak person prone to sin like us. Many people imagine that saints do not share in Adam's fall, that virtue is natural to them, and that they do good effortlessly and painlessly. That is totally erroneous. The saints are people like us, in the sense that they have a nature prone to evil like ours; like us, they find in themselves the seeds of all vices, all passions, and they have to struggle against the same enemies we do: the flesh, the world, the devil and sin. They are subject to the same temptations, and most of the time, their trials have been greater than ours. They are weak like us, they run into the same obstacles, the same dangers, the same difficulties in keeping themselves in God's grace and doing good. Virtue costs them, and it is only by doing continual violence to themselves that they practice it and remain faithful to grace.

5. The saints are always happy and never complain. They never complain about the weather and the inclemency of the seasons. Like the prophet, they say, «Rain, bless the Lord; winds and storms, bless the Lord; summer heat and winter cold, bless the Lord; snow and ice, bless the Lord.» They patiently and merrily endure inconveniences of cold and heat; for them, everything is another reason to bless God and practice mortification. They are happy in whatever country obedience sends them to, because they find God, the only object of their love, everywhere. Sensual men, totally preoccupied with satisfying human nature, spend their lives protecting themselves against the inclemency of the climate and the seasons; they complain because the country does not suit them, because it is too cold, because the heat is suffocating and draining. In the final analysis, they

complain because they don't have the sixth character of sanctity developed in the preceding chapter: they are not mortified.

6. The saints never complain of their assignment. Whatever it may be, they love it, because God, in the person of the superior, has entrusted it to them. If it is difficult, they love it twice as much, because it is more meritorious; if it is very humble, it is one more reason for them to love it even more, because it is an occasion for them to practice humility. One never hears from their mouth the sort of complaints that are so common among imperfect people: «I'm not made for that kind of work; it doesn't suit my tastes, it's beyond my strength and my ability»; or else, «It's too difficult; that class is too large for me; I can take a higher class; I'm being dishonored and sacrificed by being given this assignment, by being sent cooking, etc.»

Men lacking in virtue often want to do what they cannot or should not do; their assignment is a torture for them, and just knowing that they are obliged to do something is enough to give them an aversion for it. They complain about their assignment out of inconstancy, whim, ambition, a desire to better themselves, or to put an end to this or that difficulty they are experiencing. Such people are like invalids who are feverish, and who are constantly changing position without ever managing to find a comfortable one.

7. The saints never complain about their superiors, because they see in them only the person of Jesus Christ, and because they receive their orders as coming from God himself. They never consider the superior's personal qualities; they see in him only one thing—the authority God has entrusted to him by putting him where he is. They never allow themselves to examine and judge the orders they are given; they leave that examination and judgment to the superior himself, and all they think about is obeying. Being full of such maxims, everything that comes to them from the superior looks good to them, and they are never tempted to complain.

Restless spirits, on the contrary—those who are lacking in virtue—easily complain, are discouraged by trifles, and take offense at a word or gesture of the superior. Since all they see in him is just another man, they find him full of defects and complain of all sorts of things. They moan and lament, sometimes that the superior is too young and because in their opinion he lacks prudence, administrative ability and concern; sometimes that he is old, and therefore difficult, too absolutist, too abrupt, and does not pay sufficient attention to the remarks people make to him. They complain about a permission they were refused, or because they were obliged to observe the Rule, because they were reprimanded for their defects, etc. How unfortunate is the superior who has subjects without virtue or with bad spirit! How happy he is, on the other hand, when he has holy religious to guide!

8. The saints never complain about their confrères, nor about the people with whom they live. In their dealings with their neighbor they always keep in mind the words of St. Paul, «You should be clothed with sincere compassion...Bear with one another» (Col 3:12). So they are full of goodness towards everyone; their heart produces only sentiments of compassion, indulgence and pity for their neighbors' misfortunes; they never let suspicions, rash judgments, envy, or jealousy to enter their mind or heart. They put up with their neighbor's defects without murmuring or complaint and help him to correct himself of them by their good example, their charitable advice and their prayers. They put up with his character, no matter how difficult it may be, and never let anyone even suspect how much they have to suffer in order to give way as they do and make themselves all things to everyone.

They put up with their neighbor's physical infirmities, and give him all the service his illness requires, without showing any repugnance. They put up with his faults, his bad manners, his impatience and his ingratitude, hiding all that and responding only with attention and charity at every moment. They bear their neighbor's burden, that is, his task, helping him to fulfill it; his pains and afflictions, sharing in them and alleviating them, etc. And far from complaining about their neighbor, they try to please him in every permissible way; they sacrifice their own tastes, their sleep, even their health to be useful or even simply pleasant to him.

Men with a bad character and little virtue are very different. All they see are their neighbor's defects; they always find something in him to blame, censure and criticize. A word, an oversight, the least little thing angers them, upsets them, and leads to an outburst of complaints. They want everyone else to be perfect, and they do not know how to forgive, even though they themselves are full of defects and need the indulgence of everyone else.

9. Saints never complain about their enemies and persecutors; they take revenge only by doing good. St. Catherine spent a long time caring for a woman who had smeared her reputation and who had fallen ill. St. Ajust sold his possessions and even his clothing, to relieve the misery of one of his greatest enemies. St. Ambrose provided a pension for a man who had wanted to assassinate him. St. Sabinus cured the tyrant who had just cut off his hand. St. Joan prayed continually for her enemies, so much so that people said, «If you want a large share of her prayers, all you have to do is mistreat her.»

«When certain people speak ill of me, I feel my love for them increasing,» St. Teresa used to say. That is how the saints act: they give back good for evil, they put up with everything and never complain. Their example condemns those bitter souls who shred the reputations of those against whom they have some complaint; who for months on end avoid anyone who said a harsh word to them or did something which annoyed them; who never forgive a wrong or an injury, but get revenge sooner or later, whenever they have a chance.

10. The saints never complain about their living conditions or the way they are treated. Since they seize every occasion they can find to mortify themselves, they express satisfaction with whatever kind of food is set before them, with whatever room they are assigned, with whatever furniture and clothing they are given. «Sensual men,» says one spiritual writer, «feed their bad spirit in the dining room, whereas the saints feed the spirit of mortification there, with great merit for heaven. To the saints, everything is good, and far from complaining, they want and seek everywhere whatever is worst and most painful.»

11. The saints never complain about their illnesses. With Job, they say, «God gave me health, God has taken it away, blessed be his holy name!» Like St. Paul, they exclaim, «Power is made perfect in infirmity.» Like St. Augustine, they tell God, «Cut and burn me in this life, but spare me in eternity.»

«Illness,» says St. Vincent de Paul, «is not an evil to be feared, but a very effective way for us to sanctify ourselves. To complain when God sends it our way is to complain about the good he is doing us.» The saints understood that maxim, and far from complaining about their illnesses, they thanked God for them. St. Lidwina spent thirty-eight years lying on a bed of boards, covered with sores and filled with pain, but she never complained. St. Clare was sick for twenty-eight years, without letting a single groan escape her lips. St. Theodore had a large sore on his body his whole life, and he said that God had given it to him so that he would thank him for it every day. «Sisters,» St. Teresa used to say to her nuns, «know how to put up with your infirmities without letting the whole world know about it.» She herself suffered great pains for forty years and never complained.

When men with little intelligence or virtue are ill, or when they suffer from some infirmity, instead of imitating the saints, all they know how to do is complain, fill themselves with medicine and go to bed. It is a waste of time to talk to them about their duties of state, their work, the Rule; all they can think about is their own little selves, and they think anything and everything is permitted when it is a question of easing their pain and getting better.

12. Saints never complain about their temptations or the trials through which God makes them pass, because they know that we need temptations to strengthen our virtue and to earn us merit. When they are tempted, instead of complaining, saints do three things:

a. They watch over themselves to avoid danger and they carefully fight the temptation with some act of virtue, but especially with contempt.

b. They keep themselves in good humor, holy joy and confidence in God.

c. They ask God every day for the grace never to offend him.

One of the most dangerous snares of the devil, into which weak souls often fall, is to be too afraid of temptation, to become worried and discouraged if temptations are strong and frequent. Don't let yourselves be caught in this snare, because a discouraged soul is already half-beaten. Imitate the saints, and then temptation will be for you a means of sanctification and an occasion to show God your fidelity.

13. Finally, saints never complain even about their defects, but they work ceaselessly to correct them. Their normal disposition is contentment and holy joy. But where do they get that gentle contentment and spiritual gaiety which can be seen on their faces? It springs from the holy life they lead, for a holy and pious life always has joy as its reward. The supernatural joy of virtuous souls is rooted in their good conscience. «What could be richer,» says St. Bernard, «what could be sweeter to the heart, what could be more reassuring than a good conscience!» It rejoices in the thought of heaven and the reward awaiting it. «The glory waiting for me is so great,» said St. Francis of Assisi, «that all my sufferings make me happy.»

Holy joy and contentment in the service of God are a major proof of solid virtue and sanctity, and St. Bonaventure did not hesitate to say that spiritual joy is a certain sign that sanctifying grace dwells in a soul. Dissatisfaction, irritation, complaints, and sadness, on the other hand, are a bad sign. When you see someone afflicted with that spiritual malady, pity him and pray for him, for he really needs it.

CHAPTER TWENTY-TWO

THE GREAT TEMPTATION

In an instruction on temptations and the snares the devil spreads for us to destroy our souls, Father Champagnat told the brothers, «Our life is a constant combat; every passion, vice and devil are unleashed against us. But there are three kinds of temptations that I especially want to point out to you, because they are the most common ones, and the main ones the devil uses to seduce and ruin souls.

«The first are temptations against purity, which I call dangerous temptations. The second are temptations against our vocation, which St. Ignatius calls bad temptations. The third are temptations against Our Lord, which should be called great temptations.»

I.

Temptation against purity is a very dangerous temptation, because it dwells within us, because it enters our soul through all our senses, because it easily upsets our faculties, over-stimulates our imagination, disturbs our reasoning processes, weakens our will, softens our heart and thus exposes us to the greatest danger of offending God. In addition, this temptation is the longest one; it is with us all our life, at every time and place, and it takes only an instant to consent to it, that is, to commit a serious sin.

II.

Temptation against our vocation is rightly called a bad temptation, when it is fed and maintained by a professed religious, because:

1. It is proof of an inconstant, tepid soul which has abused grace.

2. It indicates a dissatisfied religious who has lost his filial spirit and who sows bad spirit in the community.

3. It undermines piety and the whole process of striving for perfection; anyone who is not totally settled in his vocation, who is thinking about leaving it, can no longer do anything worthwhile in religious life.

4. It threatens his entire salvation and risks his entire spiritual fortune on a single play, just as some poorly-advised rich people risk and tie up their whole fortune in a single stock-market deal. In point of fact, to abandon one's vocation is to leave aside all the great means of salvation and perfection which God has given us; it is to throw oneself into the midst of the greatest danger of losing one's soul; it is to make oneself guilty of extreme ingratitude.

5. It interferes with the works of God and endangers them. Here is a brother whom God has called to religious life to give instruction and Christian education to a great number of children who were until then deprived of those benefits; if this brother is unfaithful to his vocation, if he leaves or changes it, what will become of those children whose salvation may depend on the good principles which he had the grace and the mission to impart to them? It was exactly this thought which made St. Paul say, «Woe unto me if I do not preach the gospel!» (*1 Cor* 9:16), and St. Francis Xavier: «I don't think I could have avoided hell if I had refused to go preach the gospel in Japan.»

God has always and everywhere wanted stability. That is why Jews are circumcised, Christians baptized, priests ordained, religious professed and lay people married—all lifetime commitments. Anyone who does not understand this arrangement of Providence, is not made for solid virtue and will sow nothing but disorder everywhere.

III.

The temptation which leads us to distance ourselves from Our Lord and to deprive ourselves of communion and of the Mass, is aptly termed the great temptation; for since Jesus Christ is our light, our strength, our life, our savior, our all, this temptation, by separating us from him, makes all that he has done for us useless, and destroys the work of our salvation down to its very foundations.

1. This temptation was born in heaven. St. Basil, St. Cyprian, St. Denis, Suarez and a host of theologians teach that after creating the angels, God told them about the incarnation of his Son, and commanded them to submit themselves to him and to adore him. Lucifer, being jealous that the Son of God was taking a human nature, and not being able to accept that a man was placed over him, refused to submit and revolted against God, involving a crowd of angels in his fall.

Condemned to hell for his disobedience and pride, Lucifer swore to wage perpetual war against Jesus Christ and to undermine the effects of his incarnation, by turning men away from him, and by preventing them from profiting by the redemption he was preparing for them. From that moment, he undertook the conceited project of subjecting all men to his tyranny. Losing no time, he attacked Adam as soon as he had been created and made him his slave. Puffed up by this major success, he openly declared himself God's rival and wanted to have himself adored in God's place.

To reach that goal, he spoiled all God's works, Tertullian tells us, and taught men to corrupt the use of them. He involved everything in idolatry: the stars, the elements, the plants, the animals, so that when Jesus Christ came into the world, the universe was one vast temple full of idols, and according to Bossuet's expression, «Everything was God except God himself.» So it was that for four thousand years, the devil worked to banish knowledge of God from the earth, to distance men from the redeemer they had been promised, and to plunge them into all sorts of crimes. After the death of the Savior, for three hundred years he armed every king and all the powers of the earth against Christianity, in an attempt to suffocate it and to drown it in the blood of martyrs.

2. Since the persecutions only strengthened the Church and spread the knowledge of Jesus Christ, the devil raised up heretics to distort the mysteries of the incarnation and redemption, which are the salvation of the world.

a. Arius, by denying the divinity of the Word, destroyed at one blow the mysteries of the Holy Trinity, the Incarnation and the Redemption; for if Jesus Christ was only a man, he could not have bought us back.

b. Nestorius wanted two persons in Jesus Christ, and did not accept that the Son of God became man, was born of the Blessed Virgin, suffered and died for the redemption of the human race.

c. Eutyches, another heresiarch, taught the contrary of Nestorius; in other words, he upheld the idea that after the incarnation, the human nature had been absorbed by the divinity, and that consequently there was only one nature in Jesus Christ. That heresy overturned the whole mystery of our Redemption. In fact, according to his doctrine, one would have to either deny the passion and death of Jesus Christ, or say that the divinity had suffered and died, which is blasphemy. If the divinity had absorbed his human nature, Christ could not have been our redeemer, our model, or the high priest of the New Testament, for being only God, he could not have prayed, suffered and humbled himself.

d. the Monothelites denied that there were two wills in Jesus Christ; this also destroyed the mystery of our redemption; for without a human will, Jesus Christ could not have obeyed, merited, prayed nor made satisfaction for us.

e. Pelagius denied original sin and our need of grace in order to avoid sin and do good, from whence it flows that redemption by Jesus Christ was valueless.

In all these heresies, and in a long list of others, the devil had no other aim but to undermine the mysteries of the incarnation and redemption, and thus destroy humanity by depriving us of the grace and merits of Jesus Christ.

f. Everything which reminds us of Jesus Christ or his mysteries, everything which leads us to him, horrifies Satan. That is why he raised up iconoclasts to make war on the crucifix and on all the images of the Savior, to break them, burn them, or throw them into the mud.

g. Later on he raised up Berengarius, Luther, Calvin and their disciples, to attack the sacraments, especially penance and the Eucharist, which are for us two great sources of grace and the great means of our salvation.

In a dismal vision, Satan told Luther that he hated and absolutely detested the holy Mass; he urged him to suppress it and to work to banish it from the earth.

h. Next came the Jansenists, who did not accept that Jesus Christ died for all, and who demanded such perfect dispositions for Communion that it was abandoned. The members of this sect believed they were doing well by distancing themselves from it and depriving themselves of it for years at a time and even for their entire lives.

i. The philosophy of the 18th century was the detestable fruit of all these heresies. A crowd of impious persons with depraved morals and superficial minds, and ignorant of the things of God, dared to say that Jesus Christ was a man like us, and

Voltaire carried that madness to the point of calling him a vile impostor.

j. It is fitting to add to this long list of opponents of Our Lord the [French] Revolution with its bloody persecutions, with the proscription of priests and of Catholic worship, and the impious substitution of worship of the goddess of Reason, on the altars from which Our Lord Jesus Christ had been banished.

There you have a summary of Satan's efforts through successive centuries, to ruin Jesus Christ's work of redemption and to deprive the world of it. But his fury and wickedness did not end there; not satisfied with fighting against the work of the redemption in general, he fights it in each individual, and there is no effort he does not make to separate each of us from Jesus Christ, deprive us of Holy Mass and distance us from holy communion. The means he most commonly uses to do so are:

a. The abuse and profanation of the sacraments. How sad is the fate of those who, out of shame, conceal their sins in confession, or who, for lack of contrition, instead of receiving grace and pardon, add a new crime to their first faults! The sacrilegious person imitates Judas and crucifies Jesus Christ over again. «Those who profane Our Lord reigning in heaven,» says St. Augustine, «sin more grievously than those who crucified him while he was on earth.»

Good God! What a crime it is to change redemption into perdition, communion into poison, life into an instrument of death! And is this evil really rare? Alas, the devil's hatred for the sacraments is so great, and his efforts to seduce souls are so constant, that he catches an infinite number of persons in that snare.

b. Temptations and fear of sacrilege. Why is it that pious souls are so violently tempted on the eve of receiving communion? It is solely in order to distance them from the bread of life that the devil pursues them with so much fury. As soon as he has succeeded in upsetting them, throwing them into doubt as to whether or not they have consented, as soon as he has made them resolve not to go to communion, he withdraws and leaves them in peace. He has certainly just won a beautiful victory, and he rejoices in it, because he knows from long experience that he easily makes those who deprive themselves of this divine nourishment fall into mortal sin. What a loss it is for a soul to lose communion! How many religious grow up in their defects, live in tepidity, and have little love for Jesus Christ, because they do not know the gift of God and easily withdraw from communion! How many young brothers succumb to temptation and continue the chain of their bad habits, because they abandon confession and do not frequent the holy table!

The Eucharist is a supremely effective weapon for winning the victory over temptations; it is a remedy which preserves us from serious faults, and which purifies us from venial sins. This sacrament is like a stream of fresh water, which extinguishes the fire of the passions. Often the devil does not even dare to tempt souls he sees marked with the blood of Jesus Christ. «How is it,» St. Bernard asked his religious, «that you control your passions, that you feel the fires of concupiscence less, that you preserve yourselves from sin, and that you live like angels in mortal bodies? To what do you owe this great benefit? To Jesus Christ, whom you receive so often in communion.»

c. Scruples. Good souls cruelly tortured by this evil are not rare. They are dissatisfied with their confessions and their troubled conscience does not give them a moment's rest. What is the main cause of that condition? The devil. And why does he torture these souls so? To distance them from communion, to prevent them from preparing for it and to diminish the effects and graces they could draw from it. In fact, instead of letting themselves enjoy the holy desire for communion and feelings of humility, confidence and love, they become agitated and go into endless examinations of conscience, to see whether they are not in the state of sin. The closer the moment of communion approaches, the more their heart contracts, the more their fears increase. Their whole preparation consists in fear and trembling. Communion, which should be their joy and their treasure, is a torture for them, and leaves them poor, because they are not in the right dispositions for receiving the graces that Jesus Christ wants to give them, and they do not have the good will to profit from his gifts.

d. Work. There are Christians, and even religious, who, urged on by the devil and under the pretext of pressing business, studies, manual work or even works of zeal, easily miss Holy Mass and communion. «I don't have time to go to Mass or to prepare for communion,» they say; or else, «What does one Mass more or less matter?» What a temptation! What faulty reasoning! And what sad behavior!

You don't have time to go to Mass?! What do you have to do that's more important than carrying out the exercises of piety prescribed by your rule? Your most essential task is to pray, to bless God and to sanctify yourself. Have you forgotten that you became a religious in order to have the happiness of attending Holy Mass every day? «Before all else,» St. Jane Frances de Chantal wrote to a mistress of novices, «your first and primary concern should be to teach your novices to perform as perfectly as possible the exercise of Holy Mass and communion, because these actions are the most important ones we can perform. Remind them often that God has called them to religious life so that they could piously attend Mass every day, and receive communion frequently and fervently.»

You don't have time?! Are you unaware that «piety is useful for everything,» that it teaches us to do things well and gives us success in our work?

A solidly pious religious accomplishes more, all by himself, than four tepid ones together, because God gives him knowledge about things and blesses everything that passes through his hands.

It is when we are very busy that we must be more faithful to our exercises of piety and our communions, and attend Holy Mass more piously every morning, in order to obtain from God the light, strength, graces and dedication we need in such cases to fulfill all our obligations. Anyone who does not understand this truth, no matter how talented he may be, will have only limited success and will never be able to do great things.

e. Aversion, tepidity, lack of piety. Let's go back to those ill-advised and not very devout religious who say things like, «What does one Mass more or less matter? I don't go to communion because I don't feel any devotion, because I don't get anything out of it,» and so forth. You say, «One Mass more or less doesn't matter»! That's the way the devil speaks.

Do you know what the Mass is, you who talk that way? The Mass is the act which gives God the greatest honor which can be given him; it is the work which procures the most powerful assistance for the souls in purgatory; it is the key which opens to humanity the treasure of all the merits and graces of Jesus Christ; one single Mass heard with suitable dispositions would be more than enough to pay all our debts. There is no exercise of piety which the devil fears more than Holy Mass, because this divine sacrifice destroys the strength of hell, and is for us the source of every good. Oh, what immense wealth is contained in the holy sacrifice of the Mass!

«Understand this truth well,» says St. Bernard, «by hearing one single Mass piously, we can merit more than someone who would dedicate an entire fortune to relieving the misery of the poor, more than one who would go on pilgrimage to the end of the world, who would visit the sanctuaries of the Mother of God, the Holy Land, Rome and Loreto, with the greatest devotion.»

«The reason he said that,» says the Angelic Doctor, «is that one single sacrifice of the Mass contains all the graces and treasures which the Son of God has showered so abundantly on the holy Church by the sacrifice of the cross.» The first Christians risked martyrdom to attend Holy Mass; they bribed the guards and so were able to enter the prisons and dungeons where the holy sacrifice was celebrated; and would a religious dislike being disturbed, leaving off his study, a mere nothing, to go to Mass? Is that what it means to have faith? «I would prefer,» said one very good Christian, «to lose the whole world, if I owned it, rather than lose a single Mass; for the greatest things we can do on earth is to attend Holy Mass. What consolation I feel when I have attended Mass! I have offered God a sacrifice of infinite value, I have glorified and thanked him infinitely, and I have offered a sum which can pay all my debts. So I have accomplished more by this one action than by all the other actions of my entire life.»

You also say, «I miss communions because I don't feel any devotion and I'm too imperfect»! «A religious who talks like that, that is, who misses communion because he feels tepid or cold,» says St. Norbert, «is like a man who says, 'I don't go near the fire, because I'm cold,' or 'I don't go to doctors or take medicine, because I'm sick.' Is that the way a reasonable person acts?»

«In giving us his body and blood, Jesus Christ gives us fire to eat and drink,» says St. Ephrem in a metaphoric expression which shows us that the specific power of the Eucharist is to set us on fire with divine love, to give us the piety and virtues we lack. Anyone who desires to get out of tepidity and be cured of his spiritual illnesses, should not refuse this sacred ointment. The mere thought: «This morning I received communion,» or «I'm going to receive communion tomorrow,» makes one feel inclined to do good, held back from the slippery slope of evil, and filled with all sorts of good sentiments.

To miss communion because one can reproach oneself with neglecting a few points means adding a new fault to the ones one has already committed, and wanting to continue to live in negligence and tepidity, during that particular day and for the rest of one's life.

«But I don't get anything out of communion!» Who told you that you're not getting anything out of communion? The devil, and he speaks to you like that because he sees better than you the good your communions do you. He knows that communion strengthens you in temptation and preserves you from mortal sin; he knows that communion brings you the grace of perseverance in your vocation, the graces of light and strength to fulfill your assignment properly. In order to dry up the source of grace, he treacherously suggests that, «You're not getting anything out of communion; you'd be better off if you let it go.»

Beware! If you follow that diabolical advice, you will be lost. One day, St. Gregory was saying Mass for a man who had willed some money for that purpose, and who had been dead for eighty years. When he came to the words, «Eternal rest grant to him, O Lord, and let perpetual light shine upon him,» he heard a voice saying, «I will never see that light!» «Why is that?» the saint asked. «I was damned because I missed one communion, then the devil tempted me, and I wasn't strong enough to resist because I had deprived myself of the body of Jesus Christ. So I fell into sin and was damned.»

How many Christians, how many religious, lost their fervor and the spirit of their vocation, fell into tepidity and then into mortal sin, remained there and were finally damned because they had neglected confession and missed communion! To separate souls from Jesus Christ, distance them from the sacraments and deprive them of the Mass, will infallibly cause their damnation. The devil knows that. So he does all he can and uses all his tricks to accomplish his perverse ends, to snatch souls from Jesus Christ the Redeemer and cause their eternal loss. That is why the temptation against Our Lord is the greatest, the one Satan uses most to seduce souls and destroy in them the effects of the Redemption.

CHAPTER TWENTY-THREE

THE FIVE SAYINGS OF A WISE OLD MAN, OR THE SEASONS OF RELIGIOUS LIFE

I. The First Season: Formation

From fifteen to twenty: the age of docility. During this period, the young man is like soft wax which readily takes every impression, every shape. He does not reflect on his own, or reflects very little; he simply believes firmly whatever he is told. It is the time when he most needs direction and assiduous care; but also when he is most easily led, because his faith and confidence in his superiors are usually still intact. Woe to every superior who because of his thoughtless behavior makes his subject lose those attitudes, which are such a precious support for his virtue!

From fifteen to twenty, the novice studies his vocation in a practical manner and serves his apprenticeship in the virtues of his state and in the various tasks which are entrusted to him. By trying them out this way, he sees whether the lifestyle and ministries of the Institute suit him. The superiors can also decide if he is suited for the Institute and capable of fulfilling its aims.

During this time of probation, the novice should be pruned, shaped, molded; that is, it is necessary to protect and form his heart and to lay within it the foundations of fervent piety and solid virtue; to enlighten and instruct his conscience and give him an extreme horror of sin; to bend, soften and fortify his will, and subject it to obedience and regularity, which are essential virtues for the religious state; to polish, sweeten, and if need be, reform, his character, and to judge whether it is suited for community life.

Finally, one must work on the novice until he has been molded, so to speak, to the spirit of the Institute.

The years between fifteen and twenty are for the novice a time of great combats and temptations. There are four temptations of youth, in fighting which he particularly needs to be directed and supported.

1. The first temptation of youth: the temptation against purity. To fight it, the young brother needs great openness of heart and great docility. We lay so much stress on this means because it includes all the others and puts them into practice.

The impure vice grows only in the shadows and in darkness. Like a cancer, it eats away the heart which is not frank and which walks alone. It is especially at such a man that the curse of the Holy Spirit is directed: «Woe to him that is alone» (*Eccles* 4:10). The young brother who is struggling against the impure demon must be treated with extreme kindness; he needs to be constantly encouraged, affirmed, and strengthened. Prayer, sincere and frequent confession, fervent communion, keeping constantly busy, humility, moderation in eating and drinking, plus some voluntary penances, are the remedies which will bring him victory, if he is placed in a situation in which he can readily use them.

2. The second temptation of youth: distaste for prayer. This temptation, Fr. Champagnat tells us, is very common among young people between sixteen and twenty. This is the most critical period of one's life, the time when our senses have the greatest influence on our soul, when the passions begin to make themselves felt and to wage against us that cruel war which ends only when life ends. During this period, the soul is drawn on the one hand to the attraction of sensual pleasures, weighed down on the other under the load of its own misery, and exhausted by the combats it has to maintain. Consequently, it is not interested in anything. The holiest things make no impression on it; the most frightening truths can barely arouse it from its torpor and put the

brakes on its evil inclinations. Nearly every man pays a sad tribute to this age, and even those who are naturally good and pious, feel very little of the effects of grace and piety. Nothing is more necessary and advantageous to a young man in this condition than wise and fatherly direction. This exterior means is the best way to counterbalance the tyranny of his senses; it does for him what a trellis does for a grapevine and stakes for a still-weak tree.

A young brother must also be placed in healthy air, in other words, in good surroundings, where piety reigns, where he finds confrères who give him good example and good spirit, and make his life happy; who control his reading and keep away from him the novels which can only give him frivolous tastes and a superficial mind; who make him read the lives of the saints and books which will give him esteem and love for his holy state, and sentiments of piety and virtue.

He must often be brought back to the fundamental principles and great truths of religion, so as to give sure rules to his mind, a brake to his conscience, noble and pure ideas to his heart, strength and supernatural motives to his will, and by means of all of these, a solid foundation to his virtue.

One must dedicate oneself to inspiring in him great love of Our Lord and true devotion to the Blessed Virgin, and to suggesting to him practices which will nourish and develop those precious devotions, and lead him to make frequent novenas.

He must often be reminded not to remain idle during meditation, and be obliged to keep busy reflecting and praying, even vocally, to keep himself in the presence of God, or at least to read a good book which has been selected for him.

He must often be urged to remain faithful to grace and to little things. There are three profound reasons for that, which cannot be repeated often enough to young religious.

The first is that fidelity to grace and to little things preserves us from venial sin, which is the most common destroyer of piety.

The second is that the little victories the young brother wins over himself in order to follow the Rule, to be faithful to grace and avoid little faults, prepare him for major combats and great acts of virtue, and preserve him from mortal sin, which is death to the soul, to one's vocation, and to piety.

The third is that every act of virtue, no matter how small, earns us new graces. He who thus remains faithful in the smallest duties, in the least practices of obligation or counsel, thereby obtains piety, fervor and a deep sharing in the spirit of Jesus Christ; he grows in virtue like the tree planted near running water.

3. The third temptation of youth: difficulties in one's assignment. Apprenticeship is difficult in every state of life, and is painful for everyone. It is especially difficult for young brothers, because manual work and teaching are difficult tasks which require a great deal of intelligence and devotedness.

Consequently it is necessary to entrust novices to directors with wide experience, who are really capable of forming them. First of all, their assignment, whether classroom or kitchen, must be proportioned to the young brother's intelligence, capabilities, and physical strength. It is important for the brother director to supervise him in every detail of his conduct, show himself to be kind, teach him how to do things, and be satisfied with his good will if he does not have the aptitude to do them perfectly.

Moreover, one must know how to wait, because there are subjects who develop slowly, who for some time obtain only very average results, but who, if they are followed up and formed with care and great patience, eventually become very capable men, very good teachers, and excellent religious.

4. The fourth temptation of youth: discouragement. This is one of the most common temptations; few young people are exempt from it. The devil of discouragement is very shrewd; he slips adroitly into the soul and gets into all its faculties. He takes all sorts of forms: vice, virtue, even humility, because most of the time we become discouraged under the pretext of our lack of

ability. Discouragement is a very dangerous temptation; it does to the soul what paralysis does to the body; it weakens all its faculties and makes it impossible to fight temptations. It engenders exaggerated fear, sadness, disgust, boredom, all of which are illnesses which weaken and kill piety, holy joy, confidence in God and filial spirit. Discouragement was the temptation of Judas and of every reprobate; that is why Fr. Caracciolo, the renowned Italian theologian, said that it is the cause of the damnation of all reprobates, and that no one would be damned if there were no discouragement. So one should neglect [everything] in order to put young brothers on guard against this sickness of the soul. To do that, one must make them understand clearly that:

a. Life is a constant battle, so they should expect trials and temptations.

b. The greatest saints were the most tempted and tested in every way.

c. Temptation, in God's merciful plans, is for us a means of perfection, an exercise of virtue, an occasion for gaining merit, and not an obstacle to our salvation.

d. It is natural for us to fall, and for God to pardon us and lift us up again. Consequently, our faults should not surprise us, still less discourage us, but rather lead us to throw ourselves with confidence into God's arms.

e. Our defects and even our faults can turn to our advantage by forcing us to watch over ourselves, to pray, to humble ourselves and to count only on God.

f. The steadfast person who does not become discouraged, will always manage to be skillful in his profession, carry out his ministry well and acquire solid virtues.

We must seize every opportunity which presents itself to make these principles penetrate the minds and hearts of the young brothers, to remind them of them on every occasion, to constantly strengthen their faculties, to revive their morale and renew their confidence in God. He who does not know how to distribute the bread of encouragement abundantly and in timely fashion is not fit to lead young novices, and he can easily become the cause of their downfall.

II. The Second Season: Settling In

Between the ages of twenty and thirty, a religious becomes settled in his vocation and binds himself to it by perpetual vows. So anyone who attempts to bargain at that time of life is lacking in courage, generosity and fidelity to grace, which is a very dangerous fault, because of its unpleasant consequences. He who indulges in long self-examinations, who continues to float around undecided, is risking his entire life and ruining his whole future.

The examination and testing of one's vocation must be prudent, but not dragged out too long; such slowness is not necessary; it usually inhibits the divine call and remains subject to great dangers, as Suarez tells us. To postpone one's profession beyond the usual time of probation, out of frivolous pretexts and exaggerated fear, goes against wisdom, scripture, the Fathers of the Church, and right reason.[1] On the contrary, it is wise and advantageous to give oneself early to God and to bind oneself to one's vocation after suitable trials. The man to whom Jesus Christ said, «If you will be perfect, go sell what you have, and give to the poor, and you shall have treasure in heaven; and come, follow me» (*Mt* 19:21) was only an adolescent, according to the sacred text.

---

[1] At the time when these lines were written, our Constitutions, which were still in an experimental stage, did not specify the time for perpetual profession. This sometimes led to deplorably long delays by some brothers lacking in generosity. The reflections in this section are aimed specifically at that abuse, which was fortunately suppressed by the Constitutions approved by the Holy See in 1903.

«The devil,» says St. John Chrysostom, «is the great enemy of religious life, so he uses all his deceits to make those called to that holy state lose their vocation; and when he cannot gain an advantage over them, he seeks to at least persuade them to put off carrying out their plans, and he thinks he has really accomplished something if he can delay their entrance into religious life or their profession by even a day. And how many times has this enemy of salvation succeeded, through such delays, in causing good vocations to be lost and entire lives to be ruined!»

«We see so many people,» St. Bernard wrote, «whom the false wisdom of the world has seduced, and in whom all the good intentions heaven had given them have been extinguished. 'Don't be hasty,' it told them, 'take a long time to think about it, look it over again, for you are planning something great; test yourself, talk to your friends, be careful, reflect again and again. You are going to take a step you may later regret.'

«That is earthly and carnal wisdom, a wisdom which is almost madness. That kind of wisdom is the enemy of God and of your best interests. It gives birth to tepidity and infidelity to grace; it provokes God to vomit you out of his mouth and to alienate you from his heart. How many vocations it has caused to be lost! How many good young people has it not led astray and hurled down to the bottom of hell!»

Between twenty and thirty is the time to mature and develop one's judgment, to raise one's mind and to broaden it to the fullest possible extent. If, during this period, the young man is left to himself, if he follows his own whims, if he fears direction and avoids it, he will always be a narrow-minded and incomplete person.

«Human vision,» said Fr. Champagnat, «no matter how perfect it may be, is always weak and very limited. Eyeglasses and optical instruments extend it and carry it to the depths of space. In the same way, no matter how enlightened and intelligent a brother may be, if he is left to himself and his own weak reason, his judgment will never develop or he will take the wrong road.»

During this season of life, between twenty and thirty, a young man faces three new temptations.

1. The first temptation inherent in this season is to doubt whether one has been called, and to look back after having put one's hand to the plow. The young man turns in on himself, thinks about his past life, begins to doubt his vocation; he is tempted to change his career, under the pretext that he entered and stayed in religious life without really knowing what he was doing. This is false reasoning, which only our passions and the devil can inspire in us.

Since a child of fourteen or fifteen is incapable of long and deep reflection, God does not speak to his intelligence and his reason, but to his heart. He makes that heart docile to the attractions of grace, to the advice of a wise director, a father, a mother, a friend; he gives him a taste for piety, for religious life, and the grace to follow the attraction which beckons to him. This way of calling people into religious life is full of mercy, because it preserves the child from an infinite number of faults, and puts him in a safe place away from the dangers of the world, where his virtue would have been sadly shipwrecked. It is all the more sure, because self will and human motives had nothing to do with it. To despise that special grace, to be unfaithful to that call, which one could term divine, to fail to recognize the hand of God, his protection, his merciful designs, in such a providential action, is to be guilty of great ingratitude.

2. The second temptation of this season is presumption. The young man becomes outspoken, he has a lot of confidence in himself, he relies too much on his own abilities; he wants to be consulted about decisions made about him, and about a thousand things which are none of his business; the monosyllable «I» is always in his mouth; always and everywhere, there are only «I's.»

That is pride, naked self-love—a sad defect which spoils the most beautiful personalities if it is not resisted and corrected.

3. The third, which flows from the second, is that the young man believes he can guide himself, easily ignores the directions of his superiors and follows his own will. This temptation puts him at risk of committing serious faults and rushing along wrong roads which will lead him to the abyss.

Between twenty and thirty, the young man needs just as much direction as between fifteen and twenty. Woe to him if he abandons this unique method of forming his judgment and placing himself solidly on the road to virtue and good habits!

III. The Third Season: Becoming Set in One's Ways

By the time he reaches thirty, a man is set in his ways; his tastes and habits have been formed—whatever way he has let them take root and grow in his faculties, so they will be for the rest of his life. There may be some slight changes, but he will remain fundamentally the same. If by then he is not solidly grounded in virtue, it is very much to be feared that he will never be; if by then he has the habit of some vice or other, he will have it all his life.

Has anyone ever seen a religious who has spent ten to fifteen years being habitually unfaithful to the rule, suddenly begin to love it and to become a model of regularity after thirty? Hardly ever.

Have you ever seen a religious who drags along in tepidity between twenty and thirty, disliking his exercises of piety, and easily omitting them without a good reason, become solidly pious and fervent after that age? How rare it is!

Have you ever seen a religious with a broad conscience, who does not pay attention to little things, who does not fear venial sin and commits it easily and without remorse, and who lets habits of these sorts of faults grow in his soul between twenty and thirty, later become faithful to grace, punctual in observing the Rule, and acquire a delicate and timorous conscience? That hardly ever happens.

Have you ever seen a religious who is shaky in his vocation, or who examines it over and over, who remains up in the air and undecided between twenty and thirty without becoming really set in his vocation, later change his inconstant ways and become settled once and for all in God's service and in his holy state? Don't count on it. A religious who has not sunk roots between twenty and thirty will never do so. Even if he finally makes profession, don't be totally reassured; he will always leave a door open, and hang on to some second thoughts, and the least opportunity will be enough to knock him over and throw him back into the world. «Such men,» Father Champagnat used to say, «belong to the race of whom the Holy Spirit speaks in Ecclesiasticus, when he says, 'A fool is changed like the moon' (Sir 27:11). They limp along through life and don't know how to settle into anything.»

Have you ever seen a religious play with serpents, allow impurity to take root in his heart, put up only a weak struggle against that shameful passion, pay tribute to it between twenty and thirty, and then correct himself and faithfully observe his vow of chastity? That religious, who likes serpents, will more or less play with them his whole life. Every year of his life will be soiled and blighted by some grave faults against the lovable virtue.

Finally, have you ever seen a religious between twenty and thirty who is subject to some passion like anger, love of wine, insubordination, or any other evil tendency, uproot it, correct it, and dominate it later in life? Never, or very rarely. When he reaches thirty, the young man is set in his ways, and he will stay that way all his life.

But perhaps you will ask, «Can't someone correct himself and be converted at any time in life?» Yes, that's true; grace is never lacking, one can be converted any time; but that still doesn't mean that such conversions aren't very rare. A vice which has become a habit between twenty and thirty, in spite of all the abundant helps we have to correct it, is one of the most difficult things to uproot and destroy. A religious who has abused grace for ten or fifteen years, is one of the most difficult people in the world to touch and convert. It needs a miracle of grace to perform such a feat and work such a change; so such conversions are as rare as miracles.

Atmospheric disorders in any season of the year (and especially in springtime) will endanger the harvest, spoil the year's fruit crop, and bring sterility and famine to a region. Likewise, disorders and disturbances in a single season of life are enough (especially if the season is youth) to spoil an entire life and make it sterile in terms of virtue. The religious who does not become virtuous between twenty and thirty, but lets himself slip into bad habits, is ruining his entire life; he will never be anything but the caricature of a religious.

«When we abuse grace by neglecting little things,» says St. Gregory, «we are unconsciously seduced and fall into big ones without realizing it.»

Then we sin without remorse; and once we reach that degree of perversity where we sin without remorse, there is no longer any sure cure. «The soul,» says St. John Chrysostom, «once it has been corrupted and degraded by an evil habit, has an incurable illness; it will never recover, no matter what remedies God may offer it. A sin which has become a habit is almost identified with the person; the sinner has become the sin; hence the extreme difficulty he experiences in trying to be converted. Scripture uses three frightening comparisons to express the misfortune of a person in such a state: «He put on cursing like a garment, and it went like water into his entrails, and like oil into his bones» (*Ps* 108:18).

Cursing is like a cloak to the habitual sinner, because it entirely surrounds him; it controls all his actions and words; it enters his interior like water, and there corrupts his thoughts and intentions; and finally, it soaks like oil into his bones, that is, his soul, his heart, his mind, all his faculties, to ruin and annihilate them.

Do young brothers understand that, when they say, «There's no need to rush to give myself to God and make commitments to him. We'll have plenty of time later to correct our defects, combat our passions, and follow the Rule»? Oh, you sadly mistaken men, you are talking like madmen! Have you forgotten these words of the Holy Spirit: «A young man according to his way, even when he is old he will not depart from it» (*Prov* 22:6)? And these: «His bones shall be filled with the vices of his youth, and they shall sleep with him in the dust» (*Job* 20:11)? That's what awaits you; that's what you're going to become later on.

IV. The Fourth Season: Lack of Results and Dissatisfaction or a Maximum of Aptitude and Effort

When he reaches forty, a religious is unhappy and dissatisfied if he has failed to take care of his soul, and if he is not solidly virtuous. Would you like to know why he is discontented and suffering interior pains?

1. Looking back over his past frightens him and makes him very bitter. He sees clearly that he has been unfaithful to grace, that he has misused God's gifts, and that he has not profited by the great means of salvation and perfection which were lavished on him. After twenty years of community, he sees that he is still not virtuous; after so many confessions, communions, prayers, retreats, and spiritual reading, he still has the same defects, which are still growing and becoming more deeply rooted. He senses and realizes that all these means of perfection which he has abused, have dried him up and left him full of crushing remorse and a frightful void. He trembles when he sees that he has wasted

his life on vanities, and that everything he has done was spoiled by routine and self-love, because he did it with no intention or with indirect intentions.

2. He is responsible for the present, so he is dissatisfied. With what? With everything: with his community, where he has wasted away; with his work, which has become a burden to him; with his Institute, whose spirit he has lost; with his vocation, which he no longer prizes highly; and with himself, because he knows that his sad condition is his own doing. What makes his pain and anguish even worse is the fact that he senses that God is not pleased with him, nor are his superiors or his confrères, even if there has been nothing seriously reprehensible in his exterior conduct, because he knows that he has not lived as a good religious, and has not spread the good odor of virtue and good example.

3. He is afraid of the future, from every point of view. The rule and his religious duties are his responsibility, but he no longer loves them and finds them distasteful. The yoke of Jesus Christ, which is so sweet and light for fervent souls, has become for him a crushing, insupportable burden. Everything displeases him, everything is painful for him, everything is a torture for him. The most frightful, dangerous and terrible temptations assail him; he feels strange inclinations and tendencies, which were unknown to him at the time of his great combats. There is a terrible emptiness inside him; he is becoming withdrawn from everything around him, from everything he should love, from his confrères, from his superiors, from his Institute. His heart is like tar; it adheres to creatures and is attached to what it should despise and detest. The classroom becomes unbearable for him; his residence feels like a prison; everything in community displeases him; his thoughts and tastes are all in the world.

A religious in that sad condition lives in religious life like a prisoner in his cell; like him, he looks for an opportune moment, a favorable occasion, to escape from his house, which for him is nothing more than a prison. But what will he do in the world?

One could apply to him these words of the Holy Spirit about the evil man: «He goes with a leer on his lips, winking his eye, shuffling his foot, beckoning with his finger. Deceit in his heart, always scheming evil, he sows dissension. Disaster will overtake him sharply for this, suddenly, irretrievably, his fall will come» (*Prov* 6:12).

On the contrary, between thirty and forty the good religious has made it his duty to continue to grow in solid virtue, and to learn the art of governing souls. He has carried out this formation by always remaining very closely united to his superiors, by submitting to them all the difficulties he encounters, and by faithfully following their directions. He had a practical formation, because this was the time when he filled various posts including the direction of a house. He was tried out according to his talents, at a little bit of everything of which he was judged capable. So if he showed himself to be docile and intelligent, he easily learned how to handle business matters, to lead the brothers, to direct schools and to use all his capabilities.

And since the art of governing is completely bound up with these three points: breadth, solidity and depth of intellect, goodness of heart and goodness of character, he concentrated in particular on perfecting his judgment and sanctifying his heart, so as to make it loving, generous and full of charity, to reform and polish his character so as to easily make himself all things to all, to adopt every means to be of use to his neighbor and accomplish as much good as possible. Now, when a brother who has allowed himself to be formed, pruned and directed this way by his superiors, and who has worked on himself as much as he could, reaches the age of forty, he is capable of everything pertaining to his vocation.

V. The Fifth Season: Decadence or Holiness

If a religious is not fervent, pious and truly virtuous by the time he reaches fifty, he will always be a big baby. One often sees his intellectual capacity dwindle even before that age, so that by fifty, he no longer has enough to be able to continue his ministry, and must be retired. His idleness has made him lose the knowledge he had acquired; his infidelity to grace and his neglect in nourishing his mind with holy truths have made him lose his religious spirit and religious sense; his reasoning is often worse than that of a person in the world, even and especially about spiritual things. In his opinion, the young brothers and the children in the schools aren't what they used to be; he attributes all sorts of defects to them; he finds them proud, rebellious, undisciplined, and sees no virtue in them. To listen to him, the world isn't the same either; everything has changed; not realizing that he is the only one who's changed, that is, in growing old he has lost the spirit of his holy state and a considerable part of his good sense, because he did not cultivate the faculties of his soul through study and work, or maintain the qualities of his heart by piety and virtue.

Grace and the sacraments, which should have reformed his heart, expand it, make it loving and indulgent, have left it cold, hard, self-centered and insensitive to the troubles of his neighbor. Like his mind and heart, his character has also diminished; he has become suspicious, melancholy, irritable, and hypersensitive, so that any trifle offends and upsets him, sets him on fire, makes him angry and a nuisance to everyone. The faculties of his soul continue to weaken, and he reaches a point where he no longer has enough reason and virtue to command or to obey. Man is a perfectible being, it is true; he can always improve, always grow in virtue and experience; but if instead of applying himself to doing so, a religious neglects to work at his perfection, if he does not work on himself constantly, if he abuses grace, if he follows the inclinations of nature and lets himself slip into routine and tepidity, he loses his good qualities, he extinguishes the faculties of his soul, he droops, he degrades himself, and becomes a useless creature. From then on he is a worthless creature, to put it mildly.

How different is the condition of a good religious at that age! At this same stage, the fervent religious is bearing abundant fruit of merit and holiness. Having passed the four preceding stages in piety and in the activities of a zeal regulated by obedience, the holy religious does not slow down after fifty. On the contrary, he seems to receive each day an increase of grace and to be animated with ever greater ardor for the glory of God and his personal sanctification. He advances steadily; he constantly grows in his knowledge of how to handle matters both spiritual and temporal, practical or administrative, and also in experience, in virtue, in goodness of character and in every sort of perfection.

Age and infirmities, which often overwhelm his body, never affect the good qualities of his soul. The truth which fed his spirit all during his life gives him such abundant light and gives him such height and depth of intellect that he grasps the true and the just at top speed, and distinguishes truth from error surely and promptly. Piety and the sacraments have so transformed his heart and perfected his character that goodness, indulgence, generosity, compassion and mercy have become almost natural to him. His intelligence, reason, goodness of heart and lovable character grow constantly in him with the years, in spite of the infirmities and weaknesses of human nature.

Age, work and sickness may consume his body, drain his energy and strength, and nail him to a bed of pain, but they leave his faculties intact. Until the end, his intelligence shines like a light in his sunken eyes; the goodness of his heart arouses admiration in everyone by the unalterable gentleness of his behavior, and is imprinted like a seal on everything he does. Finally, his lovable character keeps him always calm, smiling, in holy joy and makes him beloved by everyone. His supernatural and human virtues truly make this religious «beloved of God and man, whose memory will be a blessing» (*Sir* 45:1).

CHAPTER TWENTY-FOUR

ON CHARITY

«This is my commandment, that you love one another» (*Jn* 15:12). Why did Jesus Christ call this his commandment?

1. Because Jesus Christ is charity, and he came from heaven specifically to bring us peace and charity, and because he prefers this commandment to all the others.

2. Because he taught us how to practice this virtue, not only by his words, but especially and far more so through his example; his life was really one continual act of charity towards us.

3. Because this commandment includes and sums up all the others; the entire law comes down to the commandment of charity. That is what St. Augustine teaches us when he tells us to «Love, and then do whatever you want.»

4. Because the religion of Jesus Christ is a religion of love and because love sums up all of religion. Through charity, we are children of God, we are all brothers and sisters, we are all one single flock, one single Church, one single family, one single body. If you remove the commandment of charity, this whole great work collapses in ruins.

5. Because charity is the sign of the disciples of Jesus Christ: «By this shall all men know that you are my disciples if you have love one for another» (*Jn* 13:35).

6. Because charity is the sign of the predestined; that is how people distinguish the children of God from the children of the devil.

7. Because this commandment will last forever, while all the others will end.

But what does it mean to love one's neighbor?

1. To love one's neighbor means to wish him well and do him good. «My little children, let us not love in word nor in tongue, but in deed and in truth» *(1 Jn* 3:18). Love is never sterile, and it says, like Rachel, «Give me children (meaning good works) or I shall die.» «What do you think I have in mind,» asks Seneca, «when I make a friend? I want someone with whom I can share my possessions, someone whom I can serve, defend, follow into exile, and for whom I can die and sacrifice myself.» To love one's neighbor means to do all that for him; that is what Jesus Christ did.

«In this we have known the charity of God,» says St. John, «because he has laid down his life for us; and we ought to lay down our lives for the brethren» *(1 Jn* 3:16).

«As for me,» says St. Paul, «I would willingly give all I have, and I would even give myself, to save your souls.»

2. To love one's neighbor means living in unity with our brothers, because we all form one single body in Jesus Christ. Now, what is more wonderful than the unity among the members of a human body? What will they not do for one another? They love each other without pretense, they never hurt one another, they relieve and serve and defend one another. To be together in the same place but not united in heart is a torment; to be united in heart but not in the same place is already a pleasure; but to be united in heart and in the same place is heaven on earth, as Hugh of St. Victor says.

«Charity,» says St. Jerome, «creates religious and gathers them under the same rule; without it, their residences are little hells and those who live in them are demons; but with it, all their houses are heavens on earth, and those who live in them are real brothers and sisters, or rather angels. That is when one can say, 'How sweet it is for brothers to live together!'»

«Even if Christians perform a thousand miracles,» says St. John Chrysostom, «if they do not love one another, if they do not agree among themselves, if they live amid dissensions and disturbances, they will look ridiculous even to pagans.»

«The devil,» says St. Bernard, «is not afraid of those people in community who perform great fasts and vigils, who practice mortification to the utmost degree, because he has destroyed many of that type; but those who live in peace, who are united to God and to their brothers—those are the ones he fears and dreads, whom he despairs of luring to himself, and whom he considers as lost to him.»

It sometimes happens that a ship at sea suddenly springs a leak and sinks. Why? Because the planks weren't tightly joined together. In the same way, the main cause of the ruin of a religious community is that its members are not well joined and united by charity. «So let those who are united by the Rule,» St. Bernard goes on to say, «be united also in spirit; let them support one another, defend one another, and help one another to bear the yoke of Jesus Christ; for the Wise Man has said, 'When a brother helps his brother, both are consoled, whereas if they begin to sting and bite each other, both will be lost.'»

3. Loving one's neighbor means putting up with his defects with great patience. «We put up with our neighbor,» says St. Gregory, «to the extent that we love him.» If you love your brothers very much, you will always put up with them, and you will not notice their defects; if you do not love them, you will have no patience with them, and your brothers' defects will affect you the way the sun affects sore eyes.

«Bear one another's burdens,» says St. Paul—put up with the difficult character, the bad moods, the illnesses, the passions and the faults of your brothers—«and so you shall fulfill the law of Jesus Christ» (*Gal* 6:2). What is that law? The law of charity which includes all the precepts. Who are those who put up with one another? Those who have charity. St. Augustine tells us that, «When deer are swimming across a body of water, each one rests his head on the rump of the one ahead of him, until the first one in line is tired; then he goes to the end of the line to enjoy the same respite he gave the others. By so doing, they all support one another in their weakness, and with that mutual support, they cross the water without incident, because charity serves as their ship. We should help, console and put up with one another in the same way.»

You are all one body in Jesus Christ, and the members of one another. Look at what the members do for one another, how they support one another, with what tenderness and haste they help one another. If a man hurts his foot, even though it's the lowest part of the body, even though the wound may be frightful to look at, full of gangrene and stinking, the other members don't recoil in horror; on the contrary, the eye looks at the foot with compassion, the hands wash and bandage it, the tongue asks other people for medication and asks the saints and even God for help. All the other members do what they can to ease, heal and support it. «Oh, members of Jesus Christ,» St. Augustine exclaims, «love one another, support one another, even put up with one another's infirmities, and don't be put off by one another's imperfections. By practicing holy charity, you will reach the kingdom of heaven.»

4. Loving one's neighbor means excusing and concealing his faults and defects. «As soon as we cover the defects of our brothers, God covers ours; as soon as we reveal them, he reveals ours and brings them out into the daylight for everyone else to see»; so says St. Pemen. We read that St. Ignatius always spoke so well about everyone, that everyone was readily convinced that he esteemed and loved them, and as a result, everyone loved and respected him. The holy abbot Connétable was called «the cloak of his brothers» because he carefully hid their defects and always tried to excuse their faults.

St. Teresa did the same thing, so her nuns were sure that wherever she was, their flanks were protected, because their Mother would defend them.

According to Horace, anyone who shreds the reputation of an absent friend, who makes known his defects or faults, who reveals secrets told him in confidence, is a bad citizen. We might add that he is a bad religious and a false brother.

To show how dangerous the slanderous tongue is, how much damage it does and how much it should be feared, Scripture compares it to a sword, a whip, a serpent's or viper's tongue, a fire, a lion, a leopard, death and hell.

St. Magdalene de' Pazzi said, «Show me a man who hides the faults and defects of his brothers, and who never soils his tongue with words against charity, and I will unhesitatingly affirm that he is a saint.»

Man's moral death begins with his tongue, that is, with his speech, and it imperceptibly takes over his will and his heart. So St. Peter had good reason to say, «He that will love life and see good days, let him refrain his tongue from evil, and his lips that they speak no guile» (*1 Pet* 3:10).

So, if you notice that your brother has committed some fault, don't allow your mind the liberty to accuse and condemn him, but rather excuse him. If you cannot excuse what he did, excuse his intention; say that he acted thoughtlessly, out of imprudence, that his fault took him by surprise, and so on. If the proof is so evident and clear that you cannot hide or excuse anything, at least blame it all on the violence of the temptation. That is the way, St. Bernard tells us, we should always look for some reason to excuse, minimize and hide our brothers' faults.

5. Loving our neighbor means warning him about his failings and helping him to correct his defects. «God,» says the Holy Spirit, «has ordered us to watch over our neighbor and has commanded us to take care of him» (cf. *Sir* 17:12). That is why Cain has been condemned down through the ages for his reply to God, «Am I my brother's keeper?» God has indeed placed in our hearts a feeling which inclines us to watch over one another.

«My brothers,» says St. Paul, «if anyone has committed a fault, be careful to lift him up again gently.» Fraternal correction, whose aim is our brothers' amendment, constitutes a precept, St. Thomas tells us, because if he who lets a wounded man die when he could have healed him by medicating and bandaging his wound, violates the law of charity, then he who refuses to use the remedy of fraternal correction when he sees his brother's soul covered with wounds caused by sin, violates charity even more.

Don't be afraid, says the Wise Man, to reprove your brother when he falls, but hold out your hand to him, to raise him up again and save him. Don't the members of our body use one another to care for and clean one another? Do as much for your brothers who have some stains or imperfections and who have been dirtied by some sins. Pliny assures us that when an elephant has fallen into a pit, all the others rush to help it to get up and climb out. And would we leave our brothers in the pit of sin?

6. Loving our neighbor means carefully avoiding quarrels, arguments and disputes. Real charity excludes quarrels, biting mockery, and altercations. The Apostle tells us, «Contend not in words, for it is to no profit, but subverts the hearers» (2 Tim 2:14). «Avoid foolish and unlearned questions,» he adds, «knowing that they beget strife. The servant of the Lord must not wrangle, but be mild toward all, capable of teaching, patient, with modesty admonishing those who resist the truth» (2 Tim 2:23-25). And the Holy Spirit says elsewhere, «It is an honor for a man to separate himself from quarrels» (Prov 20:3). By so doing, he forestalls the passing bitterness, the contempt, the cooling of affection which usually spring from that sort of debate, and he preserves himself from many sins, according to these other words of Scripture, «Refrain from every difference of opinion and you will diminish your sins.»

Nothing is more unworthy of good religious, says St. Bernard, than to argue with each other like prostitutes. The Holy Spirit had good reason to say that, «A man who withdraws from quarrels gains honor» (*Prov* 20:3). He does indeed, because he performs an act of charity by obviating the irritation and bitterness which arise from arguments, an act of humility by overcoming the very natural desire to win out over the others, and an act of prudence and good sense by maintaining peace and unity with everyone.

The great St. Ephrem rejoiced in his spiritual testament that he had never had a quarrel with anyone, but had always given in to keep the peace.

St. Moses the Ethiopian had an argument one day with St. Macarius, and used some sharp and cutting words; God punished him in exemplary fashion by allowing a demon to take possession of him, but such a filthy one that he made him spew out all sorts of dirt and excrement. That went on until Macarius took to prayer for deliverance from this diabolical possession and obtained pardon for his fault.

Such a severe punishment for such a saint underlines how much God detests such faults, and how opposed they are to charity.

7. Loving our neighbor means treating him gently and carefully avoiding everything which can displease him. Charity is the enemy of everything that can cause our neighbor not only great harm and bloody insults, but even everything which presents the appearance of even the slightest injury; of crafty malice, the least source of bitterness or displeasure, or of anything which appears capable of offending him, even slightly. A friend does not rest satisfied with not breaking his friend's arms and legs; he cannot even bring himself to scratch him, to graze his skin, because love leads him to turn away from his beloved all sorts of evils, and to obtain for him all sorts of good things. So if you see your brother is hurting, upset, worried, even slightly, by something you have done or said, stop right there and go no further. I tell you, and I will tell you a thousand times, it is better to act that way than to annoy your brother, and it is better that everything else perish, than that charity should. (St. Dorotheus)

Charity condemns bitter, rude, scornful words, and places on our lips only gentle, friendly, respectful ones, which show each one the esteem we have for him. «Judge your neighbor by yourself,» the Holy Spirit tells us. Let each one take stock of himself, and see how he would feel if someone spoke brusquely to him, or gave him a bitter answer, or haughty commands, and if he finds that such behavior would hurt him deeply, let him not act that way towards his brothers, because they are men just like himself.

One thing which makes charity really flourish is gentleness in our speech and in our way of treating other people. «A gentle word multiplies friends and appeases enemies,» says the Holy Spirit. So try to acquire that gentle spirit and always use it in your words and actions. As the Wise Man says, it makes us lovable to others, for just as it is impossible to please God without faith, as St. Bernard says, it is impossible to please other people without gentleness and affability.

8. Loving our neighbor means doing things for him every chance we get, according to these words of St. Paul: «By charity of the spirit serve one another» (*Gal* 5:13). A good brother is therefore helpful and ready to be of service; he is always ready to share others' tasks, to relieve those who are overburdened, and to make everyone happy, so that he can say with Jesus Christ, «I am in the midst of you as he who serves» (*Lk* 22:27).

«Nothing contributes more toward maintaining charity,» says St. Ambrose, «than when we follow the teaching of St. Paul and anticipate one another's needs; and when each one has more esteem for the others than for himself, the brothers anticipate the desires of their superiors, and the latter serve their brothers just as a loving mother serves her child.»

And Fr. Champagnat says, «The love which brothers owe each other should be an effective love, which consists in rendering service on every occasion, replacing one another with the children, assisting one another, helping one another in the tasks which may be entrusted to each, and being always ready to oblige.»

«Brothers,» said St. Bernard, «you must live with a true spirit of charity, which means you must support one another, help one another and serve one another, so that people can say of you what was said of the prophet Jeremiah: 'This man truly loves his brothers.'»

9. Loving our neighbor means consoling him when he is upset, being touched by his misfortunes and sharing his pain when he is suffering. «The just are naturally compassionate,» says the Wise Man; «they practice mercy every time an opportunity presents itself, so that they can say with Job, 'Compassion grew up with me and has always been my inseparable companion. It has always been a pleasure for me to ease the suffering of the poor and the sick, to console the afflicted, and to raise up those beaten down by discouragement» (cf. *Job* 30:25).

St. Paul wants all Christians, whoever they may be, to weep with those who weep and share all their pains. It is so very true that a charitable person is sensitive to others' sufferings, that the Hebrew word for good, just and holy also means mercy, tenderness and compassion. «True justice,» says St. Gregory, is always accompanied by compassion, and the false variety, by hardness and disdain.» «The hearts of the saints,» says St. Macarius, are sensitive and easily moved, but those of the devils are inflexible and their bowels are hard as rock. That is why Horace, speaking of Pluto, the god of the underworld, calls him the one who does not weep and who is not touched by the pain of those who suffer.»

«How beautiful it is,» says St. Alphonsus, «to console the afflicted, to serve the sick, to encourage and support the faint-hearted, to cheer up those who are sad and melancholy! The more you devote yourself to those works of mercy, the more you will share in the sufferings of others, and the more God will love you.»

10. Loving our neighbor means obtaining spiritual benefits for him and always giving him good example. The primary aim of charity, after all, is to obtain for our brothers the gifts of grace, and eternal salvation, because according to our Rule, we have come together in community in order to help one another to reach sanctity. Charity therefore leads us to pray constantly for our brothers, to give them good advice when they need it, to make them aware of their defects, and especially to give them good example.

«During a riot,» says Seneca, «when a crowd of people are pushing and shoving, if one falls, others fall with him; the same is true in the moral order.» In community especially, one cannot fall into some vice without being the occasion of the fall of many others. A gangrenous limb quickly endangers the other parts of the body; our head knows when our stomach is upset; one part of the body, no matter how strong it may be, is affected and weakened by its relationship with another which is sick. So a religious should, above all, give good example and avoid everything which could scandalize his neighbor.

«My son,» Our Lord said one day to a holy religious, «help me to save souls.»

«But Lord, how can I help you in such a holy and exalted ministry?»

«By your prayers and good example. Be faithful to your rule, be for all your brothers a model of obedience, piety, charity, zeal, devotedness and good spirit, and you will save them.»

11. Finally, loving our neighbor means honoring and respecting all our brothers. «Have respect for everyone,» says St. Peter (*1 Pet* 2:17). Esteem and respect all your brothers, because they are part of your family, they are called to the same vocation; like you they are children of God, servants, brothers, and members of Jesus Christ and co-heirs of the eternal glory which you will one day share with them.

Honor and respect all your brothers, because in spite of their defects, they are pious men, full of goodwill, a timorous conscience and solid virtue.

«Have a profound respect for one another,» says St. Paul (*Rom* 12:10). Such deference, given with sincerity, feeds love just as oil feeds the flame of a lamp. On the contrary, if these sincere external signs are lacking, there is no fraternal charity. Everyone naturally enjoys being shown honor and respect, because we are convinced of our own worth; that makes us very sensitive to scorn and touchy about our reputation. That's why we like those who treat us with respect and feel obliged to do the same for them, and why he who honors and respects his brothers will be honored and respected in turn. So honor and respect your brothers, because they are images of Jesus Christ. It was in that sense that St. Appolonius used to tell his religious that they should adore the brothers who came to visit them. «It is not they whom you adore,» he explained, «your veneration is not offered to them, but to God who dwells in them.» And he added, «Did you see your brother? Then you have seen your Lord and your God.»

CHAPTER TWENTY-FIVE

CORRECTION OR FRATERNAL ADMONITION

To maintain the brothers in the spirit of their state, and to forearm them against the dangers of the world, Fr. Champagnat left them very wise rules. One among them merits our particular attention—the one prescribing fraternal correction.

Being deeply convinced of this maxim of the Holy Spirit, «The Lord has ordered each of us to care for his neighbor» (cf. *Sir* 17:12), he wanted all his brothers to watch over one another in Jesus Christ. To make that task easy for them, he made it his principle never to send a brother alone. This principle has been faithfully observed in his Institute, which does not found any establishment with fewer than three brothers, because community life and reciprocal safeguards do not seem to be sufficiently guaranteed by the presence of only two brothers.

Moreover, the Founder wanted his brothers always to teach together, that is, in rooms which adjoin each other, at least in pairs, with a glass partition between them. As for their personal life of prayer and work, the brothers must have a common study hall, dormitory and dining room; all their exercises of piety and well as their studies, must be made in community. This community life is one of the most essential rules of the Institute. No brother may separate himself from the others, by day or night, during work or recreation; nor may he seek any privilege of personal independence, which is always fatal for the beneficial principle of common life and for each individual. When they travel, when they take a walk, and even when they go to church, the brothers must be together. Granted, this incessant community life is a continual sacrifice for nature, but what a salutary bulwark it is against all sorts of dangers! It is also understandable when one considers that the rule makes it a duty for the brothers charitably to make one another aware of their defects and faults, and to inform the superior of the abuses which might gain a foothold in the houses, and of the irregularities and everything in the brothers' conduct which might scandalize one's neighbor and compromise either the reputation of individuals or the honor of the Institute.

Fraternal admonition therefore assumes two forms; the first consists of giving good and charitable advice to someone who neglects to correct his defect or who easily fails against one of the rules. And in the case where this form of fraternal admonition, which is in a sense preventive, does not bring about amendment, one is obliged to have recourse to the second, which consists of informing the Brother Superior [General] in order to produce the necessary correction; this is the curative form.

The rule which prescribes that we make known to the superior the defects and failings of our brothers is nothing new or particular to our institute; it is common to all religious orders and one finds it in the constitutions of every community. For example, the Jesuit constitutions prescribe that, «He who is aware of some major fault of his brother must inform the superior, so that the latter, with prudence and fatherly solicitude, may apply a suitable remedy.»

In the Franciscan rule, we read, «If a brother knows about some failing of one of his brothers, he will inform the superior, without saying anything beforehand to the one who has committed the fault.» We find the same precept, expressed in similar terms, in the rules of St. Basil, St. Benedict, St. Pachomius, St. Augustine, and others.

1. Our Founder called fraternal admonition "the safeguard of the brothers' virtue" and "the guardian of the institute". He did not hesitate to affirm that «several owe it to this act of charity that they were able to escape great dangers and preserve their

virtue and even their vocation.» He also stated that «fraternal admonition was a bulwark for the institute against abuses and scandals. By means of it, the superior, being informed of everything reprehensible in the brothers' conduct, can take the necessary means to lead back to duty those who have veered away from it, to maintain the Rule, and to forestall or correct abuses.»

2. Fraternal admonition is a proof of friendship. «To reprove and correct,» says St. Clement, «is a sign of good will, not of hatred.» «Someone who reproves me or has me reproved,» adds St. John Chrysostom, «gives me greater proof of friendship than someone who flatters and praises me.»

«St. Francis de Sales,» said one of his friends, «often reproved me for my defects, and then he would tell me, 'I want you to be very grateful to me for that, because it is the greatest proof of friendship I can give you, and I will know that you love me if you do me the same favor; I cannot stand the least imperfection in you because I love you so much; what seem to me to be like flies in other people, look like elephants in you because of my great affection for you.'»

He who through fear of hurting his brother fails to warn him or to inform the Superior of his fault, really does not love him, and we can even say that he hates him, because he lets him perish when he could have saved him. St. Augustine says, «If your brother has a burning fever, you use every means you can think of to cure him; if it takes violent remedies, he is wasting his time pleading, resisting and arguing. You pay no attention to his resistance or his cries; you tie him down if you have to, so you can take the harsh measures which the doctor thinks necessary—and in all this you are acting reasonably and charitably. So why don't you do the same thing when your brother's soul is sick? Why do you conceal his defects? Why do you hide his faults from those who should correct them? Why are you afraid to annoy your brother by reproving him or having him reproved? Don't you know that love includes holy severity, which remedies evil no matter what? So do for your brother's soul what you do for his body; otherwise you are cruel, you are lacking in charity and you are guilty of the loss of the soul of him whose faults and defects you conceal.»

«To hide one's brother's sin from the superior,» said St. Basil, «is simply to hasten the death of an invalid, and to push over the cliff someone who is already running toward it.» A sin which one hides is like an abscess which continues to grow until it reaches the heart and kills. Now, just as it would be a great kindness to someone to lance such an abscess, and on the contrary, it would be acting like an enemy not to do so, in the same way, you are not acting like a friend when you hide your brother's fault from the superior, because you are contributing to his downfall and his spiritual death.

But perhaps you will reply that this brother is a very reasonable man and that he knows how and where to look for the remedy he needs. You are wrong; when someone is upset and in the heat of passion, he is not capable of looking for remedies. He may be reasonable about everything else, but this brother cannot be so on this point, because passion has clouded his mind. Do you think he is wiser than King David, who told God, «You have revealed to me the most hidden secrets of your wisdom»? Once the Prophet-King was tormented and blinded by passion, he had to cry out, «All my wisdom was swept away as by a wild windstorm, and I would have been lost if someone had not come to my help!» No, there is no more wisdom, no more reasoning, for someone who is controlled by some passion; a thick veil has covered his eyes and he walks only in darkness.

Other brothers, to excuse themselves from their duty of fraternal admonition, say, «I have enough to do taking care of myself. I'm not going to set myself up as other people's guardian, and I don't interfere in their affairs.» So you think you have enough to do taking care of yourself! But when you bring about your brother's cure, you are taking care of yourself, because he is part of the body of the Institute of which you are a member. Is it not in the best interest of all the members of a body to help one another? Isn't it against nature to act otherwise?

Listen to St. Augustine: «If a thorn has pierced the foot, all the other members hurry to help it; the back bends, the eyes look for it. If someone says, 'There it is,' the ears listen, the hands move to the spot to pull it out.» You are members of the body of Jesus Christ and of the body of the Institute, and your brothers are members too. So how is it that if one of them falls into some fault which could ruin him, instead of helping him to correct himself, like one member helping another, under the pretext that you have enough to do taking care of yourself, you look at him coldly, you don't give him any help, you excuse and approve of his fault by your silence? Such conduct is proof that you do not love your brother, and that you don't even love yourself.

Then you say that you don't set yourself up as other people's guardian! Do you know whom you resemble when you talk that way? Cain, the first murderer. You say that you don't set yourself up as your brothers' guardian! But you don't have to, because God himself has already entrusted that responsibility to you and your Rule makes it your duty to watch over them carefully in Jesus Christ. If you neglect that duty you will have to answer for their souls, and you will be guilty of their faults. «Yes,» said Father Champagnat, «he who neglects fraternal admonition shares in the fault of his brother. If there were no receivers of stolen goods, there would be no thieves, or hardly any; that is why the former are as guilty as the latter. It's the same in community: if there were no fences—no religious who lack fraternal charity and who cover the faults of their brothers with the cloak of treacherous indulgence, instead of making them known to the superior, there would be no serious failings against the Rule, and no abuse would be able to get into the houses.»

A certain brother who had neglected this duty, and then felt remorse, made known his fault to Fr. Champagnat, who replied, «You have faults, you repent of them, God be praised! Pray to Our Lord to forgive you, as well as the brother whose fault you concealed. If we want to have no regrets, dear friend, let us always follow the straight path. Let us not allow human respect, or misplaced indulgence, to make us lose sight of God's glory and the best interests of our brothers. Don't forget that failing to inform the superior is to fail against charity and to make oneself guilty of the fault of him who strays from his duty, and whom a warning from the superior would have put back on the right road. So, dear brother, we must make up for the past by great fidelity to the rules about fraternal charity.»

To those words full of culpable indifference, «I don't meddle in that brother's business,» St. John Chrysostom has this vigorous reply: «That's an error and a lie, because when you help him to hide his faults you are meddling in the worst possible way. You don't meddle in that brother's business! So you see your brother going astray without having enough charity to have him warned, and you think you have not sinned? The Law of Moses commanded that one help one's enemy's horse if it fell; does your brother's soul mean less to you than a beast of burden? As Jesus Christ is my witness, when you act like that you are guilty of the loss of that brother and God will make you give an account of his soul.»

3. Fraternal admonition is therefore a duty in conscience for all the brothers. It is a duty to admonish charitably anyone who breaks a rule; it is a duty to make his failings known to the superior if private admonitions have had no effect. «If your brother whom you have admonished does not correct himself,» says Jesus Christ, «tell the Church» (*Mt* 18:17), that is, the superior. To fail in this duty may sometimes be a mortal sin, not because of the rule, but because of the importance of the matter and because of the evil which may result for the erring brother and for the whole Institute. So beware of putting a brother at risk

of compromising himself, and the whole Institute with him, because of your own timidity or your fear of displeasing him. And where did you ever read that, so as not to displease an individual, one should fail in the fidelity one owes to the whole body? To whom do you have a greater obligation—to the Institute or to this brother who is going astray? It is bad, very bad, to hide others' faults, as if one were in collusion with those who commit them. That's what you should be ashamed of, rather than of being faithful to the Institute and observing the Rule.

If there are men who, through timidity, lack of zeal, or whatever other reason, are afraid to give fraternal correction, there are others who do not like to receive it and who have a strange dread of reports made to the superior. Such an attitude is a sure sign of weak virtue, and a proof that those religious don't really want to correct their defects. One authoritative teacher, speaking of that kind of religious, compares them to the devil, because they are as incorrigible as he is, and he says that one thing which distinguishes the devil from the sinner is that the sinner can still correct himself as long as he lives, whereas the devil is eternally incapable of that.

«Woe to him who walks alone,» says the Holy Spirit; «for when he falls, he has no one to lift him up» (cf. *Eccles* 4:10). What does it mean to walk alone? It means to hide one's faults and defects from the superior. A good religious has nothing closed, not even his own heart, which is always open to the one who is responsible for guiding him. To walk alone means to fear and flee correction. To walk alone means to think it wrong for our brothers to make our conduct known to the superior.

«Misery and ignominy,» says the Holy Spirit, «are the lot of every man who flees reprimands; he will be overwhelmed with evil and covered with vices, just as an unplowed field is overrun with weeds.»

«He who hates correction,» the Spirit says elsewhere, «is mad.» Such a man cannot be pruned and formed; he will become more imperfect every day; everywhere he goes he will be of no account, or a source of scandal for others.

If you were walking along a strange road and someone told you to stop and go back or you would fall over a cliff or be eaten by wild animals or murdered by robbers, you would be grateful for the information and you would thank the person who was kind enough to give it to you.

So why are you angry, when after having exposed yourself to the danger of losing your virtue or your reputation because of your visits or your contacts with certain persons, someone tells you, «Watch out! Stop those visits!»? Is that reasonable on your part? And don't say, «I'm the director. I'm older than this brother; I have more experience than he does. I know where I stand, I'll know how to stop if I have to, etc.»

You are deceiving yourself when you promise yourself that you'll stop. You are forgetting these words of the Holy Spirit: «Don't lean on your wisdom, because it is more fragile than you think.» You are also deceiving yourself when you think you understand the danger of your situation better than the brother who has admonished you or who has had you admonished; because over and above the fact that no one is a good judge in his own case, it often happens, as Abbot Josephus says, that someone who has more intelligence and education deceives himself, whereas someone who has less of either sees things more clearly. «So let no brother,» he concludes, «whatever his age or his ability, imagine that he can do without the others, and that he needs no one's admonitions.» God's greatest punishment is to remain silent, to no longer reprove, correct and punish. Woe to the religious when his superior imitates God this way; it proves that this religious is a sick person for whom everyone has given up hope.

The good religious thinks in a totally different way, and looks on fraternal correction as one of the greatest benefits of religious life. «Do you know what a convent is?,» St. Francis de Sales asks;

«It is the Academy of Careful Correction, in which each one learns to let himself be processed, planed, cut, polished and shaped, so that having become very smooth, he can join himself perfectly to God. A convent is a hospital of spiritual invalids who want to get well, and who, to be sure of becoming so, are willing to endure blood-letting, the scalpel, the lancet, the probe, the fire, the hot iron and all the bitterness of the remedies prescribed; that is why religious used to be called 'those who are healing.' The good religious has a clear understanding of that truth, and he loves his convent as a school of correction.»

«To want to be corrected,» he goes on, «is an evident sign of wisdom and a sure indication that one has made progress in virtue. In fact, just as the ability to easily digest rough food is a sign of good digestion, the love of being warned and corrected of one's defects is an indication of spiritual health and strength of soul. So when one receives reprimands with pleasure, it is solid proof that one has an aversion for vice and that the faults which one commits arise more from surprise and human weakness than from malice and deliberation. It is proof that one is working seriously to correct oneself. He who voluntarily accepts correction shows that he has a sincere desire to acquire virtue. A sick person who wants to get well courageously takes the remedies prescribed by the doctor, no matter how distasteful and bitter they may be. The religious who is really tending towards perfection, which constitutes the soul's full health and true sanctity, finds nothing difficult in order to reach that goal. He believes that the wounds inflicted by a loving Father, who like a skillful physician, wounds only in order to cure, are worth more than the caresses of any flatterer.»

St. Augustine, the most learned man of his time, wrote to St. Jerome that he was ready to receive his advice, and even that of the most insignificant person of all. «I beg you,» he told him, «to be so good as to inform me without fear, when you see that I need it. Because even though now, according to the practice of the Church, the episcopacy is more than the priesthood, since

Augustine the bishop is still in many ways below Jerome who is only a simple priest, he must neither refuse nor despise corrections, no matter where they come from, even if they come from the least of all.» We read in the life of St. Ambrose that he used to thank those who advised him of his defects, and that he received their advice as a special favor. St. Ignatius Loyola was so convinced of the necessity of fraternal correction that he wanted the superior general and provincials of his order always to have near them a religious specifically charged with observing their conduct and giving them charitable advice when they needed it.

A good superior considers the warnings and the words full of holy freedom addressed to him by his brothers as a testimony of their good will. This wise conduct forearms him against an infinite number of faults, because he is forewarned and armed by as many persons as he has brothers. One day, Ribadeneira, who was only fifteen, told St. Ignatius, who was then an old man and superior general of the Company of Jesus, that people mocked him when he preached, because he made many grammatical errors and had mannerisms which made people laugh. This advice charmed Ignatius, who answered, «Pedro, you're right; I appoint you to observe me from now on; be sure to note down all my mistakes, and I promise that I will try to avoid them.»

He who really wants to correct himself, and who aspires to perfection, would like everyone to keep his eyes open to keep him in the line of duty and to help him to arrive more surely at the goal he has set for himself.

«If I could only have the advantage,» St. Bernard used to say, «of having a hundred superiors watching over me and taking care of me. The more people I know are safeguarding me in Jesus Christ, the safer I feel. It's a strange sort of madness to become angry when someone is keeping an eye on our conduct; for my part, thank God, I'm more afraid of the teeth of the wolf than of the staff of the shepherd.»

Every good religious shares St. Bernard's opinion, and like the saints of whom we have just spoken, they love correction and cherish those persons who are charitable enough to warn them or to have them reprimanded.

CHAPTER TWENTY-SIX

SLANDER

«I beg of you, my dear brothers,» Father Champagnat told us, «with all the affection of my soul and by all the love you have for me, do all you can to ensure that charity is always maintained among you. Love one another as Jesus Christ has loved you. Be of one head and one mind. May it be said of the Little Brothers of Mary as of the first Christians: 'See how they love one another!' This is the most ardent desire of my heart.»

The love which Fr. Champagnat wanted us to have for one another should be an effective love, and he wanted it to include these four special elements: helping one another on every occasion, advising one another charitably of our defects and our failings against the Rule, putting up with one another charitably, and excusing and hiding one another's faults very carefully.

He wanted the brothers' defects to be hidden not only from outsiders but also from other members of the community. That is the source of the rule which forbids all the brothers to talk about anything reprehensible which has happened in the establishments, to share the little antipathies which they might have felt for certain brothers, and the difficult times they may have had with them.

«It is just as important,» he added, «to uphold the reputation of brothers within the community, as it is to do so in public: a brother has, in fact, even more right to the respect of his confrères than to that the public. A religious who is denigrated by the public can take comfort from the fact that he enjoys the esteem and confidence of his brothers; but if he is treated without respect by his own, by those among whom he is obliged to live, community life becomes a torture for him, so that unless he is a man of extraordinary virtue, he can no longer support it.»

To explain this statement of our founder, we will develop, with the help of scripture and the masters of the spiritual life, the three following affirmations, whose importance and truth seem to us to be fundamental and worthy of the most serious consideration by all the brothers:

I. Slander is one of the greatest dangers to religious life.

II. Slander is a great sin.

III. Slander is the cause of an infinite number of evils.

I. Slander is one of the greatest dangers to religious life.

One of the main benefits of religious life is that it puts us in the lee of almost every exterior danger of offending God. But man is still so weak that he cannot find anywhere an infallible and absolute preservative against sin, even mortal sin. Just as even the angels in heaven fell, man succumbed in the Garden of Eden, and Judas ruined himself by the most frightful sin while in the company of Jesus Christ and the Apostles.

«Let us go further and speak the whole truth: there are even certain mortal sins to which one may be more exposed in religious life than in the world; for example, the abuse of grace, sacrilege, and sins against charity. In religious life, we are more protected from avarice and ambition; but we are more inclined to complaining, quarrels, slander, and the like. Now what difference does it make by what sin we damn ourselves, if we are in fact unfortunate enough to be damned, as Bourdaloue says.»

«Slander is the easiest of all sins to commit,» St. John Chrysostom adds, «it is the one into which we fall with the least remorse, and for which we will be most severely punished. For other sins, we must have outside stimuli, but for slander, all it takes is our own will; all we need is a tongue. That is why we so easily slip into this fault.»

«There are very few persons,» adds St. Jerome, «even among religious, who don't allow themselves to be drawn into detraction. We have such an itch to talk about other people and to criticize their actions, that even those who are exempt from other vices fall into this one as into the last and most dangerous of the devil's snares.

«So monks should not think they are safe, and say, 'We do not commit serious sins in the monastery, because we are not adulterers or murderers.' I assure you that you are committing a great crime when you disparage your brother, because you kill him with your tongue. It is a great vice to be unwilling to keep quiet, and to run from cell to cell to disparage others.»

«Have nothing to do with detractors,» says the Holy Spirit (*Prov* 24:21). Why not? Because this vice, the gloss on this text tells us, causes many to be shipwrecked. «How sad it is,» St. John Chrysostom exclaimed, «to see someone so blind to his own defects that he has eyes only for those of others, and slanders solely for the pleasure of slandering. What a sad pleasure! He runs toward hell, not along the highway, but by winding side roads and unattractive paths. He is faithful to the difficult commandments and damns himself by the easiest sins to avoid!»

«A great misfortune often occurs in religious houses,» says Fr. Saint-Jure; «when someone has spoken ill of his neighbor, when someone has revealed his defects, published his faults and criticized his conduct, that person creates for himself a false and erroneous conscience. In other words, he does not think much of this fault, he does not confess it, or does so nonchalantly, without concern, contrition or reparation. To do so is to deceive oneself grievously, nourish one's secret sins, and put one's salvation in great danger.»

Father Claude Aquaviva, fifth superior general of the Society of Jesus, consulted all the priests of his institute by means of an anonymous questionnaire, asking them how and in what circumstances the members of the Society were most likely to lose charity and become guilty of mortal sins. The vast majority of the replies said it was by the sin of detraction. That was Fr. Aquaviva's own opinion, and he was so convinced of the dangers facing religious on that score that in his Treatise on how to cure illnesses of the soul he recommended that if anyone should happen to forget himself on that point, that he not go to bed until he had first gone to confession.

«In the opinion of wise and prudent men,» says Cornelius á Lapide, «many persons damn themselves by the sins of slander and calumny. Slander is all the more serious and dangerous when one does not worry about it and treats it as a trifle.»

II. Slander is a serious sin.

According to St. Thomas Aquinas, slander is of its nature a mortal sin. If lightness of matter or lack of full consent diminish the gravity of the sin, it is at least one of the most serious of venial sins, because it attacks charity and offends against justice.

«In my opinion,» says St. John Chrysostom, «the wickedness of the slanderer is greater than that of the thief, because the law of Christ, which concentrates so strongly on love of neighbor, is more concerned with people's souls than with their wallets, and because slander takes away from one's neighbor the most precious of all his possessions, his good reputation.»

But perhaps someone will say, «I am not being malicious, and what I say about my neighbor is true.» «It doesn't matter,» says St. John Chrysostom, «that you are convinced of the truth of what you say and do not speak out of a desire for revenge; you are wounding charity and you are guilty. You will not be judged according to what others have done, but according to what you have said. What makes the slanderer's fault even more serious is that he can offer no excuse.»

Other disorders, even though all are condemned by reason, can be excused or at least explained by the various causes which provoke them. The sex offender alleges the violence of his passion; the thief, his need; the murderer his irresistible impulses. The slanderer has no pretext at all to put forward; he is not attracted by financial gain, nor led astray by passion; he has no excuse.

And yet, with a single word, the slanderer inflicts a deeper wound with his tongue than if he bit his victim with his teeth. By destroying his neighbor's reputation, he commits an evil which will never be healed. So I am not afraid to state that he is more of a criminal than the assassin, and must expect a more severe punishment.

St. Bernard says that the tongue of the slanderer is a sword; it is a three-pronged spear—with a single blow it pierces three people: the one who slanders, the one listening to him, and the one being slandered. It is a poisonous snake which poisons three souls with a single bite.

«We are all the more obliged to avoid all forms of slander,» says our Founder, «since it is very easy, while speaking of other people's faults or defects, to make ourselves very guilty:

«1. Because a trifling fault is often made into a major one, or at least it keeps growing as it passes from mouth to mouth and is spread around.

«2. Because a defect, or even a slight fault which we make known, can create a bad opinion about a brother, turn those with whom he must live against him, destroy their esteem for him, and become a cause of dissension, disunity, trouble and disorder for a whole year.

«3. Because slander like that can give birth in the heart of the person slandered to hatred, aversion and resentment toward the one responsible for it, and even many years may not erase them.

«4. Because we have no scruples about such faults, we take them for trifles, and most of the time we don't even mention them in confession. By so doing we run the risk of committing sacrileges, because if often happens that slander or words against charity, which we think are light faults, are really mortal sins. Faults against charity, no matter how you look at them, are therefore extremely dangerous; that is why the brothers should be extremely careful to avoid them.»[1]

Finally, slander is a sin which greatly displeases God, according to the words of scripture, that «He who slanders is cursed by God» (cf. *Sir* 28:13), and that God «hates...him who sows discord among brothers» (*Prov* 6:19). And who sows discord and disunity, if not the slanderer? Jesus Christ pushes the slanderer away from his altar. «Go,» he says, «be reconciled with your brother. Go make reparation to him before bringing me your offering.»

The gravity of slander depends on:

1. the person who slanders, and his intention, or in other words, the passion which motivates him;

2. the matter of the slander, or of the evil one speaks. It is evident that making known a grave fault is a greater sin than if it were a slight fault;

3. the number of hearers. Who does not understand that to slander someone in front of four people is a more serious fault than to do so in front of only one;

4. the effects and consequences of the slander;

5. finally, the sort of person one slanders. Rodriguez has a frightening statement on this subject. «Theologians teach that revealing one of our neighbor's venial sins is not a mortal sin if we are speaking about lay people, since our words do not at all

---

[1] *Life of Blessed Marcellin Joseph Benedict Champagnat*, 1989 edition, p. 43

destroy their reputation. But revealing the venial sin of a religious or priest might be a mortal sin. The reason for that is that certain venial sins cast more dishonor on a religious or cleric than several grave faults would on a lay person.»

Saying that a priest, a pastor, a religious or a superior is a liar, that he has no brains, that he lacks piety or is superficial, etc., does him more harm in the minds of our hearers than if we said of some lay person that he does not fast, that he misses Mass, or the like. So the sin of slander and its malice in large part from the quality of the person slandered. This is a very good reason for never speaking ill of superiors and clerics.

III. Slander causes an infinite number of evils.

Yes, slander is in inexhaustible source of evil. «Name a single one which does not spring from it,» exclaims St. John Chrysostom; «from it arise quarrels, mistrust, dissention, hatred, enmity, the ruin of families and the overthrow of governments. That is what the Holy Spirit teaches us with these words: «The tongue of [the slanderer] has disquieted many, and scattered them from nation to nation. It has destroyed the strong cities of the rich, and has overthrown the houses of great men. It has cut in pieces the forces of the peoples, and undone strong nations» (*Sir* 28:16-18).

A slanderer is a terrible person to have in a house; he upsets everyone who lives there. He sets people at loggerheads and sows weeds. «He is,» says St. Bernard, «a fox who destroys and ravages everything.»

«What do you think of slander?» a religious once asked the holy abbot Agathon. «Slander,» the saint replied, «is a wild and burning wind, which overturns everything, consumes everything, knocks all the fruit off the tree of charity, and sows disorder everywhere.»

«The slanderer,» says St. Bernard, «is a plague victim, a leper, who spreads his evil to others and destroys their souls.»

«He is a public scourge,» adds St. Ambrose, «who wreaks havoc everywhere, like a river which overflows and ravages an entire region.»

«Religious who are slanderers,» affirms Fr. Saint-Jure, «are like the sewers of a city, into which flow all its refuse and garbage. All the imperfections and faults of a community collect in the mind of slanderous religious, who then give them off like bad odors which affect the whole house; their mouth is like an open grave full of corpses, which emits a deadly infection.»

Do you know what race the one who speaks ill of his superiors and brothers belongs to? To the race of Ham, Noah's third son, who instead of covering his father's nakedness, made fun of it. He was cursed for it; slanderers are cursed by God in the same way.

The slanderous religious is the great enemy of unity and concord; there is nothing more dangerous in a community than a slanderous religious. A religious house cannot survive if it tolerates this inordinate liberty to speak about one another.

Religious founders were so convinced of this truth that they were very severe when it came to detraction.

«Religious houses,» says St. Francis of Assisi, «will die out if this wicked vice is allowed to enter. So I want you Guardians and Superiors to be extremely careful to prevent this terrible plague from spreading among us. I therefore order you to punish severely any brother who has spoken ill of his brother.» What penance should he be given? «He who has stripped his brother of his reputation will be stripped of his religious habit, and he will not be allowed to pray with his brothers until he has made reparation for his fault.»

When St. Pachomius heard someone speaking ill of another, he immediately turned and ran away, as we run from a madman or a plague victim.

St. Bernard did not want slanderous religious to be kept; «He must be severely punished,» he said, «and sent away if he does not correct himself.»

St. Basil separated detractors from the rest of the community, like men with some contagious disease, and he severely punished those who listened to them.

St. Jerome gave orders to run away from a slanderer as from a serpent. «If you hear someone slandering someone else,» he says in his Rule, «run far away from him and avoid his company as you would that of a snake in the grass.»

«Religious with an evil tongue,» says St. Alphonsus Liguori, «should be chased out of the house or spend their entire lives locked in a cell, because they disturb everyone else's silence, devotion, concord, unity and rest. If they are allowed to roam freely, they will be the ruin of the community.»

St. Augustine hung a motto in his dining room, a warning never to speak ill of another. One day, when several priests who were eating with him slipped into this fault, the saint tried to change the conversation. When that indirect reprimand failed to silence the guilty parties, he suddenly stood up, and with holy freedom told them that he was going to walk out if they continued their slander.

The slanderous person is preparing an unhappy life for himself: everyone fears him, nobody loves him, he has no real friend in the world, because he has no charity. That is why St. Peter, who wanted all the faithful to enjoy happiness and tranquility, wrote to them, «Anyone who wants to have a happy life and to enjoy prosperity must banish malice from his tongue, deceitful conversation from his lips» (*1 Pet* 3:10).

But it is not enough not to slander. We must also, whenever we can, prevent slander or at least not listen to it; because, as St. John Chrysostom says, «to permit oneself to commit slander, or to listen to it, is one and the same thing.» «He who commits slander,» says St. Bernard, «has the devil on his tongue; he who listens to it has him in his ear.»

So what should we do when we hear slander?

1. Flee the slanderer and find some legitimate pretext for leaving his presence.

2. Reprimand him if we have authority over him, or make him aware of his fault if he is an equal.

3. If we cannot withdraw, pretend to be sleeping, or pay no attention to what is said.

Another good way to make the slanderer be quiet is to listen to him with obvious sadness; «for if you appear to be happy,» says Venerable Bede, «you will encourage the slanderer to go on; whereas if you appear sad, he will stop saying with pleasure what he sees you are listening to with pain.»

There is no point in repeating here that making known to the superior, according to Rule, the faults and defects of our brothers, is not slander, but an act of charity, whose aim is either the personal good of our confrères or the general good of the community, and consequently, the glory of God.

CHAPTER TWENTY-SEVEN

ON BEING SILENT AND RESERVED IN ONE'S SPEECH

What is the tongue? The interpreter of the heart. «As the heart is, so is the tongue,» says Cornelius. Do you want to know what a man is like? Listen to his words, for the mouth speaks from the abundance of the heart. That is why Socrates told one teenager, «Speak, young man, so that I may know you. Your words will mirror your soul for me.»

When you take the lid off a sewer, that catch-basin of filth gives off a foul odor. Likewise an evil heart lets the corruption which fills it escape through the mouth. It poisons and dirties everyone who comes into contact with it. On the contrary, a bottle which contains a delightful perfume spreads a sweet smell, and so a tongue which is at the service of a pure heart, an innocent soul, spreads around it the good odor of Jesus Christ and contributes everywhere to edification and virtue.

Whether a bottle holds wine, vinegar, oil or honey, the odor it emits reveals its contents; so the tongue betrays the soul whose organ it is, and reveals to all what the soul is like.

If a man likes to chatter about trifles, he shows that he has a superficial, frivolous, or sometimes an impudent mind. If he likes to use risqué or double-meaning words, it means that his heart is full to overflowing with sensuality. If he enjoys slandering his neighbor, it proves that his soul possesses neither charity nor justice nor a conscience. If he likes to boast, to dominate others, it means that his predominant passion is pride. In a word, as one's language is, so are one's soul and one's heart. Just as a

Spaniard speaks his own language and the Frenchman his, and people everywhere speak the language of their respective countries, so a person with a heavenly soul speaks of the things of heaven, and he who has an earthly soul speaks of the things of earth. Finally, after telling us in the book of Proverbs that «the mouth of the impious is full of malice,» the Holy Spirit also tells us why: «because his heart is full of iniquity.»

Since the tongue is such a faithful reflection of a man's interior, it is therefore very important for a brother, whose whole interior life should be involved in practicing virtue, that his use of his tongue should be regulated like all his other actions. Hence the necessity and wisdom of the rule of silence.

«Silence,» says our Rule, «is necessary in a community to maintain recollection, piety, regularity, peace, charity and love of work.»[1] Yes, silence is necessary for all of those, and we add:

I. We also need silence in order to avoid sin.

«He who uses many words,» says the Holy Spirit, «shall hurt his own soul» (*Sir* 20:8), and if you are a man of many words, you cannot avoid sin, for, «In the multitude of words, there shall not lack sin» (*Prov* 10:19).

«'I am convinced,» says St. Ambrose, «that breaking silence and the itch to talk represent for religious the shipwreck of innocence, and a cause of daily falls and faults.' The reason he gives is that it is very difficult to speak without offending God.» He drew his teaching from Holy Scripture. «Do you believe,» Job exclaims, «that a man who talks a great deal can be justified?» No, he cannot possibly preserve his soul from sin. To speak a great deal without offending God is a marvel not seen on this earth.

---

[1] *Règles Communes*, 1852, Chapter VIII, article 1.

«The tongue,» says St. Bernard, «is only a small part of us, and yet it does so much harm; it licks with flattery and kills with lies. How true it is that it is impossible to speak a great deal without sinning! When I had permission to speak to one person out of necessity, I spoke not only of necessary things but also of things which were not; I said vain and useless words, words intended to make people laugh, and in that multitude of words which soil the tongue with detraction, I wickedly discolored the good opinion which others had of virtuous persons. I never repeat things I saw or heard exactly as they were done or said; I assert one thing instead of another, or I embroider and modify it. In a word, of all my members, my tongue is the one which has done me the most harm.» St. James likewise says that there is no other organ of our body which so much helps the devil to make us commit sin as the tongue.

Why did the devil, who struck Job all over his body, not touch his tongue? Because he knew that the tongue is a wellspring and source of sins and he hoped that Job would use his to offend God.

St. Peter Damian says that «according to the Law of Moses, a container which had no cover had to be considered impure.» Now that is an image which teaches us that the soul whose mouth is not closed by silence is spoiled by the impurity of its sins. Therefore, a religious keeps himself free of sin through silence, and he ruins himself and commits a multitude of sins as soon as he lets himself slip into useless conversations.

«For more than thirty years,» St. Sisoes told his disciples, «I have prayed God with tears to preserve me by his grace from sin and from every evil act; but in spite of my tears and prayers, I have never reached the point of completely controlling my tongue, and I sin every day in my words.»

«The majority of sins,» says St. Alphonsus, «come from having spoken or from having listened to someone speak.» On Judgment

Day, how many religious will we see condemned for not having kept silence!

When someone asked him what was the most evil and most dangerous thing about anyone, Anacharsis replied that it was the tongue. So the Fathers of the Desert had good reason to say that he who does not know how to control his tongue will never be victorious over the passions of the flesh.

II. We need silence in order to live piously.

«A religious needs three things,» says the holy abbot Agathon: «the observance of silence, love of prayer and renunciation of his own will.» Now, without the first of those, he will never have the other two. «I barred my door and spoke with my beloved,» says the Spouse in the Canticle, meaning that she kept profound silence, separated herself from other creatures, and rejected all human consolation so that she might deserve to converse with God.

A religious who talks a lot, according to St. Ambrose, easily loses his taste for piety; his feeling for virtue runs out of his mouth like water from a cracked pitcher. «Isn't it true, brothers,» St. Dorotheus asked his religious, «that as soon as you open the oven door, all the heat escapes? That's exactly what happens to you when you speak unnecessarily; your talkativeness drives from your mind all the good thoughts you had.»

«The experience of those who dedicate themselves to prayer,» says St. Gregory, «is that they become deaf and dumb with regard to all things earthly; they cannot speak about them or listen to other people speak about them, because they only want to converse about the things they love.» When Moses conversed with God he almost lost his power of speech. As soon as Jeremiah began conversing with the Lord, he cried out that he was only a child and no longer knew how to speak to adults.

«But it is no less true,» says St. Alphonsus, «that those who do a lot of talking with creatures, talk little with God, because they don't know how. Without silence, there is absolutely no recollection, no fervor, no spirit of compunction; without silence, prayer becomes impossible, or at least is full of distractions. Besides, whoever speaks a lot commits many faults, at least venial ones, and willful venial sin is one of the greatest obstacles to communication with the divine.

Venial sin soils the soul; it is a leprosy which disfigures and deforms it in the sight of God, who then turns away from it and abandons it to its distractions and weakness. Venial sin saddens the Holy Spirit, keeps it from working in the soul, ruins its good feelings. Then that soul is prey to disgust, dryness, and aridity, and prayer becomes a torture for it. So it is certain that in order to live piously, one must keep silence and live in recollection.

III. We need silence in order to live virtuously.

Silence nourishes, increases and perfects all the virtues. That is why the ancient hermits regarded infractions of the rule of silence as a dangerous fault and punished them severely.

When St. Arsenius asked God what he should do to save his soul, he heard a voice which told him, «Avoid other people and be silent.» After having spent many years in the desert, he once again asked what he should do to acquire great virtue and reach perfection, and he once again heard the same voice saying, «Avoid other people and be profoundly silent.» «If any man offend not in word, he is a perfect man» (*Jas* 3:2).

On the contrary, St. Bernard remarks in his explanation of this text, he who does not know how to keep his tongue in check is not only not perfect, but has no virtue at all. According to St. Odo, the life and actions of a religious, no matter how good they may seem, merit no esteem and count for nothing, if he does not control his tongue. According to St. Peter Damian, a religious maintains his virtue and purity of heart by silence and recollection, and he loses both when he gives himself permission to speak without a clearly recognized necessity. That is why Dussaut did not hesitate to assert that not being silent, and being a bad religious, are almost the same thing. St. Isidore felt the same way. The itch to speak, the habit of joking and dissipation, he says, are a sure sign of a vain and unruly conscience, a superficial mind, a soul which is weak and devoid of virtue.

Someone once asked St. Thomas Aquinas, «What are the signs by which one can recognize a really virtuous person?» He answered, «The spirit of prudence and recollection.» Then he added, «If you see a religious who enjoys useless conversations and the trifles of the world, beware of thinking that he is a spiritual person, even if he works miracles. Why? Because his virtue has no foundation and no cement to hold it together.»

«They tell me,» St. Jerome wrote to one of his friends, «that you have left the world and entered religious life. So you have built a strong solid wall to protect yourself against the enemies of salvation. But I know you well enough to be sure of one thing: that you left a door in that wall through which the devil can enter. Let me explain. You have the great defect of speaking much. The door I mentioned is your mouth. So if you want to be protected from the dangers of the enemy, persevere in your vocation, and acquire solid virtue, seal up that door and control your tongue. Otherwise you will do no good, and you will run the risk of falling frequently.»

«Not a word was heard,» says St. Peter Damian, «during the rebuilding of the Temple of Jerusalem, which means that the edifice of virtue and perfection is raised by silence.»

Silence protects the heart and makes the soul more clear-sighted and intelligent. It is the seed of holy thoughts and of generous and heroic works; it inflames the heart with love of God, says St. Francis of Assisi.

IV. We need silence for mutual edification and to preserve regularity and discipline.

One of the main reasons why religious join together under the same rule is in order to help and edify one another and lead one another to virtue. But a dissipated religious who does not know how to keep silence, annoys and disturbs his brothers instead of edifying them and helping them to practice virtue; he becomes a stumbling block for them, and an occasion of failings and sins.

«You asked me,» says St. Bernard, «what I think about a brother who, by his example, leads the others towards laxity, disturbs them with his irregularities, annoys them with his talkativeness, his complaining and his facility for breaking silence. I think that such a brother saddens the spirit of God who dwells in his confrères, that he persecutes virtue and wages war on Jesus Christ.»

«A dissipated religious makes the devil very happy,» St. Joseph Calasanctius asserts, and St. Alphonsus replies, «Not only does he make the devil happy, but he even does the devil's work, since he prevents the others from keeping silence and living in the holy exercise of the presence of God. Wordy religious are the old familiar devils of religious houses, and they do a terrible amount of harm which they will realize only after they die.»

St. Ignatius Loyola believed that the habit of breaking silence was a sufficiently serious defect to justify sending someone away, no doubt because of the scandal and evil such a religious causes.

St. Bernard felt the same way. Here are his words, which are a commentary on the divine Master's condemnation of scandal-givers: «'He that shall scandalize one of these little ones...it were better for him that a millstone be hung around his neck and he be drowned in the depth of the sea' (Mt 18:6); it would be better for him if he had never been born. Yes, it would have been better if he had never been born into this community; it would have been better for him if someone had placed on his shoulders the heavy yoke of the world, and sent him back into it, because if he lost his soul in the world, he would not have to hear such a terrible condemnation as he would if he lost it in religious life. He who fails to give edification cannot expect anything else but a terrible condemnation, because as St. Paul says, even if he gave his body to be burnt, he could not escape damnation.» That is all the more true because a community cannot survive without the practice of silence. «It is for that reason,» says Mabillon, «that every founder, without exception, has put the rule of silence in first place as a bulwark against all dangers.»

St. Dominic called silence the foundation of his order. «It is forbidden,» he said, «to break silence, and religious should consider it a fault to speak without real necessity.» In another place, he calls silence «one of the main columns of religious houses; everything collapses if that column gives way.» Silence is the main element of religious discipline. One can never establish order in a community without the rule of silence. Faithful observance of the rule of silence was for St. Ignatius a positive proof that fervor reigned in a religious house, and that all the virtues were flourishing there. «Would you like to know,» he said, «if piety and solid virtues are present in a religious house? See if silence is observed. All the virtues dwell in a house where you find recollection.» In his history of the Church, Fleury confirmed that opinion when he wrote, «The best disciplined convents, those where there is the most virtue, are those where silence is most rigorously observed.»

Dom Calmet, who had studied this question in depth, declares without hesitation that «nothing contributes more to the loss of religious spirit and the overthrow of communities, than the non-observance of silence. When relaxation comes on that point, one can expect nothing but calamities.» St. Lawrence Justinian was so deeply convinced of that truth that he said, «A religious who neglects the rule of silence cannot avoid hurting his conscience and falling into sin, because by his bad example, he weakens regular discipline and opens the door to relaxation.»

Gentle as he was, St. Francis de Sales did not hesitate to say that, «To refuse to observe silence is to wish to disturb and overthrow order and the congregation; it is to despise the Holy Spirit who ordained it for religious houses.»

No matter how you look at the rule of silence, it is still one of the most important.

CHAPTER TWENTY-EIGHT

THE ONLY WAY TO ESTABLISH
AND MAINTAIN UNITY IN A COMMUNITY

One day, Brother Lawrence went to see Fr. Champagnat and told him with his usual simplicity, «Father, I came to tell you something that really hurts me.»

«Make yourself at home, brother, and tell me right away and frankly just what's bothering you.»

«We're six brothers in the house to which you assigned me a few days ago. Unless I'm deceiving myself, I think I can say that we observe every point of the Rule; in my opinion, the brothers are all virtuous men who work zealously at their salvation and sanctification.

«It seems to me that we all want what is good and are working to obtain it. But in spite of all that, there isn't complete unity among us.

«There is even less unity in the community of...who are our nearest neighbors, and whom we visit now and then, and this is so, even though the three brothers there may all be stricter Christians and more fervent religious than we. I've often asked myself what could be the cause of the little difficulties which exist among us. Why isn't there complete unity among brothers who are so regular and who are working so seriously at their spiritual advancement? Why do perfect charity, union of hearts and uniformity of opinions leave so much to be desired among our nearby confrères who are none the less solidly virtuous men? And that, Father, is what's upsetting me. Please cure me by telling me the reason for these domestic squabbles and how to put an end to them.»

«Brother, you're right when you say that the brothers with whom you live and those of the neighboring community are virtuous men. They really are, and I confess that it gives me great consolation to think of them as good religious. So why isn't there perfect unity among all these good brothers? I could rest satisfied with telling you that there are minor nuisances everywhere, that the most virtuous men have their defects and are prone to commit faults, since as the Holy Spirit says, the just man sins seven times a day; but I would prefer to start at the beginning of the question, treat it fully, and tell you everything I think on the subject.

«One can be solidly virtuous and have a bad character; but the defective character of a single brother is enough to disturb unity in a house and make all the members of a community suffer. One can be regular, pious, zealous for his sanctification; one can, in a word, love God and neighbor, without having the perfection of charity, that is to say, the little virtues, which are the fruits, the adornment and the crown of charity. Without the daily habitual practice of the little virtues, there is no perfect unity in communities. The neglect or absence of the little virtues is the major, and I might say the only, cause of dissensions, divisions and discord among peoples.»

«Excuse me, Father, but I don't really understand what you mean by little virtues; would you please explain them to me?»

«Well, even though it will take a while to name and define the little virtues, I will do so. Here they are:»

The first is forbearance, which excuses, minimizes and even pardons other people's faults very readily, even if one cannot be sure of receiving a similar pardon oneself. St. Bernard gives us a striking example of such an indulgent attitude. «Brothers,» he told his religious, «I am determined to love you forever, no matter what you may do to me, and even if you do not love me. So I will become attached to you, even in spite of you. If you insult me, I will be patient; I will bow my head in the face of insults; I will conquer your bad conduct with my kindness; I will reach out to those who refuse my help; I will do good to the ungrateful; I will honor those who despise me; for we are all members of one another.»

The second is charitable concealment, which appears not to notice our neighbor's defects, wrongs, mistakes and inappropriate words, and which puts up with everything without saying a word or complaining. «Conceal the defects of your brothers and put up with them,» St. Paul tells us. Why doesn't the Apostle say to reprove, correct or punish, but rather to put up with them? Because, most of the time, it is not our job to correct; that role is reserved to the superiors, so our duty is only to bear up. And also, even when one has reproved and corrected out of duty, we must still bear up, because there are defects which can be cured only by putting up with them patiently. Moreover, there are even some defects in virtuous souls which cannot be corrected despite the efforts one makes. God leaves them there in order to require an exercise of virtue by both the one who is subject to these sorts of defects and those with whom he lives.

The third is compassion, which takes on the sufferings of those who suffer in order to lessen them, which weeps with those who weep, which shares everyone's misfortunes, and which does its utmost to relieve them or to bear them itself.

The fourth is holy cheerfulness, which takes on even the joys of those who are happy in order to increase them, to obtain for one's brothers every consolation and all the happiness which flows from virtue and from community life. St. Paul offers an admirable example of this charity, which takes every possible shape in order to be useful to one's neighbor: «I became all things to all men. [I weep with those who weep, I rejoice with those who rejoice.]» Who is weak and I am not weak? Who is scandalized and I am not on fire? [I took on every form in order to serve you and win you all for Jesus Christ.] (cf. *1 Cor* 9:19-22; *2 Cor* 11:29).

St. Cyprian, following in the footsteps of the great Apostle, told his people, «My brothers and sisters, I feel for all your sufferings, I share all your joys. I am sick with the sick; my love for you makes me feel all your pains, as well as all your joys.»

The fifth is an open mind, which never imposes its opinions on anyone, but which readily accepts whatever is good and judicious in a confrère's ideas, and which applauds his discoveries and feelings without jealousy, in order to preserve unity and fraternal charity. It is the renunciation, easily granted, of one's own opinions and the antithesis of all stubbornness and intransigence in one's ideas.

«There is to be no wrangling in words,» says the Holy Spirit (*2 Tim* 2:14). But I hear someone saying, «But I'm right, and I can't stand the stupidity and mistakes of my brothers.» Listen to the answer St. Robert Bellarmine has for you: «An ounce of charity is worth more than a hundred pounds of correctness.» Express your opinion to keep the conversation going, but then let it stand on its own without defending it. St. Elias says that in that sort of battle, the winner is the one who gives in, because he has more virtue than the others. St. Ephrem avers that he always gave in discussions for the sake of the general peace, and St. Joseph Calasanctius adds, «Those who want peace should never contradict anyone.»

The sixth is charitable solicitude, which foresees others' needs in order to spare them the pain of feeling them and the humiliation of asking for help. It is goodness of heart which does not know how to say no, which is always alert to be of service, to give pleasure and to oblige everyone.

St. Hugh, bishop of Grenoble, withdrew from time to time to the Carthusian motherhouse, to live as a simple religious under the direction of St. Bruno. One time, he was given as companion a brother named William (in those days the Carthusians lived two to a cell). But Brother William complained bitterly to St. Bruno about the bishop; and do you know why? Because despite his protests, the holy bishop did the humblest and most difficult tasks, and because he acted more like his valet than his companion, rendering him the most menial services. So he insistently begged St. Bruno to moderate the saint's humility and charity, and to order that at least the minor work around their cell be shared half and half. For his part, St. Hugh insistently begged St. Bruno to permit him to satisfy his devotion and to dedicate himself to his brother's service. That is the sort of thing the saints argue about! Arguments like that are well suited to maintaining peace!

The seventh is affability, which listens to unreasonable people without showing the least annoyance, which is always ready to come to the help of those who request it, which instructs the ignorant without growing weary and with great patience.

St. Vincent de Paul offers us a rare example of this virtue. He was known to cut short a conversation he was having with some wealthy person in order to repeat something for the fifth time to a person who couldn't understand, and he said it the last time as calmly as the first. He was known to listen without the least trace of impatience to poor people who spoke hesitantly and endlessly. Though he was so overwhelmed with work he was known to let himself be interrupted thirty times a day by scrupulous people who simply repeated the same thing over and over again in different words, to hear them out with admirable patience, to write out for them sometimes in his own hand what he had said to them, to explain it to them in greater detail if they did not understand it too well, and finally, to interrupt his recitation of his breviary and his sleep in order to be of service to his neighbor.

The eighth is urbanity and politeness, which tends to show everyone signs of respect, consideration, and deference, and which always yields the first place in order to show honor to others. «Have a profound respect for one another,» says St. Paul

(*Rom* 12:10). Deference shown with sincerity maintains mutual love, just as oil feeds the flame of a lamp which produces light. Without it there is no unity or fraternal charity. Everyone is naturally pleased to see himself honored because he is secretly convinced of his own excellence, which makes him very sensitive to any sign of either contempt or honor. Hence it follows that we like people who treat us with respect, and feel obliged to do the same for them. St. John Chrysostom says, «Love and you will be loved; praise others and you will be praised; respect them and they will respect you; give in to them readily, and they will show you all sorts of deference.»

«Do not mistreat anyone, do not be lacking in esteem for anyone, and beware of showing contempt for a single one of your brothers or of treating him harshly because of his defects. Do you make fun of your hand or foot if it has a sore or is misshapen or dirty? Don't you, on the contrary, take even better care of it? Don't you treat it more gently than if it were well?

The ninth is condescension, which readily adapts itself to other people's wishes, which is flexible enough to please those who are under our authority, which readily listens to others' opinions and appears to enjoy them even though they may not always be well-founded.

«To possess condescension,» says St. Francis de Sales, «means to accommodate everyone, to the extent that the law of God and right reason permit. It is to be like a ball of warm wax, capable of taking any shape, so long as it is good; it is not seeking one's own interests but those of our neighbor and the glory of God. Condescension is the daughter of charity, and one must be very careful not to mistake it for a certain weakness of character which prevents one from reprimanding our neighbor for his faults when we are obliged to; that would not be an act of virtue, but on the contrary, participation in another's sin.»

Going along with others' moods and putting up with his neighbor were the favorite virtues of St. Francis de Sales, and he constantly suggested them to those under his direction. He often said that people would be much better off if they accommodated themselves to other people's wishes instead of trying to force everyone to go along with their moods and opinions. There was no one more gentle and compliant than he, but he was none the less very skillful and very courageous when it came to correcting and reproving others.

The tenth is dedication to the common good, which leads us to prefer the interests of the community and even those of individuals, to our own, and which sacrifices oneself for the good of one's brothers and the prosperity of the community.

The eleventh is patience, which keeps silent, always puts up with things, and never stops doing good, even to ungrateful people. Abbot St. Eucherius was so patient that he pushed this virtue to the point of thanking those who made him suffer. The quick-tempered man is like someone with a fever; the patient man, like a doctor who relieves the fever and restores happiness and peace to those who have lost them through their anger.

Beware of becoming impatient and upset at the sight of others' faults. «If you saw someone jump into the river,» says St. Bonaventure, «would it make any sense for you to jump in yourself just because he had done so?» In the same way, put up patiently with the imperfections, defects and annoying behavior of your neighbor; that is the real way to be at peace and to preserve unity with everyone.

The twelfth is equanimity of soul and of character, which guarantees that we will always be the same, and never give way to giddiness, impatience, boredom, melancholy or bad humor, but always be gentle, gay, affable and satisfied with everyone.

The little virtues are social virtues; that is, they are extremely useful to whoever lives in a society composed of rational creatures. Without them, this little world in which we live cannot be well governed, and communities are in a constant state of agitation and upset.

Without the practice of these little virtues, there can be no domestic peace, and everyone is thereby deprived of «first aid» for the thousand daily annoyances which afflict us in this valley of tears. A house in which no account is taken of the little virtues is such a miserable place! Superiors and brothers, young and old, all disagree with one another. Without love and the practice of the little virtues, it is not possible for three brothers to live together under the same roof. Without charity and the practice of the little virtues, a religious house is like a prison or like hell.

Do you want your house to be a paradise in which all hearts are united? Love the little virtues and practice them faithfully; they constitute the real happiness of a religious house.

***

Here are a few more motives which should lead us to practice the little virtues.

The first of these motives is our neighbor's weakness. Yes, all men are weak, which is why they have so many defects. One is suspicious, and he sifts through everything anyone says or does. Another is sensitive, and haunted by the notion that others have something against him, don't give him respect, don't trust him, etc., etc. A third is beleaguered by discouragement; the least little thing gets him down, makes him sad and a burden to himself and to others. A fourth is as explosive as gunpowder, and blows up at everything anyone says to him. Finally, everyone has his weak spot, everyone is subject to many little defects or imperfections which must be put up with and which provide many opportunities to practice the little virtues. It is only just and reasonable to take care of anything which is weak; so we must put up with all the weaknesses of our neighbor.

A second motive for practicing the little virtues is the lightness of the defects to be put up with. Since most religious, by reason of their virtue and often their education, are exempt from major vices and defects, then most of the time, if we take things in good part, most of what we have to put up with in our confrères are only imperfections, quirks of character, and weaknesses which in no way prevent the persons who are subject to them from being elite souls, richly endowed, with solid virtues and a timorous conscience. How easy it is for a man of good sense and virtue to put up with such weaknesses in such souls!

The third motive flows not only from the lack of gravity of the faults in question but often even from the absence of any fault. Therefore one should put up with things in our neighbor which are indifferent in themselves and which cannot be called defects. Among them are their looks, their build, their tone of voice, their posture, physical or moral weaknesses which displease us, etc. Here again we encounter the diversity of characters and their difference from our own. One is naturally serious, the other naturally cheerful; one is timid, the other bold; this one is too slow and we must always wait for him; that one is too lively and impetuous and wants to make us go at the speed of a train or of electricity. Reason and virtue demand that we live in peace in the midst of this natural diversity, and that we adapt to others' moods with flexibility, patience and condescension. To become upset over this diversity of characters would make no more sense than to become angry because someone else likes a type of food, fruit or candy which are not to our own taste.

The fourth motive is that we all need to be put up with. There is no one so wise and accomplished that he can do without others' indulgence. Today, I will have to put up patiently with someone else; tomorrow, he or somebody else will have to put up with me. How unjust it would be to demand respect and consideration from others and respond to it with rudeness and pride!

Will you say that you have no defects and that there is nothing in you which could possibly displease your neighbor? This is what you should say to anyone vain enough to talk like that: «Brother, even though you think you're perfect, and even though I think you are a good religious, I have to admit that you make me suffer terribly. You want only fresh bread, because you have no teeth; I can't stand it, because it gives me indigestion, and I would prefer stale bread. You insist that the soup be served scalding hot; I like it cooler. You won't let the cook serve salad because of your weak stomach; I could live on salad, and it's a great sacrifice for me not to have any. You won't allow anything but cooked fruit on our table; I only like it raw, and even a bit green. You can't stand the least draft, and you make us keep all the windows shut; I like lots of fresh air, and if it were up to me, and if I took care of my own needs, I would open all the doors and windows. During recreation, you want to spend the whole time sitting down; I would often like to take a walk. And there are still an infinite number of other things you need or prefer to do which wear me down and annoy me a great deal. So you are mistaken, brother, if you think that no one has anything to suffer because of you. Despite your great virtue, which I respect and admire, I can assure you that you are for me a cause of continual sacrifices and acts of patience; but I don't complain about it, because I also have my defects and need you to put up with me.»

The fifth motive for devoting ourselves to the little virtues lies in the bonds which unite us to those whom we must put up with. «Let there be no rivalry between us,» said Abram to Lot, «because we are brothers.» What a beautiful and touching reason! And in fact, for us also, the individuals whom we must put up with are our brothers in Jesus Christ. Besides, are not the members of an Institute all brothers of the same father, who is their founder? Aren't we Little Brothers of Mary, by our very title, the cherished sons of the same mother, who is the Blessed Virgin? Let us listen to our Father, who calls out to us, «Can our divine Mother remain indifferent to the fact that we harbor in our hearts some sentiments of bitterness or even antipathy against one of our brothers, whom she perhaps loves more than she does us? I beg you, do not cause that pain and that sorrow in her motherly heart.»

Moreover, the persons we must put up with are the friends of Jesus Christ; they share in our vocation, they belong to the same family we do and work for the same goals; they are our helpers in a common task and our collaborators in a common ministry. How many reasons that gives us for loving them, being of service to them, and putting up with them with total patience!

Finally, the sixth reason for practicing the little virtues is their intrinsic excellence. I regret now that I called them little; but the expression comes from St. Francis de Sales. They are little only because they refer to things which are small in themselves: a word, an act, a look, an expression of politeness; but if you examine the principle in which they are rooted and the end towards which they tend, they are very great. For a good religious, the practice of the little virtues is a continual exercise of charity towards his neighbor; and since charity is the first and most excellent of all the virtues, the habitual practice of the little virtues produces solidly virtuous men. That should be enough to make us love them and to make the practice of them dear and easy for us.

CHAPTER TWENTY-NINE

CAN WE REACH A POINT WHERE PEACE AND UNITY IN A COMMUNITY WILL NEVER BE DISTURBED?

I.

Father Champagnat, who so much wanted to see peace and unity prevail among us, but who also had much experience with human weakness, that inexhaustible source of division and trouble, once put the above question to his brothers. His own answer was that it is impossible, and he gave six reasons to back it up.

The First Cause of Disunity—diversity of characters. St. Gregory says that man is the most diversified creature in the animal kingdom. You will never see two men who have exactly the same features and shape, and that variety of face and body is found also in their characters.

Men have very different tastes and inclinations; one appears very likable, another hard and uncouth; this one is full of simplicity and candor which charms everyone; that one is secretive, deceptive or uncommunicative and no one can put up with him; this one wants unity and concord—he is always content, tranquil, at peace with himself and others; that one wants war—always dissatisfied, restless and irritable, he enjoys discord, finds something to criticize in everything, and as the Holy Spirit puts it, his hand is raised against everyone, and he cannot get along with anyone. Jacob was a peaceful, gentle man; he had a happy character, most suited for keeping the peace. Esau was hard, difficult, contrary; his father Isaac had even predicted that he would be at war all his life and always involved in quarrels. Defective characters are not rare in community. We find there [are] religious who are mockers and scoffers, who enjoy contradicting the words and actions of others, to make them look ridiculous. Some are proud, disdainful, scornful; they esteem and approve only what they themselves have done; they cannot stand hearing their confrères praised, and always find some way to put them down. Others hastily and unreservedly blame even what they don't understand; they speak bluntly, without any regard for the age, rank and merit of others. And others are rude and uncouth to one another, show no respect for one another, speak impolitely to one another, etc. All these brothers are tiresome characters who foment discord and destroy charity and perfect unity.

The Second Cause of Disunity—lack of zeal for their perfection on the part of a number of brothers. In religious houses we often see men loaded with talents and gifted with excellent qualities, who nonetheless are neither solidly virtuous nor capable of anything great. They always prove not to be up to their task, and become the cause of a thousand minor disturbances in community. What causes this state of things? Infidelity to grace: these religious fear to do violence to themselves; they don't want to take the trouble to reform their character, to correct certain little defects or quirks which spoil it, and so on. So their talents and good qualities become useless to them, or serve only to put them on the wrong road and to bring trouble into a house.

If the tiniest part of a watch breaks, the whole movement stops. If a draftee is only a ligne[1] too short, he is still deferred. In

---

[1] An old unit of measure equal to 1/12 of an inch or 2.125 millimeters.

the same way, a single defect which we do not correct, a passion we do not try to overcome, a wrong opinion which we do not want to give up, and a thousand other things of that sort, are enough to paralyze everything good in a man, make him unfaithful to his vocation, and make that religious a cause of embarrassment and a source of minor divisions, simply because everywhere he goes he is found wanting; everywhere he goes he brings his defects which make everyone suffer; in a word, everywhere he goes he is not what he should be. So you may be sure of this: a tepid religious creates trouble and divisions and destroys charity and perfect unity of hearts.

The Third Cause of Disunity—the hardness of the human heart and its tendency toward severity. Since his fall from justice through original sin, man has been evil. He believes evil rather than good, he easily exaggerates the wrongs of his neighbor and almost always increases them; he sees others' defects clearly but not their virtues. That is why St. Thomas says that gentleness and charity towards our neighbor are virtues rarer than chastity. Who can say that he has never offended against charity? One day, St. John, moved by a spirit which was not that of Jesus, asked that fire from heaven consume the Samaritans. In another situation, St. Peter put himself above all the other apostles: «Though all lose faith in you, I will never lose faith» (*Mt* 26:33). St. Paul left Mark and Barnabas because of some quarrel which had arisen among them. St. John Chrysostom and St. Epiphanius exchanged hard words, as we will see a bit later. St. Bernard was so strict with his brothers that he discouraged them, and so on. And yet, all these individuals were saints. What a rare virtue is perfect charity! The wickedness of man's heart [and] his severity towards others—in a word, his lack of charity—are the principal cause of divisions and dissensions in communities.

The Fourth Cause of Disunity—human weakness or each one's defects. A religious house is like a tree laden with blossoms; some of them drop off, while the others set and bear fruit. But look at the difference among the fruits of that same

317

tree: some are beautiful and well-developed, and a few attain magnificent size and color; others are small, underdeveloped, and bruised; and a few which are wormy shrivel up and fall from the tree.

What does all that mean? The flowers which the wind takes before they set represent the novices who do not persevere. The small, underdeveloped fruit are a figure of tepid religious who are unfaithful to grace and who drag themselves along in the practice of virtue. The beautiful fruit are an image of the great number of fervent, regular, truly virtuous religious. The fruit which is extraordinarily large, well proportioned, perfectly colored, without spots or bruises, symbolizes chosen souls, men of heroic virtue, religious who are faithful to their vocation and a real treasure for their community.

Still, since these religious who are so different in virtue are all men, they make everyone suffer; even the greatest saints give others reason to practice patience, because the one who is the most perfect is merely the one who has fewest defects. A rosebush which bears more roses than any others, and perfumes the air, still has thorns. In communities, those religious who are wiser than the others, who are loaded down with more virtues, and who spread around them the sweet perfume of sanctity, still do and say certain things, and have manners and habits which do not please everyone and are not acceptable to every type of personality, and for some they are sharp and painful thorns.

The wormy fruit which dries up or spoils represents vicious and unfaithful religious. In every community one can encounter unsettled and nasty men who demand much patience on the part of the good ones. In Adam's family there was Cain, the fratricide; in Noah's, Ham, who deserved to be cursed by his father; in Abraham's, the savage and vicious Ishmael who tried to ruin Isaac; in Isaac's, Esau who was reprimanded by God; in David's, the incestuous and parricidal Absalom; among the apostles, Judas. So who can be surprised, after such examples from such perfect settings, that in the most fervent religious institutes one can find a few perverse individuals, abnormal members of a noble family, rotten fruit on a healthy tree? The Church, says St. Jerome, is represented by Noah's ark, which held the wolf and the sheep, the lion and the lamb, the crow and the dove, and all sorts of animals both pure and impure.

Communities are like the threshing floor of the gospel, where the good grain is mixed with the chaff; like the net full of good and useless fish; like the banquet where someone among the guests did not have a wedding garment; like the group of ten virgins, some wise, some foolish; like a big house where one finds not only vessels of gold and silver but also some made of wood, clay and iron; like the field where weeds and grain grow together. That is why St. Augustine says, «So long as the Church is on earth, so long as the wheat suffers and sighs among the chaff, the ears of grain are mixed in with the weeds, the vessels of mercy stand among the vessels of indignation, we will never lack for adversaries who make us suffer and disturb our peace.» One single bad religious is enough to affect the unity of a community and to try the patience of every member of it.

The Fifth Cause of Disunity—difference of opinion about things. It often happens that men of good will unconsciously fight among themselves, and make problems for one another because of their clash of characters, differences of opinion, or the weakness of human judgment which sees only one side of things. Consequently they are mistaken in their opinions, but are without guilt in the sight of God, no matter what others may think of them. Very often, lack of precision in speech, lack of clarity in our way of expressing ourselves, or insufficient explanations lead to ambiguity and misunderstandings about the simplest questions. People don't understand one another; ultimately, everyone is right, but for lack of clarity or moderation, everyone is more or less wrong. It is very often confusion over words which causes disagreements, challenges and quarrels. How many questions, about which people could not fail to agree, but which from time immemorial have engendered disputes which are sometimes very bitter, are in the long run only arguments about words.

The following story illustrates the point: Baronius, in his annals, records an argument between St. Epiphanius and St. John Chrysostom, which fits our context perfectly. The former said he would never put up with the followers of Origen; the latter wanted to move much more slowly and protested that one should not condemn the innocent along with the guilty. Epiphanius retorted that the name of the Origenists was so infamous and their crime so black, that without any hesitation it would be an act of Christian piety to wipe out these vipers within the Church! Chrysostom observed that a good judge never condemns anyone without a hearing. Epiphanius replied that his companion was being too considerate. Chrysostom complained that the other was becoming too angry and didn't have enough patience to listen to the truth.

«Patience! You mean lack of intelligence and dissimulation!»

«No, I mean your violence and haste.»

«So? Are you afraid to condemn heretics?»

«Aren't you afraid to condemn the innocent person along with the criminal, or even to condemn the former instead of the latter?»

«I see you're leaning toward the side of Origen.»

«And I'm afraid you may be on the side of the enemies of the truth.»

«Oh, really? Well, I'm leaving, but I tell you on God's behalf that you will not die in Constantinople, that you will be sent into exile, and that you will end your days while traveling far away from your flock.»

«And I tell you on God's behalf that you will not reach your diocese and you will die at sea.»

Both were saints, both prophesied; both were right in their zeal in the defense of a holy cause. But neither was free from wrong in his manifestation of that zeal, in the excessive heat of their discussion or the sharpness of their words. Besides, don't their respective opinions seem to express, in the case of one, too much severity, and in the case of the other, extreme indulgence, and on both sides, a too absolute intransigence? Whatever, that's how their dispute ended, and each died as the other had prophesied.

Divine Providence permits such things in the saints so that they will mistrust themselves, humble themselves, confess their weakness and ignorance, and not become stubbornly set in their opinions. But are you still astonished that peace among God's children is sometimes disturbed, and there are arguments in the most edifying and best-run communities?

The Sixth Cause of Discord—the fragility of our unity. Yes, peace and concord are fragile things. In fact, it is difficult for men of conflicting characters, subject to a thousand defects, and obliged to live together, not to say or do anything which would ever disturb peace and unity. Their mentalities being so different, their wills so often opposed, their thoughts, affections and tastes must necessarily be different and give rise to differences of opinion. One esteems what another thinks should be blamed; what one approves, another feels obliged to condemn; what pleases this one is repugnant to that one. Everyone who knows how to write forms the same letters, and yet no two people form them exactly the same way. It is exactly the same with opinions, judgments and affections.

So how can we be astonished if from time to time, little clouds arise and threaten the peace. A man of good sense and virtue is no more surprised by such unpleasantness than by the changes of the weather or by the various irregularities which together make up the beauty and variety to a landscape. For the rest, if it is not possible to entirely avoid these little problems, it is relatively easy to make them a rare occurrence, and by so doing, to preserve peace and unity among us to the extent that is possible. All we have to do is take the following advice, which comes to us from the Holy Spirit.

II.

1. Imitate St. Paul, who says, «I try to be helpful to everyone at all times» (*1 Cor* 10:33). Like this great apostle, anyone who wants to live in peace in community must accommodate himself to various characters, be full of condescension, and bend easily according to circumstances, not in just a few things, but in everything. In music, although all the tones are different, they still manage to produce sweet harmonies. Likewise, in a community, even though characters are different, they should, through condescension and the spirit of charity, produce a pleasant harmony. «In all things, I seek to please everyone,» but only when it is a question of good or indifferent things, in which there is at least no sin, for when it is a question of offending God, we must know how to say with St. Paul, «If I still sought to please men, I would not be the servant of Christ» (*Gal* 1:10).

2. Being as wise as you are, put up with the imprudent (cf. *2 Cor* 11:19), the slow-witted and the imperfect. One effect of good common sense is the ability to put up with things contrary to common sense. It is a clear and certain indication of great mental capacity, high intelligence, and sure and profound judgment, to understand human nature, to be truly convinced that it is simply a composite of weaknesses, defects, needs, and imperfections of all sorts, and to be able to put up with all those things without difficulty. That is why men with good judgment and good spirit, are always and everywhere the most tolerant, the most indulgent, the least sensitive, the most peaceful, the least demanding and easiest to please. On the contrary, narrow minds, men with

mistaken or limited judgment, always have their little heads troubled by others' defects, just as Abraham's ram had his caught in the thornbush.

3. Like God's chosen ones, put on a heart full of mercy, goodness, humility, modesty and patience (cf. *Col* 3:12). A merciful heart and the spirit of compassion for our neighbor's troubles, are the most excellent dispositions for practicing the duties of charity.

Put on a heart full of mercy: have the spirit of charity and compassion for your neighbor, and show it externally. Put on: that means outwardly; in other words, be affable, honest, considerate; show your neighbor a pleasant face, one likely to attract him and win him over to you; show yourself ready to help him and please him every time you have a chance to do so; show him a face which reflects holy joy and gentle gaiety which console the afflicted, which raise up discouraged hearts; a face which is pleasant, calm, benevolent, which dissipates prejudices, sensitivity, ill humor, anger, antipathy and so on.

A heart—that means your interior; in other words, really love your neighbor, be touched by his difficulties and help him; esteem him, never think ill of him, excuse, hide and cover up his faults; let neither hatred or selfishness or jealousy, or anything of that sort, ever enter your heart; let nothing come forth from your heart but sentiments of compassion, indulgence and piety for your neighbor's misfortunes. St. Paul calls the saints «vessels of mercy» (*Rom* 9:23). Why so? Because it is characteristic of all the saints to spread mercy everywhere around them; because the heart of the saints are simply a composite of goodness, charity, gentleness, indulgence and love of neighbor.

4. Do not be overly just (*Eccles* 7:17). Minds are like clothes; if they are to be comfortable, they must not be too small. If minds are so just that they make no allowance for human nature, if they don't give a little, they are not suited to living with other people. If you see a man who is severe towards his brothers'

faults, who cannot forgive a fault which slips out, a defect of character, or the like, you may be sure, as St. Jerome says, that such a man is more just than he should be. There are so many things we must not see, or pretend not to see; so many things we must put up with; so many others we must touch only lightly.

When you have to punish someone who has failed, don't be too just, don't go beyond the limits of a gentle justice which pities the weak. What you cannot correct, put up with, for St. Paul tells us that, «We that are stronger ought to bear the infirmities of the weak and not please ourselves» (*Rom* 15:1). Some physical illnesses are incurable, some defects cannot be remedied. How, for example, can one cure a cripple or a person blind in one eye? You are wasting your time trying; such defects will never disappear. It is sometimes the same with certain defects of the mind, which are to some degree incurable, so we must put up with them with all the gentleness and tranquility we can muster.

Do not be too just, even in demanding things which are good in themselves: each one's duty or the task which he should carry out, etc. Be satisfied with what each one is capable of doing, according to his strength and talents. Be satisfied with good will, because asking a brother for more than he can give, demanding too much perfection, will throw him into discouragement and lose him.

Do not be too just, and never say, «I will never put up with being slighted; I demand the respect due to my rank, my age,» and so forth. He who carries on too much about his rights is often too just—too demanding, too sensitive. A good religious considers himself the least in the house, shows honor to all, makes himself everyone's servant, and expects nothing from anyone. Everyone can forget him or treat him like a servant; he pays no attention because he believes he is in his proper place and being treated as he deserves.

5. Always be united and think the same way as far as possible. Why as far as possible? Because among men of good

will, and even among the saints, there are minds which do not always agree, because they see things from a different point of view and each one has his own lights. In matters which are indifferent, each one may follow his own inclination. St. Augustine and St. Jerome held contrary opinions on certain open questions, and exchanged heated letters in which each upheld his point of view, but without wounding charity. The just may well disagree on certain questions, because they do not think the same way; but their wills are always in agreement, because they always want what is good and tend toward God alone; otherwise they would not be just.

«It may be that you hold some opinion contrary to truth,» St. Augustine wrote to St. Jerome; «but in defending your opinions, you must not do anything which may be contrary to charity. And even when one is certain that he is in the truth, he must still uphold it with charity.»

St. Paul wrote to the Ephesians, «I...beseech you that you walk worthy of the vocation in which you are called, with all humility and mildness, with patience, supporting one another in charity, careful to keep the unity of the Spirit in the bond of peace» (*Eph* 4:1-3). «Finally,» adds St. Peter, «be all of one mind, having compassion for one another, being lovers of the brotherhood, merciful, modest, humble» (*1 Pet* 3:8). These almost identical words from the two apostles show us how effectively we may maintain unity among us by all striving to think the same way and to preserve the unity of a single spirit. That is also the wish our Founder bequeathed to us in his spiritual testament: «Be of one heart and one mind.»

6. «Honor everyone,» says St. Peter (*1 Pet* 2:17), and you will preserve unity, which is such a fragile thing. Esteem and honor all your brothers, because they are servants of Jesus Christ, temples of the Holy Spirit, children of God, very noble, very excellent creatures. They are elite souls consecrated to divine service and worship; souls predestined for great perfection, for great glory in

heaven; souls who for the most part are loaded with virtues; souls whom God loves as the apple of his eye and whom he overwhelms with his blessings.

Honor and respect all your brothers, because they are part of your family; because they are called to the same vocation; because they share your table, your work, your merits; because they are members of the same society and because to despise a single one of them is to despise and offend all the others.

Honor and respect your older brothers, because they superior to you in age, in virtue, in practical wisdom, in common sense, in experience, in dignity, and because it is a duty for everyone everywhere to respect white hairs and honor old age.

Honor and respect the young brothers, because they are simple and candid; because they are the wealth and hope of the society; because they expect you to give good example; because you are all more or less in charge of their education; and because it is from you that they should acquire good breeding, good manners, family spirit and the spirit of charity, which is a spirit of honesty and mutual respect.

Honor and respect your equals, remembering that uncouth behavior, improper familiarity, and forgetfulness of the proprieties and consideration, breed contempt, kill friendship, produce quarrels and give rise to discord.

Honor and respect all your brothers, especially the infirm, the imperfect, the narrow minded, those who have most defects of soul and body, remembering that whatever is weak and suffering merits consideration and encouragement; that this brother who is unwell in mind or body is one of your members, part of yourself. Now, do you despise your foot when it hurts? Do you make fun of your hand when it has sores, when it is misshapen or dirty? Do you not treat these sick members with more consideration, gentleness, care and respect than those that are healthy?

Honor and respect all your brothers, because they have every right to demand that duty of charity from you. All intelligent beings, humans, angels and God himself, are so sensitive on that point that Our Lord, who endured the insults of the Jews with divine patience, did complain about this one, telling them, «You have not given me the honor that is my due.»

Honor and respect all your brothers in order to preserve charity. In point of fact, marks of honor and deference, sincerely given, foster mutual love and domestic peace, just as oil feeds the flame of a lamp. Whence it follows that without this respect and mutual deference, there is absolutely no family spirit or fraternal charity.

Honor and respect all your brothers, because you want them to honor and respect you; it will be done to you as you have done to others.

«Render to all their due. Tribute to whom tribute is due, or customs or fear or honor. Owe no one anything except to love one another» (*Rom* 13:7-8). What is our debt towards our neighbor? It includes honor, respect, consideration, good manners, marks of esteem and affection, help whenever needed and above all, edification and good example. Now, this debt should be paid daily, if we don't want to die insolvent, and if we really want to be paid back.

Honor and respect all your brothers, says the Holy Spirit, «so as to imitate God who governs us with great lenience (cf. Wis 12:18) and who leads the just by the right way, gives them knowledge of holy things... helps them against their oppressors, and helps them acquire spiritual wealth» (cf. *Wis* 10:10-11).

Honor and respect all your brothers so as to imitate Jesus Christ and be filled with his spirit. I am, he tells us, like a flowering vine; I spread everywhere the good odor of humility and charity. My dealings with men are accompanied with respect like a perfume which scents every heart. «When I mention Jesus,» says St. Bernard, «I picture a man who is gentle, modest, kindly, helpful, etc., very remarkable for his consideration and urbanity.»

7. Finally, meditate on this saying of Jesus Christ and make it your rule of conduct: «Blessed are the peacemakers, for they shall be called children of God» (*Mt* 5:9). St. John Chrysostom says that in community, those who reconcile minds which are in opposition, and who bring peace, do the work of Jesus Christ, who came into the world to reconcile us with God and among ourselves, and to put an end to all dissension. By devoting themselves to such an excellent and godly task, they deserve to be called God's children. They are the columns, the adornment and the treasure of a community. Those, on the other hand, who bring trouble and division, are its scourge and pestilence; they ought to be punished and isolated.

CHAPTER THIRTY

TRIALS OR THE TESTING OF FRATERNAL CHARITY

The verb «to test» or «to try» has various implications: to examine, investigate, purify, shape, separate, choose or reject. In the crucible of trial, St. Augustine tells us, the chaff is distinguished and separated from the grain. Iron loses its rust; gold is purified and becomes more brilliant; straw is burned up, consumed, destroyed. There is a truth one should never lose sight of—namely, that God wants to save us by means of contradictions, suffering and the cross, which is why St. John said that, «Jesus came with water and blood» (*1 Jn* 5:6). Water signifies human nature; blood, the sufferings which must immolate it. That is the only reason why God has left within us the effects of original sin, so that they may test our virtue.

According to the principles of faith, everything works out for the benefit of God's chosen ones—our weaknesses, misfortunes, passions, sinful inclinations, and defects should serve as stepping stones to raise us to God. «Vices don't go to heaven,» St. Augustine tells us, «but they raise us there if we fight them and trample them underfoot.» Even the devils' wickedness, in God's designs, should help to test and perfect our virtue and lead us to heaven.

When Duke Robert of Normandy arrived in Palestine to visit the holy places, he encountered four Saracens who wanted to rob and kill him. As it turned out, he stared them down, terrified them with his show of strength, and forced them to carry him to Jerusalem in a sedan chair. Along the way he met one of his friends who was returning from there and who asked if he had any messages to send home. «Yes,» Robert answered, «tell them you saw the Duke of Normandy being carried to heaven by four devils.» That is a graphic image of the strong soul which overcomes and floors its passions and wins out over its trials. It turns its great enemy, the devil, into the artisan of its good fortune and the pedestal of its glory.

We can divide trials into four categories:

1. those coming directly from the devil; that is to say, temptations with which he assails us to lead us to do wrong;

2. those coming from our peers or from our dealings with our neighbor;

3. those which come from the work entrusted to us;

4. finally, those which come from ourselves, such as our character defects, intellectual limitations, and physical ailments.

Here we will discuss only the second type of trials, which include:

- Our neighbor's defects, which we must put up with charitably and patiently, and differences of personality to which we must accommodate ourselves and blend into our own.

- The physical ailments of our brothers and students, towards which we must never show repugnance, but which we must rather alleviate to the extent that this is our responsibility.

- Irregularity and bad example, which we must never imitate nor even approve of.

- Ingratitude, which must never prevent us from continuing to do good or be of assistance to our neighbor.

- Divergent ideas on matters of opinion, argumentativeness, lack of respect, etc.

- Persecution and slander on the part of the wicked or of those who wish to be our enemies.

If you are wondering why God permits these trials which flow from our dealings with our neighbor, we will point out here the three main ones, which we will call the aims of Providence.

1. To correct our defects. In the designs of Divine Providence, contradictions work to the advantage of good people the way in which a jeweler's file removes encrustations from a piece of gold, or a sculptor's chisel polishes his statue, or a gardener's clippers prune and shape his trees. St. John of the Cross understood this perfectly, which is why he told his religious, «Imagine that your brothers are so many sculptors armed with the hammer and chisel of their own defects, in order to correct yours, and that you have been set before them like a block of marble destined, in the mind of God, to become a statue representing Christ crucified with all his virtues.»

Our neighbor's defects thus serve to correct our own, and it is the same with religious as with the stones in a river bed which become polished as they rub against one another. Plutarch used to say, «No man will ever become truly virtuous unless he has a sincere friend or a great enemy.» A sincere friend will make us aware of our defects; but, apart from the fact that such friends are hard to find, it can happen that charity will let him see only our virtues, and make him too indulgent with our defects.

On the other hand, an enemy, or an irregular and contentious brother, noticing them in great detail, will reproach us for them, will constantly throw them in our face, and will force us, so to speak, to correct them. This sort of confrontation is painful, but useful, which is why St. Alphonsus said, «Critical and difficult spirits, who are full of defects, are useful in community: they give the others practice in patience, and force them to watch themselves, which helps them to avoid a host of faults and to correct their defects.

2. To test our virtues, develop them and perfect them. It is a common enough error, even among spiritual persons, to think that possessing a particular virtue consists in the absence of the

contrary vice. But there is a big difference between having the habit of a virtue and not performing acts of the vice opposed to it. Virtue is a habit, and that habit is formed in us only by oft-repeated acts. It is not enough, for example, to abstain from acts of anger in order to have the virtue of meekness; we must also perform acts of that virtue on occasions which would normally arouse our irascible faculty.

Fleeing from vice is one path toward virtue, but it is not virtue itself. That a person is meek when nothing irritates, offends or contradicts him, is no great marvel; on the contrary, it would be strange if he were bitter and irritable in spite of the kindness, submission and deference of those around him. Bees use their stingers on those who disturb them but don't hurt those who come near their hive without bothering them. Cats use velvet paws on those who pet them, but are quick to use their claws on those who mistreat them. There are persons who appear to be very gentle, so long as everyone does what they want; but touch those mountains and you will see smoke and fire—you will realize that there are live coals beneath those ashes.

The touchstone for distinguishing true goodness from false is the way someone puts up with insults and contradictions. It is not hard to be good to those who are good to us, but to be good to those who persecute us and to speak with moderation, gentleness and affability to those who make fun of us, blame us, insult or calumniate us—that is proof positive that a person is gifted with true goodness, that he possesses to a high degree the virtues of charity and meekness. So let us never forget the truth that virtue is acquired by frequently repeated acts, and that the strongest and most perfect virtue is the one that grows like the lily amid the thorns of difficulties.

«It is no great thing,» says St. Francis de Sales, «for a religious to appear meek, and to commit few faults when he is not subjected to anything which might anger him and try his patience. If I hear someone say, 'There is a holy religious!,' I immediately ask, 'Does he have any responsibility in the community?' If the answer is negative, I don't think much of his sanctity, for there is a big difference between the virtue of this religious, and that of another who is really tested, either interiorly by the temptations he experiences, or exteriorly by the contradictions he has to put up with, because solid virtue is never acquired in time of peace, when we are not tested by temptations to the contrary.» There are unfortunately a great number of souls who are weak and not too well informed about the ways of God, who do not understand this truth. They think virtue consists in being peaceful and tranquil without trials or combats. Such ignorance is very dangerous for them and can even become fatal.

It makes them consider as an obstacle to their perfection what is really an essential means to it, and it leads them to fail against charity by being scandalized by their neighbor's defects. «The life of the saints,» says St. Augustine, «cannot be lacking in contradictions and combats, because their spiritual advancement takes place amid trials. The elect advance in virtue through temptation; what the devil suggests to destroy them, God turns to their glory.»

St. Leo the Great assures us that, «Virtue fades away when it has no adversaries; there are never any great virtues without great trials.» St. Jerome comments that, «Charity toward our neighbor increases in strength and in merit to the extent that we repeat acts of it.» «Whence it follows,» says St. Fulgentius, «that if we stop practicing a virtue because we have no occasion to do so, we lose it.»

«Do not think,» replies St. Augustine, «that there is no particular reason why there are very imperfect and even wicked people in the world. Every imperfect or wicked person is on earth in order to correct himself or to test the good ones.» By means of wicked people and those full of defects, God forms and teaches his saints and prepares them for glory. The persecutions of the wicked, or the defects of imperfect people, are the file which scrapes away the rust of the saints, the chisel which polishes them, the pruning hook which cuts away everything defective in them.

«By means of the wicked,» says Origen, «God develops the virtues of the saints and makes them shine. If the malice of the former were done away with, the virtues of the latter would not be so heroic nor so resplendent; they would be neither so striking nor so meritorious. Take away the malice, the envy, the perversity of Joseph's brothers, and by that very fact you deprive that holy patriarch of all the acts of virtue and all the merits which his brothers' wickedness added to his crown.»

«The world,» St. Basil observes, «is a battlefield. We see virtue fighting on one side, and crime on the other; on one side, pride and insolence, and on the other, humility and modesty; on one side, anger, outbursts of temper, cutting words, and on the other, patience and meekness; on one side, unreasonable demands, licentiousness, injustice, and on the other, leniency, charitable forbearance and charity, which revenges itself by pardoning, doing good and responding to evil with nothing but helpful service. This is how the vices, defects and contrariness of the wicked give good people such strong and persevering virtues.»

«And so God,» St. Augustine concludes, «permits and puts up with the vices and defects of disorderly persons, in order to give good people the means to practice patience, mortification, constancy and all sorts of other virtues.»

«For,» says St. Bede, «it is absolutely certain that no one can become an Abel if the malice of a Cain does not try his patience and virtue.»

People who lack intelligence, depth of judgment and virtue, are astonished and sometimes even scandalized to find so many problems in community, so many weak souls, so many religious who are imperfect and full of defects. They imagined that religious houses held only saints and souls who no longer shared the weakness of human nature. This dangerous illusion leads them to judge their brothers' conduct severely, to magnify their imperfections, to attribute to them a thousand defects, to regard as defects what are merely quirks of character, and not to see their virtues. To be cured of such an illusion, these religious, whoever they are, must often recall the following principles, which are confirmed by experience:

a. Religious houses, according to St. Francis de Sales, are hospitals to which spiritually ill people come to be cured; so one should not be astonished to find there weak souls full of defects.

b. Solidly virtuous persons carefully count and consider their brothers' virtues and all their good qualities, but they hardly notice or pay any attention to their defects. But wicked, imperfect and mean-spirited persons see only the bad side of their neighbor; they do not notice his virtues, which means that their judgments about their brothers are usually unjust.

c. In the designs of Providence, personal defects should contribute to the building up of our perfection.[1] Whence it follows that God, in his mercy, often allows certain defects to persist in very holy persons, as a perpetual test for their virtue, a means of progress and a source of merits.

d. Our neighbor's defects serve to test the virtue of every member of the community and give them a powerful means of sanctification. That is why St. Pachomius said, «Our spiritual life and death depend to some extent on our neighbor. How so? If we win him over to God by our good example, if we patiently put up with his defects, if we practice charity toward him, we save ourselves and we advance in virtue with giant steps. If we do the opposite, we sin against Jesus Christ and we are lost.»

---

[1] Bossuet says, «Let those fear to discover the defects of holy souls, who do not know how powerful is the arm of God, to make those defects serve not only for his glory, but also for the perfection of his elect. As for us, we know what St. Peter's denials did for him; what the persecutions he inflicted on the Church did for Paul; what his errors did for St. Augustine».

St. Francis de Sales speaks in the same vein: «Half of our sanctification comes from our dealings with our neighbor, because by putting up with one another and pardoning one another, we practice all the virtues and bring them to perfection. Now, if our neighbor had no defects, what would we have to put up with? Take away our neighbors' defects, and tell me where we will find occasions to practice the most beautiful virtues. If our brothers were perfect, if we had to live with angels, where would be our patience, meekness, mortification, charity, and all the beautiful virtues which flow from them? We would never have a chance to practice them.»

St. Bernard was so convinced of this that he even dared to tell superiors, «If your community has only good religious, all of them men of good character, you must buy a wicked one, with a hard, difficult, bad-tempered, contradictory character, so as to give yourself and all your brothers opportunities to train yourselves in meekness, patience, charity and all the beautiful social virtues. Virtue remains weak so long as it is not tested by being badly treated by our neighbor; annoying relations are the crucible in which charity, patience and meekness are tested. That is where you see to what degree a soul possesses them.»

But it is not necessary to pay his weight in gold for a defective and irregular religious, for we are all thorns in one another's side. Just as there is no rose without thorns, so there is no religious without defects; the holiest is not the one who has none at all, nor even at times the one who has the fewest, but the one who watches himself most closely and who best combats them. We all have defects; so we all test one another's virtue.

«The most united and fervent communities,» says Ven. Fr. Liebermann, «have never been able to withdraw from unpleasant contacts with people; if two angels had to live together under human conditions, there would be clouds in the sky within twenty-four hours.» «No matter how carefully subjects are chosen,» remarks St. Jane Frances de Chantal with the voice of experience, «God always permits there to be a couple of unpleasant personalities in each house, to test the others. Far from complaining about this arrangement on the part of Divine Providence, we should be grateful for it, since it offers us an opportunity to practice the most beautiful virtues.»

Fr. Champagnat tells us that, «There are three ways in which our neighbor helps us to go to God: first, he leads us to God by the good odor of his virtues and the good example he gives us; second, he leads us to God by his defects, which we must put up with, conceal and excuse, and which often make us practice patience, meekness, charity and a thousand other virtues; third, he also leads us to God by the opportunities he gives us to practice zeal on his behalf by warning, admonishing and helping him to correct himself.»

From all this, it is easy to understand how badly mistaken superiors are when they think it a misfortune to have defective subjects to correct and reform, and who try to avoid that task by asking that these men be changed, at the expense of their duty and their own spiritual best interests. By so doing, they deprive themselves of a chance to practice virtue and of a great means of sanctification, and they fail in charity towards those whose change they request. It is to no one's advantage to readily transfer defective subjects whose conduct or character leave something to be desired.

A good superior does not readily request such changes. It is against charity to hand on to another director a brother about whom one has reason to complain. And besides, one very rarely finds men with no defects. Perhaps his replacement will be worse. So it is more simple, reasonable and charitable to work at forming or reforming the subjects one has. When a coachman frequently requests a change of horses, one eventually begins to suspect that he does not know his trade.

Father Balthazar Alvarez, who thoroughly understood the merit attached to putting up with a subject and forming him, asked his provincials to send cantankerous and difficult religious to his school, so that he could win them over with his prudence and meekness, and also to give himself a chance to practice virtue. Others do just the opposite, and get rid of imperfect or difficult subjects as quickly as they can; but sad to say, these spiritual invalids, who are thus paraded from house to house, constantly changing doctors and treatments, become weaker all the time and eventually lose their vocation. A little charitable zeal, patience, tolerance and abnegation would have been a much wiser move and would sooner or later have produced very different results.

St. Vincent de Paul wrote to one of his religious, who had complained about a confrère placed under his authority and asked that he be transferred, «Put up meekly with that confrère about whom you spoke to me. You may not have the defects which you criticize in him, but you have others which he has to put up with. If you did not have this brother, you would have nothing to suffer, your charity would get no exercise and would not grow, your life would bear no resemblance to that of Jesus Christ, who wanted crude disciples with many defects. Now, do you know why Jesus Christ acted that way? To be the model of superiors and to teach them that it is by putting up with the defects of their inferiors that they acquire much merit, perfect themselves in virtue, make themselves pleasing to God and win souls for him.»

3. Finally, by helping us to correct our defects and by giving us opportunities to train ourselves to solid virtue, trials flowing from our dealings with our neighbor increase our merit and prepare for us greater glory in heaven. This is why St. Bonaventure said that it is very useful for good people, so long as they are living in this world, to mingle with imperfect people who are full of defects. The latter are an occasion of great merit and a great reward for good people.

In fact, good people feel sorry for the weaknesses or faults of the imperfect and the wicked; they exercise zeal in their regard by working to correct them and train them to virtue; they watch over themselves so as not to imitate or offend them; and they are often tested in a salutary manner, even by the persecutions they have to suffer at their hands; finally, they humble themselves by recognizing that it is to God alone that they owe the fact that they do not commit similar faults. It is clear that if good people did not have opportunities to perform all these acts of virtue, they would have less merit, their virtues would be less strong, less brilliant and less perfect, and consequently, their eternal reward would be less great.

St. Jerome set such great store by putting up with one's neighbor's defects that he preferred it to the merits of the contemplative life. A very virtuous member of an influential Roman family once wrote him to ask to be received into the convent he had founded in Bethlehem. Among her reasons for leaving the world, she alleged that her mother, even though she was very pious, was a great obstacle to her perfection, and because of her bad character, put her at risk of committing many faults. The holy doctor replied, «If your mother is the way you say she is, stay with her, because by putting up with her and patiently suffering everything she does to upset you, you will better train yourself in meekness, charity, obedience, mortification, and self-renunciation, and you will earn more merit than in any novitiate.»

Such opportunities to practice virtue and make oneself pleasing to God are more highly valued than treasure by souls who want to advance in virtue. Being convinced of that, St. Dorotheus considered putting up with one's neighbor, and the practice of virtue which necessarily flows from it, as a mark of predestination. «No one,» he said, «knows if he is deserving of love or hatred; that is a secret hidden in the heart of God. However, we almost come to know it when we have love for our brothers, that is to say, when we help them in their need, put up with them patiently, and help them to correct their defects, because anyone who loves his brother in this way loves God. Now, he who possesses God's love is in the state of grace, deserves to be loved, and bears on his forehead the seal of the elect.»

So, let us say it again, since we can never be sufficiently convinced of this truth: in God's eyes, our defects are part of his plan for our sanctification; our neighbor's defects are a gift for us, and a source of heavenly merit and glory because they test our virtue. So we must thank God for having left them that way, and apply ourselves to making good use of the precious means of perfection which are given us through them, by showing ourselves full of charity and forbearance towards our neighbor, and by putting up with him very patiently.

CHAPTER THIRTY-ONE

WHAT LIFE IN A RELIGIOUS COMMUNITY SHOULD BE LIKE

After visiting a certain community of the institute, Father Champagnat was not at all satisfied with what he had seen, so he told the brother director, «I am not pleased with your community.»

«What did you notice that was wrong, Father?»

«Your community has no religious life, no family life. Happiness cannot be found there; your brothers' virtue cannot survive there…» After explaining what he meant in a few words, he said good-bye to the brothers, leaving them very much affected by the reprimand they had just received.

On our journey, the state of that community naturally came up in the conversation, and from what Father told me, I realized how very upset he was that he could not make the brother director understand the remarks he had made to him. A few days later he sent for me, and told me, «I had the impression, brother, that you understood everything that was lacking and against religious spirit in the community we just visited together. I think I am going to send you back there to remind the brothers of the observations I made to them, and to explain them at greater length, because we have a duty not to leave them in the sad state they are in.»

After thinking about what I had seen in that community, and still more what I had heard from Father's mouth, I told him, «It seems to me, Father, that that community leaves something to be desired especially in the area of family spirit; so in my opinion, we have to stir up that spirit among the brothers.»

«Perfect!,» he replied. «You have grasped my thought and you understand what is wrong with that community. Go now, and may God give you the grace to remedy the situation.»

After receiving Father's blessing, I went to that community to carry out the mission entrusted to me. What I told those brothers can be summarized in one sentence: To be happy in community and to sanctify ourselves there, we have to find family life there. Now, family life is summed up in these two phrases: a fatherly attitude on the part of the superior, a filial spirit on the part of his brothers.

I. The Fatherly Attitude of the Superior

1. God himself gives us the first example, the first lesson in family life, with the words, «Let us make man in our image and likeness.» The Eternal Father does not say, «I make,» or «Make,» but rather, «Let us make,» let us unite to create man; let each person play his part in this work and cooperate in it in perfect unity with the others. And, in fact, that is what happens: the Father contributes authority and power; the Son, intelligence; the Holy Spirit, love. Creation is therefore the result of unity, a family production.

The same is true of the Redemption. The Father so loves the world that he gives his Son to save it. The Son, imitating his Father, loves humankind to the point of giving his life to redeem them. The Holy Spirit cooperates in this divine ministry, because it is through his operation that the Incarnation takes place, it is he who descends on the apostles to complete the work of the Redemption, to sanctify humankind and apply to them the merits of the Passion of Jesus Christ.

We are baptized in the name of the Father, Son and Holy Spirit, because the three divine persons joined together to rehabilitate us in the supernatural order, to redeem us and sanctify us. So, whether in the work of our creation, our redemption or our sanctification, we see the three divine persons always acting in harmony, and giving us a sublime lesson in family spirit through this constant example of the most perfect unity.

This unity is an image of the kind that should reign in all our communities. The work of education is a cooperation in the rehabilitation of fallen nature: one man alone would not suffice; every member of the community must work together at it. One brings to this common undertaking his power, his authority: he directs; another brings the resources of his intelligence and his talents; a third, those of his love, his caring, his devotedness, his meekness and his piety. From this joining together, from this cooperation, there results an authority which is always strong, no matter in whose hands it reposes, an impulsion towards good so strong that no one can resist it, an ensemble of action, virtue and strength which will maintain discipline, edify the children and never permit them to sidestep their duty and the path of good spirit. Unity, perfect harmony among the members of a community, is the strength and prosperity of the school, the peace and happiness of individuals, the virtue and spirit of Jesus Christ. A community like that is heaven on earth.

2. Jesus Christ, in his apostolic life, gives us the second lesson in family life. He lives, prays and works with his apostles, treating them as his children, his brothers, his friends, as second selves. Still more, he acts in turn as their teacher and their servant, instructing and serving them with great patience; he tells them, «I am in the midst of you as he that serves» (*Lk* 22:27). There you have real family life, the real sentiments of a good father who loves his children, who devotes himself to their best interests and who lives only for them. That is how every good superior has always acted.

3. St. Paul, the perfect imitator of Jesus Christ, lived this same family life with his disciples and the first Christians. He

liked to think of himself as a loving mother in the midst of her children. «My little children,» he exclaimed, «I am totally devoted to you; it is through love that I am bringing you up, teaching you, giving birth to you in Jesus Christ. In this ministry of spiritual fatherhood, I do not seek my own interests but the salvation of your souls. I make myself all things to each one of you in order to be of use to you; I adopt all sorts of measures in order to be acceptable to you, and I try to please everyone in order to win you all over to Jesus Christ.» What an admirable model he is of family life and of the attitudes which should characterize every superior!

4. Filled with the same spirit, St. Peter, the prince of the apostles, gave this lesson in family life to all shepherds of souls and all superiors. «Feed—that is to say, govern, direct—the flock of God…, not by constraint but through love, not out of self interest but out of devotedness, not by lording it over your inferiors, by adopting the attitudes and tone of a master, but by showing yourself their father and making yourself a model for them» (cf. *1 Pet* 5:2-3). The whole of family spirit is set forth in these sacred texts, which we do not need to multiply here.

5. Every holy superior strove to imitate such examples. St. Vincent de Paul lived with his subjects like the best of fathers with his children. He paid so much attention to them that not a single one of them, according to his biographer, did not believe that he loved him tenderly. He was affable, kindly, always ready to provide for their needs, always ready to listen to those who needed to speak with him; he never spoke ill of the absent; he never reproved or corrected anyone without having first warned him in friendly fashion and without having heard what he had to say in his own defense.

St. Macarius was ingenious in finding ways to please his brothers and satisfy them. His greatest preoccupation, along with helping them to grow in virtue, was to make them happy and contented, to help them find the yoke of Jesus Christ easy and light, and to help them enjoy, through the fervor of a holy life, the hundredfold of consolations promised by our divine Savior to all those who are truly at his service.

The great motto of St. Bernard was that the superior should not command like an employer but govern like a father. In his exhortations, he liked to compare himself to a mother; he called his confrères his eyes, his heart; he did not command or require anything for which he himself did not set the example. This behavior won the hearts of all his religious, who loved him as their father and obeyed him with holy joy.

St. Honoratus is an exceptional model of the fatherly attitude which should animate every community superior, and of the sort of family life which makes religious happy. He made his own the satisfactions and misfortunes of all his religious—their gains, their losses, their progress, their virtues, and even their faults. He rejoiced with those who were joyful and wept with those who were sad or upset. He was diligent, active, indefatigable in helping, consoling and encouraging. He reproved this one privately, that one publicly; this one with severity, that one with caresses. If he commanded, or even demanded in certain circumstances, he always did so with respect, cordiality, affability and politeness. He was always on the lookout to see that this one was not overwhelmed by too much work, that that one was not tempted because of lack of work. He knew so well how to foresee what was good or bad for each, according to their various temperaments, that one would have said he carried them all in his heart. And as a result, all his thoughts and attention aimed at making his confrères happy and at cultivating their souls as he did his own.

From what we have just said, it is easy to conclude that:

1. To establish and maintain family spirit in his community, a superior must show himself to be his brothers' father and love them all in Jesus Christ with tender charity. He must give them good example, always be the first at the community exercises,

show that he is happy to be with them, to live with them, to work and relax with them, and not try to be different in any way unless it be by greater fidelity to the Rule.

2. Just as a good father lives only for his children, the perfect superior lives only for his subjects; he is ingenious in winning their esteem, pleasing them, making life happy for them, piety easy, virtue desirable.

3. He is eager to help them to succeed in their work and to make their task easy, to train them and help them to progress in the knowledge proper to their state, as well as to provide them with everything they need.

4. His vigilance carefully eliminates everything which could detract from mutual respect, fraternal charity, and politeness—in a word, everything which might disturb the cordiality, harmony and unity which are characteristic of family life.

II. A Filial Spirit on the Part of the Brothers

Filial spirit is the second condition for family life; it is the contribution which the brothers must make. But what is filial spirit? It is the love of a son for a tender father, a religious respect, a profound veneration for his authority and for everything that comes from him. It is a total confidence which makes one regard and accept all his decisions as most fitting; it is perfect docility to his orders and to his direction, and absolute dedication to all his wishes and to everything which might please him.

These feelings are shown by constant acts of kindness, esteem, and willing accommodation; by gentle, polite and respectful words, and by all the signs of respect due to a superior; by sustained and obsequious attention to satisfying him, being pleasing to him, making things easier for him, and rendering him every possible service; by unity, conformity of opinions and attitudes, by doing everything not only according to his orders but even according to his intentions, insofar as they are known to us.

The principle which produces, enlivens, preserves and develops these constitutive elements of filial spirit, is faith. Through faith, we believe that the superior stands in God's place and represents Jesus Christ, and that consequently, it is God who speaks or commands through his mouth. Through faith, we believe that it is God himself, Jesus Christ, whom we obey or disobey, according to these words, «He who hears you, hears me; he who despises you despises me» (*Lk* 10:16).

On the one hand, family life requires that the superior be totally devoted to his brothers, that he live only for them, that he use his time and talents to form, instruct and direct them; that he solicitously see to their temporal and spiritual needs, and that he consider it a duty to win their confidence, be pleasing to them and make them content and happy.

On the other hand, family life reciprocally requires that the brothers be entirely devoted to their superior, that they most carefully avoid everything which might with good reason displease or upset him or cause him the least pain; that they apply themselves to lightening the burden of his authority, to making his responsibility easy and his life happy, insofar as they are able.

Family life is a sharing of goods and evils. «In the institute,» said our Founder, «it is not only material goods which should be held in common; goods of the spirit, that is to say, each one's talents, should also be used for everyone's advantage. I will say the same for goods of the body: strength and health, and goods of the soul: our virtues. So he who possesses special knowledge and the gift of teaching or directing a class, should share them with his confrères. He who is strong and robust should console those who are sick or in poor health; finally, each one should act so that all the spiritual goods which God has bestowed on him may profit all his brothers, by praying for them and giving them good example.»

Family spirit does still more; it makes one's own the various goods bestowed on others. So a religious should feel content, blessed and happy because of all the gifts, virtues, talents, qualities and advantages of every sort which he sees in his brothers. He should rejoice over them, and bless God for them; he should taste and share the honor, glory and satisfaction which flow from them, just as a mother shares the goods and compliments bestowed on her child.

In the same way, pain, sufferings, afflictions and adversities should be held in common. Each one must therefore take his share of them, and offer himself to comfort or console him who is suffering, to assist him who is in need, to help him who is overworked, to carry his share of the problems which affect the whole community or which weigh heavily on certain brothers.

III. The Enemies of Family Life

Four things in particular disturb and can ruin family life.

1. Sick or unruly members. Every member of the body has its proper place and function. Any member which becomes dislocated or refuses to carry out its proper function disturbs the harmony of the body, wearies and overburdens the other members.

The feet are made to carry the body and the eyes to lead it. If the latter wanted to carry the body and the feet to enlighten it, there would be nothing but trouble and confusion. In the same way, a brother who does not stay in his place, who usurps that of the superior and begins to give orders and commands to the other brothers, to deal with the public, to carry out in the school acts reserved to the brother director, such as changing classes, giving permission to be absent, or dismissing certain students, is an unruly member, a usurper, who is failing seriously in his duty, scandalizing his brothers and disturbing family life.

The director who does not respect the rights and position of his brothers, who interferes with their communication with the major superiors, who forbids them to punish the children when necessary, who prevents a subdirector from fulfilling the obligations of his office, who hides everything from him and does not allow him to carry out the part of the administration of the house which falls to him according to the Rule, who takes everything for himself, who wants to do everything instead of being satisfied with ordering, directing and leading, is a sick head. He is an unbalanced head, whose reason is disturbed, and who, instead of procuring the success of his school and the spiritual happiness of his community by his benign influence, spreads confusion, uneasiness and discontent and paralyzes the efforts everyone else is making to do good.

Every paralyzed or unwell member makes the others suffer and is a burden to them. Every brother who neglects his task in the community or performs it poorly, who acts according to his own whims and not according to the directives given by the brother director, disturbs and ruins family life. He makes his confrères suffer, overburdens them, and detracts from the common good and the prosperity of the house. This truth is so evident from experience that there is no point in belaboring it further.

2. The selfish member. It is a law of nature that all the members of the human body work together for the common good. Hence the eyes see for the whole body, the stomach digests for all the members, the heart distributes and circulates blood and life-force in all the arteries and veins, the hands work and serve every part of the body. Any member or organ which would sidestep that law or refuse to follow that order of things, and which would take care only of itself, would perturb the entire body.

That is exactly what the selfish person does. He sees only his own personality, thinks only of his own interests and works only for himself. He is always looking for his own well-being, for whatever can satisfy his tastes and needs, and sometimes his passions. Lacking in charity, and in the feelings of compassion, forbearance and goodness which characterize beautiful souls, the selfish person is hard-hearted and has feelings of steel; he does not feel his brothers' pain, nor see their needs; he does nothing to relieve them, and doesn't even think of them. Selfishness is the enemy of the spirit of charity, the death of family life.

The good religious, on the contrary, imitates the members of the human body: he works for the common good, he always puts community interests ahead of his personal satisfaction. Being entirely devoted to his brothers, he thinks only of being useful to them, of foreseeing and meeting their needs; he sacrifices himself to make them joyful and happy. He always forgets himself, and puts all the others ahead of himself. He takes the tasks that are hardest, the things that are less satisfying for his bodily needs, and leaves for the others whatever is easier and better.

Listen to this story about Brother Pascal, and when occasion arises, imitate the example which he left us. One day, one of his students brought him a bottle of liqueur and some chocolates. While he was telling the boy to give them to brother director or the brother in charge of buying for the house, one of his confrères said to him, «Keep them for yourself, so you can use them when you need them.»

«What kind of advice is that?» Brother Pascal replied energetically. «You want me to accept a personal gift? To break my Rule and my vows? Never, never! Do you think I'm selfish? Well, you're wrong; if I have anything good, I want my brothers to share it with me. And I intend to take my full share of whatever is unpleasant around the house. As far as I'm concerned, it's equality and fraternal charity that make community life pleasant.»

And we might add that that is what family life is all about.

Later on, when he was director of the house in Digoin, Saône-et-Loire, one of his relatives, who knew how poor his health was, also gave him some sweets, but on condition that he eat them all himself and in private.

«A gift under those conditions,» Brother Pascal answered, «is not a gift, but an insult. You can set all the conditions you want; as for me, I'll enjoy sharing what you give me with my brothers, and that enjoyment will be so sweet that it will do me a hundred times more good than if I ate them all myself.»

Brother Jean-Pierre Martinol, director of Boulieu, Ardèche, visited La Valla one day in 1824. When he was leaving very early the next morning, Fr. Champagnat told him, «Since the brother who cooks isn't up yet, take this roll; it's blessed bread I was given last Sunday as celebrant at High Mass. You can eat it as you go, for breakfast.»

«No, Father,» the brother replied, «I will take it to my brothers and we will eat it together with great pleasure, because everything that comes to us from you or from our motherhouse in La Valla is sweet and pleasant and does us a great deal of good. I am very glad to be able to make my brothers happy this way; I am sure that I will make them jump for joy and that we will talk about nothing but you and our brothers in La Valla all during dinner.»

Being touched by such sentiments, Father exclaimed, «My dear brother, you make me weep for joy when you talk like that; those are truly the sentiments of family spirit which should animate all the Brothers of Mary. If we carefully preserve those sentiments and that spirit, we will enjoy the happiness of religious life to the full.»

3. The dissatisfied member, who is filled with bad spirit.

First of all, what is «bad spirit»? It is a blindness of the soul, a negative attitude born of pride which makes us see things other than they really are. The result is that the judgments we form about them are usually wrong.

It is a reservoir of peevishness which produces a shifty and inconstant character; an irritating penchant for criticizing, complaining, rash judgment and backbiting; a secret aversion for authority and for everything which flows from it; a resistance to dependence which leads one to blame the superior, to always have something to say about whatever he does or orders, and to try to exempt oneself from his direction.

It is a license to say whatever one pleases, an evil disposition to criticize the superior and make trouble for him, to lord it over others, to lead them to criticize, complain and become insubordinate.

There is nothing more opposed, more contrary, to family life than bad spirit. St. Bernard said that, «Bad spirit is a poison which taints all the social virtues which make up family spirit. It is a poison from hell; the devil is its father and model. He demonstrated that from the beginning by fomenting war and sowing weeds in heaven. A religious afflicted with this sad defect does in community what Lucifer did in heaven, what the serpent did in the Garden of Eden—he brings trouble, confusion, and misfortune by destroying family spirit.»

This detestable vice kills all the religious virtues. Religious life is a life of obedience. A man with bad spirit is devoted to his own will and cannot stand being dependent on anyone. Religious life is humble and modest. A man with bad spirit is a son of pride, and loves only vanity, human glory and praise. He always wants to be seen and to be in charge.

Religious life is a life of charity, peace, unity, and mutual support. The man with bad spirit, who is essentially selfish, divides men, shatters their unity, and brings dissension and discord wherever he goes.

Religious life, from the point of view of the brothers, is filial love and affectionate devotedness toward the superior. The man with bad spirit is the ego personified and put in the place of authority, the ego criticizing and blaming everything that comes from authority. If the superior is zealous about maintaining the rule, he calls him a tyrant; if he overlooks certain things or holds off in order to restore order by means of gentleness, he accuses him of being lax, of tolerating disorder and destroying discipline; if he is economical, he calls him miserly, or complains that he has no charity; if he is generous, he calls him a spendthrift. The accursed ego adores itself and finds nothing good except what it has thought and done itself.

Religious life is a life of family, sociability and fraternal charity. The man with bad spirit has all the defects contrary to the beautiful social virtues. He is hypersensitive, carping, fastidious, takes offense at everything, is irritated and insulted by trifles; a word, a gesture, a look, an indifferent action performed without the least evil intent wounds him, upsets him and leaves him brooding for days on end. Now, is there anything more likely to kill family life than a combination of such defects? Therefore, a religious with bad spirit is a torment, a heavy cross for his superior, a thornbush for his brothers, the scourge of his community and the destroyer of family life.

«What can one expect from a religious who has bad spirit?» St. John Climacus asks. «Nothing good,» he replies, «except for his miserable fate. He is a gangrenous member who threatens to infect all the others; he is a member which must be severed, cut off and thrown into the world, if you don't want his poison to spread through the whole body.» Family life is impossible so long as he is around.

4. Members who are really strangers. There are two types of them:

First, the servant brother. Our Founder often said that no one can be happy in community if he comes and stays simply as a servant; he has to be a member of the family. Holy Scripture teaches us that a man must leave his father and mother in order to be united with his wife. Well, if a religious wants to be happy in his state, if he wants to experience the consolations of religious life and family life, he too must leave his father, mother, brothers, sisters and everything else he has in the world, and become attached to his superiors, his confrères and the Institute, which becomes his family.

So he who does not give himself totally to his community and who does not work to develop towards it the sentiments of a well-brought-up child, is not a religious, but only a servant. He is an outsider to the family, to which he contributes only discord and disturbance. Such a man has no filial spirit; he looks on his superior as a taskmaster and an irritating overseer. He has no affection or charity towards his brothers; he thinks of them as strangers, and shows them neither consideration, politeness nor kindness. He is totally involved in himself, his own interests, and works only for himself; he is not concerned about others and could care less whether they are overworked or suffering. He does his work simply to get it out of the way, because he is indifferent to the interests of the community, and has the same reaction whether it prospers or meets with reverses.

It would be hard to think of an unhappier person than a religious without family spirit; that is to say, one who is not devoted to his community and his Institute, who guards his affections just like a stranger whose goods and treasure lie elsewhere. What is even more irritating is that he makes those around him unhappy—he disturbs their spiritual joy and ruins the harmony of the community; he compromises the success of the school; he becomes an embarrassment for all his brothers and a source of ruination for the Institute.

A holy old priest, who was saying good-bye to the brothers who were leaving for their retreat, said to their director, «Come back soon, and bring me four brothers.»

«There's never been any question of reducing the staff,» replied the director, «so we'll certainly be five coming back.»

The priest said nothing, but when the brothers returned, he explained what he had meant. Seeing the five in front of him, he said, «Did you bring me four brothers?» And without waiting for an answer, he added, «My friends, last year we had only three brothers. Two didn't count, because they didn't have the spirit of their state and did not live the family life. When I used to go to your house, I rarely found them with the others. I never saw them do their share of work in the garden or around the house. They had their own teaching methods. From their way of acting it was easy to see that they were schoolteachers, but not brothers, and that they were not much concerned about the education and supervision of the children. They were included in the community but they were not members of it; they did less than nothing for the good of the place, because they paralyzed their confrères' efforts and zeal. I expect better things from our newcomers. I am totally devoted to your school; but I must tell you that I like only real brothers, because experience has taught me that they are the only ones who edify my parish and do good among our children.»

The good priest had sized things up well; he had judged those two brothers accurately, because they were in fact men lacking in virtue and religious spirit, and difficult characters not suited for religious life.

A brother complained to his confessor, who was a holy religious, that his profession had been postponed, and he asked what he should do. «I don't see anything in the forum of conscience,» the priest told him, «which would prevent you from making your vows; but the dispositions which I, as your confessor, know you have, are not enough for me to tell you that you could make such a commitment with total security. There is one point on which you should build yourself up: that is, knowing whether you have the spirit and qualities of your state.

«Do you love your Institute? Do you love your brothers? Do you have a filial spirit, a family spirit? Is your character suited for community life? Only your superior can really tell you if you have all those things in sufficient quantity, because he is the only one who has followed you and knows your external conduct. Religious life is not a good place for someone who lacks those qualities. Such a man suffers in religious life and earns little merit; what is even more regrettable is that he makes everyone else suffer because he destroys family spirit.»

That's a beautiful reply, on which those preparing for profession, and those councilors who decide on admission to vows, could not meditate too often.

Second, outsiders—Our Rule tells us that outsiders cannot be allowed to recreate with the brothers in the school or any part of their residence. Why is that? Because every member who is not a part of the body, who is a stranger to it, disturbs and weakens family spirit. The brothers are not comfortable in the presence of outsiders; they shut themselves up behind a wall of reserve which is out of keeping with the relaxed atmosphere of a family setting. Outsiders are to the body of the community what an artificial limb is to the human body. Even if it were gold-plated—that is, if that person were an excellent Christian, even a priest—he is still an artificial limb which does not perfectly harmonize with the others, which deforms the body, hampers its movements, and disturbs common life and freedom. Family life rejects any artificial limbs and will not tolerate any of them.

Every director who allows outsiders into his community, or who gives private lessons, whether to children or adults, in the brothers' study hall, during study or recreation, is disturbing family life, doing something detrimental to his brothers, and exposing them to serious danger.

Every brother who invites his parents to wherever he is stationed, and keeps them there as long as he can, shows that his family spirit is weak, that his heart and affections are not with his religious family, and that his community cannot count on him entirely. Every outsider who gets into a family and disturbs its tranquility imposes constraints on its members, interferes with family life, and diminishes everyone's happiness. Superiors and brothers must therefore carefully keep lay people out of the community, no matter who they may be, even their own parents.

Finally, the happiness of community life is the responsibility of all the members. Each one is bound to do his part, and each one enjoys that happiness to the extent of the efforts and sacrifices he makes to obtain it for the others. So if you spread contentment in the house where you are, you will enjoy it yourself. Nothing is more just: people must give you what you give them, and treat you as you treat them. «Always treat others as you would like them to treat you; that is the meaning of the Law and the prophets» (*Mt* 7:12). «The amount you measure out is the amount you will be given back» (*Lk* 6:38). You will reap what you have sowed.

So then, if you sow peace, contentment and happiness among your brothers, they will give you peace, happiness and contentment. If you stir up trouble, you will get trouble back; if you sow the wind, you will reap the whirlwind. It is like another version of «an eye for an eye,» according to which we almost always get back what we have done to others.

CHAPTER THIRTY-TWO

ON THE VIRTUES OF FAMILY LIFE

St. Basil's answer to the question, «What are the advantages of community life?» included, among other things, that it is preferable to the eremitical or contemplative life because it makes us practice charity more perfectly, and charity is the first and greatest of all the virtues. And in truth, real family life is charity in action, a habitual exercise of charity in all its aspects. St. Paul had an admirable grasp of this truth, and he taught it to the first Christians in these words: «Charity is patient, is kind.»

«Charity envies not, deals not perversely, is not puffed up, is not ambitious, seeks not her own, is not provoked to anger, thinks no evil, rejoices not in iniquity but rejoices with the truth, bears all things, believes all things, hopes all things, endures all things» (*1 Cor* 13:4-7). From these specifics, it is easy to see that charity takes in all the social virtues, all the rules of family life, all the feelings which superiors and brothers should have, and consequently, everything which can guarantee the happiness of both.

A brief explanation of these aspects of charity will clarify that statement.

1. Charity is patient. He who has this virtue puts up uncomplainingly with the wrongs done him, the scorn, insults, biting mockery, lack of respect and all the other discourteous behavior of his brothers. Like St. Ambrose, he says, «When someone reproaches me, insults me, provokes me to anger and argument, I remain silent and I am not ashamed to become mute, because the one who is acting that way is doing wrong and I don't want to resemble him.»

A brother who has patient charity never punishes a student out of ill-humor, in a moment of excitement or irritation. He also avoids all bitter and offensive words which might offend against charity or even politeness.

He accepts uncomplainingly the difficulties which flow from his profession as a teacher; he puts up with opposition from society, with his students' ignorance, grossness, ingratitude and all their other defects; and he patiently suffers, in union with Jesus Christ, everything disagreeable in his ministry which is one of complete charity.

He never becomes discouraged, despite his lack of success in teaching, and he never stops repeating the same things, giving the same advice and the same corrections, even though the results are barely perceptible. He reminds himself that he must cultivate, weed, plant, prune and water, but that God is the one who gives the increase.

He never repays evil with evil, but following the advice of the apostle, he blesses those who curse him, prays for those who persecute him, presents his left cheek to him who strikes him on the right, and counts among his friends those who censure his conduct and calumniate him.

That is what St. Stephen the abbot did: he thanked those who made him suffer, and wrote down in his notebook the names of those who insulted and persecuted him, in order to pray for them.

When he was threatened, insulted and called a hypocrite by a brutal man whom he had put up with patiently for a long time, St. Francis de Sales told him, «Let me assure you that, even if you put out one of my eyes, I will still look at you with the other just as affectionately as if you were my best friend.»

Eager as they are to become pleasing to God, the saints look for occasions to practice charity by patiently putting up with their neighbor.

When he was mistreated by the members of his community, St. Philip Neri, instead of showing displeasure or complaining about them to their superior general, treated them with respect and did everything he possibly could for them. When one of his friends urged him to leave that house, he replied, «I will not, because I don't want to run away from the cross which God sends me.» However, when he realized that he could not win over these bad religious by his charity and humility, and that far from softening, they were becoming more unmanageable, he turned to Jesus Christ, and looking at the crucifix, he said, «Jesus, why don't you listen to me? I've been asking you so long and so insistently for charity and patience! Why haven't you answered me?»

«I will give you those beautiful virtues,» Jesus replied, «but this is the way I want you to acquire them.»

From then on, that place where he found the opportunity to practice patience and charity became a garden of delights for the saint; he spent thirty years there and left it only on orders from the Sovereign Pontiff.

Not so long ago, one of our best directors told me, «I miss the young brother you just transferred from here. I miss him, not because he did his work well, since he did it rather poorly, but because he was very useful to me, for testing my patience and meekness.» Beautiful words and lofty sentiments, which reveal a very special soul, a soul that knows the «science of the saints,» that is faithful to grace and knows how to profit from every opportunity of growing in virtue.

2. Charity is meek. According to St. Thomas Aquinas, meekness is a virtue that presupposes a noble soul. In fact, those who have it rise above whatever anyone may say or do to them. Even at the very moment when they are being insulted in word or deed, they remain calm and never lose their peace of soul.

«Nothing edifies our neighbor,» says St. Francis de Sales, «so much as kindness and meekness.»

In the words of St. Vincent de Paul, «Affability and meekness are admirable helps to maintaining peace, concord and union of hearts.»

And St. Jane Frances de Chantal says, «The older I get, the more I can see that meekness is the virtue which wins over other people and makes our dealings with them easy and pleasant.»

Meekness sweetens conversations and nourishes concord. Everyone loves this virtue, so I am not surprised to read in the life of St. Francis Xavier that many people went to see him for the sole purpose of experiencing his remarkable meekness and goodness of character.

That is how a Little Brother of Mary acts if he wants to make progress in this virtue and live a real family life. Following the advice of St. Francis de Sales, he sees his neighbor leaning on the Savior's breast, and always keeps in mind these words of the divine Master, «As long as you did it to one of these my least brethren, you did it to me» (*Mt* 25:40). Now, with such a faith-filled attitude, how can he not love his neighbor? How can he not treat him with meekness and kindness?

Being convinced that disputes, quarrels, sharp words, and the refusal to tolerate different opinions are the scourges of conversation, he faithfully follows the maxim of a pagan philosopher: «In conversation, show respect and deference toward your superiors, meekness toward your equals, and kindness toward your inferiors.»

He especially tries to practice meekness in his words, his actions, and in all his dealings with his neighbor. He likes the adage of St. Francis de Sales, «Our tongue should remain motionless whenever our mind is upset,» and makes it his rule of conduct. When he has to deal with someone who is irritable or in a bad mood, he remembers the words of the Holy Spirit, «A mild answer turns away wrath» (*Prov* 15:1). He either remains silent, or answers with extreme meekness. When St. John the abbot was insulted by one of his religious, he did not answer. «Why don't you impose silence on that spiteful brother?» someone asked him. The saint replied, «When the house is on fire, why throw more wood on it? Meekness and silence will do more to calm that brother than correction can.»

A good brother stands by these sayings of St. Francis de Sales: «You can catch more flies with an ounce of honey than with a hundred barrels of vinegar,» and «Sugar never spoils the sauce, but too much salt or vinegar often does.» So in his dealings with his brothers and the children, he always takes the path of meekness, suggestion and persuasion, and carefully avoids constraint, rigidity and whatever might offend anyone.

3. Charity is kind. Charity is shown by good works, St. John tells us; any other proof of kindness is open to question. Some people say, «I love my neighbor, and to prove it, I smile at him and act very politely towards him.» «That's all very good,» says St. Bernard, «but that's just the minimum degree of charity.»

Another says, «I do better than that, because my brothers are so dear to me that I make it my duty to help them every chance I have.» This second degree is better, but still not enough.

«Well then,» says a third, «I love my brothers so much that I use my possessions to assist them.» «Now there,» says St. Bernard, «is an act which announces a very high and very excellent degree of charity; but it is still not the most perfect. There is still a fourth degree beyond that. What is it? It is to be able to say in all honesty, like St. Paul, 'Be followers of me as I also am of Christ' (1 Cor 4:16 and 11:1); in other words, just as Jesus Christ gave his work, his strength, his blood, his merits, his life for us, and sacrificed himself totally for the good and salvation of us all, so am I ready to sacrifice my work, my strength, my health and my life for my brothers.» It is therefore very true that charity is kind, because it gives all and keeps nothing for itself.

4. Charity is never envious. A brother who is truly charitable regards his brothers' goods as his own; he does not know the

words «mine» and «yours.» Like our Founder, he says, «Don't speak to me of 'yours' or 'mine', because whatever is mine belongs to all my brothers, and what belongs to my brothers is also mine, because we're in this together.» So he rejoices in his brothers' success, thanks God for the good they do and is upset by their reverses as much as by his own. He is not only not hurt, but even glad, to admit that others are more talented than he. He is not angry that they are more esteemed and honored and given preference over him. He is content to see them promoted while he remains in lower and more humble assignments. Like Jonathas he willingly says, «You will command, I will follow you and obey.» In heaven there is so much charity that each of the blessed rejoices as much in the glory of the other saints as in his own. The same holds for the good religious: he is gladdened and enriched by the gifts, talents and advantages of his brothers and rejoices in them as in his own.

One holy religious, realizing that he was being affected by the envy another person felt toward him, decided to take care of him and become his humble servant. So he began to make this man's bed, shine his shoes, brush his clothes, sweep his room and do all sorts of favors for him. Through this humble and charitable way of acting, he cured his brother's envy, won his confidence and affection, and turned him into his best friend.

5. Charity is not ambitious. A Little Brother of Mary who wants to imitate his divine Mother does not desire the first places, responsibilities and honors. If he is raised to them, he feels doubly obliged to practice humility, according to the words of the Holy Spirit, «The higher you are raised, the smaller you must make yourself.»

His whole ambition is to remain hidden and to live in dependence. It is no sacrifice for him to leave a position, but rather a joy and a pleasure. He willingly takes on manual work. He is particularly drawn to the lower classes and to every assignment likely to humiliate human nature. He does not seek to lord it over his brothers, but to serve them, to make himself everyone's servant. If he is appointed through obedience to direct them, he makes them feel his authority only through his good example and kindness. He controls them the way a loving mother controls her children, or a Sister of Charity her patients—through charity, kindness, and all sorts of solicitude and attention.

Pope Sixtus V, who had been a monk in the monastery of the Holy Apostles in Rome, informed the religious of that house, through their Cardinal Protector, that he wanted to grant each one a special favor, and invited them to think about what they wanted to ask for. The monks, being very flattered by this offer, all went to the Vatican, where the pope, seated on the papal throne, with a secretary at his left to write down the brothers' requests, had them come up one by one to kiss his feet and present their requests. Most of them don't deserve mention because they were hardly edifying; but we do want to recall three of them because they pertain to our topic and can serve as a lesson for us.

One brother asked for a papal decree, forbidding all his brothers, under pain of excommunication, to argue with him, insult him or say anything unpleasant to him. «He had good reason,» the historian remarks, «to request that protection, because he was a proud and insolent man, with a disagreeable personality, who gave his brothers frequent opportunity to practice patience.» Since their kindness towards him could not soften him or make him more reasonable, they were obliged to keep him in his place and rid themselves of his abuse by following the principle of «an eye for an eye,» which is why someone said under his breath, «The favor he needs is a prison or a torturer to give him a dose of his own medicine.»

Another one asked that his family, which was one of the most outstanding among the nobility of the Kingdom of Naples, be linked to the pope's family, the Perrettis. «I'm perfectly willing,» the pope replied, «but since there should be some proportion

365

between your family and mine, take off your monk's habit and go tend the pigs for a while, as I did when I was growing up. Only on that condition can you and I become relatives.» The monk, who had a doctorate and was provincial, blushed and wanted to die from embarrassment at the lesson he had been given to cure his ambition, and he was very careful not to accept the offered deal.

Finally, a very pious lay brother, who had been cook in his monastery for thirty years, told the pope, «Holy Father, it is a great joy for me to see you as head of the Church after having seen you a simple religious. Personally, I don't need anything, and all I want is your blessing. But since Your Holiness wanted me included among those presenting petitions to you, I ask you, very humbly, to have a fountain built for us, because our monastery is greatly inconvenienced by lack of water; you suffered from it yourself when we had the honor of counting you as one of our own.» This request was the only one the pope approved, and even today one can see in the monastery courtyard the magnificent fountain put up through his generosity as a reward for the good brother's family spirit.

The other brothers' requests brought the pope to tears. «I did not expect any of you,» he told them, «to be thinking of his own interests; I thought you would have in mind nothing but the common good. Shouldn't the vow of obedience you made oblige you to renounce everything which concerns you personally? Can real religious, with honor and good conscience, want something which is not advantageous to the order in general? Your greed has tied my hands; I would feel as if I'd committed a crime if I were weak enough to abet it through my generosity.»

6. Charity is not vain. No one is truly charitable if he is not humble. That is why Fr. Champagnat said that, «It is impossible to practice charity, to live in peace with one's brothers, to put up with their defects, to give in to them when necessary to keep the

peace, and not to be humble. There is no better way to combat pride than to practice fraternal charity and obedience.

«Show me a community where the brothers allow themselves to be guided by obedience, where they help, respect and support one another—in a word, where they love one another, for charity takes in everything—and there will never be divisions among them. They will be perfectly united. But a community where there are vain, hypersensitive, proud brothers will be like hell, because pride breeds insubordination, disputes and everything which stirs up trouble and discord among men.»

Pride sowed disorder, revolt and division among the angels in heaven, among human beings in the Garden of Eden, and it does the same thing wherever it appears. So, he who wants to live in peace with his brothers does not dissemble when he speaks; he says things simply, just as he sees them. He is not vain in his words, and is never caught boasting or even speaking about himself. Far from showing off his talents and good qualities, he hides them and does good quietly. He is so discreet and modest in everything he does, that his left hand is unaware of the good works his right hand performs. His clean and simple appearance never gives any indication of a vain or superficial person.

7. Charity never rejoices in misfortune, but rejoices in good things. He who loves his brothers is upset when he sees them oppressed, persecuted, and scorned, and he is as sensitive to their difficulties as he is to his own. He is often more hurt by others' sufferings than by his own. He thanks God and rejoices when good things happen to them, for three reasons: 1) because they reveal the glory of God, which he loves and seeks above all; 2) because they are to his brothers' advantage; 3) because he considers that what is good for his brothers is good for him as well, and he shares in it. When one businessman enters into partnership with others, the latters' business acumen and the profits they make don't upset him; far from it. They are a motive

of rejoicing, for him, because it all increases the profits of the partnership in which he shares like the others.

8. Charity never suspects evil. «The two most common and widespread vices,» says Cornelius à Lapide, «are excessive severity and excessive leniency—severity towards others and leniency towards oneself.» St. Augustine was well aware of that and expressed it forcefully: «People are curious enough to pry into others' lives and judge them, but slow to reform their own.»

And Jesus asks us, «Why do you see the speck in your brother's eye and never notice the plank in your own? How can you say to your brother, 'Let me take the speck out of your eye' when all the time there is a plank in your own? Hypocrite! Take the plank out of your own eye first, and then you will see clearly enough to take the speck out of your brother's eye» (*Mt* 7:3-5).

Those are good descriptions of the two great evils of which we have just spoken: judging our neighbor rigorously and forgiving ourselves for everything; seeing a speck in someone else's eye, while not seeing the plank in our own. Flaunting our virtues while tactlessly censuring others, and being shamefully indulgent toward our own vices. And finally, devoting all our zeal to harassing our neighbor to correct his little defects which offend us, while allowing our own to grow totally unchecked and letting ourselves go in extreme relaxation.

A brother who is truly charitable does not act that way. He closes his eyes to his brothers' defects and sees only their virtues. He never interprets another's actions unfavorably and sees everything in a good light. A healthy stomach converts the coarsest and most indigestible food into useful juices, but an unhealthy one converts the best food into bile and heartburn. In the same way, an upright and charitable soul interprets everything in a good light, whereas one without charity poisons everything and interprets everything negatively.

Even when he sees his brother commit a real fault, a charitable man does not condemn him. In such a case, if he cannot excuse the action, he excuses the intention, and believes that his neighbor fell through ignorance or surprise. Or else he says, like that virtuous religious of whom St. Bernard speaks, who, seeing his brother commit a sin, sighed, «Ah, well—what he does today, I'll do tomorrow, unless God comes to my help.»

Another holy religious, who was appointed visitor to his brothers, said to himself as he entered a messy room, «How lucky this brother is to be so unconcerned about exterior things, and to have his mind so fixed on heaven that he no longer thinks of the things of earth!» And when he went into an orderly room, «How concerned my brother must be about the purity of his soul!» He never judged anyone negatively, and never said, «This one is negligent, that one is too fussy, too worldly, too vain, etc..» That's the way people without virtue talk.

9. Charity tolerates everything, puts up with everything. Yes, the charitable brother is broad-minded and accommodating. He easily accepts the fact that people don't treat him with politeness, respect or esteem, because he knows that these slights are often the result of lack of education, or performed without malice or bad intention. So he does not show himself to be overly thin-skinned, sensitive or punctilious.

He puts up with his brothers' defects, helps them to correct them through his good example, his charitable advice and his fervent prayers, which will obtain that grace for them.

He puts up with the imperfections, weaknesses and lack of progress of imperfect souls, leading them very gently toward perfection. In order to do so, he is very careful not to demand too much of them, or to load them down with burdens they cannot carry, for fear of discouraging them and making them abandon the path of virtue.

He puts up with, or at least punishes very lightly, little children's character defects or faults they commit through surprise or giddiness, which age, education, and their companions will eventually correct.

Sometimes he even puts up with serious faults for a while, in order to correct them more aptly and effectively later on, when a more favorable occasion presents itself.

«Why do you put up with such-and-such a defect in that brother?» someone once asked a superior. «What are you waiting for to reprimand him?»

«I'm waiting for four things,» replied the prudent superior. «First, for a beautiful, clear, sunny day, because I've learned from experience that dull, dark days have a noticeable effect on certain characters and make them very unlikely to a profit from any correction. Second, for a moment when this brother is cheerful, contented and well-disposed to accept the correction he deserves. Third, for God to prepare his heart and to begin to teach him a lesson, so that all I'll have to do is second the movement of grace. Fourth, for myself to be well prepared, and to receive the grace to perform such a difficult act.»

An admirable reply which all those appointed to direct others can never meditate on too often.

10. Finally, charity believes everything. A charitable brother believes the following six points in particular:

a. He believes all the good things he hears about his neighbor, everything said to their credit.

b. He believes that he is the least virtuous, that all the others are better than he and more perfect in the sight of God. That is why he always takes the last place and willingly makes himself the servant of all.

c. He believes that the bad things said about his neighbor are generally false, or at least that they are always exaggerated and built up. That is why he never listens to calumny or backbiting, and his ears are permanently closed to the comments of their detractors.

d. He believes, or at least he willingly accepts, the excuses of his brothers and students. Far from enjoying finding them guilty, he is pleased to see that they are not, or at least less so than had been alleged.

e. He firmly believes the words of St. Peter, «Charity covers a multitude of sins» (*1 Pet* 4:8). In accord with this guideline, a single solid virtue he notes in his brothers makes him overlook all their little defects, and that charity covers all the rest.

f. He believes that charity is the first, most excellent and most necessary virtue, and that everything must therefore be done to preserve and increase it. Since it is preserved and augmented only through actions, he constantly practices it. And remembering the significant statement of the great apostle, «Give to each one his due» (*Rom* 13:7), he pays to each his daily debt. What are those daily debts? They are:

1. love, respect and honor in practice;

2. putting up with their defects, whatever they may be;

3. fraternal correction, if occasion arises;

4. help, assistance and service when needed;

5. prayer, constantly bringing before God his brothers' spiritual needs;

6. lastly, edification and good example at all times.

That is how a good Little Brother of Mary practices charity; and that charity makes him and his brothers happy, and makes the beauty of family life a reality for all.

CHAPTER THIRTY-THREE

IN UNITY THERE IS STRENGTH

«Brothers united among themselves,» says the Holy Spirit, «are like a strong city; they are like the iron bars which hold closed the city gates and which the enemy cannot break» (cf. *Prov.* 18:19). Father Champagnat had a special liking for that maxim; he had meditated deeply on it, which is why he so much recommended unity and fraternal charity to his followers. In one of his circular letters, he wrote, «I desire that the unity and charity of which the beloved disciple speaks should always reign among you, that those who must obey perform that duty with humility, and that those who command do so with gentle charity. In this way, the joy and peace of the Holy Spirit will always be with you.»

«You are well aware,» he wrote to the brothers of one community, «that I love you all in Jesus Christ; that is why I so strongly desire and wish that you be united, that you love one another as children of the same father who is God, the same mother who is the Church, and to put it into one word, as children of Mary.»

On another occasion, he invited and called the brothers to the retreat with these words: «How enjoyable it is for me to think that in a few days I shall have the pleasure of clasping you in my arms while saying with the psalmist, 'How good and how pleasant it is for brothers to live together in unity' (*Ps* 132:1). It is a sweet consolation for me to see you gathered, with one heart and one soul, as members of one single family, all of you seeking only the glory of God and the interests of his holy religion, and all fighting under the same banner, that of his holy Mother.»

Following the example of Jesus Christ, unity was the last lesson our Father gave his children on his death bed. «I beg of you, my dear brothers,» he told them, «with all the affection of my soul, and by all the love you have for me, do all you can to ensure that charity is always maintained among you. Love one another as Jesus Christ has loved you. Be of one heart and one mind. The most ardent desire of my heart at this, the last moment of my life, is that it may always be said of the Little Brothers of Mary as of the first Christians: 'See how they love one another; see how united they are'» (cf. Spiritual Testament).

Realizing that in unity there is strength, that it guarantees the brothers' obedience, the prosperity and good government of a community, he never failed to recommend on many occasions to Brother François, his successor, and to those who were to assist him in directing the brothers, to be on good terms with one another and to remain united. «You will have many problems,» he told them; «but have confidence—God will be with you if you remain united, because it is his work that you are doing.»

Brother François and his two assistants, as much out of affection for their Father as out of virtue and a sense of duty in conscience, faithfully followed this advice of Fr. Champagnat. Their unity was total, constant and inalterable. It was the source of their strength and their glory; it gave them total authority over the brothers, and was the main cause of all the good they did for the Institute. It is that which we commemorate here under the heading, «In Unity There Is Strength,» so that it may serve as a model for all the brothers, especially those who are called to govern the congregation.

Brother François, Brother Louis-Marie and Brother Jean-Baptiste were all about the same age, and were elected during Father Champagnat's lifetime by all the perpetually professed brothers, ninety-two in number, to govern the Institute, the first as superior general and the other two as his assistants. After this election, over which he himself presided with Ven. Father Colin,

Fr. Champagnat appeared very satisfied with the results of the balloting, and spoke these words: «I am pleased with this choice; these are just the men I wanted. May God be blessed for their election!»

These three brothers were among the oldest; they had lived with the Founder for a long time and had helped him in the government of the Institute, and they had been specially trained by him. His examples and teaching had not been wasted on them; they were deeply imbued with his principles; his spirit had passed whole and entire into each of them, and it was this spirit which was the soul of their administration and of all the works they were given to perform.

The government of the Institute was confided to them at the most crucial moment and in the most difficult circumstances; that is to say, at the death of the Founder, when the congregation had the greatest need of wise and enlightened leaders to direct it, when it was necessary to record the traditions of the past, to review the rules and teaching methods, to apply all the Founder's principles and to put the final touches to his work. It is easy to see that their task was difficult, and if they fulfilled it completely, that was due especially to their unity.

One extraordinary thing worth noting: these three men, with very different personalities, governed the Institute together for more than twenty years, without allowing any divergence of opinion to be detected, without anyone being able to notice even once that one of them thought differently from the others. No matter which of them one dealt with, there were always the same words, the same viewpoint, the same understanding of things, the same way of doing business—in a word, the same spirit and the same direction. Never did one of them grant what another had refused; never did one blame or even give any indication of disapproval of what another had said or done. Listening to them or watching them act, one would have thought they had only one soul; at the very least, one was forced to admit that a single spirit animated all three. This perfect unity, which was to their glory, was so well known that all three exerted the same authority, and it was known that there was no going back, no appeal from whatever was decided, promised or done by any one of them.

One of the most capable and most spiritual brothers, full of admiration and astonishment at the sight of such perfect and consistent unity, amid so many occasions, if not of division, at least of divergence of opinion and ways of acting, stated, «It would be more difficult to divide those three men than to plant a rosebush in the middle of the ocean.» A picturesque expression, but very apt for showing how intimate their unity was, what the brothers thought of it, and what influence it exerted on them to keep them in a spirit of submission and obedience.

A highly-respected priest, who had had several matters to settle with the administration, told one brother director, «Your 'three-in-one' are the most striking confirmation I have ever seen of the words of the Holy Spirit, 'A threefold cord is not easily broken'» (*Eccles* 4:12).

What makes this unity more admirable and praiseworthy is that it remained inalterable despite circumstances which could easily have broken or at least weakened it. Brother François, who was almost always sick and unable to act, was forcibly obliged to leave the entire burden of administration to his assistants, who divided the work between them, took care of business matters, directed the brothers, decided everything, and provided for everything, with such a perfect spirit of unity, and such self-abnegation, that Brother François' authority, far from diminishing, continued to increase, and the brothers hardly noticed that he stepped back and acted only through his assistants.

To show how touched it was by the example of such unity, the Chapter of 1860 unanimously voted that a portrait should be painted of these three brothers united in the same spirit, to remind all the brothers of something so well suited to serve them as a lesson and model. Happy and blessed are the houses of the institute where this model will be imitated and will become the brothers' rule of conduct. Peace, consolation, holy joy, happiness and the hundredfold of good things promised by Jesus Christ will be the inheritance of all the members of those communities. The prosperity of the schools, the good spirit of the students, the confidence of the public, the benevolent protection of the authorities, are all accessories which always follow in houses where unity and charity reign.

Unity is absolutely necessary if any good is to be accomplished; it was in unity that God made all things. When he wanted to create human beings, he said to himself, «Let us make man in our own image and likeness» (*Gen* 1:26). This greatest work of all involved deliberation, consent and agreement on the part of the three divine persons. We see the same unity in mankind's redemption: the Father sends the Son as a gift to men and women; the adorable mystery of the Incarnation is accomplished through the operation of the Holy Spirit; the Son sacrifices himself, but according to the will of the Father. In the name of the three divine persons, we are reborn, baptized, and become God's children.

Jesus founded his church in unity. Among the apostles, only Peter is chosen, «so that, through a single established head, all division might be avoided,» says St. Jerome. Our Lord held so strongly to this unity for his church, that he forcefully requested it from his Father: «Holy Father, keep in your name those you have given me, that they may be one as we also are» (*Jn* 17:11, 21).

Why hold so tenaciously to such unity? Because unity is life, and dualism is death; because unity is virtue and dualism is sin and disorder. Because unity is strength, prosperity and progress, and dualism is weakness, decadence and nothingness. Unity creates the order and admirable beauty which reign in heaven. Unity gives the soul virtue and sanctity; unity gives the body strength and health; unity strengthens families, cities, kingdoms.

Discord shatters and destroys everything; it leads to conflicts and wars of destruction.

«Every kingdom divided against itself shall be made desolate; and every city or house divided against itself shall not stand» (*Mt* 12:25). Hell itself subsists only through unity; if Satan were divided against himself, his kingdom could not survive.

Unity makes for strength and progress. Even paganism knew this truth, and Sallust says, «Little things grow through concord, and the greatest are ruined and annihilated through discord.» Someone asked Agesilaus why the city of Sparta was not fortified. Motioning toward its perfectly united citizenry, he replied, «There are the ramparts of the city.»

«The unity of ten persons means that any one of them is ten, because each one is in the ten, and the ten are in each one,» says St. John Chrysostom. «That is why each one has twenty hands, twenty eyes, and breathes and acts through ten souls; for each one takes as much care of the others as of himself. That is why the eyes, hands and feet of all ten serve each one; each one serves the others as he does himself. In this way, a single person can do much, because he can do as much as ten; and if one is a hundred, a thousand or even more, it is still the same thing.»

Unity produces happiness. Where there is concord, there is Jesus Christ, there is God, there is the Holy Trinity, and consequently, there reign joy and perfect happiness. The unity of heaven produces the beatitude of the saints. «There,» says St. Augustine, «there is no envy, no difference of desires; the unity of love reigns in all.»

«And that unity of love so bonds the saints among themselves,» adds St. Gregory, «that each of the elect who has not received a certain gift himself, rejoices that someone else has received it; he is as happy as if he himself possessed it.»

The grace of unity is the pledge of everything good. «I will give them one heart and one way,» says the Holy Spirit, «and in this way, strength, prosperity, peace and in a word, everything good, will be with them» (cf. *Jer* 32:39).

On the other hand, take away unity and you have nothing but ruins; separate the branch from the trunk and it no longer bears fruit; separate the brook from its source and it dries up. A building resists the wind and remains standing only because all its parts are united; take away the cement that binds them and everything immediately collapses.

Concord is likewise the bond which unites the members of a community. Take away concord and men tear each other to bits like wild beasts—no more charity, no more justice, no more indulgence, no more happiness. Everything goes when unity goes, and hell enters the house.

O holy unity, how necessary you are, how much good you contain! O holy unity, which our holy Father so often recommended to us. Come dwell among us, always reign over us; we all want to live under your lovable control. O holy unity, of which our first brothers left us such moving examples, we are ready to make any sacrifice in order to keep you! Be always with us; grant that we may have only one heart and one mind, and that people may always say of us, «See how they love one another; see how united they are!»

CHAPTER THIRTY-FOUR

ASSIGNMENTS

The brothers' assignments were a cause of great preoccupation on Fr. Champagnat's part. «Assignments,» he used to say, are a superior's most important and most difficult task. It is the most important, because the prosperity of a community during the year, the contentment of the brothers, peace and unity among them, and the success of the school, all depend on it. A single man who is not in his proper place or who is not up to his task, is sometimes enough to spread uneasiness in the community, to paralyze the zeal and dedication of the other brothers, to halt the progress of the children and jeopardize the work of their education.

«It is the most difficult task, because it demands of the superior perfect knowledge of the men he is using, of the state and needs of the communities, of the spirit of the local population and the attitudes of the local authorities. Without that knowledge, he will run the risk of making assignments which will prove to be for him a source of embarrassment during the year, a cause of disturbance and disorder for the communities, often a cause of ruin for the brothers, and a good motive for dissatisfaction and complaints on the part of the authorities or the benefactors of the schools.»

When he is assigning the brothers, the superior must take a thousand things into account: each one's character, virtue, defects, needs, capacity, aptitude, health, and often enough even his tastes, whims or prejudices. Without such precautions, he would run the risk of putting a brother in the wrong place, jeopardizing his success, or endangering his virtue and vocation.

For example, if you put melancholic temperaments together, you will have mourning and Great Silence in that house all year long. If you put together difficult, fussy, hypersensitive men, they will be constantly spying on each other, suspecting each other, and becoming upset over nothing. If you put together men who are inconstant and prone to discouragement, the least little obstacle, the slightest difficulties, will be enough to make them unhappy, to prevent them from doing their work, and to induce them to write to complain at every moment. Put together men who are vain and unduly self-willed, and instead of peace, unity and charity, you will have troubles and war in the house. In a word, if you put together men with a bad character or little virtue, they will all cause each other constant pain and continual sacrifices.

On the contrary, if you give men with a happy character as companions to a brother with a sad temperament, you will make his life happy and cure him of his melancholy. If you entrust a hypersensitive brother to a very reasonable director who is never offended by others' whims, you will spare that brother a thousand regrets and a host of faults, and in time you will correct him of his hypersensitivity. If you place an inconstant brother with a weak will and a not-too-generous heart with a director who has a strong and noble soul, who is afraid of nothing, the latter will be the benevolent tutor of the weak brother; he will revive his courage and strengthen his will in good. If you put a vain and proud brother with a director who is solidly humble and who possesses truly Christian simplicity, you will break his pride and offer him the most favorable opportunity to recognize his silly vanity and to acquire the spirit of humility and simplicity which is proper to a Little Brother of Mary. Finally, as St. Vincent de Paul says, it is certain that «the best way to correct someone of a defect or a vice is to place him with men who have the contrary virtues.»

Being deeply convinced of these principles, Father Champagnat first drew up a rough draft of the assignments, then took a few days to reflect on the groupings he had just set up, and to recommend them to God. He then submitted his draft to his council and asked each of them to comment on the way he had arranged things. Only after that did he settle definitively on each one's community assignment and work.

St. Ignatius Loyola used to say that a wise man does things as if everything depended on his hard work and he could expect his undertakings to succeed only because of his own efforts; but then he counts so much on God that he expects everything to come from his protection. That was the way Fr. Champagnat thought and acted; he did not neglect anything which would help him make wise assignments; but he did not count on his own intelligence and arrangements; he counted only on God's blessings.

«We have had plenty of discussion, arrangements and precautions,» he used to tell his council, «so as to give each brother what most suits him; we think we have made good matches and arrangements. But let's beware of relying on our own prudence; if God doesn't lend a hand and doesn't bless these arrangements, we will have done nothing, and the arrangements we think are the wisest will be the least successful. So let us beg Our Lord to bless our work, because *Nisi Dominus ædificaverit domum, in vanum laboraverunt qui ædificant eam.*» Then he took the assignment list, placed it on the altar during Mass and for several days, he and the whole community prayed fervently to obtain God's protection on the arrangements he had made.

Before reading the list to the assembled brothers and informing them of their destinations, he shared with them the following reflections and recommendations: «My dear brothers, I am going to tell you the house which has been selected for you, and the work which Divine Providence entrusts to you this year. I have done everything which depended on me to give each of you a task proportionate to his strength and talents, to place you with confrères who may make your life happy and help you to sanctify yourself. But remember that success in your work, your peace and your contentment, depend in large measure on you yourselves.»

You will succeed or fail; you will be happy or unhappy, depending on whether you behave well or ill. So your fate is in your own hands, and it will be whatever you make it. If you want God to bless you and give you a happy year, faithfully follow the following recommendations:

First, accept the house and assignment selected for you with a great spirit of faith, as coming to you from God. The more your assignment goes against your preferences, the more disagreeable and difficult your task is, the more you must love it and rely on God to accomplish it. Do you know what happens when obedience calls you to a house or gives you a task? If you accept them submissively, God immediately gives you the graces you need to succeed and to do good there, and the more difficult and humble your assignment, the more abundant are those graces.

Second, be on guard against any prejudice towards the confrères given to you, and do not listen to the unfavorable reports others may give you about them. But perhaps you will say, «They assure me that this brother director is hard to please; that that confrère is a difficult character and nobody can get along with him.» Remember that such reports are never exact, and that most of the time, the ones who are doing the complaining are those most at fault. And even if it were true that a certain brother has not been able to get along with another, that doesn't mean that you won't be able to do so. Your personality is totally different from that of the brother who's complaining, so you may find yourself well off where he was unhappy.

Third, remember that your happiness and contentment during the year depend on you. If you are pious, regular, and working at your perfection, God will bless you and overwhelm you with consolations, and you will win the hearts of all your brothers. If you are obedient to your director, charitable, forbearing, respectful and obliging to your confrères, they will all love you, they will all work to make you happy, they will pay you back a hundredfold for the favors and the little bit of good you do them.

But if instead of acting that way, you give free rein to your defects, if you are a nuisance to your brothers, if you hurt them, if you offend them, if you refuse to help them out, if you scandalize them by your infidelity to the Rule, you will be unhappy, and you will have no right to complain, because it will be done to you as you have done to others, as Jesus Christ said. God will treat you according to your works, and he will permit the law of «an eye for an eye» to be applied to you. If you are a thorn in others' side, if you prick them, snap at them and despise them, they will do the same to you, and every day they will inflict new pains on you, even if they have no intention of offending you.

Fourth, don't forget that the prosperity of the house where you are placed depends on you and the way in which you fulfill your task. A few comparisons will help you understand that. A year is good and fertile when each season fulfills its task; that is to say, when winter gives snow and ice; summer, heat and dryness; spring, moisture; and autumn, mild temperatures. If a single season is upset, the harvest may be in danger and the whole year's crops spoiled.

In the same way, a religious house prospers and does good when each member of the community fulfills his task; the negligence or bad conduct of a single member can upset the whole house and nullify everyone else's efforts. If a single wheel is missing from a clock, if a single piece is broken or out of place, it will make the clock run fast or slow or stop altogether, make it a useless piece of furniture, and confuse the community schedule. Likewise, a single brother who does not do his duty, who abandons or neglects his work, threatens the success of the school, halts the progress of the establishment and disturbs the whole community.

In the human body, a sick or paralyzed member makes all the others suffer and becomes a burden to them. In a community, which is a moral body, a single brother who does his work poorly, and whose conduct leaves something to be desired, makes all the others suffer and overburdens them, because they have to do what his laziness leads him to neglect. So it is certain that the prosperity of a community depends on the way in which each one does his work, and that those who neglect it out of lack of dedication, or who do it poorly for whatever other reason, annoy their brothers, overburden them, and impede the progress of that establishment.

Fifth, I am sure that you would be terrified if I told you in detail all the evil done by a brother who, out of laziness, indocility, inconstancy, bad will—in a word, through his own fault—does his work poorly and has to be transferred. Listen to this:

a. He deprives himself of the good he could do, and of the merits he could acquire in his task, if he did it acceptably and according to his capacity.

b. He buries the talents which God has given him and abuses the graces which are bestowed on him so that he may succeed and may procure God's glory through his assignment.

c. This abuse of the talents and gifts he has received, this infidelity to grace, this resistance to the will of God, are for him the cause and the source of a host of faults, which he cannot fail to commit—murmuring, complaints, spite, discouragement, shirking part of his task and duties, lack of submission to his brother director, lack of patience, etc.

d. He makes himself guilty of an injustice towards his students, towards the town, the benefactors and the populace, if he is teaching; or towards the institute, if he has some other assignment. How many times I have heard good brothers directors say, «That brother cook has burned twice as much coal as his predecessor; he has run up enormous expenses for groceries, because he begrudges the work involved in preparing his vegetables, he doesn't take care of things and lets them spoil, and yet we're less well fed than last year.»

e. He scandalizes his brothers, his students, and all those who witness his disedifying conduct.

f. He overburdens his confrères, impedes the progress of the school, makes the public lose confidence in it, and harms the whole institute.

g. He destroys the regularity of the houses and the discipline of the schools, because a brother who does his work poorly creates disorder wherever he goes.

h. He creates a thousand problems and a thousand crosses for the major superiors, who tie themselves into knots in order to assign him and reassign him, in hopes of finding a task which suits him.

i. He disturbs the peace and happiness of the brothers, even in the houses where he is not stationed, because often enough, several brothers have to be changed so that he can be put somewhere; several houses and several classes are thereby disturbed and turned upside down because of him, so he is the cause of all the unpleasantness which follows.

j. He is guilty of all the expenses he occasions, because these various changes cannot be carried out without a substantial outlay of money. Finally, by acting the way he does, he makes himself unhappy and despised, and spends his life doing nothing, disturbing others, and spoiling whatever is entrusted to him.

Sixth, would you like to know, brothers, what you should do in order to fulfill your task well and avoid all those changes?

a. You must love that task, whatever it may be, and in order to do that, you must remember that it is God who has entrusted it to you, that it is by means of that task that he wants you to glorify him and work at your salvation and so earn heaven.

b. You must allow yourself to be guided, putting aside your own way of doing things, your own personal methods, in order to take on those of the Institute and to follow the advice of your brother director.

c. You must be totally dedicated to your task, and pray to God and the Blessed Virgin every day to bless your work and your efforts.

It was in the light of these recommendations that Father Champagnat used to read the assignment list. All the brothers listened to him in profound silence, and then each one left, determined not to have to be transferred during the year.

CHAPTER THIRTY-FIVE

WHAT IT MEANS TO EDUCATE A CHILD

When he founded his Institute, Father Champagnat did not intend merely to provide primary instruction for children, nor even to teach them as well the truths of religion, but also to give them an education.

«If it were merely a question of teaching the children human wisdom,» he used to say, «we would not need brothers, because lay teachers would be enough for that task. If we claimed to give only religious instruction, we could rest satisfied with being merely catechists and gathering the children an hour every day. But we want to do more; we want to bring up children, which means giving them a complete education. To do that, we must be instructors, we must live among the children and they must spend a great deal of time with us.»

But what does it mean to educate a child? Does it mean to care for him, meet his needs, and allow him to lack nothing in terms of food and clothing? No. Does it mean to teach him to read and write, and give him the knowledge he may need later on in his business dealings? No. Education is a higher task than that. Does it mean teaching him a trade and making him capable of exercising a profession? No, no. Education is not apprenticeship. Does it mean making him honest and polite, training him in the social graces, and teaching him to live in society? No. All that is good and necessary for a child, but it is not education properly speaking; it is only its outer shell, its least important element.

Giving a child all these good things and advantages educates his body, but it does not educate his soul; it teaches him to live for time, but not for eternity; it prepares him for the world, for this earth, but not for God who is his only aim, nor for heaven which is his destiny and his true homeland.

Since God created humankind in innocence and justice, if Adam had not rebelled against his Creator, his nature would not have been altered and his children would not have needed an education. At birth they would have possessed all the perfection of their being, or at least they would have attained it by themselves as their faculties developed. But as a result of their original degradation, human beings are born with the seeds of all the vices, as well as of all the virtues. They are lilies, but lilies surrounded by thorns; they are a vineyard, but one which needs to be pruned; they are the Father's field, in which he sowed good seed, but in which his enemy has sowed weeds. The aim of education is precisely to uproot those thorns, to prune that vineyard, to cultivate and weed that field.

So let us now explain in some detail in what the work of education consists.

I.

Educating a child means enlightening his mind and helping him to know religion; that is, the goal of humankind, the need for salvation, death, judgment, heaven, hell, eternity, sin, the commandments of God and of the Church, the life of Jesus Christ, his mysteries, his virtues, his sufferings, what he did for our salvation, the sacraments he instituted, the abundant redemption he acquired for us, what we must do to apply it to ourselves and to bear worthily our identity as God's children, in order to merit the eternal glory which has been destined for us and which Jesus went on ahead to prepare for us.

II.

Educating a child means reforming his evil inclinations, correcting his vices and defects, such as pride, indocility, duplicity, egoism, gluttony, rudeness, ingratitude, licentiousness, thievery, laziness, etc., etc.

Now, one must try to stifle these vices and others like them as quickly as possible as soon as they appear; the serpent must be killed before it can grow; the sickness must be treated before it becomes a fatal illness. At the first moment one discovers a defect in a child, a gentle reprimand, a light penance are enough to cure the evil and kill the bad seed. But if you let this precocious defect grow, it will become a habit which all your efforts will not be able to correct.

Newborn defects and vices, which we do not think amount to much and which for that reason we neglect to repress, are, says Tertullian, the seeds of sins which foretell a life of crime. Thorns don't prick when they begin to grow; snakes have no venom when they are born; but with time, the points of thorns become solid and sharp as swords, and snakes become more venomous as they grow older. So it is with a child's vices and defects; if they are allowed to grow and develop, they become tyrannical passions, criminal habits which can withstand everything and which can no longer be corrected.

III.

Educating a child means training his heart and developing all his good dispositions. It means casting into that heart the seeds of all the virtues and working to make it docile, humble, compassionate, charitable, grateful, gentle, patient, generous and constant. It means giving [the heart] the means to practice those virtues, to make them grow and bring them to their perfection.

The heart of a child is virgin soil which is receiving seed for the first time. If that heart is well cultivated, well prepared, if that seed is good, it will produce abundant and lasting fruit. The prudent gardener bends, grafts and controls his tree while it is young and tender. The potter makes his vessel before the clay hardens. In the same way, a child must be trained to virtue when he is young, flexible and innocent, when good principles are easily imprinted in his mind and heart. At first he will do good only because he is commanded to; but soon enough, when his reason has been trained, he will do it out of love and by choice, in such a way that he will give himself to virtue not only painlessly but even with pleasure.

Experience constantly proves, as Pius V tells us, that children trained in virtue from their earliest years almost always lead a Christian, pure, exemplary life, and sometimes reach the heights of sanctity, whereas others, whose cultivation has been neglected, lead a life deprived of virtue but full of vices and disorders which destroy them.

IV.

Educating a child means forming his conscience. To do that, one must:

1. Give him solid religious instruction, and make him understand clearly that he must always act according to the principles of God's law, motives of faith, and the movements of his conscience, and not according to the opinions of the world.

2. Inspire in him a great horror of sin, implant deeply within him the adage that sin is the greatest of all evils, and that virtue is the only real good.

3. Teach him that virtue and sin flow from the heart, that it is the heart which consents to evil or which produces acts of virtue; and that he must therefore watch over its thoughts, desires, and affections; that it is not enough to be an honest man, nor even to

observe God's law exteriorly and to be faithful to it in the sight of others, but that he must love and observe it everywhere and never do anything against the promptings of his conscience.

4. Inspire in him a great love of truth and an extreme aversion for falsehood, and often urge him to be fully and entirely sincere in confession.

V.

Educating a child means training him in piety; that means making him understand the need, necessity and advantages of prayer; accustoming him from infancy to pray with respect, modesty, attention and recollection; giving him an inclination for the practices of Christian piety and leading him to find his happiness, consolation and strength in his religious exercises and in prayer.

We will never stop repeating that when it comes to education, piety is everything. When we are fortunate enough to make it penetrate the heart of the child, it makes all the virtues sprout there, and like a fire, it visibly consumes and destroys all vices and defects. Make a child pious, make him pray, make him receive the sacraments, inspire in him a tender love for Jesus and great devotion to the Blessed Virgin, and you will make him good, docile, honest, courageous, active, meek, humble and constant. Make him pious and you will see his character become open, frank, lovable and obliging. Make him pious, and as his love for God grows, you will see his defects fade away, melt, disappear just as snow melts and disappears under the burning heat of the sun. So cast a strong dose of piety into the heart of the child; it will make all the virtues you want to give him germinate there; it will kill all the vices and defects you are trying to destroy.

VI.

Giving religious education means making virtue and religion loved. A child will love religion and become attached to it out of conviction and conscience, if he clearly understands these four truths:

1. Religion is the greatest grace God has given to human beings.

2. Each commandment of God is a real gift and a source of happiness for us, even from a temporal viewpoint.

3. Religion combats only our enemies—the devil, sin, vices and evil passions which degrade and vilify us and become the source of all our difficulties.

4. Only virtue makes us happy, even here below. Duty and happiness are synonymous, and therefore inseparable. That is a maxim we must engrave so deeply in the souls of the children that they will make it their invariable rule of conduct for their entire life.

It is a truth of faith and of experience that joy, consolation and happiness are the lot of the virtuous man, just as is it certain that remorse, anguish and tribulation follow everywhere the man who does evil and gives himself up to vice.

VII.

Educating a child means training his will, teaching him to obey. The great scourge of our time is independence. Each one wants to do his own will, and believes he is better equipped to command than to obey. Children refuse to submit to their parents; subjects revolt against their rulers; most Christians despise the laws of God and of the Church; in a word, there is insubordination everywhere.

So we do a great service to religion, to the Church, to society, to the family and especially to the child, when we bend his will and make him learn to obey. Now, to train a child to obedience, we must:

1. Never order or forbid anything which is not just and reasonable; never command him to do anything which makes his reason rebel or which smacks of injustice, tyranny or even whim, because such orders can only disturb the child's mind and give him a deep contempt for his teacher and a strong revulsion for what he commands.

2. Avoid commanding or forbidding too many things at the same time; a multiplicity of commands or prohibitions produces confusion, breeds discouragement in the child's heart, and makes him forget or disdain some of the prohibitions or orders. Besides, the only result of any unnecessary constraint is discouragement and the beginnings of bad spirit.

3. Never command anything which is too difficult or impossible, because exaggerated demands annoy children, and make them stubborn and rebellious rather than docile.

4. Require the full and entire performance of whatever just and reasonable things were commanded. To issue orders or assign homework or penances, and not to insist that they be performed, will make the child disobedient, ruin his will, and accustom him to taking no account of the orders and prohibitions he receives.

5. Establish strong discipline in the school and demand the children's entire submission to the regulations. This discipline is one of the things most likely to strengthen the will, to give it energy, to help it to acquire the habit of obedience and holy violence which one must do to himself in order to be faithful to grace, to struggle against the passions and to practice virtue.

This discipline also constantly exercises the will through the sacrifices it imposes at every moment. It obliges the child to call a halt to his dissipation, to keep silence, to keep himself recollected, to pay attention to the teacher's lessons, to watch his deportment, to repress his impatience, to arrive exactly on time, to study his lessons, to do his homework, to be respectful to his teacher and honest and polite and helpful to his fellow students, to bend and adapt his character to a thousand things which annoy it. These multiple acts of obedience, this series of little triumphs the child gains over himself and his defects, are the real way to form his will, to make it strong and flexible at the same time, and to give it constancy.

VIII.

Education also, and especially, means training the child's judgment. Of all the faculties, the judgment is the one which it is most important to protect, train and develop. A poor judgment, or a badly trained one, is a false standard which leads to a host of errors and injustices. And in fact, what can a man do without good common sense, tact and *savoir-faire*? Nothing. He is not fit for either temporal or spiritual things; he is incapable of either Christian or social virtues. Before one can be virtuous and capable, one must be a human being; and where there is no reason, there is no human being.

Judgment is doubtless a gift of nature, which no one can give to someone who has not received it. But judgment is subject to improvement, and like the other faculties of the soul, it can always grow, develop and increase. So it is very important to cultivate this faculty in the child, and to equip him to continue himself to extend and perfect his reason. To do so:

1. Accustom him to think before speaking, before giving an opinion about anything. Since wrong opinions always come from an incomplete grasp of things and a faulty way of looking at them, haste is what puts us most at risk of this intellectual illness. When we look too quickly, we can see only superficially.

2. Often repeat to him St. Augustine's famous maxim, «Reflection is the source of everything good.» Habituate him to regulating his conduct and judgment according to the major

principles of Christian morality, which is the true light of the mind, the torch of reason and the source of wisdom.

3. In your instructions, give him practice in grasping the main point, the principal aim of any question, story or lesson, and don't let him get lost in non-essential details.

4. Bring him back frequently to the details of his conduct; make him see how he has offended against common sense and tact, how he has let go of the main thing in order to go after details, has dropped the solid for the glittering, or principles for changing or false opinions.

5. Make him apply himself to studies and work which demand reflection; train him to combine his ideas, to put them together, to draw consequences from principles and to acquire as clear an understanding as possible of everything submitted for his opinion, whether in his school work or in the thousand unexpected happenings of daily life.

6. Tell him over and over again that reason, wisdom, and virtue are three inseparable things which are always found in the middle, never at the extremes, and that consequently, reason and good judgment exclude all exaggeration, all imaginary perfection, every kind of excess.

7. Preserve the child in innocence and the practice of virtue, because the passions blind the mind and falsify the judgment.

IX.

Educating a child also means molding and polishing his character. A good character is a great blessing from heaven; it is a treasure and a source of happiness for a family. Inversely, a bad character is a misfortune for the one who has received it, and for all those with whom he lives; it is a cause of discord and a scourge for a family. But, thank God, character can be modified, improved and corrected. Yes, the character which shows the greatest number of defects can be reformed by a good education. To carry out that difficult task, the teacher must:

1. Study the child's character, his tastes, his inclinations, his defects, his aptitudes. Otherwise, how can he know what must be reformed? How can he cultivate, develop and perfect his good qualities?

2. Give the child appropriate and respectful freedom, because if the child is too constrained, it will be impossible to know his defects and correct them.

3. Wage an incessant war on egoism, hardness, pride, insolence, vulgarity, over-sensitivity and other similar vices, which spoil one's character and never fail to produce disorder and to disturb the peace, and the spirit of cooperation and charity.

4. Devote himself to making the child honest, obliging, agreeable, affable, respectful, and grateful, and teach him how to behave towards everyone, particularly towards his parents, his superiors and everyone who comes into contact with him.

X.

To work at educating a child means to maintain constant vigilance over him, surround him with attention, so as to preserve him from vice, to keep bad companions, bad example and every kind of bad contact away from him, and so as to defend him against whatever might become a danger for his innocence, threaten his virtue, or spoil his mind by giving him false principles.

XI.

To give a child an education means to inspire him with love of work, to give him habits of order and cleanliness, to make him understand that the source of well-being, wealth and ease is found only in work, economy, modesty and temperance.

XII.

To give a child an education means giving him the knowledge he will need in his position and station in life, making him love that station, no matter how modest it may be, and teaching him how to improve it, to make it pleasant and honorable, and to sanctify it.

XIII.

To work at imparting a good education also means seeing to the child's physical development as well as his intellectual, moral and religious growth. It means pursuing and insuring the perfection of his body concurrently with that of his soul; watching over his health in order to preserve it from all dangerous influences; keeping his members healthy, making them acquire the strength and vigor of which they are capable; in a word, it means preserving the child from any accident, from anything which might alter his temperament or endanger the perfect integrity of his senses and his entire person.

XIV.

Finally, to educate a child means to give him the means to acquire the total perfection of his being, making this child a complete person. Since men and women enjoy the privilege of always being able to advance and perfect themselves, so as to become perfect as the heavenly Father is perfect, the teacher must do what is necessary to insure that a student never leaves his hands without having understood that he himself must carry on the work of his education, continue to instruct himself, to reform himself by means of vigilance over himself, by combating his passions, by correcting his defects, and by applying himself to becoming constantly better and more virtuous.

399

***

That is the aim of education, that is the august ministry confided to the teacher of Christian youth. This work is most holy and most sublime because it is the continuation of the work of God in its most noble and elevated aspect, the sanctification of souls. It is the holiest work, because it deals with forming saints and the elect for heaven. It is the most difficult and demands the greatest devotedness; it cost Jesus Christ his blood and his life, and the teacher can be the co-worker of Jesus Christ and help him to save souls only by sacrificing and immolating himself.

It is therefore evident from the preceding that teaching children to read and write, or teaching them grammar, arithmetic, history, and geography, or even making them recite the catechism, is not really bringing them up. The teacher whose concern is limited to that is not completely fulfilling his task or his duties towards his students. He is leaving out the most important part, which is to give them an education, which means forming them to virtue, correcting their defects, making them love religion, habituating them to its various practices—in a word, making them pious Christians who are faithful to their duties.

The father of Socrates, who was a sculptor, showed his son a block of marble and told him, «There is a man inside this block; I'm going to bring him out with blows from my hammer.» When someone brings you a child who is still ignorant, crude, uneducated, living only the life of the senses, you can say with even more reason than Socrates' father, «There is a man there, a good father, a good citizen, a Christian, a disciple of Jesus Christ, a saint, a soul chosen for heaven, and I am going to bring him out; I am going to teach him his duty, his destiny, reform him and turn him into what he can and should be.»

A child arrives slowly at the full unfolding of his personality and the perfect use of his intelligence. He reaches that stage only through communication with his peers who enjoy the same gifts.

So he needs the help of others to improve himself and acquire the integral use of his faculties. But he needs it above all in order to be trained to do good and to be prepared to receive the principles of faith, the graces and virtues which are necessary for him to arrive at his supernatural destiny.

Man is the usual agent, the great means which God commonly uses to raise man, and still more, to save man. This glorious mission is always difficult, often painful and bloody—one cannot save souls except by devoting oneself and sometimes by sacrificing oneself for them. And yet, God has found this ministry so sublime that he conferred its glory on his own Son, for the Word became flesh to be man's teacher, model and savior. What a glory for a brother to be associated with him in this mission!

CHAPTER THIRTY-SIX

THE NECESSITY OF EDUCATION

«What will this child turn out to be?» (*Lk* 1:66). That was the question St. John the Baptizer's parents asked at the birth of the holy Precursor; that is the question everyone naturally asks when a child comes into the world. The Holy Spirit answered that question when he taught us that a human being follows the first path taken, and will not leave it even in old age. What will become of this child?

He will become what education makes him—a good Christian and a virtuous citizen if he is well brought up; a vicious person, an enemy of God and religion, a disturber of the public peace, if he is left to himself and left without education.

I.

«Education,» says an Arab proverb, «is the diadem of the child,» which means that the child's entire future, his success, what he will become in the world, what he will do for good or for evil, depends on education. Moreover, society is constantly increasing with the children the schools pour into it, just as the ocean is fed by the rivers which discharge into it. So we can state that the diadem of society is found in education, and that education is the mold from which society takes its shape—its spirit and its principles.

So it was not without good reason that someone said many years ago that, «Education is everything; it is the individual, society, religion; everything comes from it, both good and evil, just as the river comes from its source and the oak from the acorn.» Even paganism recognized that truth; Plato held that good education is the foundation of society and of every nation. «Education in one's early years,» he added, «is absolutely necessary in order to form one's entire life; it is the most important matter with which the State can become involved, and the first duty of the chief executive of a city is to see to it that children are raised honorably and holily from their earliest years on.»

That is precisely why, in all times and places, good and evil fight for control of the educational empire with such stubborn tenacity. Behind the apparently simple question as to who shall teach a child reading, writing, arithmetic, etc., there lies hidden, in the final analysis, the question of domination, the triumph of good or evil. For the rest of his life, the child will belong to one or the other, to whichever first gained possession of his heart. If the majority of children are raised in a Christian manner, the reign of good is assured; on the contrary, if they remain without education, or receive a bad one, the reign of evil will prevail and the whole of society will be headed for its ruin.

II.

Education does for the child what cultivation does for the soil; no matter how good a piece of land may be, if it is left uncultivated it produces only brambles and thornbushes. In the same manner, no matter how well-disposed a child may be, no matter how many good qualities he may have, if he does not have an education, if his good qualities are not developed, he will grow up without virtues. His life will produce nothing good at all, or it will produce only wild fruit, dead works.

It is obvious that cultivation is absolutely necessary to clear a field of its weeds, brambles and thorns, and to prepare the earth to produce strong plants. Education is likewise indispensable for correcting children's nascent defects, reforming their inclinations, and preparing their souls to produce the fruits of virtue.

What is the life of a man who has not received an education, who has not been trained to good manners, piety and virtue? It is a year without springtime; summer will find nothing to ripen, autumn will offer nothing to harvest, and the whole course of such a life will be a gloomy winter in which everything remains frozen, the light is never bright, and nature is always barren.

Whence comes the flood of passions which threatens to overwhelm the world today? Whence comes the precocious perversity of so many young people who are the scourge of society? From lack of education, or from an education without religious principles. «Why,» St. Bernard asked, «why do we see so many old people who are so addicted to vice or stripped of all virtues? Because they did not receive an education or because they were badly brought up; because when they were young, no one corrected their vices and turned their hearts toward virtue.»

III.

Education does for a child what pruning does for a fruit tree; it is pruning which gives the tree its beauty and makes for the quantity and good quality of its fruit. Besides, the more a tree is cared for, pruned, and shaped, the more abundant, excellent and delicious its fruit. Any tree which is not pruned produces only wood or a poor grade of fruit. Likewise, it is education which develops a child's good dispositions and prepares all the faculties of his soul for great virtues. So if education does not reform a child, if it does not correct or trim away from him whatever is defective, the passions whose seed he bore at birth will grow with age; they will stifle all the good qualities he received from nature and will leave behind only gross vices which will dishonor him.

«A man's soul needs to be pruned like a vine,» says St. Antoninus. «A vine left to itself and untended is the plant which most quickly returns to its wild state. The same is true in a man; all it takes to make him degenerate and fall back into barbarism and the folly of paganism is to deprive him of the benefit of instruction and Christian education.»

IV.

A young shrub can be given any shape whatever. It can be bent in all directions and will easily take and maintain whatever direction it is given. But if one tries to straighten it when it is big, it will break rather than bend. That is a faithful image of a child and of the good effects which education produces in him. When a child is young, one can easily bend his rebellious will, painlessly correct his evil tendencies, and readily reform all his character defects; but once he is big, there is no longer any way to change him. So shape a child, and shape him early; that is the sure and infallible way to guarantee him a life full of virtues and good works.

V.

Education is to the child what a faithful guide is to an inexperienced traveler. If the traveler is well guided, he will reach his destination safely and without much trouble. But if he takes the wrong road, he may fall over a cliff or die under an assassin's knife or in the jaws of wild beasts.

VI.

Life is like a journey; everything depends on the first steps. One can be sure of arriving safely if one has taken the right road; but if one goes astray at the very outset, one will be as often lost as on the right track.

«Children,» says Gerson, «find themselves at a crossroads, ready to follow whichever they are told to. So it is extremely important to show them the road of virtue very early on, and to teach them to follow it, because they will stay on the one they have been shown for the rest of their lives. Two masters are calling them to follow them, Jesus Christ and the devil. If you win them over to Jesus Christ, if you teach them to follow him on the road to heaven, they will belong to Jesus Christ their whole life, and they will walk steadily along the path of virtue. On the contrary, if they are allowed to take the road of vice, if they are pushed along it by bad example or bad advice, they will belong to the devil and they will follow him right to hell.

«Look how difficult it is to convert Jews, Muslims, heretics and schismatics. Why are they so attached to error? Because they absorbed it with their mother's milk, and education has, so to speak, imbedded in their brains the false opinions of their ancestors. Why are they so faithful in following the wrong roads which are leading them toward hell? Because they are kept on those roads by the principles which their earliest education gave them.»

VII.

Education does for the child what a pilot does for a ship. A ship without a pilot will inevitably break up on the rocks or sink in the depths of the ocean. A young man entering the world without a Christian education which forewarns him against the dangers he will find there, is a ship launched on the sea without a pilot to steer it, without a compass to guide it. A plaything of every vice, tossed around by every wave, he will crash into every reef until he finally sinks into the abyss. There is no hiding the fact that it is lack of education or poor education which has peopled the world with criminals and enemies of society, and hell with lost souls. He who takes the road to hell in his youth will follow it until he arrives at that frightful abode.

VIII.

Education is for a child what the foundation is for a building. A building without a foundation will never stand. If the foundation is defective, if it is not built on something solid or on rock, the building will be overturned by the wind or will collapse the first time rain softens the earth. The foundation of human life is laid in infancy.

«At that age,» says St. John Chrysostom, «it depends entirely on the education given, because in infancy we are formed for good or for evil, and we acquire habits we will have all our lives. It is education which should imprint on our mind the religious principles which should always guide our conduct; it is education which should sow in our hearts the seeds of the virtues which should lead us to salvation and make us into good Christians, predestined souls; it is education which should give us the knowledge we need for the position and state in life to which Providence will call us; in a word, it is education which should prepare us for success in everything entrusted to us. If education is lacking to us, or if for whatever reason, it does not give us those benefits, our life has no foundation whatever, it is spoiled from the outset and it will be nothing but a long succession of faults and calamities.»

IX.

If you want to poison a fountain, you need only throw poison into its source. To take over a kingdom, you need only seize its main cities; from them, you can arrange free access to the whole country. In the same way, to corrupt a child's whole life, you need only leave him without education or teach him false principles.

These principles will spread their evil and their venom to all the faculties of his soul and will spoil all his actions and all his virtues.

What can we expect from a child left to himself or badly brought up, except a life of disorder and crime? The older he gets, the deeper he will slide into vice, and he will eventually despise everything. At first he will sin only out of weakness; then he will become impassioned about evil, proud and satisfied with his own excesses.

«Detestable habits will be formed,» says St. Ambrose, «and finding no resistance, they will grow so strong as to become insurmountable.» Then, if you tell him to reform his irregular inclinations and to change his life, he will reply, «I'm too old to change; I was brought up this way, I can't act any differently.» Every uncorrected vice strengthens the passions; passion corrupts judgment, judgment perverts the will, the depraved will enjoys evil, which becomes a habit; and once a habit is formed, there arises a sort of need for vice and sin. To make us realize how strong and deplorable such habits are, Holy Scripture uses these strong and frightening words, which should make all dissolute young people tremble: «His bones shall be filled with the vices of his youth, and they shall sleep with him in the dust» (*Job* 20:11), because they are so ingrained in their nature and have become so inherent to their being.

Czar Peter the Great, emperor of Russia, often said, «I was very badly brought up. Far from repressing the outbursts of my natural ferocity, people flattered me because of it. I feel it now and I am embarrassed by it, but the force of habit is so strong that I cannot control my anger and cruelty. I, who changed the customs of my people—I cannot change myself!»

X.

Education does for a child what a canal does for water. «Just as water easily follows the course prepared for it,» says St. Jerome, «so a young child acquires the habits you want to give him, allows himself to be led, and follows the path he is made to take.»

«Man,» says the Holy Spirit, «will follow his first path, and will not leave it, even in his old age.» The experience of all the ages confirms this truth; there is no one who does not know that even if age has cooled his imagination, ripened his judgment and added to his knowledge, it has still left him with his earliest habits. So every man finds himself, in terms of vices and virtues, just about where he was in his youth: Christian or impious, sober or intemperate, chaste or dissolute—in a word, whatever his education made him. When it comes to habits and conduct, we can tell what people were in their youth by what they are today, just as we can project what a child will later become by the way he behaves at the end of his education.

Of all the nineteen kings of Israel, there is not a single one who was not extremely wicked from his youth, and not one of them returned to God and was converted before his death. Judah also had nineteen kings from Solomon until the Babylonian captivity. Only five of them were good: Asa, Jehoshaphat, Jotham, Hezekiah and Josiah; all the rest were wicked. Those who were good began that way in their youth and remained so their entire life. Most of those who were wicked began to live a bad life in their youth, and never changed, which shows how true that oracle of the Holy Spirit really is: «Instruct a child in the way he should go, and when he grows old he will not leave it» (*Prov* 22:6).

XI.

Finally, education is for the child what seed is for the earth. You can reap from a field only what you have sowed there; if the seed is wheat, you will gather wheat; if it is weeds, you will harvest weeds. The hearts of children are virgin soil which is receiving seed for the first time; if those hearts are well prepared and well cultivated, if the seed scattered there is good, it will produce abundant and lasting fruit. «Things learned in childhood,» says St. Irenaeus, «grow in the mind with age and are never forgotten.»

«In the same way,» St. Ambrose adds, «that the habit of reading, when acquired in childhood, becomes so natural that we do it without the slightest difficulty and never lose it, so it is that when divine precepts are impressed on us in our youth, they become the guides of our conduct, and we retain and follow them all our life.»

XII.

Conclusion. So let us say it again: the life of a child is totally dependent upon his education. If he does not have one, or if it teaches him false principles, the child will be full of vices and will take the road to hell from his earliest years, and his footsteps along the slippery road of vice will hurl him into every excess and infallibly lead him to eternal death.

On the contrary, a good education is never without some fruit, even for those who turn aside from the good principles they received. The holy truths deeply engraved in their souls can never be entirely erased. The winds of passion will shake the tree, knock loose its flowers, even break a few branches, but in vain; the stripped trunk will stand firm on its roots and receive their nourishing sap, which will eventually make it produce new limbs and bear abundant fruit. The many conversions we have witnessed, the return to a good moral life and to virtue, are certainly the result of Christian education, the fruit produced by the seeds of faith and piety sowed early on in the hearts of children.

Dionysius the Tyrant, having in his power the son of his enemy Dion, thought up a singular revenge against the father, which was all the more cruel for seeming so mild. Instead of killing the child or throwing him into a vile prison, he set out to corrupt all the good qualities of his soul. To that end, he let him grow up without education, left him to his own devices, and gave orders that he be permitted to do whatever he wanted. The young man, carried away by his passions, gave himself up to every vice. When the tyrant saw that the lad had developed the way he intended, he sent him back to his father. He was placed in the hands of wise and virtuous teachers and tutors, who spared no pains to try to make him change, but all their efforts were futile. Rather than correct himself, he killed himself by jumping from the roof of his father's house.

CHAPTER THIRTY-SEVEN

WHAT IT MEANS TO TEACH CATECHISM WELL

In his instructions to the brothers, Father Champagnat often repeated that, «A catechism lesson—I mean a well-taught catechism lesson—is worth more than the greatest penances you could perform.»

A young brother, whose curiosity was piqued by the expression, «a well-taught catechism lesson,» stood up and asked timidly, «Excuse me, Father, for daring to ask you, but would you please tell us just what 'a well-taught catechism lesson' means.»

«Gladly,» Father replied. «In my opinion, a well-taught catechism lesson means: first, one well-prepared by study; second, one watered by prayer; third, one backed up by good example; and fourth, one brought down to the children's level by good teaching methods and dedicated zeal.»

In this chapter, we will develop Father's reply, often with his own words, for he himself explained it many times.

I. A well-taught catechism lesson is one well prepared by study.

It is certain that the results of a catechism lesson will always be in proportion to its preparation. He who sows sparingly, reaps sparingly; he who sows nothing, reaps nothing. The brother who, out of respect for the word of God and zeal for the sanctification of the children, carefully studies our religion and prepares every day what he wants to say to his students, will always produce some results; his instructions will never be without some effect.

On the contrary, he who does not prepare his catechism lesson renders it useless for the children; as a result of the laziness which prevents him from studying and planning what he will say, they will not listen to him nor be touched by what he says. And how could anyone listen attentively to his instructions if he did not put any attention into preparing them? How can he come up with interesting questions if he has not planned them; how can he make his students love a topic, a subject, a truth in which he himself is not interested? He has no right to complain of his student's lack of attention, and still less of his lack of results, since he did not guarantee any by doing the necessary work of preparation.

It is very risky for a brother to dare to teach catechism without preparation. It is a lack of respect for God and the holy truths of our religion. It puts him at risk of saying something incorrect. It inclines the children to disgust and aversion for his lessons and sometimes even for religion itself.

St. Jean-Baptiste de la Salle says that, «A brother must diligently study religion, because ignorance on his part would be criminal, since it would be the cause of the ignorance of those entrusted to him.» And in fact, one cannot teach without having learned, and one learns only through studying, because human knowledge, and still more the truths of religion, cannot be guessed at. How is it possible to instruct others when one is ignorant of what one is obliged to teach? We must have gathered in secret before disbursing in public. We must be a source in order to become a river. «No one,» says St. Gregory, «can teach what he does not know, and our reason teaches us that before instructing others, especially in religious matters, we must be well instructed in them ourselves.»

«It is a shameful thing,» says Father Champagnat, «for a brother not to know religion well; it would be a real scandal if he were less capable of teaching catechism than other subjects. A brother cannot neglect the study of the catechism without making himself guilty, and negligence on this point is a fault which has terrible consequences. First of all, it means he will never know his religion himself and will be a superficial person all his life. It also makes it impossible for him to give the children religious instruction and train them in virtue. It means abandoning the end of the Institute. It means making our schools totally secular. In a word, it means failing in the first and most important duty of a teacher, which is above all to give religious instruction and Christian education.

«Do we reflect on these consequences, which are as rigorous as they are unavoidable, when we neglect to study the catechism? If we did think of them, we would rarely find a legitimate reason to exempt ourselves from doing so. Some say they don't have time. An idle excuse, since they find time to study other subjects; besides, you cannot lack time because according to your Rule you have an hour consecrated to that study, and you are not permitted to use it for anything else on your own initiative. Others maintain as an excuse that they have read all the catechisms in their library several times. Studying religion does not consist only of reading that kind of books, but also in the faithful reading of ascetical works, the lives of the saints and church history, and then meditating on what one has read.»

This habitual study and meditation on religion is the remote preparation for teaching catechism. As proximate preparation, we must also:

1. Learn by heart or at least read very attentively and reflectively the lesson we have to explain.

2. Note the most important points to which we must particularly draw the students' attention.

3. Foresee the secondary questions which could be asked on each of these points, linking them together so as to develop the truth and help even the least intelligent to grasp it.

4. Prepare the stories and comparisons which will clarify and confirm one's explanations.

5. Decide what practices to recommend at the end of each instruction.

That is the sort of preparation required if catechism is to be well taught and produce abundant results for salvation.

II. A well-taught catechism is one well-watered by prayer.

«Your instructions, your good advice, even your corrections,» Father Champagnat used to say, «are seeds which you sow in the minds and hearts of your children, but in order to sprout and bear fruit, those seeds have to be watered with prayer. Without moisture, the earth produces nothing; without prayer we can do nothing, either for others or for ourselves. The more defects certain children have, the more difficult they are to deal with, the less they profit from your instruction and concern, the more you must pray for them; children like that can be won over to God only by prayer.»

A brother needs prayer in order to touch hearts. Study gives us knowledge of religion; prayer gives the warmth and impressiveness which penetrates and softens hearts. «One word from a pious catechist on fire with the love of God,» says St. Alphonsus, «produces more results than a hundred conferences by a tepid theologian.»

«To impress hearts and win them to God,» adds St. Vincent de Paul, «we need burning words, which are like rays from the fire of divine love. It is prolonged prayer and meditation which set on fire the hearts of gospel workers; it is at the foot of the crucifix or at the side of Our Lord or before the Blessed Sacrament that a catechist acquires that impressiveness which touches others, that heavenly fire which enlightens, enkindles and converts hearts.»

«The way to become convinced of the truths of salvation,» says St. Jean-Baptiste de La Salle, «is to draw them from their source, which is God himself. That is why a day spent in regularity, recollection, fervor, and the exact performance of all the religious exercises, is the best preparation for teaching catechism.»

A brother who does not have the spirit of piety will never accomplish anything great. He may make noise, but he will never obtain any results. We are sometimes astonished to see certain classes in which, in terms of piety, everything is dull and flat, despite the teacher's talents and efforts; while in others, the children give great consolation. We offer a lot of extraneous reasons; the real one is the teacher's lack of piety. St. Gregory says that, «Unless the Holy Spirit himself teaches within, and speaks to the inner ear of the hearers, the catechist's voice echoes uselessly in their bodily ears.»

How many brothers, after having talked a great deal all year long, and taken a great deal of trouble, have not succeeded even one single time in producing in the children the slightest desire to become better? Why have so many classes and so much effort had so little effect? Because the hearts of the teachers were not touched; because they did not draw from mental prayer the sentiments which move souls; because the Holy Spirit did not give life to the words which came from their mouths.

Piety gives us experience with spiritual things. The science of spiritual things is both experiential and practical. He who speaks only from books speaks coldly and very imperfectly. St. Thomas teaches that we can judge a thing in two ways, either because we know it in its nature through our own experience, or because we know it through speculation and reading. The first way is, without fear of contradiction, much more perfect and much surer than the second. A chaste person, for example, knows the value and pleasure of chastity much differently than a dissolute moralist. The same is true of pain; we have a much better idea of the pain, heat and discomfort caused by fever from having one ourselves, than from all the doctor's talk. Stick your finger into the fire, and that test will tell you what it is, better than all the conferences anyone could give you about its properties.

«He who tastes honey,» says St. Alphonsus, «knows it better than all the philosophers who think about it and explain its nature. Likewise, the wisdom of the saints is not acquired from books, but from prayer, where the teacher is Jesus Christ and the textbook is the Savior's cross and wounds.»

«Draw near to God in prayer,» says the psalmist, «and you will be enlightened» (cf. *Ps* 33:6). That is where he will give you knowledge of spiritual things, and where he will teach you the discernment of spirits and the best ways to combat the children's vices and correct their defects, and make them love religion.

St. Alphonsus says that, «We sometimes learn more in one hour of mental prayer than in ten years of studying from books.» St. Albert the Great thought the same way; he used to say, «When it comes to divine science, we make more progress through piety than through study.» He backed up his opinion with the words of the Book of Wisdom, «I wished, and understanding was given to me; I called upon God, and the spirit of wisdom came upon me» (*Wis* 7:7).

Holy Scripture confirms that teaching in another place, when it says that the mind of a saint «sometimes discovers the truth better than seven watchmen standing in a high. Taste and see how sweet the Lord is» (cf. *Ps* 33:9). The Holy Spirit does not say, «study, read books,» but «taste»; that is to say, learn from experience, practice your religion, love God, serve him faithfully, and you will learn for yourself how lovable he is, how beautiful virtue is, and how happy they are who practice it. So the more we love God, the more we know him and the more capable we are of making him known and loved.

III. A well-taught catechism is one backed up or confirmed by good example.

Good example is the first lesson a brother should give his students. «Let your light shine before men,» Jesus Christ says, «so that they may see your good works and glorify your Father who is in heaven» (*Mt* 5:16), and also imitate you. Why does Our Lord, who in other contexts tells us to conceal our good works, who urges us to pray in secret and to give alms in such a way that our left hand doesn't know what our right hand is doing, order us to let our light, that is to say our good actions, shine before others? St. Augustine says, «He does this to teach us that those who are entrusted with leading others must not only be pious and holy, but must also be seen to be so; for just as their own conscience must be pure in order to insure their salvation, so must they enjoy a reputation for being virtuous, in order to obtain the salvation of others.»

St. Paul wrote to his disciple Timothy, «Be an example to all the believers in the way you speak and behave, and in your love, your faith, and your purity...Take great care about what you do and what you teach; always do this, and in this way you will save both yourself and those who listen to you» (*1 Tim* 4:12,16). A brother's first duty is to teach the children by his example; his actions should be a sort of continual catechism which teaches the children to live in a Christian manner. His conduct should be a living gospel, in which each student can read how he should behave in order to imitate Jesus Christ and be a perfect Christian. In a word, a brother should live in such a way that he may say to those whom he teaches what Paul said to the faithful: «Take me for your model, as I take Christ» (*1 Cor* 11:1).

Good example is the quickest way to lead children to virtue, for three reasons:

1. Because people, and particularly children, have more faith in what they see than in what they hear; that is why one good example is worth more than a hundred lessons.

2. Because example shows that what we are teaching is feasible; it is also what most touches the child and convinces him to do good.

3. Because children are natural imitators. St. Basil says that, «Children are like parrots and monkeys; the parrot repeats what it hears, the monkey does what it sees done. A child does the same thing.»

Thus, children learn far more through their eyes than through their ears; they are curious by nature, and their eager eyes look everywhere for instruction and examples. But whom do they look at? At those who teach them and whom they regard as models they can imitate in all things. So a brother may be sure that he has as many supervisors and imitators as he has students; he should never forget that they are constantly observing his behavior and that they follow and watch him everywhere. Without his even realizing it, they are studying his character and his good and bad qualities, and think they can imitate whatever they see him doing.

So it is not enough for a brother to make the children repeat the catechism every day, nor even to develop its teaching with explanations. He must necessarily back up his teaching with the example of every virtue. «Do you want your children to do good?» St. Jean-Baptiste de La Salle used to ask his brothers. «Then do good yourselves; you will inspire in them much more love of virtue and the desire to practice it by your example of sensible and controlled behavior than by all the words you could possibly speak to them.»

IV. A well-taught catechism is one brought down to the children's level by good teaching methods and dedicated zeal.

To really teach his children, a brother's lessons must exhibit three characteristics: method, brevity, and clarity.

Method. Nothing pleases children more, and helps them more to retain the truth you teach them, than method. If a lesson, even one which is very good and full of striking and enlightening stories, is not methodical, it is like a conglomeration of magnificent objects thrown together in total confusion. On the other hand, a methodical lesson is like a park full of trees planted in checkerboard fashion, from each of whose intersections one can easily see all the rows in both directions. In the first case, one can wander all day among the various objects, discovering something new at every moment, but never getting more than a confused idea of the whole collection. In the second case, the eye can put everything into perspective and get a detailed picture of it that is not easy to forget.

A subject can be subdivided and organized in various ways:

- by distinguishing and enumerating the qualities of the topic; for example, charity is:

  a. the greatest,

  b. the most perfect,

  c. the most profitable,

  d. the most enjoyable,

  e. the most necessary, virtue;

- or by considering its various effects; mortal sin:

  a. kills the soul,

  b. makes us God's enemies,

  c. makes us deserving of the pains of hell;

- or by multiplying motivations; we should love Jesus Christ:

a. because he is God,

b. because he has first loved us,

c. because he died for us,

d. because he has overwhelmed us with gifts, etc.

And we can also divide a topic according to various circumstances. St. Francis de Sales says that we can look at any mystery under these headings: (1) why? (2) by whom? (3) how.

For example:

Who was born?	The Savior, the Messiah.
Why?	To save us and to become our model.
How?	Poor, naked, cold, in a stable, etc.

Each of these questions or main ideas can be developed and ·explained in turn by means of whatever secondary questions may be necessary or useful.

Brevity, which consists in:

a. Giving to the explanation of the lesson only the time indicated in the Rule, or the time the children need in order to understand it.

b. Speaking little and making the children speak a lot.

c. Making your secondary questions short, clear and precise.

d. Never getting off the topic, avoiding all questions which might be indiscreet, rash, subtle or over the children's heads.

Clarity, which stems from simplicity of thought and precision of expression. If thoughts are to be clear, they must be at the children's level, and so much in tune with their intelligence that they present the truth in a way that they cannot possibly fail to grasp, if they are paying attention.

Clarity of expression means expressing one's thoughts in clear terms and simple style, avoiding all symbolic, far-fetched, technical expressions—anything which would only serve to complicate things and confuse the children's minds.

Father Champagnat sent for a brother whom he had heard using some rather flowery words in his catechism class. He told him, «I was very annoyed at your silly pretentiousness during your lesson. Why don't you use words which are more likely to make you understood? What do words like «celestial Sion» mean to your students! Wouldn't you have been better understood if you had said «paradise»? If you were humble and zealous, you would speak simply so as to be understood by the youngest and most ignorant children.»

CHAPTER THIRTY-EIGHT

THE RESPECT WE OWE A CHILD

Even in antiquity it was an accepted principle that reserve and respect held first place in the education of children. One Roman author left us the well-known maxim: *Maxima debetur puero reverentia*—a child deserves the greatest respect.

If our ancestors, despite the limitations of their paganism, so well understood that a child's innocence deserves to be protected by very special reserve, should the attitude of Christian educators be any different? The souls entrusted to them were created in God's image, redeemed by the blood of Jesus Christ, purified by baptism, clothed with candor and innocence, and sanctified by the Holy Spirit who dwells in them. With what respect, with what prudence the educator should therefore surround children who wear such a halo! That is why it is *à propos* to examine the claims the child has to this special kind of respect, or putting it another way, to examine what a child is and what we must particularly respect in him.

I. What Is This Child We Must Respect?

1. He is the noblest and most perfect of visible creatures; he is «God's greatest miracle,» as St. Augustine says; he is «something great,» as the Wise Man exclaims.

He is the masterpiece of the divine hands; he is so noble and excellent that God has commanded an angel to guard, serve and care for him. This child is not only the work of God's hands, he is God's glory.[1] The rays and the goodness of the divine face shine upon him.[2] He is full of fiery energy, because his origin is completely heavenly.

He is God's representative on earth; all visible creatures are subject to him; all have been placed beneath his feet; everything is at his disposal; everything was made to serve him. He is the king of the universe, crowned with honor and glory,[3] in soul and body, by God who has given him justice, original integrity, immortality, and control of the whole world, as Bossuet says. For his sake God created the world, preserves it, and gives life to all creatures. The heavens spread out their splendors and roll majestically above his head, the sun fills the universe with its bright light, the stars never stop shedding their gentle and benign influence here below, the winds blow, the air becomes thick with clouds, the rain falls, the rivers run, the earth produces all sorts of plants, the animals live and reproduce, all of nature works—for his health and happiness and for his use.

2. A child is the image and likeness of God. Like God, he is a trinity: he has life, intelligence, reason and love; these qualities constitute the basis of his being. Like the Father, he has existence; like the Son, he has intelligence; like the Holy Spirit, he has love; like Father, Son and Holy Spirit, he has in his being, in his intelligence, in his love, one single happiness and one single life. You cannot take anything from him without taking everything from him. Created in God's image, he has an intelligence of almost infinite capacity, so that he may know. The more he learns, the more he is capable of learning; he can know an entire

---

[1]«A man indeed ought not to cover his head, because he is the image and glory of God» (*1 Cor* 11:7).

[2]«The light of your countenance, O Lord, is engraved in us» (*Ps* 4:7).

[3]«You have made him a little less than the angels; you have crowned him with glory and honor» (*Ps* 8:6).

world, and imagine an infinite number of others; he knows material things and spiritual things, created things and the essence of God; he enters and penetrates everywhere, speaks about everything, and uses his principles to reason about even the most occult things.

His memory is like an encyclopedia of innumerable ideas, like a huge room which contains heaven, earth, the sea and everything he ever knew, as St. Augustine puts it. His will can love all sorts of good things, even an infinite good; that will is so noble, so generous, that it cannot be satisfied by any other good except God alone. His freedom is so absolute and so powerful that it cannot be forced by all the creatures in the world; even all the angels together could not force it to will what he does not want to; only God has dominion over it. Finally, that child, that sublime creature, bears in the depth of his nature, in the loftiness and power and harmony of his faculties, and in his entire being, the seal and the very likeness of God.

3. A child is a son of God,[4] a son of the Most High (*Ps* 81:6). Yes, no matter how small, weak and vulnerable he may seem to you, he is not only called a son of God, but he really is one, and he is one even now, beneath the rags which cover him. Yes, God is his father and model, who wants him to become great, holy and perfect just as he is.

4. A child is the conquest and the price of the blood of God our Savior; he is a member and brother of Jesus Christ, a temple of the Holy Spirit, one in whom God takes delight. A child is the image of the child Jesus, a reminder of the childhood, the weakness, the humility and the docility of the infant God. A child is a lovable creature whom Jesus calls to himself: «Let the little children come to me» (*Mk* 10:14), whose company he enjoys:

---

[4] «As many as received him, he gave them the power to be made the sons of God, to them who believe in his name» (*Jn* 1,12).

427

«My delight is to be with the children of men» (*Prov* 8:31). A child is the friend and favorite of Jesus. St. Augustine says that just as earthly kings have favorites, so does Jesus Christ—the children whom he caresses, loves and blesses, and in whose education he is interested, because he has a very special liking and predilection for them.

5. A child is the hope of heaven, the friend and brother of the angels and saints. He is the heir of the heavenly kingdom and the eternal palms. This humble child was born to be a king, in both time and eternity. Yes, he is destined for a double kingship; if he wears his earthly crown worthily, the kingdom of heaven will one day open to him.

6. A child is one of the most lovable and most beautiful things on earth, the flower and adornment of the human race, as St. Macarius says, the first stage of life, so lovely to see, so delightful to cultivate, so easy to train to the holiest of duties. A child is a pure and simple soul who approaches religion confidently, with no secret agenda to defend, and who willingly lets himself be attracted by its motherly voice.

A child is an innocent soul whose passions have not yet disturbed his peaceful sleep, whose uprightness has not been altered by the lies and illusions of the world.

There is something about a child which hints at his heavenly origin. He has a special nobility and dignity different from that of most men. A child is the personification of simplicity, candor and innocence, the joy of the present and the hope of the future.

7. A child is your brother, your peer, bone of your bones, another self. This child has the same heavenly father as you, the same destiny, the same goal, the same hope; he is called to the same happiness. He is your traveling companion during this time of exile; he will be your co-heir and companion in your true home in heaven!

8. A child is a field God has given you to cultivate, a tender sprout, a weak plant who will one day become a great tree loaded

down with the fruit of all the virtues, casting far and wide its glorious shade.

A child is a little rivulet, a spring just bubbling up, but he may become a majestic river if you are like the skilled engineer of whom scripture speaks, if you carefully channel his docile water and never let foreign, polluted or bitter water disturb his heart.

A child is the focus of your work, your fatigue, your practice of virtue. He will be your consolation at the moment of your death, your defender before the judgment seat of God, your crown and your glory in heaven.

9. A child is God's blessing, the hope of the earth whose wealth and treasure he already is, and whose strength and glory he will one day become. He is the hope of his country and of all humanity which is renewed and rejuvenated in him. A child is above all the hope of his family, whose glory and delight he already is, and whose honor and glory he will one day become.

In a word, a child is the whole human race, all of humanity; he is humankind, no more, no less. He is entitled to respect, and must show respect to others. Such is the child you must respect.

II. What We Must Respect in a Child

We must first of all respect his innocence. But what kind of respect do we owe to that innocence? «The same respect we show to the saints and their relics,» Massillon tells us. «Nothing on earth,» says this illustrious and wise bishop, «is so great and so worthy of our homage as innocence. Let us respect that beautiful innocence of children, that precious treasure of the first grace received in baptism which they still have and which all of us have lost.

«We give public veneration to the saints who after having had the misfortune of losing it, have regained it through penance; why should we not have the same respect for children in whom this gift of justice and holiness still dwells? Let us look at them, then, with a sort of veneration, as pure temples in which dwells the glory and majesty of God, which Satan's breath has not yet tarnished. These children are precious deposits over whom we must stand watch, esteeming them as much as the relics of the martyrs which rest on our altars and which draw the homage and veneration of the faithful. If we had that faith-inspired attitude, we would not think we were lowering ourselves when we give these children the care their age and their needs require, and we would never be lacking in respect for them.»

And St. John Chrysostom exclaims, «You who are entrusted with the education of youth, do you know how much circumspection and respect you owe the child? Consult your faith; it will tell you what he is and what you owe him. On his forehead you will see the seal of his divine adoption, and it is up to you to prevent sin from deceiving him. His head and his breast are stamped with the sign of the child of God, and it is you who will answer to God if it is altered. His heart is the true sanctuary of the Holy Spirit and you are its guardian. In his heart, if you study it carefully, you will discover the seed and source of all virtues, and it is up to you to make them take root there. Jesus Christ says that the angels of God stand around this child to defend him and you share in that holy task. Now decide whether this child is worthy of your respect and if he deserves your attention.»

But what does the holy respect we owe to the innocence of the child demand of us specifically? It demands:

1. Great reserve in our speech, our actions and our behavior, so that we may not say or do anything, or let anything be perceived which might scandalize the child or make the thought of evil spring up in his mind.

2. Great vigilance to keep clear of him anything which might put him at risk of losing his precious treasure.

3. Great reserve and circumspection and rigid modesty in our contact with the child, never permitting ourselves or him any familiarity or any liberties condemned by our profession.

4. Profound veneration and high regard, which lead us always to speak to him kindly and politely and to treat him with great respect.

5. Constant attention to our own behavior, so that we always act so as to offer the child our own example of every virtue and a model of conduct which he may always imitate or admire.

Someone once asked a saintly priest who was a teacher, «How can you always remain in control of yourself and always maintain your patience, reserve and modesty, which seem to me to be beyond human nature?»

The holy priest answered, «I can do it because I never forget the wonderful advice handed down to us from times past: *Maxima debetur puero reverentia*—we owe the child great respect! Before I began teaching, I often told myself, 'God sees me!' and that salutary advice, which is given us by all the masters of the spiritual life as an excellent preservative against sin, held me back many times when I was on the edge of the abyss. But I am so weak, that that thought, no matter how spiritual it is, could not protect me against an infinite number of slight faults. Since I have been assigned to teaching a number of children, I have told myself, 'These children see me,' and the fear of becoming a source of scandal to them has made me all but impeccable.»

«But,» his friend said, «the children aren't always with you.»

«Obviously,» he replied, «but the care I take to watch over myself while in their presence, has become a habit. Besides, we can really say about them, to some extent, what we say about God: they see us in the dark, they hear us when we think we are alone.»

We have just seen how much respect we owe to the child's innocence. We know that God has entrusted this precious treasure to us and that he will ask us to account for it. How sad and frightening to think that instead of being the guardians of the virtue of these naive children, we might become their corrupters! To scandalize a child! To teach a child to do evil! Good God, what a horrible thought! That is a crime crying out to heaven for vengeance. «If it is a sacrilegious act of impiety to tear down a building dedicated to God,» says St. John Chrysostom, «it is an even more serious crime to defile an innocent soul which the Holy Spirit has made its temple. In point of fact, a soul is worth infinitely more than any building, because Jesus Christ died for it, not for piles of stone.»

«To scandalize a child,» this holy doctor continues, «to make him lose his innocence, is a greater evil than plunging a dagger into his heart. Murdering a child in its crib takes from him the bodily life he would have necessarily lost some day; but you, you snatch away from that child the life of grace, which is by nature immortal. The death the murderer inflicts on a child will be followed by a happy eternal life; and you—you hand him over, body and soul, to endless torment, to eternal fire. I can see that you grow pale at the mention of murder; then be afraid, you spiritual murderers, for you may be sure that the latter crime goes as far beyond the former as the soul is greater than the body.»

Woe to him who scandalizes one of these little ones! Note that Jesus Christ does not say, «If anyone scandalizes someone of earthly importance.» Why not? To help us to understand, St. John Chrysostom tells us, that the soul of a child is dearer to Jesus because of its innocence, because scandalizing a child is a greater evil than scandalizing an adult, and because of the child's lack of experience and the terrible impact bad example has on him.

«Whoever shall scandalize one of these little ones that believe in me, it were better for him that a millstone were hanged about his neck and he were cast into the sea» (*Mk* 9:41). «It would be better for him,» says St. Bernard, «if he had never been born into the community which he has just dishonored and tarnished; if he had never been born into the house into which he has just brought the abomination of desolation. Better for him if the heavy yoke of the world were attached to his neck and he were cast back into secular life.»

If someone scandalizes one of these little ones who believe in me, what will happen to him? How will he be punished? Listen and tremble! It would be better for him if a millstone were hung around his neck and he be thrown into the depths of the sea. «Notice,» says St. John Chrysostom, «that this punishment is pronounced with no hope of pardon. Someone who is thrown into the sea can still swim and reach safety; but if he is at the bottom of the sea, attached to a huge millstone, what hope does he have of getting loose? None whatever.»

If someone scandalizes one of these little ones who believe in me, it would be better for him if they hung around his neck one of those millstones turned by a donkey, and threw him into the sea. «The stone the donkey turns,» according to St. Gregory the Great, «symbolizes the difficulties and problems of this present life; the bottom of the sea means eternal damnation.» So anyone who corrupts children will be unhappy in this world and unhappy in the next. Anathema to him in time, anathema to him for all eternity!

«Woe to him through whom scandal comes to a little child» (cf. *Lk* 17:1). That poor child came to you as the protector and guardian of his virtue, and you have committed an outrage against that virtue and stripped him of it! He took refuge in your school as in a safe harbor, but he ran onto a reef—and you are that reef. You who should have been his guardian angel, you are Satan, you are his demon! A terrible shipwreck made him lose the most precious thing he possessed in this world, that shipwreck happened in your house, and it was you who stole his treasure!

What will that unfortunate boy do after such a loss, after such a misfortune? What will become of him? You taught him evil, so that's what he will do! You lured him into sensual pleasure; you placed him on the slippery slope of vice, and he will let himself slide down it. He will commit mortal sins by the dozen, by the hundreds, by the thousands, in thought, word and deed! What will he turn out to be? The corrupter of his companions and everyone around him! And all those crimes will be imputed to you, because you are their first cause, their first principle!

When he entered your school, it would have been better for him if he had entered the den of a lion or tiger; that ferocious animal would have torn him to pieces in an instant, but would have left him his innocence. That child, devoured by that carnivorous beast, would have lost only a fragile, perishable life; but you have made him lose both his body and his soul, the grace of God, the peace of his conscience, his salvation, heaven! Oh, infamous one, tremble lest the earth open beneath your feet and swallow you (Fr. Lejeune).

«If anyone violate the temple of God, him shall God destroy» (*1 Cor* 3:17), says St. Paul. Now what temple is holier, more pleasing to God, than the heart of an innocent child? «If according to God's law, the sinner must die,» says St. John Chrysostom, «what will happen to him who not only sins but makes others sin,» to him who teaches evil to an innocent child, to a child whom he should edify and train to virtue, to a child of whom he has been appointed guardian? To scandalize a child, to strip a child of his innocence—good God, what a crime!

A Roman lady who had dressed her son in the latest fashions was severely punished, even though she was only obeying her husband in spite of herself, because he wanted to give the boy a taste for worldly vanities in order to turn him away from his intention of consecrating himself to God. The following night, an angel visited that guilty mother and pronounced terrible threats: «Have you really dared to prefer your husband's orders to your Savior? Have you really dared place your hands on a child consecrated to God? That criminal hand will wither at once, so that by the severity of this punishment you may understand the greatness of your fault. Moreover, within five months, you will be dragged off to hell and you will see your husband and your children die, if you commit such a fault again.»

It all happened just as the angel had foretold, and the woman's sudden death was a sign that she had waited too long to do penance. «It is thus,» concludes St. Jerome, who tells this story, «that God punishes those who profane his temple.» If God inflicts such a terrible punishment on a mother for having dressed her child in vain attire, what will he to do a teacher who perverts those entrusted to him?

The story is told of a man who killed a child, and whose conscience gave him no rest; day and night, wherever he went, he seemed to hear the voice of the unfortunate one he had killed, constantly telling him, «Why did you kill me?» That voice became such a torture to him that he could not bear it. So he went to confess his crime to the judge, and begged him to condemn him to death. And the teacher who has scandalized a child—will he be able to bear the memory of his crime? Will he not ceaselessly hear in his heart the voice of the unfortunate child who will ask him throughout his life and for all eternity, «Why did you kill me? Why did you steal the innocence which would have earned heaven for me? Why did you give my soul over to the devil? Why did you hurl me into this frightful abyss? Woe! Woe! Woe for all eternity to the one who brought about my condemnation!»

CHAPTER THIRTY-NINE

A CONVERSATION ABOUT DISCIPLINE

One Thursday, while they were taking a long walk through the Mt. Pilat range, the brothers headmasters, after talking about a little bit of everything, began discussing ways to attract children to the schools and to give them a taste and liking for study.

«What works best for me,» said one of them, «are rewards; with 'good points', a holy picture, or a redeemable coupon, I get whatever I want from my children and I could make them go to the end of the world.»

Said another, «I find that emulation is the best method, because once you've been lucky enough to establish it, the children don't think of the work involved in studying, they enjoy it and they go right to it without having to be told.»

«In my opinion,» put in a third, «the teacher's ability and his dedication to teaching are worth more than all those other things.»

And a fourth added, «Personally, I find that the beautiful handwriting and drawing models I show the children work best when it comes to attracting them to the school.»

Father Champagnat, who had been listening to the conversation, interjected, «Those are all good means, but they are not enough, even taken all together, if they are not backed up and reinforced by strong fatherly discipline. Some of you don't have as high an opinion of discipline as you should, and you don't sufficiently understand its dignity and importance. Some of you even think that it drives children away from school, but the opposite is true, and everyday experience proves that a school where there is perfect order is liked by the children and well regarded by the parents.

«The reason for that is that everyone likes order, and disorder displeases everyone. In a well-disciplined school, the children are happy and relaxed, but they suffer and lose their taste for study in an undisciplined class. Lack of discipline in a class is like the predominant passion in an individual—the source of all evils, the direct or indirect cause of all the faults committed there. Lack of discipline compromises, or rather nullifies, all other means of drawing children to God and attaching them to the school. In my opinion, discipline is so necessary that without it, there cannot possibly be any instruction or education. Even Plato, pagan though he was, did not hesitate to say that the entire impact and success of education lies in well-regulated discipline.»

Let us sum up here in a few words the good effects of discipline, and how to establish it.

I. The Good Effects of Discipline

1. Discipline is the glory of any educational establishment and draws students to it. Since men easily allow themselves to be taken by external things, they will judge a school by its discipline. A strong discipline is immediately apparent, pleases everyone, wins the esteem and confidence of the public, and is often enough to establish a school's reputation and draw students to it.

2. It guarantees progress and solid instruction, by preserving the children's morals, by maintaining order and silence in class, by goading on the lazy by the emulation it sets up and by the care it takes to prevent any student from avoiding the common classwork, and by seeing to it that time is well-spent. A disciplined, well-regulated class is always a studious class, and a nursery of good students.

3. It preserves and nourishes children's piety. To do so, it sees to it that religious duties are fulfilled, it demands that

children behave respectfully and modestly during prayer and that they answer clearly and piously, it excludes all words or actions which might be a danger to faith, weaken respect for religion and lessen fidelity to the practices of Christian piety.

4. It preserves the children's morals, as well as their health, by maintaining continual vigilance over them, by never leaving them alone, by protecting them from bad companions and from laziness, and by keeping them constantly busy.

5. It instills good spirit in children because it gives them holy respect for their teachers, combats all their defects and passions and inspires docility, trust, mutual love and all the virtues which make up family spirit.

6. It forestalls children's faults and thus helps them to avoid punishment. The more discipline there is in a class, the fewer penances are given there. Brothers who have a weak character or who don't want to take the trouble to maintain order by means of vigilance, assiduity and exact conformity to the regulations are those who most easily let themselves go and mistreat children.

7. Discipline trains a child's will and gives him energy to resist evil and to combat vicious tendencies. It prepares him to practice virtue, helps him acquire the habit of doing his duty and makes him receptive to the impulses of grace. Why is it that most people today are inconstant and sensual, can't refuse themselves anything, and can't put up with anything that goes contrary to human nature? It's because they were raised without discipline and were never taught to obey, to do violence to themselves or to combat their evil inclinations. To subject a child to strong but fatherly discipline, to accustom him to obedience, is to do him a very great favor.

8. It preserves the teacher's health. When discipline reigns in a class, the fact that the students pay attention dispenses the teacher from having to repeat the same thing several times and from having to speak loudly, which spares and protects his chest and throat. When there is good discipline in a class, order, calm,.

peace and good spirit reign there, thus assuring the teacher of perfect tranquility and sparing him the emotional outbursts and mental anguish of all kinds which sap one's strength and health. In a word, in a well-disciplined class, there is a hundred times less trouble and a hundred times more consolation than in one where discipline is lacking. Hence it is easy to see that discipline conserves the teacher's strength and protects his health.

II. How to Establish Discipline

How can one obtain that strong, fatherly discipline which produces such wonderful effects? Fatherly religious discipline, which of itself trains a child's will and all his faculties, is the fruit of moral authority.

There are two sorts of authority: legal and moral. Legal authority is conferred by an office. It suffices for maintaining military discipline and training soldiers, but it is powerless when it comes to forming Christians.

Legal authority has three attributes: it can command, punish and reward. Now in a classroom, where there is question not of dominating children by force but of training them to virtue and to doing their work out of religious attitudes and the call of conscience, legal authority with its power to command, punish and reward is only a very secondary means of maintaining discipline. And if that authority is used badly, if it is used without intelligence or prudence, if it makes itself too much felt, it annoys children, gives them a bad spirit and sows disorder in a class.

Moral authority, which truly raises a child, is the influence the teacher exerts over his students by his virtue, his capability, his good conduct and the wisdom with which he governs. This kind of authority produces respect, esteem, trust, love, gratitude, submission, fear of displeasing the teacher and a desire to please him, to make him happy and to be pleasing to him.

This kind of authority is acquired:

1. Through virtue and exemplary conduct.

2. By ability and devotedness to the instruction of children. When Cyrus asked his grandfather Atarxerxes how to rule over the various nations of his empire and win their esteem and love, the latter told him, «Show yourself to be always the most virtuous and the most capable, and they will submit to you without difficulty.»

3. Through reason, judgment, and common sense. Virtue, reason and ability bear the scepter of the world; they dominate everywhere; no one refuses to submit to their sway, which is why one of the ancients said, «It is always the most virtuous and most reasonable man who governs; he makes laws even without intending to; others copy his attitudes and submit to his authority without even being aware of it.»

4. Through gravity, modesty, restraint and reserve in dealing with children.

5. By being careful to respect oneself and the children.

6. By being attentive to concealing one's own defects, faults, imperfections and lack of ability.

7. By very moderate use of punishments and rewards; by carefully avoiding every act of brutality or even too much severity.

8. By such wise and prudent behavior that the children may never have occasion to blame their teacher or accuse him of anything.

Those are the means for acquiring moral authority. It is the only kind of authority which produces education; it alone can succeed in forming children and making good Christians and good citizens of them.

Moral authority is not strong enough when it does not guarantee the teacher the respect, docility and love of his students. Moral authority is necessarily weak when children are not convinced that their teacher is a virtuous, capable, sensible man, and that he feels fatherly affection for them.

Authority is too weak when it is not respected by the monitors and those whom the teacher has chosen to replace him. Likewise, discipline is too weak when it is not maintained during the teacher's absence. So when you see that order and discipline become shaky and disappear as soon as the teacher is out of sight, it is a sign that he has no moral authority over his students, and that he controls them only through physical force. In a class like that, no education is possible, and the teacher is simply a policeman.

CHAPTER FORTY

SUPERVISION

I. Some Reflections Which Should Encourage Vigilance

In the first section of this chapter we will develop four sayings of Father Champagnat which are very well suited to convince the brothers of the need for supervision and to give them an active and enlightened spirit of vigilance. The second section will discuss the goal of supervision and put forward the main areas in which it should be exercised. Finally, the third section will give various practical rules for carrying out this major duty, for any teacher concerned with giving his students a good education and preserving their souls and bodies from the innumerable dangers which threaten them.

1. A brother is the guardian angel of his children. Innocence is the foremost of all goods and the most excellent of all gifts. A child preserved in his baptismal innocence is in God's eyes a treasure more precious than all the kingdoms of the world. But this beautiful innocence is surrounded by enemies who have sworn to destroy it. A child does not know the price of that precious virtue; he carries it in a fragile container without realizing the dangers he is running and the snares laid for him on every side to make him fall and deprive him of his treasure.

Now, since a child is not capable of preserving this possession of infinite merit, God has entrusted its care to a Christian educator and has placed it in his hands on deposit; he has made him its guardian and defender. «I have made you,» he tells him through Ezekiel, «a watchman for the house of Israel» (*Ezek*

3:17), in other words, for the group of children you are responsible for raising.

In explaining these words, St. John Chrysostom says, «Just as a lookout is stationed in a high place to watch the enemy's movements from afar, so that the army camped on the plain will not be taken by surprise, so those who are entrusted with watching over and educating children are appointed above all to carefully watch for the maneuvers of the enemy of our salvation, to remove from their path the snares and dangers which the devil prepares for them to make them fall into his net.»

Rollin says that, «The teacher is a guardian angel for the children, and there is not a single moment when he is not responsible for their conduct, so long as they are under his direction.»

Speaking to his brothers, St. Jean-Baptiste de la Salle adds, «In a sense, we can say that each of you is a bishop—the caretaker, that is, of the flock which God has entrusted to him—and that consequently each of you is rigorously obliged to watch over every member of it.»

A brother should picture himself as a general who has been put in charge of a place being attacked by an enemy, and who does not rest for a moment in order to prevent its capture; or else as a helmsman who constantly raises his eyes to check his course by the stars, or lowers them to check for reefs in his path which could wreck his ship; or even as a shepherd who never rests when he has to defend his flock against wolves and who takes every precaution to keep his sheep away from polluted pastures.

He can even learn something from watching the devil, whose vigilance is as menacing as his is protective. That enemy of salvation never lets these tender children out of his sight; he follows them everywhere and is constantly looking for opportunities to take them by surprise. Should a religious be less zealous for their salvation than this monster is for their destruction? Can he rest easy so long as the roaring lion is constantly on the prowl to devour the souls which will fall to him through the former's negligence?

2. God will demand an accounting from each brother of the children he entrusted to him. Supervision is one of the most important aspects of the education of children. It is one of the most demanding duties of a teacher, and one in which negligence could lead to the most unfortunate results. Those who neglect to fulfill it would expose themselves to terrible punishments.

«If lack of vigilance,» says Rollin, «gives an opening to the enemy who ceaselessly prowls around children, to steal the precious treasure of their innocence, what will a teacher say to Jesus Christ when he asks him to account for their souls, and when he reproaches him for having been less vigilant in guarding· them than the devil was in seeking to ruin them?»

God himself tells us, «I will ask you an accounting for the souls you have allowed to perish.» And in another place, «If the sentinel saw the sword approaching, and did not sound the trumpet; and if because the people did not protect themselves the sword took their lives, he in turn will be surprised in his iniquity, and I will demand the blood of him who should have preserved them from that misfortune.»

In entrusting a child to a teacher, God tells the latter, as Jacob did his sons when he entrusted Benjamin to them, «Swear to me that you will take care of this child; I will hold you to account for him, and you know that if you do not bring him back to me innocent, I will never forgive you» (cf. *Gen* 43).

«Your children,» says St. John Chrysostom, «are a deposit which has been entrusted to you. You will give an account of them before God, so watch carefully over their conduct, their actions, their companions, and their contacts, and do not expect any mercy from God if you neglect that duty.»

3. Vigilance should be one of a brother's principal virtues. The spirit of vigilance, attentiveness and exactitude should mold the character of a teacher. Rollin tells us that, «Vigilance and

attentiveness hold first place among the virtues of a good teacher. He cannot carry them too far, provided that he acts without annoyance, constraint or affectation.»

It is not only during class that a brother must supervise the children; his eyes and his attention should follow them everywhere—outdoors, indoors, during recreation, at school, in the street, in the church, night and day. The vigilance of a good teacher never sleeps, and, for fear that the demon may snatch from these dear children the treasure of innocence, it follows them at every moment and in every place.

It knows that it was while the householder's servants were sleeping that the enemy came and sowed the weeds which would one day choke the good grain. It knows that it was while Samson was asleep that Delilah handed him over to his enemies, and that it is by distracting the teacher that the devil seduces his students. It knows that the wolves rejoice when the shepherds doze off, and that, as St. Ambrose says, «It is then that the wily tempter strikes a fatal blow, under cover of the faulty security of the watchman.» It knows that the devil is constantly prowling around children like a roaring lion, hoping to devour them, and that he needs only a momentary negligence on the part of the shepherd to destroy them.

It knows that the naive, trusting, compliant, sensitive, carefree child easily accepts every impression and lets himself be easily seduced, and that he consequently needs to be followed and directed; that paternal vigilance constantly follows him and directs him along the path of good. It knows that recreation time, in a school where there are children to supervise, is not a time when one is permitted to be idle or to amuse oneself, and that it is then that one must redouble his zeal and his activity. And so, without appearing to notice, nothing escapes it: improper or gross words, dangerous or too intimate relationships, suspicious gestures, slipping away furtively, conversations carried on too long, sensual movements during games, and anything likely to offend against decency. It is constantly in the midst of the children to point them out and make them avoid them.

This vigilance should extend to all the children, to all their senses, to all their actions, so that it finally drives away the thought of evil by always making it impossible to commit. «You will behave,» Our Lord told St. Mary Magdalen de Pazzi, «within the limits of your own power and the grace I will give you, as if you had as many eyes as you will have souls entrusted to your care.» It should be the same for a brother; he should have as many eyes as there are children, so that not one of them will be overlooked or left to himself, and so that the actions, words, and I would almost say all the thoughts, of all those children placed in his care, may be revealed to him, as it were, in some mysterious way.

4. Without this active vigilance, it is not possible to safeguard the children's morals. «Young people get carried away,» says St. John Chrysostom. «You cannot give them too much protection against their natural enthusiasm, nor set up too many precautions, supports and supervision. If you want to preserve their innocence, spare neither warnings nor reprimands nor any of the means which authority places in your hands.»

Whatever may be the good qualities and dispositions of your children, watch over them day and night, never leave them masters of their own actions, supervise even their very thoughts; without all that, you have no hope of keeping them pure (cf. *Sir* 30:11). In point of fact, the finest wine, if not carefully watched, soon turns to vinegar; the most delicious fruit degenerates if the tree that bears it is not pruned and cultivated; the fattest sheep waste away if they are not kept healthy by the vigilant care of the shepherd.

Without assiduous supervision and care, you cannot expect to preserve the innocence in the heart of a child, that virtue which is so precious, so delicate, so important for his happiness, not only in eternity but during his lifetime, so necessary for his advancement in piety, his progress in studies, and even for his health and his very life. Without assiduous vigilance, the child will learn the science of evil without your even being aware of it— that science which, like a pestilential vapor straight from hell, burns and kills the flower of purity at the moment when it was coming to birth; that science which corrupts and degrades even the best of natures; that science which makes a child contract deplorable habits which he may never get rid of; that science which from earliest youth, prepares him for every excess of wantonness and debauchery, and for an old age afflicted by infirmities and a shameful death.

And what does it take to lose that beautiful innocence and bring on so much unhappiness? One single moment of negligence. It needs only a spark to start that fire, and the human heart is made of tinder! One look was enough to turn David into an adulterer and murderer. One conversation, one thoughtless action, one reading done out of curiosity, one suspicious contact, one stepping out of class, one momentary absence during recreation, during which the children are left to themselves— those have all too often been the first and only causes of the loss of so many young people.

II. The Object of Supervision

What in particular should we supervise? The main aim of supervision is to keep a child clear of everything that can interfere with his education, to prevent his falling by removing from him the occasions which would lead him to do so, to prevent the fire of his passions from being kindled by taking away its fuel, to close his mind to dangerous thoughts by keeping far from him whatever might give rise to them. The main areas on which our supervision should focus are:

1. The child's companions. Bad companions are the most natural source and the most common cause of corruption (Cardinal de La Luzerne).

A closer than normal relationship between two children, especially if they are of different ages and if both are not very virtuous and very obedient; the urge to seek each other out, to be side by side, in class or elsewhere, and out of sight of the teacher; their attitude and the way they speak with each other: a smile, a gesture, a wink, or whatever else gives an impression of immodesty—all these are indications that something out of order may be going on.

In such cases, without telling them what you think or suspect, you must advise them not to show so much familiarity and to be more modest. The way they receive that advice and put it into practice will show you what is in their hearts. Whatever may be the case, continual supervision is a must in order to preserve these children's virtue, because it is in danger. Therefore the teacher should never lose sight of them.

But in order to prevent such relationships from being formed, or to put an end to them, the brothers must be careful to change the students' seating often, and to separate, in the classroom, dormitory, dining room, chapel and church, children from the same town, neighborhood or street, and those who have shown some propensity for this sort of relationship. They must also see to it that these sorts of children are not together too often during recreation or on outings; one must find some pretext or plausible reason to keep them apart and to make them play or travel with others.

2. Watch their posture. Children's posture is usually a good indication of what they are like. A child who is often surprised in a suspicious posture, especially if he blushes and suddenly gets back to his work, should be reprimanded and watched very closely. Great care should be taken to train children in proper dress and in good manners and propriety. They should be taught

the rules of modesty and habituated to practicing them. In class, they should always keep their body upright and not bent over, with their hands on the desk and not beneath it, and their feet nearly joined. During recreation and on outings, they must be required to be always decently attired, not to put their hands in their pants pockets, and not to have their clothing open in an improper fashion. Any behavior contrary to these rules and any others they are given, of which they should often be reminded, any gesture, any sign of passion, must be stopped and even punished.

3. Supervise the bad students. Contagious diseases are spread by contact. A single dissolute student, like bad yeast, can spoil an entire class, a whole school full of young people. This is a plague which spreads rapidly and which brings infection and death to all those who come near it. How many children born with a pleasant temperament, gifted with virtuous inclinations, fortified with religious principles they received at home or at school, saw all of that fade away and disappear through meeting and associating with a vicious and corruptive companion!

So one of the most important elements of supervision is never to allow a student capable of perverting others to remain in a school. In such cases, the dangerous and incorrigible student should always be expelled. If you need to be convinced of that, change the scene and ask yourself if you would allow a student with a contagious disease to remain with the others. Is the contagion of vice any less dangerous, or its effects less tragic? Can a teacher with religious principles stand the frightening thought that God will one day demand an accounting of all the souls lost in his school because, whether from self-interest or complacency or softness, he did not expel the corrupters?

St. Jean-Baptiste de la Salle says, «Never put up with libertines among those you are teaching, because virtue and good morals must be the heritage of all your students, if you want God to bless you and make your school prosper.»

4. Watch over their conversations, tastes and inclinations. Our Lord tells us that the mouth speaks from the abundance of the heart. A child whose heart is spoiled, will always let that appear somehow in his speech, and a vigilant teacher, who hears everything, weighs everything, becomes aware of everything, will soon know which ones need special supervision in that area. Every double-meaning, indecent or simply too unguarded word must be severely punished.

The child who is inclined to laziness, to light and dangerous reading, to intemperance, to fits of temper or outbursts of anger, must be followed closely, because such inclinations indicate morals which are highly suspect. The same holds for those whose clothing smacks of vanity, those who like to look at themselves in the mirror, or who spend too much time fixing their hair. Bishop Dupanloup writes that a very experienced man once told him, «You may be sure that a student who begins to comb his hair constantly and is always adjusting his tie, will soon become a poor student, and most of the time he is on the verge of some moral difficulty.»

Sneaky, uncommunicative children, who do not like to play, who keep to themselves, who speak softly, or whisper in the ear of this one and that one, or who always try to avoid the teacher and keep out of his sight, are usually corrupt. If one is not careful, they soon become the bane of an educational institution. These sorts of children should always be the object of special supervision; otherwise their evil instincts will rapidly develop and spread like a fire.

5. Whatever might constitute a danger for children's morals. Innocence is a flower which lives only on precautions. To preserve it in children, your supervision must create a sort of rampart around them, which keeps away from them whatever might tarnish their lovable purity, and every situation which might become harmful to them. The most effective remedy, the only sure one against temptations, as you should know from

personal experience, is to distance yourself from them. What good is it to urge your children to behave, to flee sin, if you leave them the possibility of seeing evil and doing it. To hold a hungry convalescent to his diet, you do not allow him near a table full of food. You do not tear down the wall around your garden while asking that no one steal anything. So you have to:

a. keep the minds of your children off every indecent thought, off everything which might remind them of evil, off everything which might give them an inopportune impression;

b. watch them so closely that you always know what they are doing, what they are saying, what they like and what they want;

c. from time to time, check their lockers and desks, their trunks and the other places where they put their belongings, to reassure yourself that there are no bad books, songs, pictures or other objects dangerous to their morals. A child who is caught hiding such things must be punished, and even expelled if there is a second offense and if he has tried to lend them out or to spread them among his fellow-students;

d. on outings, avoid having the children go through places where they would be exposed to seeing or hearing things which might scandalize them or arouse in their minds the thought of evil.

6. Watch over yourselves. This vigilance over oneself demands of the teacher:

a. great reserve in his speech, so as to avoid not only any licentious expressions, but even any which are too free or spoken thoughtlessly;

b. great self control in his actions, gestures and bearing, so as to avoid whatever might offend against the strictest modesty;

c. great attention to behaving in such a way that everything about him is edifying and may be for the children an example of virtue;

d. great exactness in starting class on time, in always being with the students during recreation, and anywhere else where supervision is needed.

This multiplicity and continuity of vigilance certainly requires sacrifice, but it is absolutely necessary, because unless one's attentive care keeps blocked up all the ways by which the knowledge of evil may enter, the serpent will slip in through the opening which has been overlooked. How many children have been lost for lack of that sustained supervision.

Supervision is the responsibility not only of him who is specifically charged with that office; it is a duty for all the brothers. No one can in conscience leave this task entirely to the official prefect. Everyone must cooperate and all are responsible for the conduct of the children, no matter which class they belong to.

Every brother who allows evil to be committed, through neglect of supervision or failure to reprimand children he may have caught doing wrong, makes himself guilty and will bring before the judgment seat of God the sins he allows to be committed and the faults he tolerates, even though the children do not belong to his class. Nothing therefore can dispense a brother from supervising the children, and if he fails to do so, he should confess it as a fault which may at times be serious.

III. Rules to Follow in Order to Supervise Well

1. Vigilance is one of the most essential qualities for an educator of youth. It should be such as to easily take in the whole classroom, everything that happens there, and each student in particular.

2. The brother's attention must never be absorbed by any single thing, or by the exercise being done at the moment. Hence, while explaining a lesson, correcting an assignment, or doing whatever else, he must give general attention to the entire

classroom, to direct and control everything going on there, to maintain order and discipline, and to keep each one busy at his duty.

Anyone whose mind is not capable of exercising simultaneously both general attention over the class as a whole and particular attention to each assignment being done there, but who is rather totally absorbed by one specific thing, is not fit for teaching. It is to be feared that many reprehensible things will happen in his classroom without his ever being aware of them.

3. During class time, a brother must remain constantly seated at his desk, except during writing lessons and on other rare occasions. This is the only way to keep all the children always in sight and to be able to remain aware of everything they are doing.

Walking around the classroom is an imprudence which could have serious consequences, because experience proves that the children will take advantage of the moment when the teacher cannot see them and when his back is turned to them, to fool around, talk, make signs to one another, disturb, and do evil.

4. He must not leave the classroom without grave necessity, and even such cases, he must always appoint someone capable to replace him and maintain order, and he must return as quickly as possible.

Anyone who readily leaves the classroom to speak with parents or for whatever other reason may be sure that he is putting the children at risk and that he is opening a door through which the devil can come into their midst and bring them the contagion of all vices.

5. He must never forget that he is in the classroom only for the benefit of the children, that all his time must be devoted to their instruction and education. Consequently, he must never busy himself with his own interests, nor take up any task which might lessen the attention he owes his students or prevent him from seeing everything going on in the school.

6. He must not lose sight of any children who are standing in a circle reciting their lessons from memory, or doing arithmetic at the blackboard, or looking at the maps. He will insist that they keep their arms crossed, or hold their books in both hands, and that they stay in one place.

To stand in the center of a circle when hearing them recite their lessons, or to become so absorbed in explaining an arithmetic problem that he loses sight of them, is a lack of prudence which allows the enemy of salvation to lay traps for their innocence.

7. His attentiveness to the whole class and to each child in particular should be doubled during exercises and changes of lesson. So as not to be distracted at such moments, he must never speak to anyone, nor busy himself with anything whatever apart from the exercise to be performed.

8. He must take care to see that each child is always seated in his own place and he must never let anyone leave it without permission.

9. He must keep them constantly busy; this is the best way to maintain silence, order and discipline, and to preserve the children from evil.

10. He must firmly insist that the children return home in good order, two by two, and that they not stop along the way. This is one of the most important points, because everyone knows that it is while they are on their way to and from school that the children become perverted and teach each other evil things.

11. Each row should have its monitor to note the students who misbehave, and the brother should require a daily account of the conduct of each one.

According to the acts of the Councils of Tours, religious and clerics to whom is entrusted the education of children, must see to it that they are housed together and sleep in common dormitories, and are never left alone for a single moment by their principal or teacher.

12. Following these wise prescriptions of the Councils, boarding students must never be left to themselves. By day, by night, in class, during recreation, in the dining room, in the dormitory, in the locker room, wherever, at least one brother must follow them to supervise and direct them.

13. During recreation, the brother prefect must stay in the midst of the children, but he must never play with them, nor chat with a few students or with the other brothers. His total attention must be given to supervision. Therefore, he must carefully avoid being distracted or doing any work which might interfere with the attention he must give to the children's conduct.

14. He should be ingenious in managing to place himself so as to see all the children: to observe them, hear what they are saying, see what they are doing, keep them together, make them play, and prevent them from getting their clothes torn or dirty, or from quarreling or hurting themselves in any way. That is the prefect's duty during recreations.

15. In the hallways or corridors, going to class or to the dormitory, in the street when they are going to Mass or on outings, he must never allow any children to lag behind him, but must make them all walk ahead. He himself must not walk behind them, but to one side, so as to see the whole line and easily notice those who might create disorder, break ranks, or create a disturbance.

16. It is good to offer children a variety of games, to satisfy their various tastes, but one must never tolerate any games for money, nor any which might endanger their morals, or which require too violent exercise which might endanger the children's health.

17. Games are the best way to keep children usefully occupied during recreation, so all must be obliged to play, with complete freedom to choose whichever of the permissible games they

prefer. One must never tolerate certain children spending their recreations in groups, chatting and arguing, still less that they go aside in twos or threes to talk.

18. It must be the rule that older boys play with older boys, young ones with young ones. On the way to church or on walks, the older ones will always remain together, and the younger ones likewise.

19. No child may slip away from the others, nor go to the dormitory or locker room without permission. If a child must be allowed to go to either of those places, care should be taken to see that he is not meeting another child there.

20. On outings, it is necessary:

a. to establish beforehand the place and time, and the orderliness and conduct expected of the students;

b. to require them to remain in line, both coming and going, not to speak too loudly, and not to lag behind or get ahead of the others;

c. once they have arrived at the spot where they are to stop and play, to indicate the boundaries beyond which no one may go;

d. to watch carefully to see that no child slips away from the others or hides behind the hedges;

e. to keep the children from throwing stones, or snowballs in winter, from damaging the trees, stealing fruit, walking through freshly-sown fields—in a word, from causing any damage or harm of any kind.

21. It is usually while on outings that children, if not carefully supervised, bond together intimately, share confidences, transmit bad spirit and their defects, and teach one another to do wrong. So the brothers must be doubly watchful on such occasions; if there are several of them with the children, they must not remain together, nor spend their time talking among themselves, but

spread out through the group, so as to more readily see the children and hear what they are saying.

22. Boarding students may not go into town unless accompanied by a near relative. It is not prudent to let them go out with cousins of either sex, still less with other boys from their town, or with friends who have come to visit.

23. A brother must always be present when the children are getting up and going to bed, to make sure that they observe the rules of decency and modesty while dressing, undressing and changing.

24. The children must never dress while on their bed, but standing beside it and facing the wall.

25. A brother must supervise the toilets while the children are using them after rising or before retiring, and at any other time during the day when several boys are there together.

26. The number of toilets should be proportionate to the number of students. Great care must be taken to see that two boys never go into the same stall, that they do not speak in the bathroom, that they stay there only a short time, and that their leaving the room during class time is carefully controlled.

27. Familiarity between older and younger students must not be tolerated. There are also certain ways of playing, such as grabbing one another around the waist, or piling up in heaps, which must not be permitted, because they could very easily become dangerous.

28. A young child in need of help of any kind must never be entrusted to an older student, because it is precisely the older ones who upset and corrupt the little ones.

* * *

Finally, while keeping the children at their tasks, a brother who has the true spirit of his state will know how to have compassion on their weakness. That means he will always speak to them kindly, correct them gently, and allow them a reasonable amount of freedom in order to get to know them better. For the rest, if supervision must be exact and continuous, it should not for all that be nervous, mistrustful, tense, or prone to unfounded conjectures. That would be against justice and charity, and would become revolting to the children, who will certainly become aware of it.

Supervision should be calm, without disturbance or constraint or affectation; it should be simple and relaxed, so that the children do not realize that they are being so closely followed, and so that they think someone is always with them in order to be of assistance rather than to watch them. Supervision will be all the more perfect if carried out this way. Besides, just as one must not omit anything which contributes to careful supervision, one must not take exaggerated precautions either, because while we want to preserve their morals, we must be careful that the children do not become two-faced or hypocritical, which easily happens if they think that they are not trusted.

CHAPTER FORTY-ONE

WHAT IS A TEACHER?

In society, each person holds a certain place and performs a certain service. From this point of view, everything is honorable, because everything is useful and contributes to the common good. However, it must be recognized that certain social functions are more honorable and loftier than others. Some serve the soul, others the body; and just as the soul is superior to the body, so the service of souls is a ministry superior to the one whose only object is the service of the body. Hence it follows that the priest and the educator, who are concerned with souls, carry out the two highest human ministries.

Education is such an elevated task that the Fathers of the Church and the most serious authors who have discussed it have all affirmed that the educator's task is a judgeship, a parenthood and an apostolate.

1. St. John Chrysostom states that this judgeship is as far above the civil judiciary as heaven is above earth; and there is even more to it than that. The civil judiciary offers you no teaching at all about true wisdom, nor teachers who tell you what the soul is, what the world is, what will become of us after this present life, where we will go when we leave this earth, and how we can practice virtue here below. In every good school, on the other hand, all these important things are taught; that is why it is called a school of religion, a chair for the education of souls, a tribunal where the soul judges itself, and a gymnasium where we train for the race which leads to heaven.

Civil magistrates judge the guilty and condemn public crimes; but they shed no light on, nor do they follow to the very depths of conscience, the first thought, the first temptation to vice; that is the task of the educator. The judge punishes evil; the teacher does even more: he forestalls and smothers it at its birth, in its very seed. Judges often punish without correcting; the teacher worthy of the name more often corrects without punishing. When evil is done, he does not demand the death of the guilty party, but of the evil itself.

If a country owes its gratitude to the judges who deliver it from evil citizens, how much does it not owe to the educator who prepares good and virtuous citizens for it, who will one day be its strength and its glory! «So I can say once again,» states Bishop Dupanloup, «that the teacher is also a judge, and the judgeship he holds, as well as the work entrusted to him, hold the first place in society.»

2. An educator of youth is not only a judge of the highest order; he is far more than that—he is a father. Yes, a teacher is a second father, whose vocation is assuredly not superior to that of the first, but whose devotedness may perhaps be more generous, since it is freer and more disinterested, and whose inclination, if it is less natural, is just as highly inspired, and whose aptitude, finally, is often greater and more perfect.

The educator shares essentially in what is most noble in the divine parenthood. He is, to the extent that it pleases God to share his power with him, what holy scripture says so well about God himself: «the father of souls.» Nothing fits him better than this magnificent name. Even the pagans had the same lofty idea: «Let young people be aware,» said one philosopher, «that teachers are the fathers, not of their bodies, but of their souls.» That is what inspired the statement attributed to Alexander the Great, that he owed no less to his teacher Aristotle than to his father Philip, because if he was indebted to Philip for the gift of life, he was indebted to Aristotle for knowing how to live honorably.

3. The Church has always seen education as an apostolate, like the priesthood. «I do not hesitate to state,» says Bishop

Dupanloup, «that the holiest priest, the one most dedicated to souls in his holy ministry, often has less extensive and less profound influence than the teacher on the soul and destiny of a child that he is educating.»

The priest is rarely present among the children; his contacts and conversations with these young souls are few and far between; he cannot follow them in the various activities of their lives. But the teacher is something else again; he holds in his hands, so to speak, the child's total existence, his whole life, every day, every hour, his entire present and his entire future. He has such frequent contacts with the child, the most natural close relationship; his influence is always alive, always present; in a word, it is perpetual and universal. Without a doubt, the confessor repairs wrongs done and does immense and admirable good to the soul, but he makes very little direct contribution to developing the child's faculties, and rarely any toward forming his character and correcting his defects in detail.

It is from his teacher that the child learns simultaneously how to use his time, develop his intelligence, acquire ideas and constantly improve his attitudes. The teacher is always with the child; he watches over and directs his activity all day long. So the child thinks only of him, hears only him, works at first hand only for him, depends entirely on him for what most closely affects his mind and his heart: blame or praise, shame or honor, the pleasure of learning, work, success.

Hence, the teacher's impact on the child is immense, whether he is improving his faculties through teaching, or whether he is contributing to the formation of his character and morals through discipline during the various activities of the day. As for defects, the teacher follows them closely and catches them in the very act, discerns them, defines them, knows them better than the child himself, even sooner and better than the confessor. One's confessor especially knows one's faults properly so called, and wipes them out; he suggests acts of virtue and encourages them.

The teacher goes beyond that: he has in-depth knowledge of his students' qualities and vices, and works, if I may put it that way, on the spot and diligently, to uproot the latter and develop the former. The confessor forms one's conscience with the highest authority. The teacher does just as much, no doubt from a lower level, but with an authority which is still very great. The confessor heals the wounds of the soul, draws down graces, imparts supernatural life. The teacher prepares within the child strong and vigorous faculties for the supernatural life; he inspires love of what is beautiful and true; he forms a mind which is clean, pure, upright, for the truths of faith; an energetic will, a generous, grateful, filial heart; a character which is firm and strong in the struggle for virtue.

Hence, education is not a matter of speculation, nor a trade; it is a real apostolate which seeks out souls to win them over to God.

In the area of speculation, the teacher becomes a master; he is a man carrying out a trade. In the apostolate, the teacher is a father; he is a shepherd fulfilling a sacred ministry; he is the man of God, the apostle who devotes himself and forgets himself in order to save souls.

In the area of speculation, the children are students whom one instructs at a reasonable profit for oneself. This is exploitation— one means among many of making money. In the apostolate, they are children that one loves, that one raises for God and for whom one sacrifices his concern, his health, even his very life.

The apostolate means fatherly care, pastoral devotedness, apostolic zeal. Schools where the apostolate dictates the education offered are a family, and a very Christian family. God is present, and the authority of God, which is fatherly and motherly to the highest degree, and care and solicitude for souls. Yes, in a school like that, one is primarily concerned with souls, to win them over to God.

From what we have just said, it should be clear that the ministry of the Christian teacher is very noble, very exalted and very difficult. In point of fact, imparting a good and virtuous education is no easy business, and it does not happen automatically. «It is a masterpiece of human reason,» says Cardinal de la Luzerne; «it requires long and assiduous attention which flows from great wisdom.» It is not enough simply to throw into the soul the seeds of virtue; they must be cultivated with care, constancy and intelligence, until one has harvested their fruit. It is not enough to teach religious principles; they must be so deeply engraved that they can never be erased. It is not enough to make religion known; one must make it loved. One must not only strengthen weak human nature, but also reform human nature prone to evil.

What a combination of seemingly irreconcilable qualities this great undertaking demands!

- Authority which grants all the freedom needed to develop character but which refuses what might spoil it;
- Gentleness without weakness;
- Severity without harshness;
- Seriousness without brusqueness;
- Kindness and good-naturedness without familiarity;
- A great desire for success tempered by a patience which nothing can dishearten or discourage;
- A vigilance which nothing escapes, with a wisdom which often seems to overlook things;
- Reserve which does not detract from frankness;
- Firmness which is never opinionated;
- Sagacity for discerning inclinations without ever showing its hand;
- Prudence which knows what to excuse and what to punish and the right moment to do each;
- Cleverness which never degenerates into slyness and which influences others' minds without antagonizing them;

- A pleasant manner which makes lessons enjoyable without detracting from their solidity;
- An indulgence which evokes love, coupled with an exactitude and justice which inspire fear;
- A condescension which adapts itself to others' inclinations without favoring them too much;
- Skill in using certain inclinations to overcome others, and in strengthening the good ones and weakening the bad;
- Far-sightedness which anticipates dangerous situations;
- Presence of mind which is never disconcerted by unexpected happenings or students' embarrassing questions.

«To be a good teacher, one would have to be a perfect human being» (La Luzerne).

Even if not all our brothers have been blessed with all the qualities listed above, which Cardinal de la Luzerne would require even of layteachers, they should at least work at acquiring solid virtue, fervent piety, great love for children, total dedication, and constant, firm and vigilant zeal for preserving their innocence and correcting their defects.

Solid virtue. Of all the lessons you can and should give your students, the first, principal and most meritorious one for you, and the most effective for them, is your example. Teaching sinks in more easily and penetrates more deeply through the eyes than through the ears. Words may persuade people, but example wins them over; its authority, all the stronger for being gentler, unites and presents in one package teaching, exhortation and encouragement.

Children are born imitators; nature made them that way so that they could learn through the language of action. Watch children doing calligraphy or painting; they learn by copying the works of others. Children learn morality the same way, by imitating their teachers' actions. That is why a teacher should be able to serve as a model for all his students, so that, seeing in him an example of virtue, they need only imitate him.

Therefore, his teaching and all his words must always be in accord with his works, so that his disciples may respect him and so that no one may have anything bad to say about him, following St. Paul's advice, «In everything you do make yourself an example to them of working for good: when you are teaching, be an example to them in your sincerity and earnestness and in keeping all that you say so wholesome that nobody can make objections to it; and then any opponent will be at a loss, with no accusation to make against us» (*Tit* 2:7-8).

But there is another, deeper, reason which must be explained. What is education? It is a handing on of the moral life; it is an authentic fatherhood, as we have already said. Now, is it not one of the fundamental laws of life that it can be transmitted only under certain conditions of identity or resemblance? In the physical world, plants and animals reproduce only within their own species, and as they communicate life, they communicate with it their general shape, needs and abilities.

Well, with rare exceptions, moral life is transmitted under analogous conditions. In order to pass it on to others, parents and teachers must first be gifted with it themselves; as the proverb says, «you cannot give what you do not have.» They must, moreover, possess this moral life—that is to say, virtue—in all its fullness, with no intermingling of weaknesses or blemishes; otherwise they would communicate it to the child only in an altered or incomplete form.

Everyone knows that at birth each of us has either vigorous and healthy blood, or tainted blood which is the source and carrier of all sorts of hereditary illnesses. Well, we affirm that education transmits to us either moral vigor or dangerous germs. In a word, the moral life and virtue are transmitted under the same conditions in which they exist, weak or strong, depending on whether the educator is tepid or fervent in doing good. That is why we have the proverb, «Like father, like son.» Like teacher, like student; that is the rule, and exceptions only serve to prove it.

The Creator himself in a sense intended to formulate this law of paternity when he said, «Let us make human beings in our image and likeness.» God drew from himself a breath of life and breathed it into the man. The momentous fatherhood of education is exercised in the same manner. The teacher should also draw from the depths of his soul true ideas, good, noble and virtuous sentiments—everything which makes up the moral life. If all of that is only in his words and not in his way of acting, it will be only useless noise, a dead letter, rather than life bringing forth life, and virtue producing virtue. If instead of what makes for life, there are in his heart only elements of death, vice, sin, indifference, greed, and the spirit of the world, the child will feel their influence, and barring a special grace of preservation, his soul will reproduce their image to a greater or lesser degree.

This moral life enters us like a breath; it is breathed in like air; it escapes from souls which possess it by unseen emanations, just as perfume escapes from a flower. It is a word, a look, an attitude, a smile; it is above all that multi-faceted ensemble of relationships, habits, and ways of speaking which serve as exits and passageways for life to communicate itself to other souls.

But in the moral order, death goes on just as life does. It is not always the result of some unfortunate mishap which one can see and name. It often slips into souls and penetrates them invisibly, because it also slips out of them like a deadly exhalation, by the same route along which life passes. Hence the expressions, «the contagion of vice» and «the sweet smell of virtue.»

In order to teach virtue, or rather to inspire and communicate it, one must be virtuous; otherwise one is a charlatan and a professional liar, which is the worst form of degradation. Being convinced of this, Bishop Borderie of Versailles once told a young priest, «To become a saint, when one is entrusted with the education of young people, it is enough not to be a hypocrite or a liar. It is enough to practice what one preaches and to take one's own advice; you recommend moral purity to the children, so be very pure and irreproachable yourself. You tell them to love truth, to be obedient, humble, docile, pious; be for them a model of all those virtues.

«To give wise advice to children and then contradict one's teachings by bad example, is a shame and a crime. It is like caressing them with one hand and slapping them with the other. Words must match actions; if one's conduct is in conflict with one's words, the latter will be of no use to the child and will only serve to condemn the teacher.» Every brother assigned to teaching should therefore be able to say, «Since I have been appointed to guide young people, I will leave them examples of virtue.»

Fervent piety. To fully grasp the necessity of piety, one must remember that God holds the first place in education.

a. He holds the first place because he is mankind's first teacher. Yes, God himself, before all others, works at educating us. He is essentially a teacher, which is why the prophet Isaiah said, «Everyone will be taught by God.» First of all, there are three areas in which it pleased God to be our first and only teacher; these three areas are thought, consciousness and speech. The greatest geniuses have never been able to explain how these are acquired. Willy-nilly, we must therefore recognize God's own illumination.

God does not work at education in any visible manner. Exteriorly, this work is entrusted to ordinary teachers: «Paul planted, Apollos watered»; teachers do what they can, but neither he who plants nor he who waters counts for anything. There is only one person who truly counts in a man's education: he who gives the increase, which is to say, he who develops strengthens, enlightens, brings up—and that means God.

«He works invisibly in us,» says Fénelon, «like a miner working in the bowels of the earth. And although we do not see him and do not attribute anything to him, it is he who does everything. He works continuously in the depths of the soul, just as he works in the depths of plowed fields to make them produce crops; if he did not do so, everything would die and all human work would be useless.»

So the teacher is only God's coworker in the task of education; but to be fit to work together with God, one must obviously be closely united to him and share generously in his Spirit. One can attain to that union and that participation in his spirit only through piety and frequent communication with God. Besides, the first means of success in education is the grace and gift of teaching. But every perfect gift, every grace, comes from above, from the Father of lights. Without divine assistance, the most sustained and painful effort produces no effect; whereas with that help, the smallest efforts are crowned with success.

Only fervent piety can obtain for us that help, that grace, that gift of teaching, without which we can do nothing. Therefore the teacher who is not pious is not fit for teaching; he will never succeed at it. He may be able to teach others reading, writing and arithmetic; at the very most he may succeed in planting some words from the catechism in the children's memories; but he will never inspire them to virtue nor form their souls.

b. God holds the first place in education because children must be brought up for God. «Animals deprived of reason would suffice to bring up children for a merely natural life,» says Cardinal de la Luzerne. «Infidels deprived of the light of faith are capable of doing the work of bringing them up for a merely social life. But to bring up a child for God, for the Church, for heaven—only the priest, the Christian father and the deeply pious and religious teacher are fit for that task.»

Education is an interior task, because it is involved above all with souls. To bring up a child means to be occupied with his soul, to raise it to God; with his mind, to enlighten it and give it solid religious principles and knowledge of Jesus Christ; with his heart, to purify and ennoble it and form it to virtue; with his will, to give it strength and energy, to make it docile, pliable and constant; with his conscience to enlighten and form it and give it a horror of evil; with all his moral faculties, to develop them and make them capable of raising themselves to a supernatural plane, meaning the practice of solid Christian virtues.

At the moment when someone entrusts a child to you, imagine Jesus Christ saying to you, as Pharaoh's daughter said of Moses whom she had just taken from the Nile, «Take this child and raise him for me; I will repay you for your work. This is the most valuable thing I have on earth; I entrust him to you to preserve him from evil and to teach him to do good. This child is the price of my blood; teach him what his soul cost me, what I did to save it. Raise him for heaven, because he is made to reign with me.»

Now, it is evident that work like that cannot be accomplished by human means. Only grace and virtue are capable of it, but that grace and that virtue can be obtained only through prayer. So piety is absolutely necessary for a teacher.

c. God holds first place in education because the child absolutely needs his help in order to work personally at his education. Piety is the first thing a child needs to carry on the work of his education. He needs it to strengthen his weakness and to struggle against wrong, evil tendencies, the devil's temptations, human respect, and the bad example of his fellow students. If he lacks piety, he will be weak on such occasions. On the other hand, virtues are not acquired without effort and defects are not corrected without a struggle.

The child has to make a sustained effort against his own nature; we can help and encourage him, but in the final analysis, it is up to him to uproot evil, cultivate good, correct his defects and develop his qualities. But without piety, all of that is beyond his strength. Piety makes duty pleasant and easy; it strengthens and enlivens everything in a young man. It is what gives virtues their

471

sap, their vigor and their beauty. What children do out of fear, out of strict duty, because they cannot avoid it, is always annoying to them—hard, painful, sometimes overwhelming. But when they act out of piety and love of God, everything is pleasant and easy.

A child without piety, even if he is hard-working and steady, is very difficult to raise and instruct. He becomes tired, loses interest, grows discouraged; he mistrusts his teachers, he cannot put up with setbacks or disappointments; he takes offense, his feelings are hurt, he is always changing, he cannot make a decision about anything important, nor settle down to anything anywhere. A pious child is certainly not without defects, but he knows them, regrets them and works at correcting them; if he falls, he gets up without sulking over his faults and without trying to hide them.

It is normal for piety to impart wonderful strength and firmness. It sometimes gives children between twelve and fifteen years of age a maturity of character and mind and a strength of spirit which are astonishing. It makes them studious, prudent, self-controlled, upright, and firm with themselves. It makes them the best of friends, the staunchest students in the world; they remain simple and lovable, without becoming haughty or hardened. Their piety makes them all things to everyone; while raising their intelligence, it enlarges their heart and develops all their faculties to the point where one can say of them what Bernardin de Saint-Pierre wrote about a child: «Every day, piety develops the beauty of his soul through indelible graces which show in his face.»

d. Again, the first place in education belongs to God because it is only with his help that the teacher can properly carry out this august ministry. As we said before, no one can give what he does not possess; so how can a teacher inspire a child to piety if he himself is not very pious? How will he make known the excellence, necessity and benefits of prayer if he does not know them himself or has only a superficial awareness of them? Is a teacher without piety capable of even making children pray properly? No; he may act like an usher and maintain a certain amount of order, but he will never make children adopt the posture and respectful tone which prayer requires; he will never be able to suggest to them the intentions and the pious feelings which sustain and give life to piety.

A student may have followed the routine of a Christian school for many years, and without him or his teachers realizing it, still not be very Christian or very pious. How can that be? Because his actions were not inspired by his conscience. He acted from imitation or routine; he went wherever the others went; he followed the crowd with indifference; when that movement ceased, when the child found himself alone, he thought no more about the religious practices of his school days. The voice of his conscience did not replace the now-silent bell, nor his own will the directives of his teachers. He abandoned prayer, dropped Mass and the sacraments, and soon, going with the current, he committed evil and unresistingly followed the impulses which led him in that direction.

Such are the results of an education given by a teacher lacking in piety and virtue; he could not communicate what he did not have himself, he was not intent on engraving good principles in the child's mind or on forming his conscience; he did not know how to make him understand the need, value and necessity of prayer; so he should not be surprised if the results of his work are zero.

One of the most important factors in inspiring piety is to see that religious exercises are well performed, that all the children answer the prayers with respect and pronounce each word, each syllable, in a simple, normal, recollected voice. There is nothing sadder than prayers said hastily, without modesty, not in unison, or with a dryness and an attitude which announce that they are putting up with the act of praying, but that they do not like it and that their heart is not in it.

A brother who does not attach full importance to the exercises of piety, who fails to take suitable means to make the children pray piously, who does not give the example during prayer, who does not have a serious and modest posture or who is busy with something which has nothing to do with the holy exercises, is seriously at fault; he is destroying the pious sentiments in the children's hearts and jeopardizing the entire work of their education.

So the teacher must pray, he must be solidly pious, he must teach his children to pray, train them to pray well, and teach them to invoke their heavenly Father every day. Every teacher who does not pray, who does not have the gift of piety and who does not know how to inspire the children he is bringing up with love of prayer, is a teacher incapable of performing the noble mission entrusted to him.

Great love for his task and for children. To succeed in the noble ministry of teaching, one must have great esteem for that task, and one must love children. One must dedicate the entire strength of one's being, one's mind, one's heart, one's activity, one's whole life, to the accomplishment of one's duty. One must not share oneself; that is to say, become weakened and divided. The teacher's total affection and concern must be directed toward his students. If he carries out his mission as though it were a trade, or like a mercenary; if he does not love what he does, nor his students; if he does not give himself totally to their education, he will not do a bit of good.

Education does not consist of either discipline or teaching; it is not imparted by courses in politeness or even in religion, but by constant daily contact between students and their teachers, by personal advice, attention to details, encouragement, corrections, and all the other sorts of lessons to which this uninterrupted contact gives rise.

But in order to cultivate these young souls this way, one by one, with the assiduousness their needs and their frailty require, one must love children. When one loves them, one does more for them; one does better, with less difficulty and greater success. Why?

Because words and actions which are inspired by true affection carry with them a special, penetrating, irresistible force. A teacher who loves can warn and advise; the love which comes through in his words gives them more charm and force; his advice is received as a sign of friendship, and followed with docility. A teacher who loves can reprimand and punish, because there is neither prejudice nor rigor in his severity, and the student is more upset about having disappointed his teacher, whom he knows loves him, than about the punishment he received.

So love your students; fight ceaselessly against the indifference, weariness and annoyance their faults so easily arouse in you. Without closing your eyes to their defects, because you must correct them, nor to their faults since you must often punish them, keep in mind at the same time all the pleasant qualities they have, which deserve your attention. Look at the innocence which shines in their peaceful faces and unwrinkled brows, the naiveté of their statements, the sincerity of their contrition even though it may not last long, the honesty of their resolutions even though they break them quickly, the generosity of their efforts even though it is rarely sustained for long. Give them credit for the good they do, no matter how imperfect, and for all the evil they do not do.

Finally, whatever they may do, keep loving them as long as they are with you, since this is the only way to work with any success at reforming them. Love them all equally—no outcasts, no favorites; or rather, let each of them think he is favored and privileged because he receives personal proof of your affection. Who entrusted these children to you? God and their families. Now, God is all love for human beings, and whoever governs in his name should imitate his providence and share his love. Their fathers and mothers have entrusted these children to you, but are you unaware that the heart of a father or a mother is an unquenchable furnace of love? Then in the name of God and of their families, love these children; only then will you be worthy and capable of raising them.

Devotedness. What is devotedness? It is the fruit of love. To devote oneself is to hand oneself over unreservedly, to forget oneself, to take no account of oneself and to sacrifice oneself entirely. It is as St. Paul says: after having given everything, one must still give oneself.

«Be a father; no, that is not enough—be a mother,» was how Fénelon put it; and that said it all. St. Paul said it before him: «We are not tutors, we are fathers; I was among you as a father, speaking to you tenderly as to my own children.»

«There is not a single moment,» says Rollin, «when a teacher is not responsible for the souls of the children entrusted to him. If his absence or inattention gives the enemy an opportunity to steal the precious treasure of their innocence, what will he say to Jesus Christ, who will ask him to give an account of their souls? He must therefore never lose sight of them. But what is that continual vigilance, if not devotedness?» In fact, only fatherly devotedness is equal to the task; any teacher who does not feel inspired in the depth of his heart to be so devoted, will inevitably be found wanting.

For example, why does a teacher decide to take care of the weak students in his class as well as the strong ones, and to give them even more attention precisely because they are weak, and to act so that, without slowing too much the progress of the better students, he does not leave behind any of these poor children who give so little satisfaction to his self-love?

That definitely demands fatherly devotedness, because only fathers and mothers never leave their little children behind, pace themselves to their weakness, wait for them if need be, and never sacrifice some for the sake of the others, saying as did Jacob, «I cannot walk so quickly; you know I have little children.» Only devotedness can patiently put up with the weaknesses, the shocking natural defects and the ingratitude of children. Only devotedness can eventually endear him to them, attract them, raise them to his level because only devotedness stooped down to their level. Only devotedness transforms them, because it alone can identify with these young souls, as would a father or mother. In a word, only devotedness can carry out properly the task of education. Devotedness is the most clairvoyant and penetrating teacher; it possesses a skill which nothing can replace.

But one devotes oneself only because one loves, so love is therefore the basis of all devotedness. When the Son of God became the teacher of the whole human race, he devoted himself to raising us to the level of our original destiny. Love was the supreme inspiration for that tremendous devotion; that is why the Apostle says, «Then the charity of God appeared and revealed itself in all its splendor.» When Jesus Christ sent his apostles to carry on his work, he thrice asked them for the witness of love and devotion, so as to make us understand that in order to carry out the beautiful and laborious ministry of education, one must first of all love God and souls.

To take on the raising of children without loving them, to carry out that ministry with distaste and negligence, is a great misfortune and a great responsibility.

«If a shoemaker,» Plato tells us, «is a poor shoemaker, or becomes one through his own fault; if he pretends to be a shoemaker without really being one, none of that will wreak great damage on the State. All that will happen is that a few Athenians will be less well shod. But if the teachers of youth are such in name only, if they perform their task badly, the results will be something else again. The poor product which comes from their hands are ignorant and vicious generations who endanger the future of the country.»

Love and devotedness need salt and life in order to be truly useful to a child. What is the salt of love and devotedness? A wise firmness which protects against softness and deadly self-indulgence.

Firmness is the moral strength, the strength of mind and character with which a teacher exercises the rights of authority wisely. It is first of all strength of mind, that is, wisdom in giving counsel, joined to decisiveness in thought. It is not the enemy of reflection, but once the latter is completed, it cuts short all hesitation and produces action without beating around the bush. Secondly, it is strength of character, by which we must understand that resolute and temperate will, which is none the less unshakable in its moderation, which inspires respect, confidence and submission, and which forestalls or discourages all resistance.

Unlike physical force, which can easily stifle the exterior manifestations of vices and base instincts, but is powerless to correct them, firmness, understood in the sense we are talking about, acts on the children's souls and truly educates them. It is necessary in order to bring about progress and to make both teachers and students work; to maintain silence, good order and recollection, without which there can be no serious work or sustained concentration; to maintain the rule in its entirety; to never allow or tolerate the slightest wrong, the slightest fault. One can and one even must pardon at times, or pretend not to notice, but without ever approving or tolerating what is contrary to good order. The principles of virtue and justice must never bend.

«But there is a false firmness,» as Bossuet tells us. «What is it? It is hardness, rigidity, stubbornness, the power of commanding pushed too far. Never to be patient, to obstinately insist on being obeyed at any price, not to ever know how to wait or delay, to shatter everything, first of all usually means jeopardizing everything and shattering oneself. It shows weakness, because one is not master of oneself, which is the greatest of weaknesses.

There is no real power if one is not first of all master of oneself, nor profitable firmness if one is not first of all firm against one's own passions.» So, in the work of education, never do anything through caprice or violence or in a fit of anger; but do everything reasonably, consciously, reflectively, prudently—that is real firmness, and also the source and foundation of a teacher's entire authority. Anyone who possesses it within himself deserves to exercise it over others. Anyone who is not master of his own heart is not strong in any way, for his very principles are weak. In a word, all firmness which is not directed and guided by a healthy reason and upright judgment is not a virtue, but a passion or an outburst of caprice. All firmness which is not rooted in goodness is false firmness; all firmness not founded on devotedness is not worthy of the name, and its effects are deplorable, especially in the field of education.

Constant zeal for enlightening, correcting and forming the child with all patience. Plutarch says that, «For the earth to produce an abundant harvest, three things are needed: good cultivation, a good worker, good seed. The earth is the child; the worker is the one who raises him; the seed is the good principles he should receive.»

So holy truths should be strongly imprinted in children's minds, and divine precepts deeply engraved in their hearts. Your lessons would soon be forgotten and lost if they were not repeated. Your instructions will not last long if they are not frequent. (I said frequent, not long!) A child's attention is too flighty to be fixed for long on anything. When you give him your lessons, don't give him boredom as well. The child is a plant which benefits infinitely more from each morning's watering than from abundant rains which come only occasionally.

One's earliest years are when lessons and principles of faith are most easily engraved in one's memory, when Christian virtues strike the mind most strongly; when feelings of piety move the heart most powerfully. A seal is easily impressed on soft wax; in the same way, the image of God is most easily impressed on a young soul. It takes time, effort and a sharp chisel to carve anything in stone. When there are not yet any prejudices to dispel, nor passions to suppress, nor habits to relearn, it is easier to work on the soul and train it to the holy duties of the Christian.

Watch how the knowledgeable gardener chooses the time when his young tree still has its original uprightness, to attach it to a support which will prevent it from bending. And the potter doesn't wait either for the clay to harden before working it. So it is when the child is young that he must be formed and given good principles. If you let a child grow up in ignorance and vice, the Holy Spirit predicts that you will never again be able to make him submit to the law of God, nor form him to virtue.

Just as plants, flowers and fruit are contained in tiny seeds, so the seeds of all the virtues and vices are already present in little children. The whole value of education lies in cultivating the former and uprooting the latter. Therefore, a good teacher is concerned not only with disorders that disturb discipline, nor even with the children's personal faults which may wound their conscience; he works mostly at correcting their defects.

Is there anyone who doesn't know that defects are the roots of faults? Defects are the shoots which grow back again and again so long as they have not been pulled up by the roots. Even pagans understood that truth, and as Plato said, «It is by struggling against his inner tendencies and against his defects, and by repressing them, that a young man acquires perfection. Without those combats, he will not become even half virtuous.»

Education is a form of cultivation, and good cultivation includes two elements: the first consists in cutting off useless branches and removing rotten fruit from the plant. That is an image of repressing and cutting back disorders and faults; it is good and useful, but it is not everything. One must arrive at the second part, which consists in grafting a better tree onto that wild stock. This graft is a symbol of the virtues one must inspire and inject into the child.

But there is one thing the Christian educator should never forget: defects can hardly ever be corrected except in youth. All moralists speak with one voice to affirm that truth. As St. Paul says, one reaps in maturity only what one sowed in his earliest years.

Even when wisdom is finally acquired, we commit, even while deploring them, new faults which are the sad result of older ones. Fénelon tells us that when people want to give up doing evil, evil still seems to pursue them for a long time. They still have bad habits and a weakened nature; they have no flexibility and almost no natural resources against their defects. Like trees whose rough and knotty trunks have become hardened with the years and can no longer straighten up, men of a certain age can no longer react against certain habits which have grown old with them, and which have seeped into the very marrow of their bones. Often enough, they know them, but it's too late; they bewail them, but in vain. Youth is therefore the only age when a man can do anything he needs to himself in order to correct himself.

One truth we must admit and never lose sight of is that our defects are the foundation of all the misfortunes, all the regrets, all the weaknesses, all the major mistakes, all the disappointments and all the great troubles of life. That is a powerful enough motive to convince a zealous teacher to work consistently to correct and root out his students' defects.

Yes, among people of every social class and standing, every superiority or inferiority, every happiness or unhappiness in life, is dictated by their qualities and their defects. If such and such a man had realized he had a certain defect, or had not nourished it, if his teacher had helped him to correct it, he would have become an honor to his family, he would have made them happy; instead, he dishonored them and became their disgrace.

Imagine a family with a very common defect, a tendency to contrariness. If it shows itself in little things, it banishes peace and happiness; if in big things, it leads to scandalous dissensions.

Imagine a man who has the vice of laziness, or who lacks order, but still has important business to conduct; his firm will be ruined in short order.

If education does not correct that proud, vain child, his haughty pretensions, whims and tyrannical ways will one day make him the scourge of his family.

And there's another who early on shows a free and independent spirit, who despises the authority of his parents and teachers. When he grows up, if education has not reformed him, he will revolt against the laws of his country, teach insubordination and preach disorder.

That other has a pronounced inclination toward things forbidden by the sixth commandment. If you don't watch him, if you let him give himself up easily to the desires of his disordered heart, in a short while he will lose his body, he will lose his soul, and through his bad example he will bring about the loss of many other souls. But one day, God and society will demand an account from his teacher for what he should have done to correct such vices and to bring up virtuously the children who were entrusted to him.

There is, moreover, a sad commentary to make on how small defects weaken and eventually ruin great characters. So one must never flatter nor even neglect a single defect, no matter how weak or slight it may seem. Every defect which is flattered or merely neglected grows and expands in secret, and eventually becomes a vice. Since original sin, there is no bad seed within us so small, so unnoticed, that it will not tend to grow, and if not combated, to invade everything, take over everything, corrupt everything. On the other hand, there is not a single good disposition in us which will not tend to become weaker if it is not maintained and strengthened. That is also why one must never neglect any good quality, because a virtue, no matter how small, will die if neglected.

In nature, whatever grows successfully, whatever rises gracefully during its years of full vigor, must have suffered when young from being controlled and constrained. If a tree is to have a pleasing shape and bear fruit, it must not only be surrounded with thorn bushes when it is young, to keep animals away, but its branches must also be trained to grow in the right direction, and any suckers which would drain its strength must be pruned. So we must use the knife, which seems deadly but which really confers gracefulness and fruitfulness, because the elegant shape of its branches and the abundance of beautiful fruit are due to the hand, apparently cruel, which has not spared it either salutary constraint nor necessary wounds.

But great discernment is needed in repressing and correcting defects, so that severity does not degenerate into rigidity, and gentleness into weakness. Either extreme produces the most serious negative consequences which will ruin the whole educational process. Corrections which are too soft or too harsh will end up having no effect at all. Skillful blows will make iron malleable and bend it the way we want it; but awkward blows will break it.

He who does not know how to moderate and temper reprimands and punishments makes children used to them; he embitters their mind, and instead of correcting a defect, gives them an even greater one.

Prudence measures warnings and penalties, especially according to the child's character. It breaks the rigidity of one by stronger penalties, but it fears to shatter another by severe punishment. It does not treat him whose inclination is toward good the same as him who naturally tends toward vice; it varies the type and gravity of the punishment according to the defects and faults involved. It restrains the hot-headed, humbles the proud, stirs up the lazy, encourages the timid.

You inexperienced teachers, who do not know any better than to hand out punishments for anything and everything, who multiply them, who make them more severe without good reason, you flatter yourselves that with your exaggerated severity, that you are making a student more obedient. You may perhaps bring about that result, but at the detriment of his character and spirit. You may make him bend, but you are taking all the spring out of him; your excessive severity will brutalize him; you may obtain his obedience, but you will lose his confidence; you will make him submissive only by making him sneaky. You teach him to distrust you, and to hide his faults from you much more than to avoid them. Look at any intelligent sculptor; he uses only necessary means, and avoids any useless force which might damage his work. Punishment is the last resort in education, so it must be used only when all others prove ineffective. The rarer you make it, the more effective it will be.

Finally, the more religious education is, the less it will need to be severe. If his conscience is well formed, if piety takes over his heart, a child will automatically submit to obedience and to all his other duties; he will watch over his disordered tendencies and defects, and correct them. Only piety, fear of God, and the holy practices of religion can impose on the child's eyes, tongue and all his senses that salutary restraint, that brake of conscience which are the best protectors of innocence and virtue.

IVE Press

New York—2010